Civil Rights
in
Imperial Russia

EDITED BY
OLGA CRISP
AND
LINDA EDMONDSON

CLARENDON PRESS · OXFORD
1989

Oxford University Press, Walton Street, Oxford OX2 6DP
Oxford New York Toronto
Delhi Bombay Calcutta Madras Karachi
Petaling Jaya Singapore Hong Kong Tokyo
Nairobi Dar es Salaam Cape Town
Melbourne Auckland
and associated companies in
Berlin Ibadan

Oxford is a trade mark of Oxford University Press

Published in the United States
by Oxford University Press

British Library Cataloguing in Publication Data
Civil rights in Imperial Russia.
1. Russia. Civil rights, 1855–1917
I. Crisp, Olga   II. Edmondson, Linda Harriet
323.4'0947
ISBN 0–19–822867–8

Library of Congress Cataloging-in-Publication Data
Civil rights in imperial Russia / edited by Olga Crisp
and Linda Edmondson.
Includes bibliographies and index.
1. Civil rights—Soviet Union—History.
2. Soviet Union—Politics and government—1855–1881.
3. Soviet Union—Politics and government—1881–1894.
4. Soviet Union—Politics and government—1894–1917.
I. Crisp, Olga.   II. Edmondson, Linda Harriet.
JC599.S58C575   1989   323.1'47—dc19   88–28812
ISBN 0–19–822867–8

Set by Hope Services, Abingdon
Printed in Great Britain by
Biddles Ltd., Guildford and King's Lynn

PREFACE

In western political thought over the past three centuries, the assumption has taken hold that legitimate political authority in any state rests to a considerable degree on its respect for the personal rights of its citizens. Regimes which have failed to guarantee civil rights (or worse, have actively violated them) have not only been abhorred but have increasingly been seen to stand outside western civilization, and reasons have been adduced to explain their anomalous position. In the nineteenth and early twentieth centuries, the prime example of a European state which, by its disregard of civil rights, was believed to forfeit its place in the civilized western world was the Russian Empire, the 'gendarme of Europe'. 'He must have sojourned in that solitude without repose, that prison without leisure, which is called Russia,' wrote the Marquis de Custine in 1839, 'to feel all the liberty enjoyed in the other European countries, whatever form of government they may have adopted . . . whoever has well examined that country will be content to live any where else.'[1]

From Custine's day to the collapse of the Romanov dynasty, and from the October Revolution to our own day, analysis of Russia's political traditions has invariably emphasized the separateness of Russia from the West, the absence of pluralist political institutions, and the lack of a culture guaranteeing the maximum individual freedom and privacy compatible with the needs of society. A whole generation of western scholars after 1945 made this their point of departure; their writings sought to understand why such a development had occurred and how it had determined the structure and dynamics of politics and society in the Soviet Union.

The tendency to distinguish Russian, and later, Soviet experience from that of the West has been reinforced in this century by a socialist critique of natural rights theory which has denied the universality of the latter, and has counterposed a

---

[1] Marquis de Custine, *Russia*, 2nd edn. (London, 1844), iii. 353.

theory of rights based on the satisfaction of basic human needs and the individual's responsibilities to the collective. Arguing from this standpoint, several writers have proposed that the categories of rights which western liberals regard as essential to any society are not only alien to Russia's past, but also inadequate for a modern society, above all in their failure to recognize the right to subsistence as a fundamental human right assuming priority over all others.[2]

Both the liberal and the socialist interpretations of civil rights in Russian history have been defended with conviction, but they have usually been debated within the context of other historical problems. Historians in general have only recently begun to respond to the rapidly growing literature on rights in the fields of law, philosophy, politics, and international relations by examining past societies from this perspective. Reawakened interest on the part of historians in the problem of the individual's relationship to the state, together with a heightened awareness in western societies of the vulnerability of personal rights even in a constitutional regime, have been accompanied by a welcome reappraisal of the monolithic concept of 'the West' (even of 'Western Europe') and an appreciation of the diversity of political and legal traditions in those countries. One consequence of this process is that we are able to view Russia's history with greater relativity; from this perspective, the study of civil rights in Russia is no longer an eccentric excursion into the byways of history, but a topic of immediate relevance to all historians.

The intention in this volume of essays is to take a close look at the question of civil rights in the history of the Russian Empire during the last half-century of tsarist rule. We do not expect to overturn the prevailing view that respect for citizens' rights was poorly developed at all levels of Russian society; indeed, most of the essays in this book will tend to confirm the conventional wisdom. But it gives us the opportunity to cast a new light on familiar themes in Russian history, separating the issue of civil rights from the study of government and law where it has

---

[2] For a discussion of those writers who argue that the western concept of rights cannot apply to the Soviet Union (nor to Russia before 1917), see D.S. Lane, 'Human Rights under State Socialism', *Political Studies*, 32/3 (Sept. 1984); for a recent advocate of subsistence rights taking priority over other human rights, see R. J. Vincent, *Human Rights and International Relations* (Cambridge, 1986).

traditionally resided, and placing it in the territory of historians whose preoccupations have mostly been quite different. In doing so, we not only begin to appreciate the connections between the civil rights theme and a host of problems which hitherto have not appeared to be closely related to it (land tenure, for example, or popular protest); we are also forced to question certain assumptions which have been made about the nature of civil rights and citizenship in an autocratic state. Several essays in this collection suggest that in spite of the unfavourable political environment, a concern for civil rights was rather more apparent than historians have been inclined to perceive.

The essays are very varied, both in their approach to the subject and in their underlying assumptions. They fall into two broad categories: those which examine the concept of civil rights as a 'package', and those which discuss specific aspects of civil rights. In the first group belongs W. E. Butler's introductory essay, which provides us with a general definition of civil rights (less straightforward a task than might be imagined), and surveys the theory and practice of civil rights in late imperial Russia and their legacy for Soviet constitutional development. Also in this group are three essays which examine the concept from the point of view of a particular section of society (S. A. Smith's discussion of working-class attitudes to rights) or at a particular moment in history (Linda Edmondson's essay on civil rights rhetoric in the 1905 Revolution, and H. J. White's on the Provisional Government of 1917).

Each of the essays in the second group develops a single theme in relation to civil rights. G. R. Swain discusses freedom of association and the problems of trade-union organization from 1906 to 1914, and Caspar Ferenczi demonstrates the relative freedom exercised by the periodical press in these same years, despite the continued existence of censorship and the use of administrative and criminal sanctions against writers, editors, and publishers. Peter Waldron analyses government policy on religious toleration in the last sixty years of the empire and the shifts in its attitude to non-Orthodox groups; Raymond Pearson considers the problems of the national minorities, faced with assertive Russification in an empire which recognized no rights, but only privileges; and John Klier looks at the fluctuations in the legislative treatment of the Jewish inhabitants of the empire.

Three essays raise the problem of property rights. Richard Wortman argues that the Russian intelligentsia's conceptions of civil rights were deficient in failing to recognize the ownership of property as an inalienable right of the citizen; Olga Crisp develops this theme in her study of the debate over peasant land tenure before and after the emancipation of the serfs, linking it to the problem of peasant collective responsibility for taxation and the consequent legal restrictions on their freedom of movement. William Wagner's essay discusses proposals for the improvement of women's property and inheritance rights, and their rights within the family, as part of a general attempt by Russian jurists to establish civil equality and security of the individual's personal and property rights within the Russian Empire.

The remaining essays in this volume address the subject from the perspective of two 'enemies of civil rights', to use D. C. B. Lieven's words. His essay discusses the security police, its functions, techniques, and personnel, analysing both its effectiveness and the consequences of its activities for civil rights. Alan Wood's contribution describes the development of forced labour and Siberian exile as central features of the tsarist penal system.

All the essays raise important questions about civil rights: the possibility or otherwise of protecting the rights of individuals and groups in an autocratic state; the potential conflict between the individual and the collective; the debate on property ownership as an inalienable right; the distinction between rights and privileges; the extent to which the attainment of civil rights mattered to groups engaged in social and political protest; even the very definition of civil rights. Such issues provided the debating ground for a very stimulating conference held in London in 1985, from which these essays derive. We should like to thank all those who took part in an event which was both lively and enjoyable, including three participants whose contributions have been, or are to be, published elsewhere.[3]

[3] Beatrice Farnsworth's paper, 'Peasant Women and their Civil Rights prior to 1917', was published in somewhat altered form as 'The Litigious Daughter-in-Law: Family Relations in Rural Russia in the Second Half of the Nineteenth Century', *Slavic Review*, 45/1 (Spring 1986); William C. Fuller's paper, 'The Russian Revolution of 1905 and Military Justice', forms ch. 6 of his book, *Civil–Military Conflict in Imperial Russia, 1881–1914* (Princeton, 1986); and Dittmar Dahlmann's paper, 'The Peasants and the Civil Rights Problem in 1905', has been revised for publication in German.

We should also like to record our gratitude to the Economic and Social Research Council for its support of the research project on civil rights in Russia before 1917 which gave rise to this conference, and for its additional funding of the conference itself. Our gratitude must also be expressed to the Nuffield Foundation and the BUAS/NASEES Ford Foundation sub-grant committee for their funding of the conference; to the Deutscher Akademischer Austauschdienst; to the Centre for Russian and East European Studies, University of Birmingham, for providing an ideal environment in which to prepare the manuscript of this book; and to the School of Slavonic and East European Studies, University of London, for giving a home to the research project and generous hospitality for the conference.

O.C. and L.E.

Birmingham
1988

CONTENTS

NOTES ON TRANSLITERATION AND
˙DATES

Transliteration of Russian follows the British System, with minor modifications. Book and periodical titles published before 1918 are transliterated in the notes according to their original spelling (e.g. -ago, instead of -ogo). Personal names are transliterated in the text in their Russian spelling, with the following exceptions: non-Russian names are given in their original form (Witte, Plehve, Reutern, Feldstein, etc.); rulers are referred to by their anglicized names (Alexander I, Catherine the Great, etc.), but their uncrowned heirs are given in the Russian form (Aleksandr Nikolaevich, not Alexander Nikolaevich). Place names are given without diacritical marks (Kharkov, Ryazan), or in their Western spelling (Kronstadt).

Dates are given according to the Julian calendar, unless otherwise stated; twelve days behind the western calendar in the nineteenth century, thirteen in the twentieth.

NOTES ON CONTRIBUTORS

W. E. Butler is Professor of Comparative Law at the University of London and Director of the Centre for the Study of Socialist Legal Systems, University College, London. He is the author of numerous works on Soviet law and on international and comparative law, including *Soviet Law* (2nd edn., London, 1988).

Olga Crisp is Emeritus Professor of Russian Economic History at the University of London. Among her many published works are *Studies in the Russian Economy before 1914* (London, 1976), and 'Labour and Industrialization in Russia', in the *Cambridge Economic History of Europe*, vii (Cambridge, 1978). She was the director of the project on civil rights in Russia before 1917 which was funded by the Economic and Social Research Council from 1982 to 1985.

Linda Edmondson is Honorary Research Fellow at the Centre for Russian and East European Studies, University of Birmingham. She is the author of *Feminism in Russia, 1900–1917* (London and Stanford, 1984), and is now writing a book on civil rights in the 1905 Revolution. She was the research fellow on the ESRC project on civil rights in Russia.

Caspar Ferenczi is Lecturer at the Institute of East European History, University of Heidelberg. His books include *Aussenpolitik und Öffentlichkeit in Russland 1906–1912* (Husum, 1982), and *Nationalismus und Neoslawismus in Russland vor dem Ersten Weltkrieg* (Berlin, 1984). He has written on Stalinism and the contemporary Soviet Union, and is preparing a book on Russian Freemasonry in the eighteenth century.

John D. Klier is Professor of History at Fort Hays State University, Kansas. He is the author of *Russia Gathers her Jews: The Origins of the 'Jewish Question' in Russia, 1772–1825* (DeKalb, Ill., 1987), and he has written extensively on the 'Jewish question' in nineteenth-century Russia.

D. C. B. Lieven is Senior Lecturer in Russian Government at the

London School of Economics and Political Science. He is the author of *Russia and the Origins of the First World War* (London, 1983), and *Russia's Rulers under the Old Regime* (London and New Haven, 1988). He is currently writing a book on the European aristocracy between 1815 and 1914.

Raymond Pearson is Senior Lecturer in History at the University of Ulster at Coleraine. His works include *Revolution in Russia* (Dublin, 1973), *The Russian Moderates and the Crisis of Tsarism, 1914–17* (London, 1977), and *National Minorities in Eastern Europe, 1848–1945* (London, 1983). He has recently completed *Russia and Eastern Europe, 1789–1985: A Bibliographical Guide.*

S. A. Smith is Senior Lecturer in History at the University of Essex. His publications include *Red Petrograd: Revolution in the Factories, 1917–18* (Cambridge, 1983), and (ed. and introd.) *Oktyabr'skaya revolyutsiya i fabzavkomy* (New York, 1983). He is currently working on a history of labour in Shanghai, 1895–1927.

G. R. Swain is Senior Lecturer in European History at Bristol Polytechnic. He is the author of *Russian Social Democracy and the Legal Labour Movement, 1906–14* (London, 1983), and he is currently engaged on research into aspects of the history of the Communist International.

William G. Wagner is Associate Professor of History at Williams College, Massachusetts. He is the author of several articles on Russian legal history since 1861. He is co-editor of a new translation of Chernyshevskii's *What is to be Done?*, and is completing a monograph, *In Pursuit of Orderly Change: Law, Marriage and Property in Late Imperial Russia.*

Peter Waldron was formerly Lecturer in Modern History at the University College, Cork. He is co-author of *The Emergence of the Modern Russian State, 1855–1881* (London, 1988), and he is now working on a biography of Stolypin.

H. J. White is Lecturer in Soviet Government at the London School of Economics and Political Science. He is completing a study of the 1917 Revolution in the provinces. In 1984–5 he was a research assistant on the ESRC project on civil rights in Russia.

Alan Wood is Lecturer in Russian History at the University of

Lancaster, and convener of the British Universities Siberian Studies seminar. Among his publications are (ed.) *Siberia: Problems and Prospects for Regional Development* (London, 1987), and *Origins of the Russian Revolution, 1861–1917* (London, 1987). He is writing a history of the Siberian exile system.

Richard Wortman is Professor of History at Columbia University. His publications include *The Crisis of Russian Populism* (Cambridge, 1967), and *The Development of a Russian Legal Consciousness* (Chicago, 1976). He is currently working on a study of tsarist ritual and imagery.

Civil Rights in Russia:
Legal Standards in Gestation

W. E. BUTLER

RATHER than dwelling upon minutiae of some of the legal aspects of civil rights, this essay undertakes a rather broad exposition of the larger issues implicit in the subject, and singles out aspects that a jurist or legally trained historian sees. At times, therefore, it touches upon legal and constitutional theory, but in a manner that one hopes will be instructive for the historian of the period.

The expression 'civil rights' is used here in the broadest sense that has become common in modern international practice. The 1966 United Nations covenants encompass civil, political, economic, social, and cultural rights, amounting in aggregate to what is widely referred to in brief as civil rights. The term is not employed in its narrower meaning of the legal capacity granted under the civil law to natural and corporate personalities, rights, and duties that in continental and socialist legal systems, for example, would be governed by the civil code.

What are Civil Rights?

An absolute categorical definition of civil rights has proved to be exceptionally elusive. The problem is hardly ambiguity, for few, if any, modern legal systems fail to accord civil rights to their constituents, so that the substance of civil rights is to be found in constitutions, legislation, international treaties, international customary law (according to some), and in the common law; rather, the difficulty has been the diversity in concepts of justice, of right, of equality, of values, all of which in any society contribute to the configuration of civil rights that are accorded, the reasons they are guaranteed, the limitations on their exercise, and the priorities to be acknowledged when two or more civil rights conflict with one another.

The history of human society could be seen in part as a continuing quest for the realization of civil rights. Some of the major landmarks are known to every child of school age: the Magna Carta; the Declaration of Independence and the Constitution of the United States of America; the Declaration of the Rights of Man; Woodrow Wilson's Fourteen Points; some of the early Soviet revolutionary documents, including the 1918 RSFSR Constitution; the Covenant of the League of Nations; the United Nations Charter; the Universal Declaration of Human Rights; and the international covenants of 1966. This collection of essays addresses aspects of the historical development of civil rights in Russia during the last six or seven decades of imperial rule, a slice, so to speak, of the larger perspective just mentioned, and an era that culminated in the appearance of three of the landmarks mentioned above.

Modern international concepts of human rights constitute part of the backdrop against which Russian experience is to be comprehended and evaluated, and to which Russian experience has contributed, for better and for worse. The international covenants dispose of one issue persuasively—for the twentieth century at least—and in doing so invite us to ask what the range of Russian attitudes on that issue was: to wit, where do civil rights originate? The answer given by the covenants relates to the human condition: the 'equal and inalienable rights of all members of the human family' derive from 'the inherent dignity of the human person'; those rights, the covenants stipulate, are 'the foundation of freedom, justice, and peace in the world'.[1] The ideal of free human beings enjoying civil and political freedom and freedom from fear and want, the covenants add, can be achieved only if conditions are created whereby everyone may enjoy the rights in the covenants. Through the medium of an international treaty, the covenants seek to fix a minimum standard below which no state may fall without being held accountable for a breach of international law by the other contracting parties.

In the era of late imperial Russia, civil rights as a generic

[1] *The International Covenants on Human Rights and Optional Protocol* (United Nations; New York, n.d.), 3. Both covenants contain this identical formulation.

phenomenon were strongly associated with parliamentary or republican forms of government. To be sure, absolutist monarchs granted certain civil rights to their subjects, but by sufferance rather than by right. All of the major civil landmarks from the Magna Carta to the Declaration of the Rights of Man have been linked to movements or philosophies antithetical to an absolutist state. Russia in this sense remained one of the great anachronisms in the earliest twentieth century in striving to preserve the all-powerful status of the tsar. In the eyes of many legal philosophers it would be untenable to speak of 'civil rights' under these circumstances; unless the rights can, in principle and in practice, be invoked against the state as well as against individual citizens or corporate entities, they are merely principles or tolerances subject to withdrawal at the whim of the grantor. Others would take a more particularistic view by suggesting that even an absolutist form of government may acknowledge and protect the civil rights of individuals *vis-à-vis* one another while excluding the possibility of having those rights invoked against its own person.

It has been commonplace to explain civil rights simply by enumerating them—equality before the law, inviolability of the person and the home, freedom of conscience and religion, and so on—but the thoughtful citizen will quickly appreciate that a realization of the enumerated rights is possible only with reference to their origin and the values underlying their *raison d'être*. For the historian examining the existence and realization of civil rights in imperial Russia, it is equally essential to explore carefully the reasons for the failure to grant civil rights or for the limitations imposed on the exercise of those rights that can be said to exist. It is the Russian concept of social community in the largest sense that is under analysis for these purposes, and an awareness of reciprocal rights and obligations is a part of this feeling of community. The international covenants, it should be added, in endeavouring to fix a minimum standard for civil rights, are undertaking to inculcate a sense of international society, and this accounts for the reference to all members of the human family.

The Quest for Constitutionalism

Most advanced societies have reduced to written form the limitations on the exercise of state power and authority with respect to citizens, and the rights enjoyed by individuals. The written form is commonly called a constitution, or has come to be treated as a document enjoying constitutional stature. The United Kingdom is remarkable and exceptional in relying upon the common law and international conventions as the principal repositories of civil rights accorded under English law, although many in Britain now believe that the time is ripe to introduce a written constitution.

American and French examples of constitutionalism of the late eighteenth century had a profound impact upon nineteenth-century movements for socio-political reform in Russia. A. D. Radishchev had found inspiration in the United States Constitution. The Decembrists presumed to draft a constitution, and for a brief time it appeared that Alexander I might embrace the limited schemes for a constitutional monarchy prepared by M. M. Speranskii (1809) and N. N. Novosil'tsev (1820). Subsequent Russian rulers held off the trend towards constitutional monarchies rampant in continental Europe, but many western students of Russian legal history believe that the seeds for legal constraints upon autocracy, made manifest in the abolition of serfdom in 1861, the judiciary reforms of 1864, and eventually the Basic Law of 1906 (also known as the Fundamental Laws), were sown with the development in the late eighteenth and early nineteenth centuries of legal education, a legal profession, and eventually a civil service with substantial numbers of legally trained individuals.[2] The so-called 'golden age' of Russian law is closely identified with the success of Russian defence counsel in defending individuals charged with 'political' offences before juries established in accordance with the judiciary reforms.[3]

The Basic Law of 1906 represents the most advanced statement of civil rights acknowledged by Russian legislation,

[2] R. Wortman, *The Development of a Russian Legal Consciousness* (Chicago, 1976).

[3] S. Kucherov, *Courts, Lawyers and Trials under the Last Three Tsars* (New York, 1953).

and it is here that we must look for the premises underlying civil rights and the particular rights actually accorded.

As a whole, of course, the Basic Law represented a limitation of the monarchy that was forced upon a reluctant government by the exigencies of the Russo-Japanese War of 1904–5 and the concomitant domestic unrest and civil strife. Conceptually, however, the autocracy was acknowledged. Chapter 1 (4) of the Basic Law prescribed: 'To the All-Russian Emperor belongs the Supreme Autocratic Power. To obey his power, not only by reason of wrath, but also for conscience's sake, is commanded by God himself.'[4] The tsar, in other words, ruled by divine right and commanded obedience to his wishes by virtue of that status. By enumerating the particular areas in which he exercised jurisdiction or functions, together with those areas in which the State Duma or other agencies or officials acted, the draftsmen achieved their object of autocratic limitation in the interests of more representative, democratic, and responsive government. One clause of relevance to civil rights generally is Chapter 1 (23), wherein the emperor is authorized to grant 'favours in special cases which do not fall under the operation of general laws, if legally protected interests and *civil rights* of none are infringed by it' (my emphasis).

The rights and duties of Russian subjects are treated principally but not exclusively, in Chapter 8 points 69–83. The main exception is the freedom of religion, mentioned in three separate points of the Basic Law, and perhaps the most venerable of the civil rights to be unequivocally acknowledged in Russian legislation, dating back to the first edition of the *Svod zakonov* in 1832. The matter is first raised in Chapter 7 (66), 'On Faith', which declares that all subjects of the Russian state not belonging to the Established Church, whether subjects by birth or admittance, as well as foreigners who are in Russian service or who are in Russia temporarily, may enjoy the free exercise of their faith and may worship according to its rites. In point 67 of the same chapter it is made clear that this freedom of religion extends not only to Christians of foreign confessions, but also to

---

[4] M. Szeftel, *The Russian Constitution of April 23, 1906: Political Institutions of the Duma Monarchy* (Brussels, 1976). All references to the 1906 Basic Law are drawn from the Szeftel translation.

Jews, Muslims, and pagans, so that, the Basic Law continues: 'all races residing in Russia praise God Almighty in different languages according to the [religious] law and confession of their forefathers, blessing the reign of Russian Monarchs, and beseeching the Creator of the Universe to increase the prosperity and consolidate the strength of the Empire'. Those seemingly unequivocal guarantees (so long as prayers are offered in support of the autocrat) appear to be attenuated by Chapter 9 (81), which states: 'Russian subjects enjoy freedom of religion. The conditions under which they may avail themselves of this freedom are determined by law.' As for members of the imperial family, whose civil rights were prescribed by Chapter 5 of the Organic Law on the Imperial Family, the marriage of a man who might succeed to the throne to a person of another faith required her conversion to Orthodoxy.

Chapter 8, devoted to the rights and duties of Russian subjects, contained fifteen points and commenced with duties: the duty to defend the throne and fatherland, and the duty of males, without distinction of social status, to perform military service. In modern times, equality of sexes would render even the latter duty discriminatory against women. Civil duties were included: to pay the taxes established by law, and to perform certain public services (*povinnosti*), for example, to render assistance during natural disasters.

The rights accorded to Russian subjects under the Basic Law, excluding the freedom of religion discussed above, fall into three basic categories. The first of these (points 72–4) appertained to legal proceedings. No one could be prosecuted for a criminal act other than in accordance with the procedure determined by law; and no one could be detained or placed under guard other than in the instances provided for by law. Criminal laws were not retroactive in character. Individuals were to be tried and punished for the criminal acts provided for by the legislation that was in force when the act was committed; except, however, that new legislation abolishing crimes could be retroactive in character.

The second category (points 75 and 77) encompassed property in its broad sense. A person's place of domicile was inviolable. In the absence of the master's consent, searches or seizures could be carried out only in the instances and procedure established by law. Property was also inviolable, in that it could not be expropriated for state or public benefit unless the owner was accorded just and adequate compensation.

In the third category (points 76, 78–80) fall the rights of movement, assembly, speech, and association. Unless established otherwise by special laws, Russian subjects were at liberty to choose their place of residence freely, to acquire and transfer property freely, and to travel unhindered beyond the limits of the state. Under the Basic Law, Russian subjects had the right to hold meetings, peacefully and without arms, for purposes not contrary to law. Everyone, within the limits prescribed by law, might express his thoughts orally or in writing, and circulate them in print or otherwise. Russian subjects were also granted the right to form societies and unions for purposes not contrary to law.

Foreigners (*inostrantsy*) who sojourned in Russia enjoyed the rights of Russian subjects within the limitations provided by law, but aliens (*inorodtsy*) did not.

The Realization of Civil Rights

This is not the place to dwell upon the extent to which civil rights could in fact be exercised before and after the 1906 Basic Law. Suffice it to observe that individual Russian legislative enactments of the late eighteenth and early nineteenth centuries made provision for freedom of worship, alluded to freedom of speech within certain organizations or associations (e.g. the Academy of Sciences), and in the course of regulating censorship simultaneously shaped the general contours for the freedom of the press. The introduction of trial by jury and adversary proceedings by the 1864 judiciary reform act, preceded by the emancipation of the serfs three years earlier, accentuated notions of individual legal personality and concomitant rights. A multitude of enactments dealt with civil rights in the early twentieth century as preparation for, and in pursuance of, the 1906 Basic Law. The Russian government's intention to broaden civil rights was announced on 12 December 1904. The Manifesto of 17 October 1905 inaugurating the transformation of the Russian Empire into a constitutional monarchy declared that the government should: 'grant the populace immutable foundations of civil liberty in accordance with the principles of genuine personal inviolability, freedom of conscience, speech, assembly, and association'. The rights of Old Believers, sectarians, and converts to another Christian denomination were broadened in April 1905, and eighteen months later they were authorized to form legally recognized religious communities. Censorship was relaxed substantially in a series of decrees. In 1906 restrictions were eased on the right of private and limited public gatherings, although constraints on meetings of associations remained considerable. Also in 1906 freedom of movement was expanded for the peasantry and city dwellers, and the possibility of public-service employment for this category of the populace was enlarged.

Full implementation of the basic rights laid down in the 1906 Basic Law achieved little progress in the successive State Dumas convoked between 1906 and 1917. Sundry bills were introduced in a liberal reformist spirit, but those which were passed were either blocked in the State Council or vetoed by the Tsar. It remains a matter for historical speculation as to whether, in the absence of war and revolution, the fledgling Russian constitutional system might have developed freedoms of press, association, assembly, speech, and personal inviolability in sufficient measure to become a full-fledged constitutional democracy.

The Legacy of Pre-Revolutionary Russian Civil Rights

Of what contemporary significance is the pre-revolutionary Russian experience with civil rights? Apart from contributing to a more profound knowledge of Russian society, of Russian law, of the Russian polity, is something more to be learned from a study of Russian experience with civil liberties, such as it was? The record of struggle for civil rights in Russia is not unimpressive, but it surely does not overshadow that of Western Europe and America; and the record of achievement is rather a dismal one, sufficiently so that the popular image of civil liberties in pre-revolutionary Russia is that, quite simply, few existed. The history of Russian civil rights is one of struggle and oppression, not of attainment and example, and there is very little feeling for the true balance between the theory of absolute autocracy and the legal presumptions designed to give effect to it on the one hand, and the genuine human condition expressed in the limitations—physical, moral, spiritual, institutional—on the actual effectuation of autocracy. Autocracy was always an ideal only approximated to in pre-1917 Russia; dismissing Russian civil rights as non-existent or inconsequential is not merely to lose sight of a major arena for political and social reform, but also to indulge in a kind of axiomatic negativism that likewise continues to obscure our perceptions of modern realities in the Soviet Union.

The true legacy of Russian civil rights lies in the possible contributions, both positive and negative, to the modern civil rights tradition in the Soviet Union, and to the fashioning of international human rights standards. With regard to modern Soviet legislation and practices, there are a number of elements of legal style which seem to have their roots in the Russian past. We shall dwell on two of these, one more or less positive and the other more or less negative. Both go to the heart of the movements for socio-political reform in Russia, and both have arguably left an enduring imprint upon modern civil rights.

To begin with the more or less positive development, the Russian revolutions of 1917 brought to the forefront social forces which believed that the social and economic rights of the individual were at least as important as his political rights, and suggested that the latter could not exist independently of the former. All four models of the Soviet Constitution since 1918 have asserted the importance of socio-economic rights, and a very substantial body of states, including the United Kingdom, have in the post-war world come to accept at least their equivalence to political rights in the 1966 international covenants. The 1977–8 Soviet Constitutions enumerate socio-economic rights first: the right to labour, leisure, health protection, material security, housing, education, use of the achievements of culture, and artistic and inventive creativity, among others.[5] These are not rights that can be found in the Basic Law of 1906 or other pre-revolutionary legislation; their *raison d'être* lies partly in the Russian civil rights movements, the social injustices experienced at the time, and the values cherished which led to these principles

---

[5] All 36 Soviet Constitutions are translated in W. E. Butler, *Collected Legislation of the USSR and Constituent Union Republics* (Dobbs Ferry, NY, 1985–).

being accorded such high priority when compared to others. It would be invidious to ascribe responsibility for international acceptance of this dimension of civil rights to any individual country, but there can be little doubt that Russian pre-revolutionary circumstances and Russian revolutionary experiences have played a role. It is appropriate for the social historian to explore both the Russian roots of that contribution and the extent to which a distinctively Russian concept of socio-economic rights and their balancing may persist.

The more or less negative contribution relates to legal limitations or restrictions upon the exercise of political civil rights. The rights enumerated in the 1906 Basic Law, to choose freely one's place of residence or occupation, to acquire and transfer property, to travel abroad without hindrance, to hold meetings, to express one's views orally or in writing, to form societies and unions, and to exercise freedom of religion, were all conditioned by clauses of limitation: 'for purposes not contrary to law'; 'within the limits fixed by law'; and so forth. Russian law in fact imposed severe and numerous restrictions on the exercise of all these 'rights'—often sufficiently onerous to ask whether the right had wholly disappeared amongst the limitations and exceptions. Censorship persisted through the late imperial period; it was rather a matter of degree which ebbed and flowed—Karl Marx's *Das Kapital* managed to see the light of day, but Hugo Grotius's *On the Law of War and Peace* contrived to appear only in a much truncated version (1902). For almost the last four decades of imperial rule, Russia lived under a state of emergency legislation (1881) which authorized sweeping restrictions of individual liberties. Public assemblies in either closed or open premises were stringently curtailed. Even under the reform enactments of 1906, police permission was required for open-air meetings, and for assemblies in closed premises detailed information about the agenda had to be supplied to the police at least three days in advance.

As for associations, prior permission from the authorities was necessary before they could be formed, and after 1906 compulsory registration was required. Many segments of the populace lived under severe legal constraints or disabilities. The peasantry and some urban dwellers were limited in where they could live and what occupations they could pursue. The Jewish population was the target of special restrictions affecting residence, freedom of movement, access to education and professions, and property ownership. Many observers believe that the government's attitude towards the Jewish population was responsible for its failure unequivocally to grant Russian subjects equal civil rights and duties when drafting the 1906 Basic Law. Even the imperial family was not exempted from certain restrictions: point 222 (Chapter 5) of the 1906 Basic Law empowered 'The reigning Emperor, as unlimited Autocrat . . . in any adverse event to deprive the disobedient [member of the imperial house] of the rights set out in this law . . .'.

The personal inviolability of individual citizens guaranteed in the 1906 Basic Law meant little so long as the state of emergency was in effect, for although the regulations varied slightly from one period to another, the renewals of the state of emergency enabled Russian subjects to be exposed to arbitrary search and seizure, banishment, or trial by a military court for certain offences. The arbitrariness of administrative officials remained essentially unchecked by legal restraints.

In this complex of limitations and restrictions lie some of the most objectionable features of the imperial era with respect to civil rights; some doubtless represented an autocratic reflex against currents in Russian society that were perceived as a threat, or a potential threat, to the existence of the monarchy, but others—restrictions on Jews, the movement of peasants, occupations, and the like—cannot plausibly be attributed to such an apprehension. Soviet Russia, however, inherited them all, discarded some, and preserved and reshaped others for its own ends.

Thus, the Soviet Constitutions contain, as do the constitutions of all members of the family of socialist legal systems, words of limitation with respect to civil rights that inject a qualification of purpose: the freedom of speech, press, and assembly, for example, must be exercised 'in accordance with the interests of the people and with a view to strengthening and developing the socialist system . . .'. Social and economic rights may contain the same qualification: the freedom of scientific, technical, and artistic creativity is guaranteed 'in accordance with the aims of communist construction . . .'. While in some instances the element of purpose operates to secure state support or enforcement of rights, in others it can be employed to stifle a diversity of expression or opinion that other societies regard as indispensable to the true exercise of civil rights, and wholly compatible with the standards laid down by the international covenants.

It is here perhaps that the ultimate success or failure of the international covenants will rest—in the ability of the Soviet Union and other socialist legal systems to incorporate in their social revolutions a greater degree of the tolerance of political, religious, and ideological pluralities which has served the Anglo-American tradition so effectively, and to recognize, as some East European jurists are beginning to acknowledge, that even within the socialist framework of human rights the individual requires protection against the state as well as affirmative state action on behalf of his rights. A better understanding of the historical roots of the Russian equation of the two may contribute in a positive way to the contemporary civil rights movement.

No modern political society gives unfettered rein to individual rights or society's rights. Neither does the international system require states to destabilize their domestic orders in order to secure human liberties. Where we disagree is in the equation that is struck by different societies when these rights conflict or overlap.

Property Rights, Populism, and Russian Political Culture

RICHARD WORTMAN

In his famous critique of the 'legal obtuseness' of the Russian intelligentsia, Bogdan Kistyakovskii wrote: 'The spiritual leaders of the Russian intelligentsia have constantly either completely ignored the *legal* [*pravovye*] interests of the individual, or have expressed open hostility towards them.' Individual rights, he thought, could come to Russia only with the introduction of constitutional government. Kistyakovskii reserved his sharpest criticism for two of the leading ideologists of populism, Alexander Herzen and Nikolai Mikhailovskii. Both Herzen and Mikhailovskii, he claimed, had subordinated political freedom and the legal guarantees of the individual to the goal of social equality.[1]

Kistyakovskii's defence of individual rights made no mention of property rights. Indeed, he too looked forward to a socialist order, and valued the right of property no more than the thinkers he had attacked.[2] In this respect, his thought was typical of the intellectuals who led the movement against the autocracy in the first years of the twentieth century. The programmes of the Constitutional Democrats as well as the various socialist parties included demands for such rights as freedom of speech, assembly, and the press as well as the right to domicile. But none of them mentioned the second of the rights of the Declaration of the Rights of Man, the right to property. The omission of property rights by groups seeking to defend the dignity and freedom of the individual points to a distinctive feature of the struggle for civil rights in Russia. For whether or not one deems property rights essential for human freedom, the assertion of civil

---

[1] B. A. Kistyakovskii, 'V zashchitu prava', *Vekhi* (Moscow, 1909), 132–5.

[2] On Kistyakovskii's conceptions of right, see S. E. Heuman, 'A Socialist Conception of Human Rights: A Model from Prerevolutionary Russia', in A. Pollis and P. Schwab (eds.), *Human Rights: Cultural and Ideological Perspectives* (New York, 1982), 50–3; Kistyakovskii, 'V zashchitu', pp. 142–3.

rights in opposition to property rights places the Russian experience outside the western tradition that was supposed to serve as its model.

The hostility to property reflected in part the socialist orientation of the Russian intelligentsia. But before 1905 the right of property had few consistent defenders in any political camp in Russia. Property rights were associated with the bourgeois West or the system of serfdom. Russians of divergent political persuasions favoured the peasant commune with its principles of common ownership, even if their visions of its true character and ideal form differed. To be sure, there was an undercurrent of opposition to the commune in liberal circles and in the administration. But it was only the peasant uprisings of 1905 and 1906 that made the virtues of private holding clear to the Tsar, his most influential officials, and the majority of the landed nobility.[3]

Private property, of course, developed as a basis for the Russian agrarian and industrial economy in the late eighteenth and nineteenth centuries. But the notion of individual property *rights* lacked ethical justification in Russian political culture, and retained a strong stigma throughout this period. Conservatives saw in it the seed of social discord and breakdown. Liberals and socialists could not reconcile private property in land with the concepts of equality or freedom. The word 'property' conveyed the sense of oppression and exploitation, of an illegitimate usurpation of the possession of all, under the auspices of arbitrary and brutal political authority. Landed property symbolized not a basis for the individual's freedom, but a constraint which, by tying him to a particular place, debased his concerns to the mundane and trivial and destroyed his spiritual freedom. They felt, like Ivan Ivanych in Chekhov's story 'Gooseberries', that 'a man does not need three *arshins* of land, not an estate in the country, but the whole globe, all of nature where he can freely display all the features and peculiarities of his free spirit'.

Like other western concepts, the concept of property rights in Russia was transformed by a political culture which attached to it its own connotations and associations. In the West, the modern sense of property came into usage during the French Revolution.

[3] V. Leontovitsch, *Geschichte des Liberalismus in Russland* (Frankfurt-on-Main, 1957), 153.

Article 17 of the Declaration of the Rights of Man described property as 'an inviolable and sacred right', yet justified the abolition of seigneurial rights by providing that individuals could be deprived of their property 'when a legally stated public necessity obviously requires it, and under the condition of a just and prior indemnity'. This provision established a semantic continuity between old and new conceptions of property under the rubric of 'natural' right. As William Sewell has shown, it created a successful transition from the old feudal conception of property as an attribute of privilege to the new sense of property as a belonging rightfully held by all individuals.

Under the rubric of natural right, the National Assembly extended the right of property to the middle classes. Detached from its feudal origins, the concept of property rights was transformed into an attribute of freedom. The Assembly defined property as 'a set of physically palpable possessions that a person had annexed to himself by his labor and was free to use in any way that did not infringe on the liberty of other citizens'. It meant an extension of 'personhood' to be guaranteed 'the same liberty as all other aspects of his person'.[4]

In Russia, the transition from property as an attribute of privilege to property as an attribute of freedom never took place. Indeed, property rights remained an alien element in Russian historical development, and never became a fully legitimate aspect of privilege. Slavophile writers in the nineteenth century extolled the absence of a tradition of Roman law and the prevalence of an orthodox collective spirit which, they claimed, shaped the institutions of the people. But this was a romanticized view of secular developments. It was the prevalence of the state as a moral and legal entity in the Russian past, not deep religious feelings, that prevented property rights from gaining the esteem they held in the West.

In Russia, the notion of property developed from rights to land extended by the tsarist state. There was no tradition of feudal law to justify these grants. Before Peter the Great, servitors held land either as conditional grants for service, or in hereditary tenure, but both were obliged to serve. Private property was justified by an ethos of service to the public weal, embodied in the state.

[4] W. H. Sewell, Jun., *Work and Revolution in France: The Language of Labor from the Old Regime to 1848* (Cambridge, 1980), 134–6.

When Peter the Great eliminated what had become an obsolete distinction and made all lands hereditary in 1714, he enforced a requirement of compulsory lifetime service for the nobility. In the 1760s the nobility gained freedom from compulsory service, but the connection between land and service retained its force. Their estates remained 'unfree landed property', granted on an assumption of a moral, if not a legal, obligation to serve.[5]

When Catherine the Great granted the nobility the right of property in the Charter of 1785 and other laws of her reign, she was using a western concept without historical roots in the Russian past. From its inception, the right of property became associated with the consolidation of the nobility's power over their peasants and the abuses of the serf system. The Charter of the Nobility of 1785 uses the word 'right' (*pravo*) only in regard to property. The word *pravo* approximated property to the other noble right which was not mentioned in the charter, 'bondage right' (*krepostnoe pravo*), or serfdom. Other concessions in the charter were termed the 'personal privileges' (*lichnye preimushchestva*) of noblemen. In the vocabulary of early nineteenth-century autocracy, the word 'right' meant merely a firmer and more important form of privilege.

The property rights bestowed by the tsarist state became identified with its despotic authority. The serf-owner served as an agent of the state, performing police, judicial, and fiscal functions. The government, in turn, used the army to protect the landlord from peasant unruliness and violence. Property, in this sense, remained an attribute of authority. It carried none of the redeeming sense of autonomy that it held in the West. It could not promote the liberal values of individualism and self-reliance. Herzen sneered at Russian conceptions of property: 'What really can be said on behalf of the inviolability of the landlord's private property—the landlord, the whipper-of-men, who mixes up in his concept of property, the garden plot and the peasant woman, boots and the *starosta*?'[6]

Noble property rights remained a troubling inconsistency in the system of official values. During the first half of the nineteenth century, Alexander I and Nicholas I sought to limit

[5] A. V. Romanovich-Slavatinskii, *Dvoryanstvo v Rossii ot nachala XVIII veka do otmeny krepostnago prava* (St Petersburg, 1870), 238–9.
[6] Quoted in V. Chernov, *Zemlya i pravo* (Petrograd, 1917), 17.

the landlords' power over their serfs and extend property rights to the peasants as well. Such efforts aroused the fears not only of the gentry, but also of many officials: peasant property independent of state authority might threaten the political order. Thus, in the Committee of 1839, Count Kiselev recommended giving the peasants land in use rather than as property. Peasants owning land in hereditary tenure, he warned, might demand a role in government. As 'an unrestrained majority', they would 'destroy the equilibrium of the parts of the state organism'.[7]

During the eighteenth and nineteenth centuries, service continued to provide the ethos of the Russian nobility and state, even when honoured mainly in the breach. 'Service became the expression of a social and moral ideal', Marc Raeff wrote. They and their ancestors had earned their nobility and land by service, predominantly in the army, and their *raison d'être* continued to be service to the state rather than their own independence or honour. The notion that private property provided the basis of political virtue, which proved to be so crucial in the evolution of western political theory, was weakly developed in Russia. The nobility's virtue was expressed in their acts of sacrifice for the fatherland, not in their possession of land. Nikolai Karamzin wrote in his famous *Memoir* that the Russian gentry 'were never anything except a brotherhood of outstanding men serving the grand princes or tsars'.[8]

Service to the state also provided the principal secular legitimization of the monarch's power in Russia. From Peter the Great onwards, Russian emperors and empresses were depicted as servants of the nation who worked for 'the general welfare'.[9] The tsar represented the general good, and his absolute power enabled him to remain above the interests of particular groups and individuals. After the Decembrist uprising of 1825 these claims assumed moral and religious overtones. Mikhail Speranskii taught the Tsarevich, Aleksandr Nikolaevich, that the aim of society was not the mere satisfaction of particular interests. Life in society should be a preparation for the supreme truth, 'the

[7] Leontovitsch, *Geschichte des Liberalismus*, p. 108.

[8] Raeff, *Origins of the Russian Intelligentsia* (New York, 1966), 119. R. Pipes, *Karamzin's Memoir on Ancient and Modern Russia: A Translation and Analysis* (New York, 1969), 200.

[9] N. I. Pavlenko, 'Idei absolyutizma v zakonodatel'stve XVIII v.', *Absolyutizm v Rossii XVII–XVIII vv.* (Moscow, 1964), 389–427.

threshold of the highest being'. The government was the conscience of society, introducing ideas of justice and duty and ensuring their observance. 'Just as conscience in the internal moral order is the organ of divine justice, so the supreme authority is the organ of eternal truth in the social order when it is pure and correct.'[10]

The emperor was to live not for himself or particular interests, but for the nation. From his religious instruction, Aleksandr Nikolaevich learned that 'the ruler should have no purpose but the welfare of his subjects and he should not distinguish between his advantage and theirs, not to speak of allowing the two to come into conflict'. Christ was to be his example.[11]

Later in the century the tsar's mission as the secular embodiment of the truth was emphasized all the more by monarchist writers. Lev Tikhomirov, the former populist, stressed the ethical essence of autocracy, which placed social good above individual interest, and obligation above right. He cited Mikhail Katkov's description of 'the psychology of right': 'Only that right is fruitful which reflects nothing but an obligation. . . . There is no benefit in the fact that I have the right to do something if I do not feel obliged to do what I may.' The tsar had to act as an instrument of divine justice. 'Most important, the tsar must not have personal motivations. He is the executor of the Supreme Will. Where the Supreme Will indicates the need for punishment and severity, the tsar should be severe and should punish. He is only the instrument of justice.'[12]

The tsar's presumed power to transcend human weakness provided grounds for critiques of parliamentary government, which, monarchist writers claimed, defended not only the material interests of particular groups. Speranskii taught Alexander II that constitutional government inevitably fell into the hands of the monied classes and advanced their interests to the detriment of the good of all. Alexander III's tutor and adviser, Konstantin Pobedonostsev, claimed that representative institutions turned into the despotism of unprincipled politicians and

[10] *Gody ucheniya ego Imperatorskago vysochestva naslednika tsesarevicha Aleksandra Nikolaevicha: Sbornik Russkago istoricheskago obshchestva*, 30 (1880), 342–4, 366–7, 436–8.

[11] Ibid. 100–1, 106.

[12] L. A. Tikhomirov, *Monarkhicheskaya gosudarstvennost'* (Buenos Aires, 1968), 454, 612.

the mob, and could not attain the lofty moral plane of autocracy.[13]

The ethos of autocracy asserted the supremacy of the moral and political sphere over the economic. The tsar's role as the moral guardian of Russian society endowed him with obligations to preserve equity in the relations between groups in Russian society. As an impartial arbiter, he was supposed to stand above economic interest and social conflict, and enforce equity and justice.[14] During the eighteenth century, the tsarist state regulated and closely supervised the economic relationships between estates. What Reinhard Bendix described as 'the ideology of the masters' implied that the authorities must ensure that the good of the state and the maintenance of authority take precedence over the interest of the individual producer. The administration intervened in disputes between labour and management as the protector of the interests of all the people; it both reinforced the authority of the managers and rectified some of the workers' grievances.[15]

This perspective led tsarist officials in the nineteenth century to view the peasant commune as an embodiment of the values of the state, ensuring both equity and order. The commune guaranteed each peasant a plot of land, and presumably served as a safeguard against impoverishment and the appearance of a potentially restless proletariat.[16] The commune encouraged the subordination of individualistic impulse to the good of the group, and promoted the ethical goals of the autocracy. The Minister of Finance, Egor Kankrin, expressed this sentiment when he wrote in 1837: 'The people's custom of equal division of the land among all settlers and inhabitants of one area is a sign of popular good will and fraternal union in which one should take pride, and

---

[13] *Gody ucheniya*, pp. 366–7; C. P. Pobedonostsev, *Reflections of a Russian Statesman* (Ann Arbor, 1968), 266.

[14] Contrast this view with the dominant attitude in the United States in the nineteenth century: 'It was a century which put all the energy and attention it could into economic interests. . . . In most affairs one senses that men turned to non-economic issues grudgingly or as a form of diversion and excitement or in spurts of bad conscience over neglected problems' (J. W. Hurst, *Law and the Conditions of Freedom in the Nineteenth-Century United States* (Madison, Wis., 1956), 29).

[15] R. Bendix, *Work and Authority in Industry* (New York, 1956), 166–74.

[16] A. Gerschenkron, 'Russia: Agrarian Policies and Industrialization, 1861–1917', *Cambridge Economic History*, 6/2 (1965), 750; P. A. Zaionchkovskii, *Otmena krepostnogo prava v Rossii* (Moscow, 1968), 150.

which bears the splendid imprint of deep Christian feeling.'[17]

The justification of the emancipation of the serfs in 1861 followed the traditional pattern of subordinating the interests of the specific estates to the good of all. The state clearly encroached on the property rights of the landed nobility by assigning lands, with compensation, to the peasantry. Alexander, however, maintained the fiction that property rights remained sacrosanct by presenting the emancipation as a response to the initiative of the nobility itself. The initial rescripts were issued in response to contrived or intentionally misinterpreted 'requests' from provincial noble assemblies. Official statements then described the reform as a great act of national sacrifice. The Emancipation Edict referred to the nobility's 'sacrifice for the benefit of the fatherland', asserting that they had 'voluntarily renounced their rights to the persons of the serfs'. The emancipation, thus, tampered with noble property rights in order to defend them.[18]

With the emancipation, the government began strenuous efforts to convince the peasantry that they should not expect a redivision of all the lands, the 'black partition' that they longed for. The edict referred to 'misunderstandings' that had arisen in the countryside, and reminded the peasants that 'he who freely enjoys the blessings of society should mutually serve society by fulfilling certain obligations'. After quoting Paul's admonition in the Letter to the Romans to 'obey the powers that be' and to give everyone his due, it declared that 'the legally acquired rights of the landlords cannot be taken from them without proper compensation or voluntary concession'. In subsequent years, Alexander made it clear that he considered the defence of property rights to be inseparable from the autocratic order. In his rescript to the Chairman of the Committee of Ministers, Prince P. P. Gagarin, he emphasized the importance to the welfare of the state and each of its citizens of 'the complete inviolability of the right of property in all its forms, defined by the general laws and the statute of 19 February 1861'.[19]

[17] M. Tugan-Baranovskii, *Russkaya fabrika v proshlom i nastoyashchem* (Moscow, 1922), 222.

[18] On the contrived noble initiative see D. Field, *The End of Serfdom: Nobility and Bureaucracy in Russia, 1855–1861* (Cambridge, Mass., 1976), 77–83; S. S. Tatishchev, *Imperator Aleksandr II: Ego zhizn' i tsarstvovanie* (St Petersburg, 1903), i. 380–1.

[19] S. S. Dmitriev (ed.), *Khrestomatiya po istorii SSSR*, iii (Moscow, 1952), 67–70.

The emancipation of the serfs involved an effort to enhance respect for private property. But this goal was not pursued consistently. The maintenance, and indeed, the strengthening of the land commune, ensured that the great majority of the peasants would not receive rights of individual property. Recent studies have shown that reformers in the Editing Commission hoped to extend the right of property to the peasantry as well and bring about the dissolution of the commune. But the reformers thought it premature to embark on a forcible dissolution of the communal system, especially since the peasantry lacked other institutional structures in the countryside. In any case, it is doubtful whether their viewpoint could have triumphed, given that both the conservative bureaucracy and most of liberal public opinion believed in the commune as a basic institution of Russian life. Another effort to dismantle the commune led to Alexander II's approval in 1874 of a resolution to find ways to introduce individual land-holding among the peasantry. But the growing international crisis and revolutionary menace precluded so drastic a reform, and the matter was dropped. After Alexander II's death, the government defended the commune as a mainstay of the autocracy and took measures for its defence.[20]

Nor did the state extend political rights to proprietors. The Emperor came to the defence of noble property rights, but insisted on maintaining his monopoly of power. In 1862 the Committee of Ministers issued a warning to the nobility, reminding them that 'the Government, at present concentrating all its attention on the reforms in various parts of the administration for the general welfare, reserves for itself the further conduct of these reforms toward their ultimate goal'. In 1865, angry at the nobility's continued requests for a role in government, Alexander issued a rescript which asserted his own 'concern to improve and perfect . . . the various branches of state administration', and his own exclusive right of initiative in reform. 'No class has the right to speak in the name of other classes. No one is called to take

---

[20] V. G. Chernukha, *Krest'yanskii vopros v pravitel'stvennoi politike Rossii* (Leningrad, 1972), 124–64. The movement to dissolve the commune in the bureaucracy is explored in D. Macey, *Government and Peasantry in Russia: The Prehistory of the Stolypin Reforms* (De Kalb, Ill., 1987). See also L. G. Zakharova, *Samoderzhavie i otmena krepostnogo prava v Rossii, 1856–1861* (Moscow, 1984), 158–9.

upon himself before ME petitions about the general welfare and needs of the state.'[21]

Yet by defending the property rights of the nobility, Alexander impugned the principle of ethical supremacy that justified his autocratic prerogatives. The leaders of the intelligentsia now claimed the title to ethical leadership that the Tsar had relinquished. Herzen looked towards a 'social monarchy' in which the tsar promoted the cause of equality. Chernyshevskii wrote: 'Only one thing is necessary: let our autocracy take to the path of economic improvement, let Alexander II finish the work begun by Alexander I and by Nicholas.' Chernyshevskii envisaged a system of agricultural and industrial co-operatives introduced and operated by the state; the state would work to transform the commune into a truly socialist institution.[22]

The leaders of the intelligentsia rose to the task of replacing the tsar as ethical leader of the nation. Herzen could not drink the toast he had prepared to the Tsar-Liberator. 'The Tsar has cheated the people', he wrote in *The Bell*. Serfdom had not been fully abolished. Nikolai Ogarev and N. N. Obruchev wrote an appeal, 'What Do the People Need?' They answered that the people needed land, freedom, and education: '*The land belongs to no one but the people*', they declared. The peasants should receive the land that they held at the moment, and they should be governed by their own representatives who would apportion taxes fairly and not oppress them like the tsar's officials.[23]

Radical writers retained the structure of tsarist thought, claiming that the autocracy had violated its own fundamental principles. By defending the landlords' rights in the emancipation, they asserted, Alexander II had undermined his claims to ethical supremacy. Their propaganda portrayed the Tsar as selfish and callous. The pamphlet 'A Conversation between the Tsar and the People', written in the early 1870s, presents Alexander as indifferent to the people's pleas for help, concerned only about the collection of tax arrears. He impatiently urges the peasants to have faith in God and to learn to accept their lot. He is unable to

---

[21] T. Emmons, *The Russian Landed Gentry and the Peasant Emancipation of 1861* (Cambridge, 1968), 396–7, 410–11.

[22] T. Dan, *The Origins of Bolshevism* (New York, 1964), 33–4; F. Venturi, *Roots of Revolution* (London, 1960), 173–4.

[23] Venturi, *Roots of Revolution*, pp. 108–10; Dmitriev, *Khrestomatiya*, iii. 101–6.

understand the peasants' condition or to act as their guardian.[24]

Populist writers influential during the 1870s asserted that property and wealth had silenced the ethical imperatives of government in Russia. Economic concerns had become paramount, as they had in the bourgeois societies of the West which Russia had now begun to resemble. From this perspective, constitutional government and the civil rights of a liberal order seemed little more than weapons of the propertied classes. Petr Lavrov wrote in his *Historical Letters* that American democracy had one feature in common with the Russian Empire or Asian khanates: 'the subjection of a considerable number of individuals to a juridical contract or to a class domination which these individuals have not discussed or concerning which they declare their disagreement'.[25] The most complete statement of populist views of government, Lavrov's *The State Element in the Society of the Future*, dismissed representative government briefly: 'The Lords and Commoners of England, her judges and coroners have become the juridical organs of the ruler of wealth over the masses. The bourgeoisie reigned in the chambers and courts of France after the great revolution.'[26]

The state, according to Lavrov, had now relinquished its principal responsibility as the protector of the security of the individual and society, and had become 'the preserver of the economic order' which had grown out of 'the international competition among monopolistic property owners'. It assisted the exploiting classes and assumed 'the role of the vampire of society'. Ethical principles could triumph only with the social revolution which would usher in an era of human solidarity. Then property would belong to all, and people would engage in work for the general good. Egoistic feelings would weaken, and altruistic feelings would grow stronger and form the bases of a common life.[27]

Populist writers looked to the peasant commune as the mainstay of altruistic feelings in Russia, and rallied to its defence against government policies that they claimed encouraged private

---

[24] *Agitatsionnaya literatura russkikh revolyutsionnykh narodnikov* (Leningrad, 1970), 462–3.

[25] P. L. Lavrov, *Historical Letters* (Berkeley, 1967), 245.

[26] Id., *Izbrannye sochineniya na sotsial'no-politicheskie temy v vos'mi tomakh* (Moscow, 1935), iv. 239.

[27] Ibid. 243, 245, 264–5.

ownership. They, like the Slavophiles, found the collective spirit in the people themselves, not in the state. Just as the Slavophiles had discerned a religious principle in the commune, the populists discovered a social ideal which they projected into the future. The absence of private property in the commune represented a potential guarantee against the prevalence of private interests in a future society. The communes' practice of repartition of the land, they believed, provided the grounds for a socialist law based on use rather than possession. The revolutionary tracts of Mikhail Bakunin promoted the communal system as the ideal of the people; inequality and oppression in existing communes resulted from the domination of the autocratic state.[28]

At the end of the 1870s the revolutionary populists recognized the importance of winning political and civil rights. But these rights were an addition to their programme, and fit uneasily with their principal goals of social and economic justice.[29] The programme of the People's Will in 1879 announced the revolutionaries' plans to introduce democratic suffrage and freedom of religion, speech, press, and assembly. But their principal goal remained the elimination of private property in land. The land was to belong to the people, they declared, but as a strategic concession they promised to regard as inviolable the persons and property of those who remained neutral to the revolutionary struggle.[30]

Nikolai Mikhailovskii presented the populists' argument for parliamentary government and individual rights in a series of articles he wrote for the illegal press. The tsarist government could no longer protect the population from the bestial oppression of the bourgeoisie, he argued. Only by transferring 'public matters' into 'public hands', by convening an 'Assembly of the Land', a *Zemskii sobor*, could the citizen's security be secured. Although Mikhailovskii assumed that democratic government would ensure political freedom, he made no mention of civil rights *per se*, nor of the institutional means of guaranteeing them. Indeed, he thought political freedom in Russia presumed

---

[28] For a comparison of populism and Slavophilism, see A. Gleason, *Young Russia: The Genesis of Russian Radicalism in the 1860s* (New York, 1980), 49–53; S. S. Volk (ed.), *Revolyutsionnoe narodnichestvo 70-kh godov XIX veka* (Moscow and Leningrad, 1965), i. 45, 51. On the notion of peasant legal norms, see Chernov, *Zemlya i pravo*, pp. 19–21, 24–5, 44–5.

[29] R. Wortman, *The Crisis of Russian Populism* (Cambridge, 1967), 82–4.

[30] Volk, *Revolyutsionnoe narodnichestvo*, ii. 170–4.

expropriation: a constitutional system could gain support from the peasantry only by promising them land. 'The Russian people will rise up to a man only for that kind of freedom that guarantees them land.' A social revolution, he suggested, was also more probable against an assembly than against a tsar: 'When is a popular uprising more likely? When at the summit of the political system sits a remote, semi-mythical tsar, whom the people in their ignorance still believe in according to custom, or when the country is being governed by elected individuals, ordinary people, without any mystical aura?'[31]

Populist writers thus introduced the notion of political rights into programmes that continued to express an egalitarian and collectivist social vision. Unlike Russian Marxists, who insisted on a bourgeois phase of development before the advent of socialism, they provided no historical grounding for these rights. They assumed that they could be imposed by a triumphant revolutionary leadership. But the decline of the revolutionary movement in the 1880s and the spread of the historical and deterministic doctrines of Marxism undermined the earlier faith in the power of the vanguard.

In the first years of the twentieth century, the resurgence of the opposition movement and the spread of peasant insurrections rekindled the revolutionary faith of the populists. Viktor Chernov provided new intellectual grounds for their assumption of the role of ethical leader of the nation. Chernov cited European critiques of Marxist theory which showed that capitalism did not always lead to economic growth. He drew the conclusion that in many countries like Russia capitalism would not develop new forms of social co-operation—as it had done in the West 'as a result of the blind play of particular interest'. In Russia it would bring only destruction and suffering. But this allowed the leaders of the intelligentsia to intervene and shape the economy according to their ideals. He summoned them to 'the vigorous work of taming and harmonizing egoistic tendencies, smoothing out of rough spots, the submerging of individual wills, the elimination of dissonances, the working out of an internal harmony. It is a labour of massive conscious creation.'[32]

[31] N. K. Mikhailovskii, *Revolyutsionnyya stat'i* (Berlin, 1906), 9–10, 18, 21.
[32] V. Chernov, 'Tipy kapitalisticheskoi i agrarnoi evolyutsii', *Russkoe bogatstvo*, 10 (1900), 243–4.

Chernov's writings expressed the populists' voluntaristic faith in the possibilities of subordinating economic processes, viewed as ineluctable by Russian Marxists, to ethical imperatives.[33] The programme of the Socialist Revolutionary party, adopted in January 1906, incorporated this central populist belief. It reaffirmed the intelligentsia's role as ethical leader, using words borrowed from Lavrov and Mikhailovskii. The destructive impact of capitalism in Russia had left the field open for moral leadership. Social progress manifested itself in 'the struggle for the establishment of social solidarity and for the complete and harmonious development of human individuality'. The struggle presumed the evolution of impersonal class antagonisms, but above all it required 'the intervention of conscious fighters for truth and justice'.[34]

The political section of the programme developed the principles advanced by the revolutionaries of the 1880s. Political freedom would be a necessary preliminary stage to the achievement of socialism. The party recognized the inalienable rights of man and the citizen—freedom of conscience, speech, press, assembly, and unionization. There would be freedom of movement, choice of work, collective refusal to work, and inviolability of person and dwelling. The agrarian section of the programme, however, reaffirmed the populists' determination to do away with private property in land. 'In the interests of socialism and the struggle against bourgeois-proprietorial principles', the party would rely upon the communal views and forms of life of the peasants. This meant the dissemination of the notion 'that the land is no one's, and that right to its use is given only by labour'. As a result, the party would work for the socialization of the land, which would be removed from commercial exchange and turned 'from the private property of separate individuals or groups into the possession of the whole people (*obshchenarodnoe dostoyanie*)'. Under the management of central and local organs of popular self-government, the land would be allotted equally, on a labour principle: 'to secure a norm of consumption on the basis of the

---

[33] On the voluntarist strain among the Socialist Revolutionaries, see M. Hildermeier, *Die Sozialrevolutionäre Partei Russlands: Agrarsozialismus und Modernisierung im Zarenreich (1900–1914)* (Cologne, 1978), 81–3.

[34] *Protokoly pervago s"ezda partii sotsialistov-revolyutsionerov* (n.p., 1906), 355, 359.

application of one's own labour, either individually or in a co-operative'.[35]

The SRs' programme thus retained the earlier populist view that property did not belong to the sphere of natural rights, but derived from the values and vocabulary of the system which had to be overthrown. The political and legal programme anticipated that the revolution would establish civil rights and the inviolability of the individual, while their agrarian programme foresaw the swift end to individual property rights in land. The programme did not conceive of any discrepancy between the introduction of freedom and civil rights, and the attack on the right of property. The socialization of the land was to take place according to the peasants' own concepts of land tenure. But the leadership assumed that the peasants shared their views, and would continue to hold land collectively. They made no provision for dissenting opinions. Moreover, the SRs both countenanced and encouraged seizures of land from the nobility, which were to take place under its own direction in order to ensure the socialization of the land. Mikhail Gots even attacked the Bolsheviks' strategy of confiscation for failing to ensure that the agrarian revolution brought the village as close as possible to socialism.[36]

The moderate populists of the *Russkoe bogatstvo* group and the Popular Socialist party shared the same determination to abolish private property in land, though they advocated more gradual and less violent methods. Aleksei Peshekhonov, the principal writer on the land question for the *Russkoe bogatstvo* and a leader of the Popular Socialists, saw private land-holding as the major obstacle to the economic well-being of Russia. Individual rights, he emphasized, were not absolute: 'Perfecting social forms, [humanity] strives not only to extend and secure the rights of each individual, but to limit them in the interests of collectivity.' His review of the reports of the gentry Committees on Agriculture made clear that noble property rights conflicted with the rights of man as he understood them: 'The "rights" that [the nobles] are storming about are, first, the right of individuals to turn fruits of the labours of all society to their own advantage

[35] Ibid. 361, 363.
[36] M. Perrie, *The Agrarian Policy of the Russian Socialist-Revolutionary Party from its Origin through the Revolution of 1905–1907* (Cambridge, 1976), 102–4.

and, second, the right of the strong classes to exploit "the very weakest" part of the population.'[37]

Peshekhonov repeated John Stuart Mill's argument that property rights derived from the labour applied to the land, and thus could not justify excluding others from the possibility of devoting their time and energy to that land. Nor could the right of property be defended on the grounds of productivity in Russia, where it had led to impoverishment and destruction of the agricultural resources of the country. Only the transfer of land to the peasants could remedy this situation. Those who laboured, he concluded, should have exclusive right to the land: 'In addition, the management of these lands should be transferred to the people in the agency of central and local representation, organized on democratic principles.'[38]

The moderate populists favoured the nationalization of land. Nationalization represented a more controlled and moderate form of land transfer than the socialization supported by Chernov and the Socialist Revolutionary party—the Popular Socialists even supported the redemption of noble lands—but it did not permit private ownership, even if the owners were to be peasants. Indeed, they opposed seizures and control by local committees, partly because they feared that local initiative without central control might result in kulak ownership in many areas. They were bitter critics of the Stolypin land reform.[39]

The 1906 programme of the Popular Socialist party was based on the populist goal of the good of the whole people by gradual methods. The party spoke for 'all labourers'. It strove for 'the welfare of the people' (*narodnoe blago*), which it would determine through 'the people's will'. 'The people's will' was to be expressed by a democratic government, which would protect individual rights. Their political programme, Ginev remarks, could have been endorsed by the Constitutional Democrats. The goal of the

---

[37] A. V. Peshekhonov, *Zemel'nyya nuzhdy derevni* (St Petersburg, 1906), 66–7, 70–1.

[38] Ibid. 67, 71, 154–5.

[39] Perrie, *Agrarian Policy*, pp. 161–2; V. N. Ginev, *Bor'ba za krest'yanstvo i krizis russkogo neonarodnichestva, 1902–1914 gg.* (Leningrad, 1983), 194–6, 210. The Popular Socialists' consistent opposition to all private landowning belies the notion that they represented the interests of a rural bourgeoisie or farmer class, as suggested by N. D. Erofeev in his *Narodnye sotsialisty v pervoi russkoi revoliutsii* (Moscow, 1979), 62–3, 71–2.

government was to be nationalization of the land, but the means were to be peaceful, involving redemption of private property by a democratically elected government. Those lands that were being worked, *trudovye khozyaistva*, would remain temporarily in the possession of their owners, and could be inherited on the principle of labour use.[40]

Populist attitudes towards private property extended far beyond their own circles and influenced many members of the Constitutional Democratic party, the principal champion of a constitutional regime in Russia. An articulate contingent of Kadet leaders, among them I. I. Petrunkevich, V. P. Obninskii, and V. E. Yakushkin, argued for reform leading to national ownership of land. Petrunkevich wanted agrarian reform to eliminate the consciousness of private property in land. On the opposite side, figures such as N. N. Kutler and L. I. Petrazhitskii opposed the commune and favoured private homesteads among the peasantry. The party had difficulty overcoming these differences and formulating an approach to land tenure. Its leaders would not accept the populist concept of a 'labour norm', but advanced instead the notion of a 'consumption norm' for determining future allotment quotas, based on each family's needs rather than the number of workers. The delegates at the Kadet party's second congress in January 1906 finally agreed to Petr Struve's proposal that land be given 'in use' rather than in property. They adopted the goal of an 'inalienable' state land fund, which would allot land according to the principle of equality.

Stolypin's measures to promote separations from the peasant communes and the development of individual homesteads posed difficult problems for the Kadet leadership, which was divided on the question of land tenure. In the Second Duma the Kadet group proposed measures that would provide the commune with more protection from individual peasants than the Stolypin projects. When Stolypin introduced the laws on the basis of the emergency provision of the Fundamental Laws, article 87, it enabled the Kadets to unite in opposition to the Prime Minister's arbitrary methods of enactment rather than to the substance of the measures.[41]

[40] Ginev, *Bor'ba za krest'yanstvo*, pp. 204–5.
[41] On the Kadets' debates on agrarian policy in 1905 and 1906, see J. E.

The liberal intellectuals of the Kadet party had difficulty in formulating a consistent position on the right of property. While most believed in private ownership in general, they refused to defend it as a right, for this would have meant the acceptance of noble land-holding and inequality of distribution in the countryside. Thus Kadet leaders, who looked upon themselves as heirs of the French Revolution, could not accept a transition between old and new forms of property like that formulated by the National Assembly. In the end, many placed their faith in the state again, not the autocracy of course, but a state based on acceptable, egalitarian, ethical principles.

As westernized an intellectual as Pavel Milyukov branded the Stolypin reforms a 'Europeanization' of the land which, he claimed, violated Russian tradition: 'The idea of private property has had a stunted development here . . . the idea [of the nationalization of the land] is no novelty for Russia . . . the principle of the nationalization of the land, in the sense of a recognition of the supreme right of the state to land, is an ancient Muscovite principle'.[42]

Among the political groups that formed before 1905, only the Marxists expressed support for the notion of private property, at least during the bourgeois stage that most of them believed must precede the socialist revolution. But this regime of private property was more of a doctrinal obligation for them than a concrete objective and they had difficulty in finding a place for it in Russian historical development. Both Plekhanov and Lenin anticipated at first that the bourgeois revolution would lead to only a moderate reform in the countryside, the return of the *otrezki*, the lands taken by the landlords at the time of the emancipation. But Marxist doctrinal constraints gave way to the revolutionary and egalitarian ethos.

When the peasants rose up in the first years of the twentieth

Zimmerman, 'Between Revolution and Reaction: the Russian Constitutional Democratic Party, October 1905 to June 1907', Ph.D. thesis (Columbia, 1967); and 'The Kadets and the Duma', in C. E. Timberlake (ed.), *Essays on Russian Liberalism* (Columbia, Mo., 1972), 136–7; W. G. Rosenberg, *Liberals in the Russian Revolution* (Princeton, 1974), 12–19. On populist influences upon the liberals in the Provisional Government, see L. Schapiro, 'The Political Thought of the First Provisional Government', in R. Pipes (ed.), *Revolutionary Russia* (Cambridge, Mass., 1968), 97–113.

[42] Leontovitsch, *Geschichte des Liberalismus*, pp. 196–9.

century and demanded all of the land, the Social Democrats could hardly pose as the defenders of noble private property, and at the second congress the party pledged its support for the peasant movement. Lenin gave up his insistence on the *otrezki*, and in his *Two Tactics of Social Democracy* he developed his concept of a democratic alliance of workers and peasants, which presumed the seizure of landlord property. To salvage the notion of a bourgeois stage, Lenin developed his notion of 'nationalization' of the land, and the Mensheviks theirs of 'municipalization' of the land. But whether the land was under the disposition of the central state or of the localities, it was clear that the Marxists' 'bourgeois' stage would scarcely bring the protection of the right of private property in Russia.[43]

In 1905 the defence of the right of property in Russia was left to the pillars of the old order, the landed nobility and the tsarist government. As peasant insurrections swept across the country, the nobility began the work of political organization, and formed the United Nobility and such political parties as the Octobrists to act on behalf of their interests. The tsarist government made the defence of noble landowning its principal cause. The identification of private property with despotism, arbitrariness, and oppression became overt as the Tsar's ministers explicitly presented private property as the mainstay of the existing order. In his speech to the First Duma, the Prime Minister, Goremykin, declared that the state could not deprive some without depriving all of their rights of private ownership: 'The inalienable and inviolable right of private property is the foundation stone of the popular well-being and social progress of all states at all stages of development. Private property is the fundamental basis of a state's existence: without the right of private property there would be no state.'[44]

In the West, property rights have historically provided the basis for other civil and political rights. Ultimately, the person has assumed the inviolability granted to property. In those western nations that have suspended the right of property selectively, there has been a respect for property rights when they

---

[43] Dan, *Origins of Bolshevism*, pp. 310–22; E. Kingston Mann, *Lenin and the Problem of Marxist Peasant Revolution* (New York and Oxford, 1985), 66–73, 92–3, 183–8.

[44] Cited in T. Riha (ed.), *Readings in Russian Civilization*, ii (Chicago, 1969), 451–2.

are not abused, an unspoken, informal respect for property as the basis of security and limitation on the power of the state. Whether it is possible to create a society that protects civil and political rights without protecting the right of property is a question sharply disputed by political theorists. Those with liberal or conservative views tend to answer the question in the negative. They point to the historical role of private property and its effect in limiting the untrammelled exercise of governmental power. Those of a more radical or socialist persuasion believe that property rights are often used to violate the rights of those without property.[45]

The Russian experience before the revolution brings to light the problem of the establishment of civil rights in a political culture that did not confer high ethical value on the right of property. In early twentieth-century Russia, property rights and civil rights belonged to antagonistic and irreconcilable political doctrines. On the one hand, the concept of property rights had become attached to the fate of the tsarist state, which disdained and violated all other rights. On the other, the champions of civil rights, with only a few exceptions, lacked a morally viable concept of property that could sustain individual freedom in the new society. Reflecting the deep political divisions in twentieth-century Russia, the terms of discourse precluded the continuity between old and new forms of property rights that has been achieved in the West. Whether under different historical conditions Russia might have evolved a legal order protecting the rights of all its citizens is an unanswerable question. But the Russian experience, as well as that of most of the non-western world in the twentieth century, belies the assumption that an individual's civil rights can be attained easily when they are not grounded in a prior tradition of respect for his or her right of property.

---

[45] For a sample of the variety of viewpoints recently advanced on this subject, see J. R. Pennock and J. W. Chapman (eds.), *Property* (New York, 1980); and V. Held (ed.), *Property, Profits and Economic Justice* (Belmont, Calif., 1980). An interesting discussion of property as a symbol of the limits on the power of the bureaucratic state is contained in J. Nedelsky, 'American Constitutionalism and the Paradox of Private Property', unpublished manuscript.

Peasant Land Tenure and Civil Rights Implications before 1906

OLGA CRISP

THIS essay will eschew the question of whether one is justified in considering civil rights in the context of an absolute state, which Russia certainly was until 1906, and some would say until 1917. Perhaps the term 'individual rights' might be more appropriate in the context of this essay. It is not accidental that the Declaration of the French National Assembly enunciated 'the Rights of Man and the Citizen', the two being distinct. 'Men are free and equal'—said the Assembly—'in respect of their natural and imprescriptible rights of liberty, property, security, and resistance to oppression.' Whether justified or not, the terms 'citizen' and 'civil rights' figured in the vocabulary of rights in Russia from the reign of Catherine II, and featured prominently in the wording of several key passages of the Emancipation Edict of 1861.

By the time the nature of peasant land tenure was being considered, upon the emancipation of the serfs, official concepts and laws relating to property in land had been enunciated and acted upon for almost a century. They were greatly influenced by the concepts of property rights current in the philosophical and political thought of Western Europe, and the economic ideas of liberalism connected with the teaching of Adam Smith.

Private enterprise economics, from the days of Adam Smith onwards, has tended to take it for granted that the main function of the state was to maintain laws of property and contract within which individuals could pursue their interests for the maximum economic advantage of everyone. Property laws were thought to be manifestly necessary, for 'who would bother to sow crops if others could push him aside at harvest time?'. The ideas of Adam Smith became 'fashionable' in Russia at almost the same time as they did in the West; as did the physiocratic ideas which stressed the importance of agriculture as the source of wealth.[1]

[1] P. S. Atiyah, *Law and Modern Society* (Oxford, 1983), 84.

Of the two western philosophical traditions of thinking about work and ownership, the one 'instrumental', the other 'self-developmental', it was the former which gained currency in eighteenth-century Russia and was the most readily adopted and expressed in official views in favour of private property in land in the course of the nineteenth century.

The instrumental tradition regarded the institution of private property, like all other social institutions, with reference to its benefit for mankind. It accepted the individual as given, and stressed the desirability of private property in terms of its efficiency in providing for his wants and his welfare.

The self-developmental tradition started not from what was good for society or 'all mankind', but from the individual and his need for an anchor in the physical world so that he could impose his will upon it and express himself as a free and independent being. It considered the individual as an end to be achieved, and stressed the importance of property as a means by which he formed himself in relation to other selves and the world of things.[2]

Locke's famous labour theory of property and of the contractual state as its preserver was the beginning of the modern instrumental tradition. The utilitarians were the most instrumentalist of all, Jeremy Bentham believing that private property was the only guarantee of abundance for some and subsistence for all.

Kant's theory was most explicitly self-developmental, and rooted property in the self as the only arrangement which would guarantee men's welfare and freedom from oppression. Hegel, like Kant, rooted property in the will, in the determination to master the physical world.

In Russia, Boris Chicherin was among the very few, if not the only one, to stand firmly in the self-developmental tradition of Kant and Hegel: 'Property stems from the nature of man as a rational and free being', he wrote. 'It is the first expression of freedom in the physical world. Further strengthening and widening of property rights is tantamount to the development and strengthening of freedom.' Chicherin was writing at a time when in Europe, and even more in Russia, ideas of social rather than private ownership were being entertained and hotly

---

[2] A. Ryan, *Property and Political Theory* (Oxford, 1984).

debated. Even in England, where individualistic ideas continued to dominate public policy and the law more confidently and for longer than elsewhere, social goals were emerging by the mid-century as the proper realm of public policy and the law. In Russia, Chicherin was uniquely clear-headed and uncompromising in his rejection of the ideas of social ownership as an 'economic, juridical, moral, and political absurdity'.[3] In general, however, Russian intellectuals, including those of pronounced liberal persuasion and vocal on the issue of fundamental civil rights, were at best equivocal with regard to property rights, even in their purely instrumental aspect. Thus it was the Russian government which, from the eighteenth century, sponsored the propagation and implementation of property rights, though in the area of practical policy the record was at times patchy, to say the least.

Under Catherine II, ideas of peasant property rights were publicly discussed and even experimented with. Whether the author of the two letters in 1765 and 1766 which instigated an essay competition on peasant property in the Free Economic Society was Catherine herself or someone else is immaterial for our purpose. What is important is that the ideas expressed in them point to an instrumental concept of property: 'Many sensible authors declare . . . that farming cannot flourish where the farmer possesses nothing of his own. All this is founded on a very simple rule: every person takes more care of his own property than of something which he has reason to fear another may take from him.' The author of the letter took 'these rules as indisputable', but expressed some uncertainty as to what type of property should be considered best in the interest of agriculture, individual or communal. The author admits that in his view

---

[3] B. N. Chicherin, *Sobstvennost' i gosudarstvo* (Moscow, 1882), pt. 1, pp. 97, 159–60. A. Kelly challenges Chicherin's right to be classed as a liberal in '"What is Real is Rational": The Political Philosophy of B. N. Chicherin', *Cahiers du monde russe et soviétique*, 18/3 (1977), 195–222. One wonders whether other contemporary Russian liberals would pass muster if equally challenged: K. D. Kavelin, for example, who seemed to have been unaware of the absurdity and inconsistency in terms of liberal thinking of his argument that as the 'serfs were as much the property of their owners as the land', emancipation of serfs without compensation would be 'unjust' and 'a very dangerous example of violation of private property, which no government can [contemplate] without shaking the legal and social order to its very foundations . . .'. *Sobranie sochinenii* (Moscow, 1882), ii. 46–7.

property is that 'which no one can take from me or my children without lawful reason, and in my opinion that alone can make me industrious . . .'.[4]

During the discussions at Catherine's Commission, the deputy of the Kozlov gentry, Grigorii Korobin, invoked specific paragraphs of Catherine's 'Great Instruction' which stressed the importance of security of property to the process of farming and emphasized what was to be understood by peasant property: 'that which he can mortgage, sell, gift, and bequeath to whomever he wishes, not having to think that it could ever be taken away . . . in short that over which he is full master [*gospodin*]'. Korobin had in view absolute property, i.e. *sobstvennost'*. Another of the deputies, Yakov Kozelskii of Ekaterinoslav province, supported Korobin in his suggestion that the serfs should be granted the right of property in land, but he had in mind contingent property, i.e. the right to hereditary possession and utilization (*vladenie i pol'zovanie*), but without the right to sell, mortgage, or bequeath without the consent of the estate owner.[5]

Thus, under Catherine the concept of the right to full property (*polnaya sobstvennost'*) as it was later codified in the *Svod zakonov* (volume x, part 1, article 420, entailing the right of possession, utilization, and disposal) was formulated, if not applied, even in relation to serfs. In relation to the nobility, absolute property rights to land and the subsoil were confirmed in the Charter of 1785.

The law of 20 February 1803 on 'Free Agriculturalists' (*Svobodnye khlebopashtsy*), which was an extension of the right given in 1801 to all non-serfs to buy unsettled land, gave estate owners the right to free serfs with an allocation of land in full individual property. It provided that the landowner who freed his serfs under this law must set aside for each householder a clearly specified parcel of land, and issue him with a plan signed by himself and the district surveyor. This provision is very significant, as one of the reasons for the weakness of the concept of property in land among the population at large right up to the

---

[4] A. I. Khodnev, *Istoriya Imperatorskago vol'nago ekonomicheskago obshchestva s 1765 do 1865 g.* (St Petersburg, 1865), 22; R. P. Bartlett, 'I. E. and the Free Economic Society's Essay Competition of 1766 on Peasant Property', Study Group on Eighteenth-Century Russia, *Newsletter*, 8 (1980), 59–60.

[5] *Sbornik Russkago istoricheskago obshchestva* (*SRIO*), xxxii, app. 28, p. 409; ibid. 87.

revolution was the chaotic situation with regard to boundaries and title-deeds. The law of 1803 is also significant in recognizing not just full property but *individual* property, as distinct from a share in joint property even if full property.[6]

That there was a clear understanding of this difference is obvious from the discussions at one of the many secret committees on the peasant question under Nicholas I. With reference to state peasants, Prince Kurakin argued that whilst land was in common ownership the individual peasant was only a *khozyain*; as soon as the holding becomes the individual property of the peasant, however, it turns him into a *gospodin*, with all the implications that this carried not only for freedom of disposal but for all other kinds of freedom.[7]

In 1848 serfs were granted the right to acquire immovable property in their own name, and not, as hitherto, in that of their masters. This property, if acquired outside the village, began to be looked upon as *individual* as distinct from joint household property, to be disposed of outside the system of customary law which applied to his village household plot and farming appurtenances. And yet in 1838, Count Kiselev, in his reform of the administration of state peasants, gave statutory validity to the system of joint tenure of land, recognized peasant self-government, and institutionalized village courts based on customary law. This was in many respects the prototype of the provisions of the 1861 Edict. Kiselev, too, was largely responsible for the provisions of the 1842 Act on 'Peasants under Obligation' (*obyazannye*) which provided for the freeing of serfs with land, not, as in 1803, on the basis of full ownership, but on the basis of heritable usufruct.[8]

The explanation of this back-sliding and Kiselev's role in it is complex. Kiselev shared Kurakin's view about the political implications of full ownership by peasants. But his main motivation seems to have been the desire to persuade as many nobles as possible to free their serfs with land. He believed that few nobles availed themselves of the provisions of the 1803 Act

[6] V. Veshnyakov, *Krest'yane sobstvenniki* (St Petersburg, 1858), 24; *Svod zakonov Rossiiskoi imperii* (St Petersburg, 1857), ix, art. 460; V. A. Aleksandrov, *Obychnoe pravo krepostnoi derevni Rossii XVIII–nachalo XIX v.* (Moscow, 1984), 233 ff.

[7] *SRIO*, lxxiv, 'Prilozhenie k zhurnalu 16. 11. 1827 and 2. 12. 1828'.

[8] V. Leontovitsch, *Geschichte des Liberalismus in Russland* (Frankfurt-on-Main, 1957), 108–10.

because it demanded the granting of full landownership rights to peasants.[9]

As regards his retention of the communal system in the state domains, he did so (by his own admission) out of recognition of the peasants' attachment to this type of land tenure and the institutions connected with it, and the undesirability of acting hastily or using coercion. However, he continued to stress his preference for private property in land, and on his initiative family heritable land-holding was to be encouraged as an experiment in areas of new settlement. The law of 9 December 1846 provided for the creation of family holdings on condition of freely given peasant consent. The boundaries of the holdings were to be clearly marked and registered, and the holdings were to be passed undivided with inventory by testamentary disposition to one designated male heir, or, in the absence of such disposition, to the oldest of the heirs.[10]

It is also worth noting that it was Kiselev who is known to have said that to 'live, work, acquire, and not to own is an unnatural condition', and that it was he who wanted solemnly to proclaim the rights of state peasants in a special charter, on the model of those granted by Catherine II to other estates. When prevented from doing so, he ordered the codification of all laws relating to state peasants, and issued them in 1850 in a special four-volume collection. Most significant were the chapters 'On the Legal Rights Conferred on Rural Dwellers' (*O pravakh sostoyaniya prisvoennykh sel'skim obyvatelyam*). Prominent among them was the right to own property, the right to inheritance, and the right to enter into contracts. Clause 7 of the second volume specified that a state peasant could not be deprived of his rights other than by court decision. According to the Soviet scholar Druzhinin, 'this should be interpreted not only as a confirmation or more exact formulation of the civil rights of state peasants, but as a proclamation of their inalienability'.[11]

It is well known that the fate of the peasant commune was hotly debated in the course of preparation of the Emancipation

[9] A. P. Zablotskii-Desyatovski, *Graf P. D. Kiselev i ego vremya* (St Petersburg, 1882), ii. 265–76.

[10] Ibid.; N. M. Druzhinin, *Gosudarstvennye krest'yane i reforma P. D. Kiseleva*, ii (Moscow, 1958), 21–3.

[11] Druzhinin, *Gosudarstvennye Krest'yane*, ii. 74–7; 'Kiselev P. D.', *Russkii biograficheskii slovar'* (St Petersburg, 1897), 702–17.

Edict. In the Editing and the Main Commission there were both partisans and convinced opponents of the commune. Those who stood for freedom of enterprise, the autonomy of the individual, and the importance of security of property for the progress of agriculture pointed to the traditionalism of the patriarchal commune, the deplorable effect of periodical land redistributions on peasant motivation and farming, the constraints on the free disposal of land and freedom of movement. P. P. Semenov Tyan-Shanskii, who was in charge of the transactions of the Editing Commissions, believed that the majority of representatives of the high bureaucracy were in favour of private property. And yet, though the edict provided for the continuation of household tenure where it existed, it endorsed communal land tenure, which at the time accounted for about four-fifths of all peasant households in European Russia.[12]

Witte rather ungraciously wrote that the view favouring the retention of the commune prevailed because of the convenience of 'managing a herd'. In other words, the commune was a convenient instrument for the day-to-day administrative and fiscal management of the countryside. However, in his memorandum to the Emperor (the famous *Zapiska*) as Chairman of the Special Committee on the Needs of Agriculture set up in 1902, he argued that the principles underlying the Emancipation Edict were for the ultimate development of private property in land, and that the preservation of the commune was meant to be temporary and was dictated by specific considerations at the time. Though Witte was not entirely impartial in his interpretation of the edict or of the documentation relating to its preparation, one is inclined to agree that there is substance to his claim that the subsequent interpretation of the legal status of the Russian village, and the official policy in this regard after the 1880s, represented a substantive departure from the spirit of the emancipation legislation, and that the policies followed were not so much based on the law as on 'the interpretation of the law' by Senate rulings. A rereading of the documentation referred to by Witte does indeed seem to suggest that many of the potentially most restrictive provisions of the edict were designed to cope

[12] P. P. Semenov Tyan-Shanskii, *Epokha osvobozhdeniya krest'yan v Rossii (1857–61) v vospominaniyakh chlena-eksperta i zaveduyushchego redaktsionnykh komissii* (St Petersburg, 1915), iii. 230.

with the problems arising from the relationship between former
landowners and their peasants once their powers over the person
of the peasant had gone, during the period of so-called
'temporary obligation', i.e. until the redemption contract had
been signed. There was a general expectation at the time that the
conclusion of redemption agreements would be a long-drawn-out
operation. It was the gentry's need for cash and the suspension of
bank credit that drove them to speed it up, even though this was
often at a financial loss to themselves. It was not, however, until
1881 that redemption became obligatory.[13]

More importantly, as regards peasant customary law, which
became a significant element of peasant 'apartheid' in law and
which the Senate subsequently used as the basis for its rulings
about the property rights of allotment land, it is clear from the
documentation that in matters of property its application was
intended to be limited to the area of inheritance (with a
maximum value specified), and in family matters to custodial
issues. Moreover, reservations were expressed about customary
law at the time, in view of its localized nature, its underdevelop-
ment, and its inapplicability as a basis for legal judgement on a
national scale. Hence the limitation of customary law to county
courts (*volost'*), and the inadmissibility of challenging their
decisions in courts of higher instance. In all other areas the laws
based on the Civil Code were to apply, although, whenever the
parties wished it, recourse to customary law could be had. The
very terms used in this regard, *dozvolyaetsya* ('it is permitted'),
ne vospreshchaetsya ('it is not forbidden'), indicate that it was
intended that the use of customary law be concessionary rather
than obligatory, once more pointing to a subsequent shift from
the spirit of the original legislation, whereby the *volost'* courts
were *obliged* to base their decisions on customary law. With
regard to inheritance of property, the wording of article 38 in the
General Statute of 1861 (*Obshchee polozhenie*) preserves the
concessionary nature of recourse to customary law; peasants are
'permitted' to have recourse to their local custom.[14]

[13] S. Yu. Vitte, *Vospominaniya* (Moscow, 1960), ii. 491, 529; id., *Zapiska po
krest'yanskomu delu* (St Petersburg, 1905), 13–60; *Materialy redaktsionnykh
komissii dlya sostavleniya polozhenii o krest'yanakh vykhodyashchikh iz krepostnoi
zavisimosti*, 2nd edn. (St Petersburg, 1860), ii, bk. 1, pp. 126–81, esp. pp. 158–9.

[14] *Materialy redaktsionnykh*, pp. 28–96, esp. pp. 58–63; Vitte, *Zapiska*, pp. 29–
39; 'Obshchee polozhenie o krest'yanakh, vyshedshikh iz krepostnoi zavisimosti',

Even though the provisions of the edict as finally promulgated were a somewhat equivocal statement of the intent of the legislators, and even though there was an unresolved ambiguity at its very basis, the edict nevertheless contained more scope for evolution towards private property with its three attributes of right of possession, utilization, and disposal than has been commonly accepted in the historiography.

Thus, article 36 of the General Statute and articles 163 and 165 of the Redemption Statute offered whole communities the possibility of breaking up the land into family holdings by a two-thirds decision of their members, and the separation of individual family holdings from communal land—if possible in one place—upon outright redemption.[15] Further, the edict retained hereditary family holdings where they existed at the time of emancipation; and though the statute provided for conversion from communal into private ownership as in clauses 36, 163, and 165 just quoted, it made no provision for conversion from private property into communal, or for reversal of the decision to go private. Intellectuals in favour of communal ownership were highly critical of precisely this aspect of the edict.[16]

The fact that clause 165 could serve only those with financial means; or that those who opted for it did not wish to exercise their full property rights, but just wanted to avoid collective responsibility for redemption payments or wished to make provision for elderly or female family members not entitled to share in allotment land; or that they faced opposition from those communities which did not wish to lose viable taxpayers etc., does not change the fact that, *de jure*, there was considerable scope for the development of private property under the provision of the 1861 Edict.[17]

Moreover, during the 1860s and 1870s the prevalent official view continued to be in favour of private property. Contrary to

Krest'yanskaya reforma v Rossii 1861 goda: Sbornik zakonodatel'nykh aktov (Moscow, 1954), 47.

[15] Krest'yanskaya reforma, p. 46; 'Polozhenie o vykupe krest'yanami vyshedshimi iz krepostnoi osedlosti i o sodeistvii pravitel'stva k priobreteniyu simi krest'yanami v sobstvennost' polevykh ugodii', ibid. 129, 130.

[16] K. D. Kavelin, Sobranie, p. 476.

[17] A. M. Anfimov, 'Krest'yanskoe zemel'noe pravo v poreformennoi Rossii', in Akademiya nauk, Sotsial'no-politcheskoe i pravovoe polozhenie krest'yanstva v dorevolyutsionnoi Rossii (Voronezh, 1983), 216–17.

conventional interpretation, the Ministries of the Interior and of Finance tended to work in tandem during this period to facilitate transfer to household property where the edict allowed for it. They also pressed for a revision of legislation away from common property in land. Even in the 1880s, when the clauses allowing for privatization were largely rescinded, the case for private property was gaining new adherents in the State Council, e.g. Polovtsov. The foundation of the Peasant Land Bank to advance credit for land purchase not only by communes but also by associations of peasants or individual peasants, similarly indicates that government policy in the 1880s was far from being monolithic.[18]

In the literature, however, there has been a tendency to give more weight to the policies that were gaining the upper hand during the 1880s and 1890s than is warranted by the evidence, to impute to them a continuity since 1861 and an ideological basis purporting to be representative of the consistent thinking of the government as a whole. Within this scenario, Stolypin's pro- gramme of 1906 appears as a radical discontinuity provoked by the revolutionary behaviour of the peasantry, marking the bank- ruptcy of policies pursued since 1861 and premissed on the stability and conservatism stemming from joint ownership. A more correct assessment of the position might be to recognize the coexistence of two currents of opinion, with one or the other gaining temporary ascendancy but neither ever being totally eclipsed.

The main difficulty in discussing peasant land tenure from the point of view of rights is how to isolate those features and legal disabilities which stemmed from an individual's status as a peasant or member of a legal estate (*soslovie*), and those which were connected with the specific manner of land-holding and the legal norms which governed it. It is common knowledge that the Russian peasant was not equal in law relative to other social groups. Indeed, in Witte's Committee on the Problems of Agriculture some deputies argued that not only was the peasant unequal in law (*neravnopravnyi*), but he in fact lacked full legal capacity (i.e. he was *nepolnopravnyi*).[19] As regards property

---

[18] V. G. Chernukha, *Krest'yanskii vopros v pravitel'stvennoi politike Rossii (60– 70 gody XIX v.)* (Leningrad, 1972), 184–204.

[19] N. N. L'vov and A. A. Stakhovich, *Nuzhdy derevni po rabotam komitetov o nuzhdakh sel'skokhozyaistvennoi promyshlennosti* (St Petersburg, 1904), i. 144.

rights, complications arise from the fact that a peasant was subject to special laws as long as he remained a member of a village community (abstracting from the ease or otherwise of changing status), but he was not subject to these laws in respect of property outside the community or transactions with persons belonging to other estates. Furthermore, even within the rural community he could be jointly responsible with others for taxes and dues and be subject to the same law and administration, but he could enjoy a different status with regard to any immovable property which he had purchased individually or as a member of an association (*tovarishchestvo*) from non-peasant owners.

The permutations and complexities—and hence the opportunities for conflicts and injustice, if not outright evasion and abuse—were myriad. And they arose because the administration, or parts of it, found it convenient to operate with categories of legal status which life in many areas had long outlived.

Most difficulties as regards the rights implications of land tenure arise from the overlapping functions and roles of three distinct units which the provisions of the Emancipation Edict, however, seemed to have rolled into one. There was, firstly, the community of peasants holding and managing land in common. This is usually referred to as *obshchinnoe pol'zovanie*, defined as such in a comment (*primechanie*) to clause 113 of the Local Statute. In the main part of the edict (*Obshchee polozhenie*), references are to 'common' or 'community' tenure (*obshchee* or *obshchestvennoe*).[20]

Then there was peasant self-government with its elected officials and assemblies of householders, the *mir* in the language of the peasants who did not use the term *obshchina*, and for whom the two units mentioned so far were often indistinguishable. The third unit was the one imposed by the edict, the village society (*sel'skoe obshchestvo*) and the larger *volost'*, which was to act as the lowest link in the country's administration, but which also in an unidentifiable way embraced the other two units. It was this overlapping of functions and roles which gave most scope for intervention, arbitrariness, and administrative practices and laws which could be oppressive and incompatible with the freedom of the individual and the security of property.

---

[20] *Krest'yanskaya reforma*, p. 207; Vitte, *Zapiska*, p. 47.

What was the standing of joint ownership in terms of property rights? Jurists were not certain about the legal status of communal property. The wording of the edict suggests that it was the property of the whole *obshchestvo* as an entity, but the standing of this entity in law, its legal personality, was not precise. Clause 36 specified the conditions under which the *obshchestvo* could acquire more property, dispose of some of it, or change its legal status.

What were the property rights of individual household members? Here, too, the legal relationship was ill-defined, and there was no provision in law for the protection of the rights of individual members against the collective. It can be argued that each household had the right of possession and utilization, whilst the community as an entity had the right of full ownership. Though not clearly formulated, this appears to have been the case when compared with the status of the land held by state peasants. Though some state peasants could acquire full property rights both under Kiselev's provisions and those of the 1866 law, in principle the bulk of state peasants remained the perpetual tenants of state-owned land. Only in 1886 were the rents payable by state peasants converted into purchase instalments, and the legal status of the land cultivated by state peasants became indistinguishable from that of former serfs.[21]

How did the position change in the 1880s and 1890s? Did the intervention of the state on the issue of the alienability of allotment land, periodical land repartitioning, or family divisions indicate a violation of the property rights of the *obshchestvo*, an assertion of the claim of the state as owner? Can it be maintained that as long as the redemption debt was not extinguished, the state as the holder of the title-deeds, so to say, was *de facto* owner, though the land was described as the property of the peasant *obshchestvo*? If this was the case, then the state had the

[21] M. A. Sirinov, 'Yuridicheskaya struktura krest'yanskago zemlevladeniya po zakonu 19-go fevralya 1861 g. i v posleduyushchee vremya', *Trudy Imperatorskago vol'nago ekonomicheskago obshchestva*, 3 (1904), 59–86; I. M. Strakhovskii, 'Sel'skoe obshchestvo i pozemel'naya obshchina', *Vestnik prava*, June 1900; 'Obshchaya sobstvennost'', *Entsiklopedicheskii slovar' Brokgauz–Efron*, xlii. 601 ff.; 'Krest'yanskoe zemlepol'zovanie', in A. A. Rittikh (ed.), *Svod trudov mestnykh komitetov* (St Petersburg, 1903), 32 ff.; A. A. Klauz, 'Obshchina-sobstvennik, i eya yuridicheskaya organizatsiya', *Vestnik Evropy*, 2 (1870), 604–19.

right to impose conditions designed to safeguard its collateral. Or was the state intervening *qua* state?

There seems to be no easy way of determining exactly where the role of the state as the holder of the title-deeds ended and that of the wielder of the highest administrative authority began; just as it is not possible to separate the land management functions of the community from its administrative, fiscal, or judicial responsibilities. Nevertheless, such measures as the law forbidding whole communities or individual householders to mortgage their allotments with private individuals or private credit institutions *even when the redemption debt was fully repaid* cannot be explained in any other way than as a crass violation of the property rights granted under the provisions of the Emancipation Edict. It points to a shift in the concept of allotment land in terms of property rights.[22]

The various rulings of the legal department of the Senate point in the same direction. Thus, whilst clause 160 of the Redemption Statute stipulated that 'the land redeemed by the whole *obshchestvo* is the property of that *obshchestvo* which has the right to distribute it among its members . . .', the Senate's clarification of 10 September 1891 runs as follows: 'on the basis of clause 160 of the Redemption Statute the land redeemed by the *obshchestvo* is the property of the whole *obshchestvo* and is in communal (*obshchinnoe*) usufruct. This land is put at the disposal of the *obshchestvo* in order to ensure the livelihood of peasants and the punctual meeting of state, local, and village dues.' This illustrates, as Professor Leontovitsch has argued, the emergence of a new concept whereby peasant allotment land was a fund which must be safeguarded to ensure the existence of peasants, or, more precisely—says Leontovitsch—their existence as peasants.[23]

Senate rulings 27 and 69 of 1900 and 1901 respectively are even more unequivocal in this respect: 'Peasant allotments . . . represent a distinct type of ownership [*vladenie*], sharply differing from property right [which implies] full command [*gospodstvo*] over property . . .'.[24] These Senate rulings were designed to clarify issues which arose in day-to-day matters relating to peasant property, above all the extent to which

[22] Sirinov, 'Yuridicheskaya struktura', p. 74.

[23] Ibid. 81; Viktor Leontovitsch, *Geschichte des Liberalismus*, p. 152.

[24] Anfimov, 'Krest'yanskoe zemel'noe pravo', pp. 211–12.

foreclosures of allotment land could be effected for the debts of whole communities or individual households. They nevertheless became the basis of a substantive shift in attitude and policy towards allotment land, which seemed to have become a protected peasant reservation for ever excluded from the general commercial circuit. Witte had this in mind when he said that the attitudes and policies adopted since the 1880s were based not on the law, but on the interpretation of the law.[25]

This shift in policy, attitudes, and concepts reflected the ascendancy of an ideological current always alive in official thinking and in society at large, based on the desirability of preserving traditional institutions and values, and with them the stability of the socio-political system. However, there was a variety of factors and developments which, in conjunction, contributed to the ascendancy of this view and the acquiescence to it of those whose outlook and concerns were often diametrically opposed to it.

Among these developments was the 'discovery' of the reality of rural life. This suggests an ignorance of rural life prior to 1861, and a tendency in the past to ascribe any shortcomings, whatever they were, to serfdom. The submissions to the Valuev Commission, the statistical study by Yanson, the gloomy reports of provincial governors clamouring for wholesale reliefs for their provinces, and the grim language of accumulating tax arrears all seemed witness to the poverty and impotence of peasant life. It is immaterial that most of the depositions to the Valuev Commission diagnosed the retention of the communal arrangements as the main source of malaise; nor that the Yanson findings were based on insufficient evidence; nor that provincial governors were painting an unduly dark picture in order to justify their failure to prevent the accumulation of arrears; nor that the arrears were often an index of unwillingness to pay rather than of inability to pay; nor that, in some areas or for some groups of peasants, the conditions were particularly grim because they still had to meet arrears of rents to former landlords, begin to make overvalued redemption payments, and pay poll tax at a time when the industrial slump reduced the opportunities for additional earnings. What is important is that all of the above contributed to a

[25] Vitte, *Zapiska*, p. 57.

profound pessimism about the viability of peasant farming.[26]

No one caught and reflected this mood better than K. D. Kavelin, the Professor of Law at Moscow University and a well-known 'liberal' and philo-peasant. For him, the majority of the great Russian peasants were failures (*neudachniki*) who must not be left to the prey of market forces which would engulf them: 'Russian peasant farming did not exist for the purpose of raising agriculture or to stimulate industry, it existed for the survival of the peasants, and peasants had to be protected to survive.' Hence the need to preserve and strengthen the peasant commune, under whose shelter the peasants would be gradually weaned towards individualism, 'saving the state expenditure on prisons and police' in the process. The few with initiative and entrepreneurial energy should be encouraged to seek scope for their talents outside the village, leaving their share of allotment land to the commune. It is uncanny to what extent Kavelin's writings anticipated the views and policies of the Ministry of the Interior, and of V. K. Plehve in particular.[27]

The counterpart of this pessimism was an exaggerated view of the all-conquering powers of capitalism and the market, and a fear of land engrossment by a few, leading to peasant landlessness and, with it, a return to rootlessness, thereby rendering null the sacrifices of centuries of serfdom designed to combat this very rootlessness and the resulting nomadism of the Russian peasantry.[28]

This fear of the market and the alleged peasant inability to cope with it were strengthened by the evidence of their growing involvement in the land market. There were those who were appalled at what they saw as the 'godless' dealing 'in *desyatins* of land as if they were so many sheep or sacks of radishes'. There was alarm at the apparent recklessness and speed with which peasants were parting with land in exchange for promissory notes. Statistical tables were compiled showing the ascending

[26] Chernukha, *Krest'yanskii vopros*, pp. 70–123; N. M. Druzhinin, *Russkaya derevnya na perelome 1861–1880 gg.* (Moscow, 1978); *Doklad vysochaishe uchrezhdennoi komissii dlya izsledovaniya nyneshnego polozheniya sel'skago khozyaistva i sel'skoi proizvoditel'nosti v Rossii*, apps. 1–7 (St Petersburg, 1873); Yu. Yanson, *Opyt statisticheskago izsledovaniya o krest'yanskikh nadelakh i platezhakh* (St Petersburg, 1881); B. G. Litvak, 'O nekotorykh spornykh voprosakh realizatsii reformy 1861 g.', *Istoricheskie zapiski*, 68 (1961), 101–2.

[27] Kavelin, *Sobranie*, ii. 281. The original article was written by Kavelin in 1876 in *Nedelya*.

[28] Ibid. 283–4.

scale of land sales by peasants availing themselves of the clauses in the edict which permitted the outright redemption of land. It was argued that unscrupulous money-lenders were advancing them the redemption price in order either to increase their own land-holdings or to exploit the debtors for their own advantage. It was feared that such sales of land would accelerate with the introduction of compulsory redemption in 1881.[29]

A further factor contributing to the shift was the growing volume of published material providing more precise information on communal arrangements and peasant property concepts as reflected in customary law, and especially on the operation of *volost'* courts. Though this information was often fragmentary and outdated, in the sense that the data reflected attitudes and concepts formed in the past but rapidly being eroded under the impact of new developments, to those fearful for the fate of the peasants it offered hope that the evil could be contained by bolstering the traditional institutions and values. Moreover, this had the added virtue of giving peasants what they seemed to want. As the associated debates both in government circles and among intellectuals also highlighted the negative features of the institution, either from the angle of agricultural productivity or from the potential for arbitrary behaviour by ignorant communal officials, government supervision was strengthened by the creation of 'land captains' and by the passing of laws designed to control land repartitioning and family divisions.[30]

The result of this shift was to eliminate whatever potentiality for evolution towards full property rights of joint peasant land tenure had been inherent in the provisions of the Emancipation Edict. But if a loss of rights had occurred, its counterpart was a

---

[29] G. P. Sazonov, *Neotchuzhdaemost' krest'yanskikh zemel' v svyazi s gosudarstvenno-ekonomicheskoi programmoi* (St Petersburg, 1889): 'Bought, sold, mortgaged, issued a promissory note against the land—all this is an everyday occurrence', he wrote (p. 61).

[30] *Trudy komissii po preobrazovaniyu volostnykh sudov*, 7 vols. (St Petersburg, 1873–4); *Trudy Imperatorskago vol'nago ekonomicheskago obshchestva*, 2/5 (1865), 421–9; 4/4 (1865), 343–6; and 1/4 (1866), 312–19; S. A. Grant, 'The Peasant Land Commune in Russian Thought, 1861–1905', Ph.D. thesis (Harvard, 1973); in 'Krestyanskiya prava i bezpravie', the lawyer E. A. Gal'perin-Ginzburg refers to the 'mystical, impenetrable, doomladen attitude to the peasant commune', and to the defence of the *samobytnost'* and *samotsennost'* of peasant communal life which paralysed action and stifled criticism of its fundamental shortcomings (*Pod znamenem prava: Sbornik statei* (Berlin, 1923), 171).

gain in security of possession, as allotment land could not be impounded for debts or tax arrears. A rise in arrears was the inevitable consequence.

However, it must not be forgotten that full property rights were available to peasants with regard to any non-allotment land that they purchased. Furthermore, whilst the shift in the concept of allotment land was taking place, the proportion of land over which peasants had full freedom of disposal was continuously on the increase—with the encouragement and the financial assistance of the government, which was thus creating space for peasant choice. This brings us to three further aspects of joint land tenure: collective responsibility for taxes and dues; the passport system; and the constraints imposed by the household (*dvor*) on its individual members.

Collective responsibility (*krugovaya poruka*) and the passport system were interrelated instruments of fiscal and social control. Their potential effect was to subordinate the individual to the community, to interfere with his freedom of movement and choice of domicile and occupation, and with his right to enjoy the fruits of his labour and effort.

Collective responsibility, or more exactly 'mutual guarantee', was a very ancient institution. Some detect its existence in the treaty between the Kievan Prince Oleg and the Byzantine Greeks. It certainly operated in Kiev Russia as provided for in *Russkaya pravda*. Throughout the centuries it had constituted a mechanism for distributing or minimizing the risks of various transactions (and not only those imposed from above). Collective responsibility for taxes and dues survived in Russia until it was abolished by statute in 1903.[31]

Dewey and Kleimola, commenting on 'the way in which the basic component of *poruka* presented in Kievan society continued to operate according to the same fundamental principles down through the centuries', invoke 'Braudelian structures' whereby 'routines [become] embedded in custom and law'. It would appear, however, that for this to occur there must exist conditions which make for continuity. The institution of collective responsibility was a convenient, if not perfect, arrangement for both sides—government and population—especially in

---

[31] 'Krugovaya poruka', *Ents. slovar' Brokgauz–Efron*, xxxvi. 836 ff.

rural communities scattered over the vast expanse of the country.[32]

Until well into the nineteenth century the government lacked the apparatus and the procedures for the assessment and apportionment of taxes to individuals. More importantly, relative poverty or lack of visible taxable wealth and the delay of monetization of the rural economy made direct relationships with individual tax- or fine-payers impracticable. Consequently, the apportionment of taxes by a single document (*oklad*) sent to a whole territorial unit (doing away with the need to enter into the material position of individual residents) was convenient and cheap, although it did not always yield optimal results.

From the point of view of the communities concerned, this was also an acceptable system, since it meant that they could avoid responsibility and sanctions more easily. The inequity of the tax per male could be adjusted to take better account of the paying capacity of individuals in a face-to-face society where the circumstances of each were well known, usually from generation to generation. Then there was a consciousness of interdependence in a social group not yet very differentiated from the material point of view. The relatively narrow margin of wealth, the hazards of the annual harvest and of disease, and the limited opportunity for change meant that no single member could feel confident of always being able to discharge responsibilities of whatever kind individually. Finally, this system of taxation allowed a certain autonomy to the community which took responsibility for the apportionment, thus keeping outsiders at bay.

As the economy developed, the state's administrative competence increased, and the conditions and opportunities of individual members began to differentiate, conflicts of interests and the oppression of more enterprising and individualistic members by the collective were bound to occur. However, it was not just *mentalité* and custom which sustained the institution when it was no longer compatible with the development of freedom, but the relative weakness—if only numerically, and

[32] H. W. Dewey and A. M. Kleimola, 'Russian Collective Consciousness: The Kievan Roots', *Slavonic and East European Review*, 62 (Apr. 1984), 190.

more pronounced in some regions than others—of the new forces which made for individualization of interests.

Collective responsibility for redemption payments was an essential plank of the Emancipation Edict. The Redemption Statute made very detailed provision for the sanctions to be applied by the *obshchestvo* in the event of arrears. These provisions gave wide-ranging powers to the community and entailed serious civil rights constraints. Debtors could be forced to accept employment, with the earnings being used to meet arrears; passports for departure could be refused or impounded, etc. (clauses 127–30). In mitigation it can be said that given that the majority of peasants had little property against which debts could be recovered, the procedures available in other societies were not practicable—debtors' prisons or the Victorian workhouses were not exactly unimpeachable models in terms of civil rights. It was this situation which, among other things, explains why N. K. Reutern, Minister of Finance from 1862 to 1878, was so unenthusiastic about communal land tenure. It prevented him from recovering arrears by selling the land of insolvent taxpayers. If only with this aim in view, he wished to encourage privatization.

In the first two decades following emancipation, the use of collective responsibility threatened the possibility of transfer to household property and the freedom of departure of members. Cash agricultural incomes were still rather low, and redemption payments in many areas were so much in excess of the rentable value of the holding that the latter, far from being an asset, was often a liability which those who could were trying to shed. Land for leasing usually cost less than the annual redemption dues, and there was the lure of the sparsely populated South. By the same token, each departure, even without land, did not add much to the income of the remaining members, but raised their individual share in the tax and redemption burden for which they were collectively responsible. Hence the community attempted to prevent anyone from leaving by invoking clause 173 of the Statute of Redemption and demanding from departing members half the redemption payment due from their plots. This would have made departure impracticable for the majority of the peasants who wished to leave. Concerted intervention by the Ministers of the Interior and of Finance with the Main

Committee on Peasant Affairs rendered clause 173 *de facto* inoperative, and it was finally formally rescinded in 1876.[33]

Collective responsibility also explains the reluctance of joint landholders, often of local governmental authorities too, to transfer their property into household tenure by advance redemption in accordance with clause 165 (prior to its abolition in the 1880s). Householders who could afford it were also those whom joint holders wanted to keep, since they were the most viable taxpayers who could be asked to meet any shortfall in redemption payments over and above their own share. There was government concern that these community attitudes would not only hamper the desired emergence of private property, but also that the invocation of collective responsibility in relation to the most enterprising and viable households would be destructive of effort, motivation, and freedom of movement. Moreover, it was found that the better off gradually began to delay their own contribution, waiting for others to pay first. Under collective responsibility, therefore, the flow of payments to the government was often less than it would have been without it.[34]

N. K. Bunge, a firm supporter of private property, which, he repeatedly maintained, could 'turn a barren rock into a blossoming garden', worked for the abolition of collective responsibility and the revision of passport legislation side by side with his measures for the repeal of the poll tax. In its social and legal significance, he ranked the abolition of this tax, which was finally effected in 1886, almost on a par with the Great Reforms. Under Bunge, the Ministry of Finance pursued policies that were designed ultimately to eliminate restrictive conditions on person and property. Simultaneously, as we have seen, credit was provided for land purchase, thus creating space for peasant choice.[35]

At the same time, the abolition of the main direct tax—the poll tax—and its replacement by indirect taxation meant that there was less need for direct interference, not only by governmental

---

[33] Chernukha, *Krest'yanskii vopros*, pp. 165 ff.; N. I. Anan'ich, 'K istorii otmeny podushnoi podati v Rossii', *Istoricheskie zapiski*, 94 (1974), 183–213; N. M. Druzhinin, 'Glavnyi komitet ob ustroistve sel'skogo sostoyaniya', Akademiya nauk, *Issledovaniya po sotsial'no-politicheskoi istorii Rossii* (Leningrad, 1971), 269–87.

[34] N. Brzheskii, *Nedoimochnost' i krugovaya poruka sel'skikh obshchestv* (St Petersburg, 1897), 408–14.

[35] Chernukha, *Krest'yanskii vopros*, pp. 196 ff.; Anan'ich, 'K istorii', pp. 184–6.

authorities but also by village assemblies. Collective responsibility could not be invoked when taxes were paid with every match struck, and every cup of tea and bottle of vodka drunk. Whatever view one may have of the unprogressive nature of indirect taxation, it was not only a flexible system of resource mobilization but also one which did not discourage individual effort, and which above all was not restrictive of freedom of movement and choice as the direct taxes in Russia were. Bunge also reduced very substantially the overall level of redemption payments, which, in conjunction with rising land prices, had the effect of gradually convincing the peasants that the land allotted to them was becoming an asset rather than the liability it was in some areas during the 1860s and 1870s. As is well known, S. Yu. Witte extended the system of indirect taxation. He also substantially developed the operations of the Peasant Land Bank by increasing its capital and easing its terms of credit. To what extent land purchases widened peasant choices and created space for the exercise of a measure of freedom is difficult to specify. Purchased land could be disposed of by sales, by testamentary bequest, and on the basis of the general civil law, and it could be used as collateral.

It was Witte who took up the attack on collective responsibility as being the 'personification of the worst features of the communal system' and of retarding 'the natural evolution of the rural economy'. Immediately on his appointment, he prepared jointly with I. N. Durnovo a revision of the passport law which would have done away with the, in his view, outdated system of classifying people as belonging to tax-paying and tax-exempt estates. As we shall see, he was not very successful. As the two issues were closely connected, Witte concentrated his attack on the *poruka* by instigating an investigation of the operation of the system, to be carried out by tax inspectors in fifty provinces in 1893.[36]

The data collected by the tax inspectors were systematized by A. A. Richter, the former director of the department that handled direct taxes and a convinced opponent of the system of common land tenure. Many of the questions put to the inspectors

---

[36] M. S. Simonova, 'Otmena krugovoi poruki', *Istoricheskie zapiski*, 83 (1969), 158–95, esp. 162; Anan'ich, 'K istorii'; N. K. Bunge, 'O finansovom polozhenii Rossii', *Istoricheskii arkhiv*, 2 (1960), 130–40.

related to the manner of allocation of direct taxes and payments within the *obshchestvo*. The answers seemed to point to the disintegration of the patriarchal commune. Land and payment were not allocated on the basis of revision souls, as the edict had provided. Instead, taxes tended to be allocated according to income and/or a variety of other criteria, ranging from revision souls to the actual number of males (*nalichnye dushi*). The old revision soul had survived only in large communes of the Black Earth zone. Voronezh was typical in this respect. In some villages, there was pressure for the acceptance of the principle of allocation based on the existing male membership of households. However, this was successfully 'opposed by those whose families were now small but who had originally received land on the basis of a large number of revision souls who do not wish to give up the land for which they had been making redemption payments for nearly thirty years'.

The data collected by the inspectors showed that under collective responsibility even prosperous peasants were in arrears, and that the wealthy often used the mutual guarantee to their own advantage. In some provinces, allotments were taken away from those in arrears and leased to wealthier peasants. In Kursk, poorer peasants leased out their allotments themselves, without waiting to be coerced to do so. Those peasants who were in arrears could not obtain passports or, if they were away, they would be threatened with recall to their place of permanent residence. Occasionally the *volost'* administration would contact the police and request them to hold back the earnings of those working in cities. Not only heads of households but also members of their families would be returned under police escort. In some areas, rural elders would receive travel allowances to check up on residents working in cities and to collect taxes; and in some others, they would hand over those who were in arrears to work in neighbouring factories.

However, there was evidence that the village assemblies were unwilling to use the coercive powers available to them. Witte ascribed this 'indifferentism' to their conviction that the duty of compulsory collection of taxes belonged to members of village and *volost'* administrations; to the practical impossibility of calling a full assembly, especially in areas with well-developed migratory trades; and finally, and most importantly, to the growth of principles of individualism which conflicted with the system of collective responsibility. He called for its abolition in the name of progress: 'collective responsibility, by restricting freedom and by subordinating individuals to the will of the collective, kills private initiative and paralyses the strivings towards a more prosperous existence'. However, when this ancient institution was formally abolished in 1903, it was not so much because there was a general consensus that this was desirable for the development of the individual and freedom, but because the accumulating arrears had convinced its most ardent defenders that collective responsibility had failed in the very aspect for which it was institutionalized. This was the most powerful argument for its abolition.[37]

Nevertheless, as a private means of distributing the risks of business transactions, the mutual guarantee continued to be resorted to by peasants when renting or purchasing land from private owners, or when making contractual arrangements of various kinds. The persistence of the institution illustrates the practice of group purchase or rental on the one hand, and the lack or inadequacy of judicial procedures for the recovery of debts or the enforcement of contracts on the other.[38]

The passport system was introduced by Peter the Great in 1719 to control the movement of those people attempting to evade the recruitment obligation. In 1724 this was complemented by special instructions connected with the introduction of the poll tax; namely, that those peasants who wished to travel more than thirty versts from their place of permanent residence required special permission to do so. The passport became a document which controlled the movement of persons belonging to tax-paying estates, and in 1763, with the introduction of a passport duty, it became a source of revenue also.[39] These three functions

[37] Simonova, 'Otmena', pp. 170–4; Vitte, *Vospominaniya*, ii. 525; Brzheskii, *Nedoimochnost'*, pp. 408–14. Many of those in favour of joint tenure believed that collective responsibility was intrinsic to it. Kavelin argued that 'if all householders are jointly owners, then they all must jointly answer for arrears and debts due from each . . . Collective responsibility and communal land tenure are indivisible: the latter inevitably implies the former.' *Sobranie*, ii. 247.

[38] An interesting illustration of peasant mentality or 'low cunning' was a refusal to pay rent for land leased under *poruka* from local estates, for 'has not the Emperor abolished the *poruka*?'.

[39] *Ents. slovar' Brokgauz–Efron*, xliv. 924 ff.; N. I. Anan'ich, 'Iz istorii zakonodatel'stva o krest'yanakh (vtoraya polovina XIX v.)', *Voprosy istorii Rossii XIX–nachala XX veka* (Leningrad, 1983), 34.

of the passport—police and administrative control, tax collection, and the production of income—remained practically unchanged throughout. The passport duty was abolished in 1897 as a way of encouraging peasants to seek earnings in industry and commerce.

When the revision of the passport system was raised by Bunge in 1886, the general feeling was that the policing function of the passport would have to stay, given the size of the country and the relatively small numbers of police and administrative personnel. It was the taxation function—and especially its legally differentiated nature—which no longer corresponded to economic and social reality. It was felt that the abolition of the poll tax on the one hand, and the desire to encourage people to move to other parts of the country in search of earnings or better conditions on the other, made the refusal of a passport to those in arrears with their taxes an unnecessary constraint. Bunge argued that the retention of the taxation function of the passport was incompatible with the principle of all-class taxation (*vsesoslovnost'*).[40]

He was not successful; neither was Witte in 1892, though his project, submitted jointly with I. N. Durnovo, was far from radical and was criticized by the Justice Minister, N. A. Manasein. Manasein believed that as long as ordinary people were dependent on their communities and the authorities for permission to leave (*pravo na otluchku*), and adult members of households could not make decisions about their place of work without the consent of the head of the household, one could hardly speak of freedom or of *vsesoslovnost'*.[41]

The final law as it emerged in 1894 provided for the issue of passports under the general denomination of *vid na zhitel'stvo*, which would serve for 'all estates as an identification document', and as a certificate of a 'right of departure' for all those persons whose travel depended on the consent of their communities. However, peasants could now have a passport for five years without need for renewal. They could not be refused a passport on account of arrears in taxes or redemption payments, but the consent of the communities was still required.[42]

[40] Anan'ich, 'Iz istorii zakonodatel'stva', p. 37; Simonova, 'Otmena', pp. 177–8; Brzheskii, *Nedoimochnost'*, pp. 107–8.

[41] Anan'ich, 'Iz istorii zakonodatel'stva', p. 40.

[42] *Polnoe sobranie zakonov Rossiiskoi imperii*, 3rd series, xiv, no. 10709 (1894), 'Vysochaishe utverzhdennoe polozhenie o vide na zhitel'stvo'.

Thus, there was a partial severance between collective responsibility for taxes and the issuing of passports, although the annual amount of local taxes was entered in the passport and had to be met by the end of the year, otherwise the police had the right to impound the passport.

Passports could also be recalled in accordance with the decisions of local communities: if members of a family incapable of work were left without means; upon the demand of the head of the household; and when a member was elected to the post of elder, though he had to be given a year's notice.

The law of 1894 also increased the distance over which peasants could travel without a passport to fifty versts, and no passport was required for agricultural work. On the other hand, workers in establishments under factory inspection required passports even if their permanent residence was within fifty versts.[43]

It was only on 5 October 1906 that the rights of former tax-paying estates were finally equalized with other members of society in this respect. As I have written elsewhere, neither the passport system nor collective responsibility for taxation and redemption payments seemed to have inhibited movement to cities and industry. The inhibiting factor was not the lack of supply but insufficient employment opportunities. However, we shall never know about those individuals who were frustrated, or those who found their position oppressive beyond endurance. Moreover, though the passport was a prominent feature of state fiscal control, one is inclined to think that many of the restrictions on individual peasants came from households asserting their claim to the earnings of household members, and indirectly from the community. It was not strictly speaking an official constraint on the freedom of movement.[44]

---

[43] Ibid., clause 19, provided that 'to unseparated members of peasant families, even those of age, *vidy na zhitel'stvo* are issued or renewed only upon consent of the head of the peasant household. In the event of his refusal . . . they can be issued by decision of the Land Captain, Peace Arbitrator . . . permanent officer of the District Authority on Peasant Affairs (*Prisutstvie*) . . .'. The provision regarding factory workers was solicited by Witte and Durnovo because the existing rule was not respected and had become 'inadequate for the needs of police supervision of factory workers'.

[44] O. Crisp, 'Labour and Industrialization in Russia', *Cambridge Economic History of Europe*, vii (Cambridge, 1978), pt. 2, pp. 308–415, esp. pp. 332–50.

The peasant has figured prominently in this essay, but inevitably we have seen him through the eyes of government officials, intellectuals, scholars. What about the peasant's authentic voice?

A number of peasants were invited to the Valuev Commission, a number sat on the Witte Committees, and they accounted for substantial proportions of deputies to the district *zemstva*. By the mid-1880s, peasant owners of private land accounted for one-half of all smallholders with electoral rights in the landowners' curia, and for one-tenth of the fully qualified electors. Some publicists have given us eyewitness accounts of the proceedings at village assemblies, reproducing peasant speech patterns and incidents which have an authentic ring about them. Nevertheless, if we wish to say something about peasant attitudes to property, we are forced to use circumstantial evidence, in other words, to see what they did.[45]

One damning or enlightening piece of evidence is 1917. Not much sign then of individualistic peasant proprietors. Instead, peasants seemed to be welcoming the return to land repartitioning —if they had ever given it up—and recognizing the right of all those who had ever had residence in the community to claim a share. Of course, participation in the breaking-up of estates is not necessarily incompatible with peasant desire for private property. Who would not yearn for a little extra land at no cost (*darovaya prirezka*)? Especially since the Russian landed proprietor had rarely been the kind of competent manager and improver to inspire respect.

Against this piece of evidence, there is the impressive record of peasant land purchases even under serfdom, and then the very extensive purchases after 1861, and especially after 1882 when the Peasant Land Bank was founded. Though the bank did sometimes foreclose, it seems that on the whole, even when peasants were falling behind with other payments, mortgage repayments were kept up. Most purchases were made by associations (*tovarishchestva*) of a few householders who pooled their resources for the purchase transaction. Between 1883 and 1905, 75 per cent of all land purchased through the Peasant Land

[45] D. Atkinson, 'The Zemstvo and the Peasantry', in T. Emmons and W. S. Vucinich (eds.), *The Zemstvo in Russia: An Experiment in Local Self-Government* (Cambridge, 1982), 86, 110 ff.; N. P. Druzhinin, *Ocherki krest'yanskoi obshchestvennoi zhizni* (St Petersburg, 1905), 43 ff.

Bank was acquired by associations. Land bought in larger parcels was cheaper; and sometimes the vendor preferred to sell it in one piece to avoid dealing with several buyers individually. As for joint purchases, the mutual guarantee was used; wealthier peasants preferred not to participate in purchases by the whole *obshchestvo*, but to organize special associations for this purpose. They disposed of the land freely, sold it, bequeathed it, rented it out, etc. Between 1883 and 1915, over two and a quarter million peasant households were involved in the buying of land through the Peasant Land Bank alone.[46]

Of course, the opportunity to purchase land, and thus to exercise an option for freedom, was not available to all. The price of land rocketed after the foundation of the Peasant Land Bank. Moreover, the deposits required represented a substantial portion of the price, and were not within the means of the poorest households. However, given the large number of households involved, they could not all have been among the richest. Furthermore, during the decades immediately following the emancipation, not only was land cheaper, but a season's work in New Russia—before the population influx and the introduction of machines—could earn the price of a *desyatin* of land or more without undue effort. Nevertheless, given that in areas such as the Central Agricultural Region the scope for land purchase was relatively limited (on account of both higher land prices and a greater percentage of poorer households), the security element was much more significant than the lure of potential freedom. Furthermore, it was not just the security of tenure of arable land, but also of access to pastures and meadows which was rightly perceived by many as essential to survival.[47]

There seems little doubt that after the first two decades, and

[46] V. N. Kashin, *Krepostnye krest'yane zemlevladel'tsy nakanune reformy* (Leningrad, 1945); V. G. Litvak, 'O zemel'noi sobstvennosti krepostnykh', *Materialy po istorii sel'skogo khozyaistva i krest'yanstva*, v (Moscow, 1962), 338–48; L. Khodskii, 'Krest'yanskoe zemlevladenie i pozemel'nyi kredit', *Narodnoe khozyaistvo*, 5 (1903), 1–51; Anfimov, 'Krest'yanskoe zemel'noe pravo', p. 215; *Obzor deyatel'nosti krest'yanskago pozemel'nago banka s 1 yanvarya po 1 sentyabr' 1907 g. i obshchie itogi za 1907 god* (St Petersburg, 1908), 3; *Otchety krest'yanskago pozemel'nago banka za 1907–1913 gg.* (St Petersburg, 1909–14); *Otchet . . . za 1915 god* (St Petersburg, 1916), app. 8.

[47] The value of the average mortgage through the Peasant Land Bank during the period 1883–1915 was 481 roubles per household, and the deposit was 155 roubles (calculated on the basis of *Otchet . . . za 1915 god*, app. 8).

especially after the reduction of redemption payments and the rise in land prices, peasants cherished their allotment. Even when it gave them little income, they valued the security it offered. Compared to the prices they had to pay for land that they bought either through the Peasant Bank or directly, the redemption payments began to look low (not that they were more eager to pay them!).[48] That they knew this is evident from a case related by L. Khodskii.

An estate was being offered for sale in Saratov province which a group of so-called 'quarter'- or 'beggar'-holder peasants (whose land was free of redemption debt) was eager to buy but did not possess the full asking price. The peasants approached the Peasant Bank and suggested that half their allotment land should be used as security. They made their calculations and presented them to the management, confident that they were offering excellent security; they quoted the current market value of the land and pointed out how much their allotment land had appreciated in value since emancipation. In pursuit of their case, they approached the head office and the Ministries of the Interior and Finance, who all recognized the soundness of their proposition. However, the bank had to turn them down because allotment land was not alienable; if they were not able to keep up the payments, the bank would not be able to foreclose.[49]

That many of the peasants understood and valued property *per se* is also clear from their use of sophisticated arguments and their spirited defence of their interests when, following emancipation, they were establishing their right to property acquired under serfdom. N. M. Druzhinin relates a case of ten families of peasants from Krasnoperovo in Vyatka province who put up a dogged fight for their full property rights to land which they had bought from the Bashkirs in 1802. They were taken over by the *Udel* department, which made them pay rents. In the process of proving their case before the governor, their title-deeds (*krepost'*) got lost. In 1856 they resumed their fight. Representatives went to St Petersburg to plead their case; it went through several court

[48] B. G. Litvak, *Russkaya derevnya v reforme 1861 goda* (Moscow, 1972), 394–9; A. V. Fadeev, 'Formirovanie kapitalizma v severnom Kavkaze v poreformennyi period', *Ezhegodnik po agrarnoi istorii vostochnoi Evropy* (1959), 251 ff.; V. I. Budaev, 'Vykup krest'yanami Smolenskoi gubernii zemli po polezheniyam 19 fevralya 1861 g.', ibid. 280–304.

[49] Khodskii, 'Krest'yanskoe zemlevladenie', pp. 48–9.

instances, was rejected, and presented again, until in 1891 the Senate gave judgement in the peasants' favour and against the *Udel*. Following this success, the peasants sued for compensation for the rents they had paid and for their costs. They won substantial recompense, though not the full claim.[50]

Thus the evidence, however circumstantial, suggests that the peasants did understand the differential value of property acquired by purchase. It gave them greater freedom of economic decision-making. Such property could be used as collateral for further purchases or for other transactions. On the other hand, a right to share in communal land, which could not be taken away from them to pay their debts, gave them greater security of tenure. Thus the two phenomena, attachment to joint land-holding and an expanding resort to the land market, could be reconciled by the peasants' desire for both security *and* freedom.

Men capable of such financial sophistication would also have perceived the difference between property which was alienable, and the allotments in joint tenure to which they had less than full rights (certainly no right of disposal and no secure rights of possession in areas where periodical redistribution was the rule). And yet Kavelin was right when he noted that there were many peasants who were buying land but still treasured their allotment. Khodskii campaigned for the removal of restrictions on allotment land so that it could be used as collateral, but he nevertheless favoured joint land tenure as providing security. Writing in 1903, when the question of peasant legal status was being aired publicly in connection with Witte's Committee, he commented: 'one could say with certainty that no peasant community would refuse to renounce the right to be flogged by the decision of their assembly (*skhod*) or by order of the authorities. But try to ask them to give up their right to manage and regulate the use of allotment by the decisions of the assembly, and you would hardly find anyone wishing to do so.'[51]

Furthermore, though there were those even in the State Council who maintained that from the peasants' point of view the

[50] N. M. Druzhinin, 'Byvshie udel'nye krest'yane posle reformy 1863 g. (1863–1883)', *Istoricheskie zapiski*, 85 (1970), 166–8; N. G. Ryndzyunskii, 'Reforma 1861 v krupnykh promyshlennykh selakh', Akademiya nauk, *Problemy sotsial'no-ekonimicheskoi istorii Rossii* (Moscow, 1971), 118–45.

[51] Kavelin, *Sobranie*, ii. 175–8; Khodskii, 'Krest'yanskoe zemlevladenie', p. 3.

redemption payments were just a tax, and that the peasants had no idea that they were actually buying the land when they were making these payments, the evidence seems to belie this. In 1896, attempting to ease the burden of accumulating arrears of redemption payments, Witte suggested rescheduling, which would have meant prolonging the redemption operation for a number of years. Normally only too eager to avail themselves of any relief going, the peasants were very reluctant to come forward on this occasion. Khodskii believed that they knew very well that they were making payments which would come to an end, and that they were not paying tax or rent, which had a way of rising indefinitely.[52]

As stated earlier, the western concept of private property as an incentive to effort and achievement on the part of the individual for the benefit of himself, his family, and 'all mankind' became current in Russia from the reign of Catherine the Great. Despite periodic lapses, it was the guiding principle of consecutive governments. It was certainly in its name that Stolypin's agrarian reforms were initiated in 1906. However, the evidence that private ownership really conferred these benefits is exceedingly patchy. The imperfect right of possession under communal ownership did not seem *per se* to have inhibited growth or discouraged improvements where there was know-how and opportunity, largely because communal arrangements were far from rigid. Furthermore, there is no conclusive proof that peasants cultivated land acquired by purchase more efficiently than the communal allotment; we do not know enough about the configuration of purchased land prior to 1906. More often than not, peasants bought parcels of land here and there to make up for a shortage of meadowland for hay, or to grow some oats for sale, or to avail themselves of an opportunity to increase their acreage when a neighbouring landowner was selling, etc. The bought land was unlikely to have been conceived of from the outset as an entity with developmental potential. On the other hand, Nifontov tells us that peasant marketings came from purchased land, whilst the allotment land served as a source of

---

[52] P. K. Shvanebakh, *Nashe podatnoe delo* (St Petersburg, 1901); Khodskii, 'Krest'yanskoe zemlevladenie', p. 18.

subsistence.[53] To conclude: though the government—with some lapses—accepted in principle the desirability of a right to private property in land, and though the peasants, whilst treasuring the security of their communal land allotment, were increasingly involved in the land market, on balance one has to say that the concept of property was more weakly developed in Russia, especially in the main provinces of eastern and central Russia, than elsewhere in Europe, and not only among the peasants. The most important reason historically was undoubtedly the land–labour ratio, which, until fairly late in the life of the Russian Empire, worked in favour of labour.

Connected with this was the state of the land market, which remained very poorly developed until late in the nineteenth century—the result of the slow commercialization of farming and its low profitability. Other factors included the underdeveloped system of land registration, and the imprecision of juridical norms, especially those governing heritable household tenure. Land transactions among peasants developed rapidly after 1861, but the shortage of surveyors and notaries, and the high cost of conveyancing and of stamp-duty, often meant the conclusion of informal transactions (*domashnyaya*) which lacked firm legal validity; property rights could thus be asserted only by being in uninterrupted and uncontested possession for a specified number of years, or else they could be subject to forfeit.[54]

The lack of clearly defined boundaries, and the intermingling of strips of not only peasant land but estate land as well, encouraged encroachment upon the property of others, and also weakened respect for property rights in general. This aspect of the law, especially with regard to forests, was rather permissive, and both officials and landowners were inconsistent in their attitude to encroachment. The underlying philosophy was one of unease about the legitimacy of the defence of property rights, especially against those less privileged than themselves.[55] 'The

[53] Rittikh (ed.), *Svod trudov*, pp. 2–32; A. S. Nifontov, *Zernovoe proizvodstvo Rossii vo vtoroi polovine XIX veka* (Moscow, 1974), 301.

[54] Rittikh (ed.), *Svod trudov*, pp. 83–96.

[55] Ibid.; A. A. Leont'ev, 'Mezhevyya nuzhdy derevni', in L'vov and Stakhovich (eds.), *Nuzhdy derevni*, pp. 234–86; I. V. Gessen, 'Iuridicheskaya pomoshch' naseleniyu', ibid. 178–203, 208–28. There was no penalty for unauthorized ploughing up of estate land, cutting timber in estate forests, or driving cattle into estate fields, etc. in the Criminal Code. The official reason was 'that given the absence

Russian soul', wrote Herzen, 'felt offended by enclosures, fences, hedges' representing exclusive possession, 'a kind of offensive insolence of the right of property'. On the other hand, the great future that Herzen prophesied for the native Russian villages would have been more likely to materialize if their fields had not been quite so open![56]

of proper boundaries, punishability of wilful seizures would provoke an avalanche of cases, not always *bona fide*'. It seems that Polish estate owners and German managers did not approve of the *gumannost'* of Russian landowners; they tended to retaliate on occasion by ordering their cattle to be driven into peasant fields. This was effective, apparently, and would persuade the villagers that it might be advisable to respect estate property. Some estate owners asked for the collective responsibility of the whole village to be invoked for encroachment upon their property, thereby emphasizing both the difficulties of seeking redress and the vitality of the institution of collective responsibility in Russian conditions.

[56] A. Gertsen, *Sochineniya*, iii (Moscow, 1956), 77.

The Trojan Mare: Women's Rights and Civil Rights in Late Imperial Russia

WILLIAM G. WAGNER

LECTURING on women in European society at St Petersburg University in 1864, Petr Redkin, a prominent jurist and later rector of the university, declared to his law students that Russian women by themselves would never be able to attain their rightful social position. 'You, my young jurists,' he exclaimed to loud applause, 'must extend a hand to Russian women and give them the possibility of occupying their appropriate place in society.'[1] Redkin's admonition to his students reflected both the changing attitude towards women among many members of Russia's emerging educated professional élite, and the idealistic hope of many jurists that the impending judicial reform would enable them to eliminate society's ills by recasting it on the basis of legality. Believing women to be particularly oppressed by law and social convention, these jurists considered them to be in special need of their chivalric protection.

While jurists were sincere in their desire to improve the lot of women, however, their proposals often represented only part of a grander design to transform Russian society in accordance with their own values, circumstances, and ideals. Reform of women's legal rights provided jurists with an opportunity for replacing the unlimited patriarchal authority and unequal status of the patrilineal kin-group with the mutual rights and obligations of the conjugal family as the basis of Russian family, property, and inheritance law. Many jurists hoped that this reformulation of the law would limit the exercise of authority in general while securing

* I would like to thank the National Endowment for the Humanities, the International Research and Exchanges Board, and the American Council of Learned Societies for fellowships and grants that made the research for this paper possible.

[1] M. V. Shimanovskii, *Petr Grigor'evich Redkin (biograficheskii ocherk)* (Odessa, 1890), 13.

the individual's personal and property rights, thereby ensuring greater social stability and prosperity. From the 1860s onwards, therefore, jurists' efforts to enlarge the individual's civil rights by expanding women's personal and inheritance rights formed part of the general struggle over social values and political ideals that racked late imperial Russia. Moreover, by emphasizing the individual's rights, personal merit, and the role of law in society, these efforts also promoted the personal and professional interests of jurists, the majority of whom were landless, well educated, and dependent primarily on their professional expertise for their livelihood and social status.[2] Paradoxically, however, the challenge to autocratic power and the traditional social order implicit in these proposals to reform the law provoked such strong conservative and clerical resistance that little improvement in women's legal rights had been achieved by the fall of the old regime.

Imperial civil law gave Russian women good grounds for lament. Based on unlimited patriarchal authority and the patrilineal kin-group, family, property, and inheritance law discriminated severely against them. Reflecting traditional practices and Orthodox doctrine, family law defined marriage as a religious institution based on patriarchal authority, unquestioning obedience, and unequal status. A wife was obliged to obey and live with her husband, who was proclaimed head of the family. She also needed her husband's consent to enter employment, to undertake higher education, to execute a bill of exchange, or to receive a separate passport (*vid na zhitel'stvo*), which was necessary for residence and often for employment. The law tempered the husband's authority only by the unenforceable admonitions to love, respect, and defend his wife, to forgive her infirmities, and to live with her in harmony. The husband's only substantive obligation was to support his wife in a fashion commensurate with his means. Designated mistress of the household, a wife was required to submit completely to her

---

[2] On the social, educational, and professional characteristics of the legal profession, see R. S. Wortman, *The Development of a Russian Legal Consciousness* (Chicago, 1976); V. R. Leikina-Svirskaya, *Intelligentsiya v Rossii vo vtoroi polovine XIX veka* (Moscow, 1971), chs. 2 and 3; ead., *Russkaya intelligentsiya v 1900–1917 godakh* (Moscow, 1981), chs. 1 and 2; and A. Sinel, 'The Socialization of the Russian Bureaucratic Elite, 1811–1917: Life at Tsarskoe Selo Lyceum and the School of Jurisprudence', *Russian History*, 3/1 (1976), 1–31.

husband and to render him pleasure, affection, and fidelity. Considered a personal affair, marital strife and a husband's efforts to discipline his wife lay outside the purview of the law. Stripped of its pious and unenforceable admonitions, then, the law completely subordinated a wife to her husband's power, and left her with virtually no means of legal redress apart from a criminal action for severe injury.[3] Few wives brought such actions against their husbands, however, not least because they would still be obliged to live together after their husbands' release from prison.[4]

Even when the husband's exercise of his authority became unbearably oppressive, Russian law offered no real means of escape, especially for Orthodox wives. Each of the recognized faiths in the empire established and enforced its own rules for divorce, and those set by the Orthodox Church were among the most stringent. The Church permitted divorce only for adultery, sexual incapacity arising before marriage, exile to Siberia due to a criminal conviction, or disappearance. Moreover, spouses guilty of adultery, abandonment, or sexual incapacity were also prohibited from remarrying.[5] As church leaders stated repeatedly, these rules were intended to discourage divorce as a violation of the holy sacrament of marriage.[6]

Restrictive laws administered by an unsympathetic body made divorce difficult to obtain for Orthodox women. In the two decades prior to the judicial reform, for example, the Orthodox Church granted an average of only twenty-three divorces per year

[3] *Svod zakonov Rossiiskoi imperii* (St Petersburg, 1857) (hereafter *SZ*; all references are to the 1857 edn. unless otherwise stated), x, pt. 1, arts. 100–8, 2202, and 1–118 generally on marriage; xi, pt. 2, *Ustav torgovyi*, art. 546; xiv, *Ustav o pasportakh*; and xv, *Ulozhenie o nakazaniyakh ugolovnykh i ispravitel'nykh*. On marriage law generally, see A. I. Zagorovskii, *Kurs semeinago prava*, 2nd edn. (Odessa, 1909); K. P. Pobedonostsev, *Kurs grazhdanskago prava*, 4th edn. (St Petersburg, 1896), ii; and N. S. Suvorov, *Uchebnik tserkovnago prava* (Moscow, 1912).

[4] I. Orshanskii, 'Lichnyya i imushchestvennyya otnosheniya suprugov', in *Izsledovaniya po russkomu pravu semeinomu i nasledstvennomu* (St Petersburg, 1877), 19–21, 188–91.

[5] The Church also reluctantly and infrequently granted annulments for certain violations of marriage procedure: *SZ*, x, pt. 1, arts. 45–60, and xi, pt. 1, *Ustav dukhovnykh del inostrannykh ispovedanii*. See also the works cited in n. 3 above.

[6] Leningrad, Tsentral'nyi gosudarstvennyi istoricheskii arkhiv SSSR (hereafter TsGIA), f. 1405, op. 542, d. 663, l. 117–23; f. 796, op. 445, d. 417, l. 1–13, pp. 4–21; f. 797, op. 91–1898, d. 53, l. 77–8; and 'Razskazy knyaza A. N. Golitsyna: Iz zapisok Yu. N. Barteneva', *Russkii arkhiv*, 2 (1886), 69–75, 101–2.

for all causes except exile. Even though the number of divorces and the rate of divorce rose substantially after the mid-1860s, both remained very low until the end of the tsarist regime.[7] Nor did marital separation provide a feasible alternative. Since formal separation was illegal, informal agreements to separate were unenforceable and left women especially in a vulnerable position. They had no right to support from their husbands, who in turn could impede their ability to support themselves by controlling their passports and refusing them permission to enter employment. A wife's children, too, could be declared illegitimate, subjecting them to harsh legal disabilities as well as branding them with a severe social stigma.[8]

Unmarried women, too, felt the strictures of patriarchal authority. The law subordinated daughters to their parents', especially to their fathers', authority, which was only limited but not terminated by marriage. Parents enjoyed extensive power to punish their daughters, and could have them confined for disobedience, although actions resulting in death or severe injury were criminally punishable. Obliged to obey their parents unconditionally and to support them when they were in need, daughters were admonished to love, honour, and respect their parents and were barred from bringing any legal actions against them.[9] Like wives, then, daughters were left largely defenceless in the face of patriarchal authority.

[7] According to the annual reports of the Chief Procurator of the Holy Synod, the number of divorces granted by the Church for all causes except exile rose to 650 in 1866, and thereafter varied between about 550 and 750 until the early 20th century when the total again rose sharply, reaching 3,532 in 1912. The rate of divorces per 1,000 marriages rose from 0.05 to 0.13 between 1841 and 1861, jumped to 1.43 in 1866, and leapt from 1.40 to 4.20 between 1900 and 1914: *Izvlechenie iz otcheta Ober-Prokurora Svyateishago Sinoda* (or slight variations of this title) St Petersburg, 1841–83); and *Vsepoddaneishii otchet Ober-Prokurora Svyateishago Sinoda po vedomstvu pravoslavnago ispovedaniya* (St Petersburg, 1884–1914).

[8] *SZ*, x, pt. 1, arts. 119–63, 1119. See the works cited in n. 5 above, and TsGIA, f. 1405, op. 542, d. 666, l. 149–58, 181–2, d. 668, l. 457–9, d. 671, l. 249–52, d. 124, l. 67, 71–3, 75, 78–9; f. 797, op. 92, d. 51, l. 1–7. See also K. K. Arsen'ev, 'Khronika: Razluchenie suprugov, kak neobkhodimyi institut brachnago prava', *Vestnik Evropy*, 3 (1884), 290–326; B'., 'Supruzheskoe pravo', *Sudebnaya gazeta*, 24 (1895), 2–4; 27 (1895), 2–4; 36 (1895), 2–4; and 40 (1895), 2–3; and M. I. Kulisher, *Razvod i polozhenie zhenshchin* (St Petersburg, 1896), esp. 148–53, 183, 208–35, 253–4.

[9] *SZ*, x, pt. 1, arts. 164–95, 226, 229–30, 294–5, 995; and xv, *Ulozhenie o nakazaniyakh ugolovnykh i ispravitel'nykh*, art. 2957. See also the works cited in n. 3 above.

Women fared no better under inheritance law. Arising from an earlier period of strong kin-groups and land tenure based largely on male service to the state, the law discriminated severely against women in order to prevent valuable property from passing away from the kin-group or clan (*rod*). In descendant lines, therefore, daughters received only one-eighth of the deceased's movable property and one-fourteenth of the immovable property in the presence of sons or their heirs. In collateral lines, females were excluded entirely by males of equal degree or their descendants, and the deceased's movable or acquired property passed only to paternal lines. Wives could claim only one-quarter of their husbands' movable property and one-seventh of their immovable property as a provision for maintenance. While these harsh provisions could be overridden by the deceased's will in the case of movable or self-acquired immovable property, they were unavoidable with regard to patrimonial property (i.e. any immovable property inherited from a kinsman), which could not be alienated to anyone but the direct heir except by sale.[10]

Only women's exclusive control over their own property provided any relief from their otherwise dismal legal position. Marriage created no community of property under imperial law. Regardless of marital status, therefore, women of age enjoyed unlimited power to use and dispose of their own property, including their dowries.[11] An outgrowth of both the clan social structure and the system of service tenure, this power was unusually extensive compared with the property rights of other European women. It was limited in practice, however, by the apparently still widespread custom of giving the wife's dowry to her husband to use for family needs.[12]

[10] *SZ*, x, pt. 1, arts. 383–1537 (but see also ix; x, part. 2; xi; and xii). In addition to the works cited in n. 3 above, see M. F. Vladimirskii-Budanov, *Obzor istorii russkago prava*, 6th edn. (St Petersburg, 1909); I. E. Il'yashenko, 'Institut rodovogo imushchestva s tochki zreniya budushchago grazhdanskago ulozheniya', *Zhurnal Ministerstva yustitisii* (hereafter *ZhMYu*), 2 (1900), 96–130; 3 (1900), 110–42; and 4 (1900), 110–36; and id., 'O prave nasledovaniya suprugov s tochki zreniya budushchago grazhdanskago ulozheniya', *Vestnik prava*, 4–5 (1902), 70–90.

[11] *SZ*, x, pt. 1, arts. 109–18; x, pt. 2, arts. 2270–74; and xi, pt. 2, *Ustav torgovyi*, arts. 1932–7. See also the works cited in nn. 3 and 10 above, and Orshanskii, 'Lichnyya i imushchestvennyya otnosheniya'.

[12] Orshanskii, 'Lichnyya i imushchestvennyya otnosheniya', pp. 100–87; A. I. Zagorovskii, 'Lichnyya i imushchestvennyya otnosheniya mezhdu suprugami', *Russkaya mysl'*, 4 (1897), 65–8; and *Grazhdanskoe ulozhenie: Proekt vysochaishe*

Beginning in the 1860s, jurists first of all harshly criticized these legal arrangements as unjust and socially dysfunctional, and then scathingly condemned them as the remnants of an outdated social order. Their criticism derived from an image of the family as a matrix of moral relationships, rights, and mutual obligations between equal individuals that contrasted sharply with the notions of patriarchal authority and unequal status underlying existing law. By the late 1870s this image dominated Russian legal writing on family, property, and inheritance law, and for most jurists had come to symbolize society's progressive development, in contrast to the backwardness embodied in the patriarchal clan. As a result, jurists increasingly demanded a reform of women's rights and of the law in general in order to limit the husband's or father's authority and to secure the rights and personal development of individual family members. Through such reform they hoped not only to improve the position of women, but also to instil a sense of legality in Russian society and to transform it in accordance with their progressive views. Thus, their proposed reforms largely reflected their own social values, conditions, and aspirations, and sometimes their political goals.

Critics of the law argued that the family's social role was to enable the fullest possible development of each individual, and to foster civic-spirited, patriotic, and productive citizens. This role could only be fulfilled, they contended, when actual family relations corresponded to the natural equality of rights, mutuality of obligations, and affection that existed between family members. By basing the law on relations of unlimited authority, unquestioning obedience, and unequal status within the patrilineal clan, Russian law distorted these relations and prevented attainment of the family's social objectives.

In a scathing review of Russian family law which he wrote in 1861, for example, the radical jurist and publicist Mikhail Filippov claimed that marriage was based on the mutual rights and obligations that were created between spouses by their voluntary union and emotional affinity.[13] Yet, he argued, the law transformed women into their husbands' slaves and encouraged

---

uchrezhdennoi redaktsionnoi komissii po sostavleniyu grazhdanskago ulozheniya (hereafter *Grazhdanskoe ulozhenie*), 2 (St Petersburg, 1902), i. 184–5.

[13] M. Filippov, 'Vzglyad na russkie grazhdanskie zakony', *Sovremennik*, 85 (1861), 523–62; and 86 (1861), 217–66.

their abuse by granting their husbands unlimited authority over them. In his estimation, a wife's right to separate property afforded her inadequate protection from mistreatment, because restrictive divorce laws and the legal obligation to live with her husband prevented her escape from an oppressive relationship. Compelling spouses to live together when the moral relations between them had broken down merely led to mutual hostility, degeneracy, and frequently violence, a situation that was hardly conducive to fostering sound morals and civic virtue. 'I am convinced', Filippov asserted, 'that only an insane person, an obscurant, an ignoramus, a callous and complete egoist' would 'demand unlimited submission, or, in other words, slavery, from [his] wife,' or would 'compulsorily, by means of the law, the court, and the police, force his wife to live with him . . . .'[14] He concluded that existing law was unjust, that it frustrated the social objective of marriage and conflicted with prevailing social attitudes, by which he meant the attitudes of reasonable and rational people like himself.

To rectify this situation, Filippov proposed to eliminate the husband's control over his wife's actions, to accord her an active social role outside the home in addition to her principal role as a mother, and to allow divorce whenever the basis for marriage no longer existed. From now on, increasing the possibility of dissolving marriage through divorce or separation became the most frequently proposed means for guaranteeing equity and preventing abuse within it.[15] Reflecting both their own professional aspirations and their distrust of the Church's ability to administer divorce laws dispassionately, later juristic critics of the law also advocated transferring jurisdiction over marital affairs to secular courts.[16]

[14] Ibid., 85 (1861), 224.

[15] Ibid. 526, 549–62; and 86 (1861), 219–40, 249. See also Orshanskii, 'Lichnyya i imushchestvennyya otnosheniya', pp. 39–71, 88–9, 194–8; K. D. Kavelin, 'Prava semeistvennyya: Ocherki yuridicheskikh otnoshenii, voznikayushchikh iz semeinago soyuza', in *Sobranie sochinenii* (St Petersburg, 1904), iv, cols. 1067–75, 1083; A. L. Borovikovskii, 'Sud i sem'ya', in *Otchet sud'i* (St Petersburg, 1892), ii. 213–20, 238–40, 263–9; id., 'Konstitutsii sem'i po proektu grazhdanskago ulozheniya', *ZhMYu*, 9 (1902), 23–6, 32–7; Zagorovskii, *Kurs*, pp. 187–208; I. M. Tyutryumov, 'Po povodu peresmotra i kodifikatsii grazhdanskikh zakonov', *Russkoe bogatstvo*, 3 (1884), 694–8; and 5–6 (1884), 475–6; and id., 'Razdel'noe zhitel'stvo suprugov', *Yurist*, 11 (1903), 364–9.

[16] Orshanskii, 'Lichnyya i imushchestvennyya otnosheniya', pp. 5–6, 28–30, 192–8; id., 'Dukhovnyi sud i semeinoe pravo', *Zhurnal grazhdanskago i torgovago prava*,

Filippov also believed that the law distorted the relationship between parents and daughters. This relationship, he asserted, derived from the emotional bonds and moral obligations arising from the event of birth. Parents thus had a moral duty to protect, nurture, and adequately educate their daughters, a duty that was also reinforced by social interest. But, Filippov contended, instead of protecting naturally weak and defenceless children, the law invited their abuse by proclaiming unlimited parental authority over them. While he and subsequent critics could devise no means for eliminating parental authority, they advocated its termination when children achieved their majority, and at least allowing minor children to turn to the courts for protection against their parents' abuse of power.[17]

Jurists likewise condemned women's inheritance rights as immoral and socially dysfunctional. The severe discrimination (especially against daughters and widows) entailed in the patrimonial system of inheritance was fundamentally unjust, they argued, and created tension and disharmony within the family by transgressing the moral obligations and bonds of equal love that united it. The wife deserved a larger portion of her husband's estate: as his freely chosen partner, she was spiritually closest to him and often helped him to increase substantially the value of his property. Similarly, they asserted that daughters should have at least an equal share with sons in their parents' inheritance: they were equally loved by their parents, and yet daughters enjoyed far fewer opportunities for gainful employment. The fact that husbands and fathers frequently resorted to illegal means to circumvent the law's inequities proved that it conflicted with

3 (1872), 449, 455–6; and 4 (1872), 616–70; and id., 'Reforma grazhdanskago suda i brachnago prava', *Zhurnal grazhdanskago i ugolovnago prava* (hereafter *ZhGiUP*), 6 (1873), 148–96; Kavelin, 'Prava semeistvennyya', cols. 1032–43, 1116–19; A. L. Borovikovskii, 'Brak i razvod po proektu grazhdanskago ulozheniya', *ZhMYu*, 8 (1902), 1–2, 10–13, 15–28, 59–62; Tyutryumov, 'Po povodu peresmotra', 3, pp. 694–80, 701–2; and 5–6, pp. 461–5; and *Grazhdanskoe ulozhenie*, 4 (1903), arts. 160–2, 165–70, 181, 189, 217–18, 224, 233 (with commentary, esp. pp. 42–52, 272–4, 278–80, 289–90, 309–26, 331–2, 341).

[17] Filippov, 'Vzglyad', 85, pp. 527–30; and 86, pp. 227, 256–65. See also Kavelin, 'Prava semeistvennyya', cols. 1111–16; Borovikovskii, 'Sud i sem'ya', pp. 298–307; I. M. Tyutryumov, 'Ogranichenie roditel'skoi vlasti', *Yurist*, 13 (1903), cols. 437–42; I. Nadezhdin, 'Vlast' roditelei nad det'mi', ibid., 8 (1902), cols. 278–85; and *Grazhdanskoe ulozhenie*, 2 (1902), arts. 3, 197–9, 253–4, 284–302 (with commentary).

prevailing social attitudes, jurists claimed, as well as undermined respect for law in general. They added that the law also retarded economic progress and reduced national prosperity by causing the constant division of estates and dispersal of capital. This effect inflicted considerable economic damage on both individual families and the state, they asserted, while fetters binding owners of patrimonial property discouraged investment and innovation.[18]

To overcome the injustices and problems of existing law, most jurists proposed the abolition of the patrimonial system of inheritance, and the reformulation of the law on the basis of individual ownership and the moral bonds within the conjugal family. Women's and men's inheritance rights would be equalized and the spouse's share of the inheritance would be greatly expanded. The rights of family members would be protected by the introduction of a system of obligatory shares similar to that of France or Austria. To ensure adequate flexibility in the law for moral and economic reasons, however, many jurists also advocated an expansion of the owner's testamentary power, a proposal that was not always easy to reconcile with a system of obligatory shares.[19]

The values and ideals inherent in these proposals for the reform of family and inheritance law clearly clashed with the principles underlying the traditional tsarist social and political order. From the later 1870s onwards, therefore, to deflect conservative criticism based on the need to preserve national traditions and existing social relations, juristic proponents of

[18] A. Lyubavskii, 'Unichtozhenie razlichiya mezhdu imushchestvami rodovymi i blagopriobretennymi', in *Yuridicheskiya monografii i izsledovaniya* (St Petersburg, 1875), iii. 9–38; id., 'Ob uravnenii nasledstvennykh prav muzhchin i zhenshchin', *ZhMYu*, 5/2 (1864), 399–424; I. Orshanskii, 'Nasledstvennyya prava russkoi zhenshchiny', *ZhGiUP*, 2 (1876), 1–38; and 3 (1876), 1–31; V. D. Spasovich, 'Sledovalo by razreshit' svobodnoe rasporyazhenie po dukhovnym zaveshchaniyam rodovymi imushchestvami', in S. I. Barshev *et al.* (eds.), *Pervyi s"ezd russkikh yuristov v Moskve v 1875 godu* (Moscow, 1882), 161–3; and *Zamechaniya o nedostatkakh deistvuyushchikh grazhdanskikh zakonov: Izdanie redaktsionnoi komissii po sostavleniyu grazhdanskago ulozheniya* (St Petersburg, 1891), nos. 1, 293–4, 305–7, 309–10, 312–13, 320, 507, 573–9, 586–605, 609–12, 720–5.

[19] In addition to the works cited in n. 18 above, see Il'yashenko, 'Institut rodovogo imushchestva'; Tyutryumov, 'Po povodu peresmotra'; P. N. Gussakovskii, 'Nasledstvennoe pravo po proektu grazhdanskago ulozheniya', *ZhMYu*, 9 (1903), 1–52; A. N. Gedda, 'Obyazatel'naya dolya v nasledstve po proektu grazhdanskago ulozheniya', ibid., 2 (1904), 56–84; K. P. Zmirlov, 'Otmena ili preobrazovanie nashikh zakonov o rodovykh imushchestv?', ibid., 4 (1898), 75–124; and *Grazhdanskoe ulozhenie*, 4 (1903), esp. introd.

reform used comparative historical methodology and sociological theories to demonstrate the historical legitimacy as well as the justice and social utility of their proposals.[20] The origin and function of existing law, these jurists asserted, lay in the particular social and economic conditions of pre-emancipation Russia. While appropriate for these conditions, they argued, the law no longer corresponded to the social needs and relationships which had arisen after the abolition of serfdom. Comparing the development of Russian and European law, reformist jurists attempted to demonstrate that existing Russian legal institutions had their counterparts in Europe's past. These studies proved that Russian institutions were not unique products of national history or character, but were simply local variants of general socio-legal institutions that existed in all societies at a similar stage of development. Since Russia was following a similar evolutionary path to that of Western Europe, the jurists concluded that their task was to adapt the universal institutions of civil law developed by European juridical science to the particular needs of contemporary Russian society.

Employing this progressive evolutionary approach, reformist jurists depicted socio-legal development as two parallel processes in which the conjugal family (*sem'ya*) gradually replaced the patrilineal clan (*rod*), and the autonomous individual gradually emerged from subordination to patriarchal authority. Jurists considered these two processes to be closely interrelated, with the conjugal family—after its restructuring on moral principles— creating the best environment for the development of each member's potential. Since women represented the most oppressed family members within this scheme, their legal status became both the measure of a society's movement along this path of development and a means for promoting further change. It was through studies employing this model, therefore, that reformist jurists sought to persuade judges and the government to complete the transition from clan to family and to liberate the individual

---

[20] On the development of these methodologies, see A. Vucinich, *Social Thought in Tsarist Russia: The Quest for a General Science of Society* (Chicago, 1976), 125–72; G. F. Shershenevich, *Nauka grazhdanskago prava v Rossii* (Kazan, 1893), 195–231; G. V. Shvekov, 'Sravnitel'nyi metod v russkoi istoriko-pravovoi nauke (istoricheskii obzor)', *Problemy istorii gosudarstva i prava* (*Trudy Vsesoyuznogo yuridicheskogo zaochnogo instituta*, 43 (Moscow, 1977), 188–223; and N. Ya. Kuprits, *Kovalevskii* (Moscow, 1978).

from patriarchal control by reforming family, property, and inheritance law. Since these jurists also claimed that family relationships both reinforced and provided the foundation for social relationships in general, their further implicit objective was the reshaping of society on the basis of the ideals embodied in their image of the family.

Although jurists disagreed over whether the state, socio-economic forces, or the Church caused the transition from clan to family, they all agreed that this transition transformed both the family's structure and the distribution of authority within it. According to these authors, as state law, religious precepts, reason, or economic development overcame the primitive conditions, instinctual nature, and physiological needs of early human society, the affection and spiritual affinity within the family began to weaken the blood ties and patriarchal authority that had bound the patrilineal clan together. The individual gradually emerged from this process with a social identity and an ability to survive apart from the clan. As the individual gained autonomy, jurists argued, marriage came to be based more on the spouses' voluntary choice and their emotional affinity with each other than on parental arrangement and calculation of the clan's interests. Having freely chosen their wives, husbands no longer considered them to be their chattels and outsiders to their clan, but thought of them as their moral and spiritual partners. As affection between spouses gained primacy over blood relationships in the clan, patriarchal authority weakened and natural affection between parents and children strengthened. As a result, jurists argued, daughters came to be loved equally with sons and were no longer considered expendable assets to be used for concluding marriage alliances. Mutual affection between family members thus eroded the clan's authoritarianism, inequality, and amorality, and gave rise to mutual rights and obligations within the conjugal family. Hence, although most jurists still recognized the husband as the head of the family, they narrowly circumscribed his power by his moral obligations and the rights of other family members.[21]

[21] Kavelin, 'Prava semeistvennyya'; id., 'Russkoe grazhdanskoe ulozhenie', *ZhGiUP* 9 (1882), 1–24; D. I. Azarevich, 'Russkii brak', ibid., 5 (1880), 82–132; and 6 (1880), 97–139; A. N. Stoyanov, *Zachatki semeinago prava u pervobytnykh narodov: Etyud po istorii zakonodatel'stv* (Kharkov, 1884); M. M. Kovalevskii, *Ocherki proiskhozhdeniya i razvitiya sem'i i sobstvennosti* (St Petersburg, 1895); id., *Rodovoi*

Applying this scheme to property and inheritance relationships, reformist jurists argued that as the individual emerged from the clan, the basis of property and inheritance shifted from the clan to the individual and the family. Patrimonial constraints on an owner's proprietary power were gradually stripped away as the individual became the focus of social and economic activity. Likewise, male preference in inheritance disappeared as mutual affection, moral obligations, and individual rights within the conjugal family displaced the blood relationships of the clan. Existing Russian law represented a transitional stage in this transformation, jurists contended, and was thus a sign of backwardness rather than a mark of national distinction. But the recent abolition of serfdom, and the earlier elimination of land tenure based on state service and of the nobility's service obligation, had done away with the last props of the patrimonial system. Since the division of society into formal social estates was now also anachronistic, they declared, individuals, including women, should be free to pursue their own and society's gain. Thus, reformist jurists concluded that existing property and inheritance law conflicted with both the principle underlying current property relations—individual ownership—and the basic unit of social organization—the conjugal family. It was therefore in the state's interest, they claimed, to help release the tremendous productive potential of individuals by eliminating the legal fetters that restrained them.[22]

byt v nastoyashchem, nedavnem i otdalennom proshlom: Opyt v oblasti sravnitel'noi etnografii i istorii prava (St Petersburg, 1905); id., Modern Customs and Ancient Laws of Russia (London, 1891), 1–68; G. F. Shershenevich, Uchebnik russkago grazhdanskago prava, 10th edn. (Moscow, 1911), 674–5, 711–20, 729–30, 760; Vladimirskii-Budanov, Obzor, pp. 409–506; Zagorovskii, Kurs, pp. 1–7, 60–9, 127–43, 182–4, 256–60; Kulisher, Razvod; and Tyutryumov, 'Po povodu peresmotra'.

[22] In addition to the works cited in n. 19 above, see Kavelin, 'Russkoe grazhdanskoe ulozhenie'; id., 'Pravo nasledovaniya: Ocherki yuridicheskikh otnoshenii, voznikayushchikh iz nasledovaniya imushchestva', in Sobranie, iv; K. P. Zmirlov, 'Znachenie rodovykh imushchestv dlya budushchago grazhdanskago ulozheniya', ZhGiUP, 3 (1889), 51–98; D. I. Azarevich, 'Svoboda i ogranichenie dukhovnykh zaveshchanii', ibid., 8 (1889), 64–115; id., 'Semeinyya imushchestvennyya otnosheniya po russkomu pravu, ibid. 4 (1883), 101–36; I. V. Gessen, 'Vliyanie zakonodatel'stva na polozhenie zhenshchin', Pravo, 51 (1908), cols. 2833–40; N. N. Tovstoles, 'Svoboda zaveshchatel'noi voli po russkomu pravu v razlichnye periody ego razvitiya', ZhMYu, 8 (1902), 63–119; id., 'Yuridicheskoe polozhenie zhenshchiny pri otkrytii nasledstva po russkomu zakonodatel'stvu', ibid. 1 (1910), 56–83; and id., 'Nasledovanie suprugov po russkomu pravu, v svyazi s procktom grazhdanskago ulozheniya', ibid. 5 (1911), 1–63.

A populistic variant of these evolutionary ideas emerged in the early 1880s. Strongly influenced by general populist idealization of the peasantry, it developed as knowledge of peasant legal customs expanded after the emancipation. None the less, jurists adopting this view shared essentially the same moralistic image of the family and evolutionary notions as their progressivist peers. They differed from the latter primarily in their belief in the reforming potential of peasant custom, and their apparent rejection of state law as a regressive rather than a progressive influence on Russian legal development. In fact, however, they too sought to persuade the state to reform imperial law in order to realize their ideals. Moreover, the principles they imputed to peasant custom turned out to be surprisingly similar to those believed to underlie European civil law. Indeed, they advocated essentially the same reforms of family, property, and inheritance law as their non-populist yet progressive counterparts, and they relied just as frequently on European law for support. This similarity between Russian peasant custom and European law, they claimed, merely demonstrated the common humanitarian principles underlying them both.[23]

The arguments used by jurists to justify a reform of the law were teleological and often circular, yet they were well suited to the predilections of lawyers committed to the idea of legality. Trained to think in terms of rights and obligations rather than authority and obedience, it is not surprising that they redefined family and inheritance relations in these terms. Moreover, while the image of the family to be found in the jurists' theories hardly corresponded to the realities of life or to the attitudes of most Russians—especially of the peasantry and lower urban classes of the second half of the nineteenth century[24]—it did bear a closer

[23] Tyutryumov, 'Po povodu peresmotra'; id. in Zamechaniya o nedostatkakh, nos. 1, 10, 14, 26, 86, 109, 293, 501, 573, 623, 642; A. Savel'ev, Yuridicheskiya otnosheniya mezhdu suprugami, po zakonam i obychayam velikorusskago naroda (Nizhnii Novgorod, 1881); N. V. Reingardt, O lichnykh i imushchestvennykh pravakh zhenshchin po russkomu zakonu (Kazan, 1885); A. M. Evreinova, O znachenii i predelakh obychnago prava pri razrabotke otdel'nykh institutov grazhdanskago ulozheniya (St Petersburg, 1883); and ead., 'Ob uravnenii prav zhenshchin pri nasledovanii (Protokoly grazhdanskago otdeleniya S.-Pb. yuridicheskago obshchestva, XLI i XLIII: Zasedaniya 1 i 15 maya)', ZhGiUP, 3 (1884), app., pp. 133–60; and 7 (1884), app., pp. 160–6.
[24] A. Efimenko, Izsledovaniya narodnoi zhizni (Moscow, 1884); V. Nazar'ev, 'Sovremennaya glush': Iz vospominanii mirovogo sud'i', Vestnik Evropy, 2 (1872),

resemblance to the family life and attitudes of those members of the educated élite who were propagating it. Thus, the theory that the humanitarian family was in the final stages of supplanting its patriarchal counterpart in tsarist society represented the projection of one social group's ideals, relations, and hopes on to the rest of society.

This theory had obvious social and political implications, despite jurists' frequent denials of political intent.[25] The restructuring of family, property, and inheritance relations on the basis of individual equality strongly suggested the replacement of formal legal estates by civil equality for all subjects. It also implied that social and political authority should be limited by civil, and perhaps political, rights. Furthermore, it supported the aspirations of jurists and other trained specialists to use their expertise to resolve social problems by influencing state policy. But most importantly, its antipathy to patriarchy struck at the very foundation of autocratic power. Thus, the values that jurists were projecting on to the family reflected their own social, professional, and often political interests.

Indeed, by the 1880s, jurists' demands for a reform of women's legal rights in fact represented a fundamental critique of the entire system of family, property, and inheritance law, and ultimately of traditional Russian society. Reform of women's rights became the Trojan Mare through which Russian civil law, and thence Russian society, would be transformed in accordance with the values, ideals, and professional aspirations of the progressive jurists. Extending the grounds for divorce, allowing marital separation, expanding the owner's proprietary powers, and introducing more flexibility in inheritance law would benefit men as well as women, and would protect them both from the abuse of arbitrary authority. For many jurists, moreover, the establishment of civil security was merely the first step towards a

609–20; Ia. Ludmer, 'Bab'i stony', *Yuridicheskii vestnik*, 11 (1884), 446–67; and 12 (1884), 658–79; *Zamechaniya o nedostatkakh*, nos. 65–77, 83, 86–96; Kulisher, *Razvod*, pp. 148–53, 183, 208–35; and N. Brzheskii, *Ocherki yuridicheskago byta krest'yan* (St Petersburg, 1902). See also R. L. Glickman, *Russian Factory Women: Workplace and Society, 1880–1914* (Berkeley, 1984), 16, 27–58, 120–3, 215–18; and G. L. Freeze, *The Russian Parish Clergy in Nineteenth-Century Russia: Crisis, Reform, and Counter-Reform* (Princeton, 1983), 57–8, 171–8, 278–9, 310–13.

[25] Borovikovskii, 'Sud i sem'ya', pp. 249–50; Kavelin, 'Prava semeistvennyya', cols. 1081–2; and K. K. [Arsen'ev?], *Vestnik Evropy*, 2 (1885), 881–3.

fundamental change in the tsarist political system. As the eminent jurist Maksim Kovalevskii declared in a debate over reform of inheritance law in the State Council in 1912, political freedom and equal political rights had to be based on civil freedom and equal civil rights.[26]

The social and political implications of these proposals to improve women's legal rights provoked strong conservative resistance. This resistance had both ideological and more practical roots. Ideologically, conservative jurists argued that existing law represented the cumulative outcome of Russia's historical development, and thus embodied unique national and Orthodox traditions. In contrast to the progressives, they interpreted the law's historical development as a sign of vitality rather than a process of disintegration. This long development proved that basic legal principles could survive for centuries, adapting successfully to constantly changing social and economic conditions. In their opinion, then, the task of jurists was to preserve these principles while modifying them to take account of current conditions and needs. To disrupt them through reform based largely on foreign models would destabilize the social and political order, as well as deflect Russia from its natural course of development.[27]

The basic principles of civil law defended by conservative jurists also had a political function. They maintained that the inherent family relationships of authority and obedience—reflected in current family law—were necessary for the preservation of

---

[26] *Gosudarstvennyi Sovet: Stenograficheskii otchet*, session 7 (St Petersburg, 1912), cols. 1611–20.

[27] Pobedonostsev, *Kurs*, i. 64–5; ii. 1–254, 443, 447–8, 487–8; V. G. Demchenko, *Zapiski po grazhdanskomu pravu: Semeistvennoe pravo* (Kiev, 1894); L. A. Kasso, *Istochniki russkago grazhdanskago prava* (Moscow, 1900); P. A. Matveev, *Krest'yane i svod zakonov (po povodu sostavleniya novago grazhdanskago ulozheniya* (Moscow, 1883); *Pervyi s"ezd russkikh yuristov*, 151–4, 158–9, 163–4, 218–20, 224–34, 238–40; *Zamechaniya o nedostatkakh*, nos. 320–3, 564–5, 583, 590; A. A. Bashmakov, 'Institut rodovykh imushchestv pered sudom russkoi yurisprudentsii', *ZhMYu*, 7 (1897), 1–34; and 8 (1897), 1–62; id., 'Institut rodovykh imushchestv nakanune ego otmeny ili preobrazovaniya', *Zhurnal yuridicheskago obshchestva pri Imp. Sanktpeterburgskom universitete*, 9 (1897), 98–130; id., 'Opyt kriticheskoi otsenki instituta obyazatel'noi doli', ibid., 7 (1897), 36–69; V. N. Nikol'skii, *Ob osnovnykh momentakh nasledovaniya* (Moscow, 1871), 73–80, 127–54; *Grazhdanskoe ulozhenie*, 4 (1903), introd., pp. 86–7, 103–44. See also A. F. Brandt, 'O rodovykh imushchestvakh', *ZhGiUP*, 6 (1888), 1–44; and 7 (1888), 1–55. Brandt later reversed his position.

order within both the family and society. The discipline and respect for authority fostered in the patriarchal family grew into social discipline and respect for state authority, which helped to maintain social stability and political order. Thus, conservatives claimed, reforms of the law which weakened this authority, especially by allowing wives to challenge or leave their husbands, threatened to undermine public order by subverting the family.[28] Likewise, they asserted, the patrimonial system of inheritance had to be preserved—albeit in a modified form—in order to ensure the politically and socially stabilizing presence of the landed nobility in the provinces. Equalizing women's inheritance rights and expanding widows' shares of inheritances, they contended, would merely exacerbate the already serious problem of excessive fragmentation of estates through inheritance that was undermining the provincial nobility. Thus conservative jurists not only rejected proposals to reduce the law's discrimination against women, but often embraced counter-proposals that increased this discrimination; for example, by entailing all noble land in favour of sons.[29]

By the 1880s, then, two conflicting views of family, property, and inheritance law had emerged within the Russian legal profession and in society generally. Each view represented a different vision of Russia's future, and had important implications for the development of women's rights. The first defined marriage and the family as matrices of mutual rights and obligations that

[28] Pobedonostsev, *Kurs*, ii. 1–126, 166–94, 210; N. Znamenskii, 'Malenkiya zametki po povodu tolkov o razvode', *Moskovskiya vedomosti*, 70 (1900), 2; and 71 (1900), 2; I. Kashkarov, 'Polurazvod i razvod', ibid., 61 (1900), 2; and 62 (1900), 2; id., 'Senatskoe reshenie otmenyayushchee zakon', ibid., 330 (1900), 2; 'Mera sodeistvuyushchaya raspadeniyu krest'yanskoi sem'i', ibid., 295 (1900), 1–2; 'Razvod', ibid., 271 (1902), 1; N. N., 'Brak, otdel'noe zhitel'stvo i razvod', *Grazhdanin*, 26 (1901), 7–9; Provintsial, 'Zametka otnositel'no proekta o razdel'nom zhitel'stve suprugov', ibid., 8 (1900), 8–9; and *Gosudarstvennyi Sovet: Komissiya*, session 8, report 2 (St Petersburg, 1913; Harvard University, International Legal Studies Library).

[29] In addition to the works cited in n. 27 above, see P. [A. D. Pazukhin?], 'Zapovednyya imeniya', *Moskovskiya vedomosti*, 26 (1889), 2; and 31 (1889), 2; ibid., 190 (1902), 1; A. Lykoshin, 'Rodovyya imushchestva i dvoryanskoe zemlevladenie', ibid., 213 (1900), 1–2; D. Bodisko, 'Dvoryanskii vopros: Vopros gosudarstvennyi', *Grazhdanin*, 37 (1897), 4–7; and 39 (1897), 3–5; id., 'Pravda i krivda o dvoryanskom voprose', *Moskovskiya vedomosti*, 70 (1898), 2; 72 (1898), 2; 78 (1898), 2–3; 84 (1898), 3; 116 (1898), 2; 118 (1898), 2; and 119 (1898), 1–2; *Sel'skoe khozyaistvo i lesovodstvo*, 202/8 (1901), 294–310; and the references cited in n. 31 below.

arose from moral relationships and that protected the individuality of each family member. While this view often accepted the ultimate primacy of male authority, it none the less emphasized that this authority should be limited to protect other family members. Only by preventing the abuse of power and by providing scope for individual development could social stability be secured and society's prosperity assured. Individual ownership of property and equality of male and female inheritance rights were stressed for similar reasons. For women, this view promised equal rights in principle and expanded rights in practice.

The second view portrayed the family as an institution based on patriarchal power, obedience to authority, and unequal status, and accepted male preference in inheritance for political reasons. These relations were believed necessary for the preservation of order in the family and of stability in society. The importance of moral relations between family members was not denied, but they were expressed in terms of the obligations of those who exercised power, the duties of those who submitted to it, and the need to suffer abuse of power patiently in order to serve the higher goal of maintaining order. This view was generally combined with a belief in the need to preserve national traditions and existing social and political structures. It also openly accepted the subordinate status of women and militated against any significant improvement in their legal rights.

Although fundamentally disagreeing over the basis and proper legal structure of the family, property, and inheritance, adherents of both views believed that these institutions fostered as well as reflected general social relations, social attitudes, and moral values. Both groups thus concluded that reform of the law could be used to alter family and property relations, and, through them, society generally. The stage was set for a conflict that reflected the general struggle over social values and political ideals that was besetting post-emancipation Russia.

This struggle was manifested in government conflict and public controversy over a series of largely unsuccessful projects for reforming the law and improving women's personal and inheritance rights that were drafted by government officials, especially jurists in the Ministry of Justice, from the 1860s to 1917. Several times during this period various government departments sought to protect mistreated wives through the reform of divorce law and the introduction of marital separation, while at the turn of the century the Ministry of Justice proposed a complete reform of inheritance law and the equalization of women's inheritance rights. Political and ecclesiastical conservatives blocked reform of marriage and divorce law until, in 1914, the Ministry of Justice finally devised a plan for separation that was acceptable to the Holy Synod.[30] Conservative government officials and noble landowners likewise prevented reform of inheritance law until, in 1912, moderate conservatives in the State Council transformed a bill to equalize women's inheritance rights into a law that protected noble landowners while improving women's rights.[31]

The improvement of women's rights figured prominently as either an objective or a justification in all these efforts to reform the law. This prominence reveals the shifting attitude towards women among much of Russia's educated élite during the late nineteenth century, to the point where appeals to male chivalry to protect oppressed women obviously provided an effective polemical device. Opponents of reform invariably denied its political or economic expediency, but seldom the justness of helping women.

[30] See *Grazhdanskoe ulozhenie*, 2 (1902); TsGIA, f. 796, op. 445, d. 409–14, 417, 421; f. 797, op. 39, d. 295, op. 87, d. 179, op. 91–1898, d. 53, op. 92, d. 51, op. 92–1906, d. 68, op. 92–1914, d. 185, op. 92–1901, d. 81a–81b, op. 96, d. 219, 271; f. 1405, op. 542, d. 662–8, 670–2; *Gosudarstvennaya Duma: Stenograficheskii otchet*, Third Duma, session 4 (St Petersburg, 1911), ii, cols. 1652–62; session 5 (St Petersburg, 1912), iii, cols. 1876–83, 3075–7; Fourth Duma, session 2 (St Petersburg, 1914), ii, cols. 362–427; *Gosudarstvennaya Duma: Prilozheniya k stenograficheskim otchetam*, Third Duma, session 5 (St Petersburg, 1911), i, no. 96; Fourth Duma, session 2 (St Petersburg, 1914), ii, no. 134; *Gosudarstvennyi Sovet: Stenograficheskii otchet*, session 8 (St Petersburg, 1913), cols. 1114–1215; and *Gosudarstvennyi Sovet: Komissiya*, session 8, report 2. See also L. Bertenson, *Fizicheskie povody k prekrashcheniyu brachnago soyuza: Nesposobnost' k brachnomu sozhitiyu. Bolezni. Durnoe ili zhestokoe obrashchenie* (Petrograd, 1917); S. P. Grigorovskii, *O razvode: Prichiny i posledstviya razvoda i brakorazvodnoe sudoproizvodstvo. Istoriko-yuridicheskie ocherki* (St Petersburg, 1911); and I. V. Gessen, 'Razdel'noe zhitel'stvo suprugov', *Pravo*, 49 (1911), vols. 2755–67; and 50 (1911), cols. 2842–51. This conflict is analysed in detail in W. G. Wagner, *In Pursuit of Orderly Change: Law, Marriage and Property in Late Imperial Russia* (forthcoming), ch. 4.

[31] A. P. Korelin, *Dvoryanstvo v poreformennoi Rossii 1861–1904 gg.* (Moscow, 1979), 261–84; Yu. B. Solov'ev, *Samoderzhavie i dvoryanstvo v kontse XIX veka* (Leningrad, 1973), 201–16, 316–26; G. Hamburg, *Politics of the Russian Nobility 1881–1905* (New Brunswick, 1984); and W. G. Wagner, 'Legislative Reform of Inheritance in Russia, 1861–1914', in W. E. Butler (ed.), *Russian Law: Historical and Political Perspectives* (Leyden, 1977), 143–76. The conflict is also treated at length in Wagner, *Orderly Change*, ch. 8.

Yet, in all cases, reform was also inextricably entangled with other social and political issues. This entanglement marshalled powerful political and institutional forces both for and against the cause of women's rights. The attempt to protect married women by amending divorce law and allowing marital separation, for example, ultimately pitted jurists and the Ministry of Justice against Orthodox prelates and the Holy Synod in a struggle for control over the power to define and enforce marriage law. Other professional groups (such as physicians) and political factions (such as feminists and the moderate, liberal, and radical political parties organized after 1905) allied with reformist jurists in this effort to secularize the law.[32] Securing women's rights in this area thus involved the resolution of fundamental questions concerning the social and political roles of the Church, and the emerging professional élite within the tsarist system. Attempts to reform inheritance law similarly embroiled jurists and the Ministry of Justice, noble landowners and conservative officials in the Ministry of the Interior, and other landowners and officials in the Ministries of Finance and Agriculture in a struggle over the social and economic objectives of property and inheritance law, and the role of the landed nobility in post-emancipation Russia.[33] Elevating women's social position by equalizing their inheritance rights likewise required a resolution of these fundamental political and economic issues. Lurking behind these disputes lay the struggle between political reformers and conservatives to

[32] In addition to the works cited in n. 30 above, see *Russkiya vedomosti*, 299 (1898), 2; and 3 (1899), 2; 'Popravki semeinago prava', *Nedelya*, 5 (1898), cols. 145–9; 'Razdel'nost' suprugov', ibid., 48 (1899), vols. 1584–7; *Vestnik Evropy*, 2 (1900), 812–18; and 4 (1900), 801–3; *Russkaya mysl'*, 2 (1898), 186–8; 12 (1902), 428–30; and 1 (1903), 38–40; I. G. [Gessen?]', 'Davno pora', *Rech'*, 297 (1910), 2; *Trudy pervago vserossiiskago zhenskago s"ezda pri Russkom zhenskom (vzaimno-blagotvoritel'nom) obshchestve v S.-Peterburge 10–16 dekabrya 1908 goda* (St Petersburg, 1909), 11, 60–2, 344–8, 359–67, 374–86, 494–5, 512–19, 549–57, 589, 742, 754–60, 768, 825; 'Zasedanie komissii Ushinskago', *Pravo*, 16 (1905), cols. 1324–9; L. H. Edmondson, *Feminism in Russia 1900–1917* (London and Stanford, 1984), 139–42; *Obshchestvo russkikh vrachei v pamyat' N. I. Pirogova: Dnevnik shestogo s"ezda russkikh vrachei* (Kiev, 1896), xii. 1, and suppl., pp. 66–9; *Obshchestvo russkikh vrachei: Dnevnik sed'mogo s"ezda* (Kazan, 1899), iii. 21–5; and xiii. 281–7; *Obshchestvo russkikh vrachei: Desyatyi s"ezd* (St Petersburg, 1907), 91–2; B. I. Vorotynskii, 'Dushevnaya bolezn' odnogo iz suprugov, kak povod k rastorzheniyu braka', *Vrach*, 45 (1898), 307–9; and 'Zhurnal zasedaniya grazhdanskago otdeleniya yuridicheskago obshchestva 24 fevralya 1896', *Zhurnal yuridicheskago obshchestra pri Imp. SPb. universitete*, 10 (1896), app., pp. 8–22.

[33] See the works cited in nn. 29 and 31 above.

resolve their ideological conflict by enshrining in law their competing images of women and the family.

Although sometimes beneficial, this wider conflict generally impeded the women's cause, because it meant that a significant improvement in women's legal rights could be achieved only with the resolution of these other issues. Given the fundamental nature of these issues, and the apparent inability of tsarist legislative institutions to deal with them, any substantial reform of women's legal position under an unchanged tsarist regime appeared problematic. This outcome is not surprising. Women are an integral part of any society; their legal rights, therefore, form only a part of larger systems of family, property, and inheritance law that reflect and define society's basic institutions and values. Thus, the legal rights enjoyed by women ultimately depend on the character of the society in which they live, their position in this society, and the values that dominate it.

In late imperial Russia, social relations and values were changing. The struggle to improve women's legal rights reflects these changes, especially in the attitudes of much of society's educated professional élite towards women, the family, and the individual. Moreover, the political connotations of proposed reforms demonstrate how many members of this élite had adopted some notion of civil rights, defined broadly as civil equality, security of the individual's personal and property rights, and legal constraints on political authority. But the limited success of these efforts to achieve reform also reveals the relative weakness of civil rights, both in concept and reality, in Russia on the eve of the revolution.

Privileges, Rights, and Russification
RAYMOND PEARSON

To present a synoptic overview of the position of the non-Russian nationalities over the last fifty years of the tsarist empire is an unenviable undertaking. Together comprising an undisputed majority of the population of the Russian Empire, the nationalities constituted what has recently been called 'a subject too vast to be covered even in outline'.[1] At the same time, the 'nationalities question' has been 'commonly underrated' historiographically, rarely receiving appropriate scholarly coverage, and typically accorded grudging and lightweight treatment in general works of history.[2] Within the overall context of historiographical neglect—mainly involuntary and adventitious on the part of the West, often deliberate and disingenuous on the Soviet side—both camps have developed their own distinctive but flawed perspectives. Sharing only the starting-point for their polarized historiographical positions—the concept of the tsarist empire as the 'prison of nations'—Soviet and western perceptions of the nationalities question have proved to be distorted by prisms of their own manufacture.

On the Soviet side, dramatic change, coming very close to an historiographical volte-face, has transformed the prevailing orthodoxy governing Russian–minority relations. In the early Soviet period, spokesmen as authoritative as Lenin and Stalin queued up to denounce the tsarist oppression of minorities as well as the 'Great Russian chauvinism' which so regrettably lingered through the Bolshevik Revolution. From the early 1930s, a significant shift was registered, as the recent celebration of 'national liberation movements' (like those headed by Shamil in the Caucasus and Kenesary Kasymov in Kazakhstan in the

---

[1] M. Raeff, *Understanding Imperial Russia: State and Society in the Old Regime* (New York, 1984), 217.

[2] H. Seton-Watson, *The Russian Empire 1801–1917* (London, 1967), p. ix. For an example of lightweight treatment, see R. Charques, *The Twilight of Imperial Russia* (London, 1958), which spends just 3 pages on non-Russians (44, 65, 183).

mid-nineteenth century) was condemned as 'bourgeois nationalist'.[3] A new formula of the 'lesser evil' was floated, suggesting that 'membership' of the tsarist empire (however unassenting) was in retrospect preferable either to stagnation in isolation or to the depredations of even more tyrannical masters. The 'lesser evil' asserted that the nationalities had generally benefited—at least in a comparative, almost counter-factual sense—from their enforced association with the Russian people. In the early 1950s, a fresh doctrine of the 'friendship of peoples' argued that not only in the Soviet but even in the pre-revolutionary era, the national minorities had never confused the tsarist regime with the Russian people, but had drawn together in a multinational alliance quite naturally led by the Russians against the tsarist yoke. Whilst retaining a solid disapproval of tsarism, Soviet historiography toned down its absolute strictures on the unpardonable iniquities of the tsarist treatment of minorities (as promoted by M. N. Pokrovskii in the late 1920s), and jettisoned the 'prison of nations' concept in favour of a 'great friendship' dogma which consistently played down present and past instances of antagonism between the Russians and the minority nationalities. Remaining the prevailing orthodoxy throughout the post-Stalin period (with substantial concessions to historical sophistication since 1956), the 'great friendship' has been imposed retrospectively on Russian–minority relations even during the tsarist empire's espousal of Russification.[4]

That the western view of the later tsarist empire has seen relatively little movement from the contemporary 'prison of nations' line is not necessarily cause for self-congratulation. Over the last fifty years of tsarist rule and for decades thereafter, western liberal opinion was to see its existing prejudices against the Romanov regime confirmed in the treatment of the nationalities. Yet, for the most part, the West focused myopically upon a

---

[3] I am grateful to Brian Pearce for making available to me the text of a personal letter from A. M. Pankratova, editor-in-chief of *Voprosy istorii*, dated 22 July 1955, expounding the new Soviet orthodoxy on the 'reactionary revolt' of Kenesary in 1837–45 (by contrast with the 'progressive national liberationist rising' in India in 1857–9, otherwise known as the 'Indian Mutiny').

[4] The authoritative study is L. Tillett, *The Great Friendship: Soviet Historians on the Non-Russian Nationalities* (Chapel Hill, 1969); but see also K. F. Shteppa, 'The "Lesser Evil" Formula', in C. E. Black (ed.), *Rewriting Russian History: Soviet Interpretations of Russia's Past*, 2nd edn. (New York, 1962), 107–20.

few highly visible minority nationalities who seized and then monopolized international attention, and made sweeping generalizations from this limited sample. Because the Jews and the Finns were so distinct from the Russians in both race and religion, their harassment after the 1880s was condemned as politically unrealistic as well as morally repugnant. With the Jewish, Finnish, and Polish minorities all mounting persuasive claims to cultural superiority over their 'Asiatic' masters, their subordination could only be interpreted as unpardonably reactionary. And because all three of these minorities featured a strong and accelerating commitment to emigration from the 1880s onwards, their experiences received eyewitness corroboration—and consequently the widest currency and publicity—in emigrant destinations in the West. What one may simplistically label the 'Jewish refugee view' of the Russians and the tsarist empire quickly established itself, retaining much of its authority in the West right up to the present.

It is only relatively recently that western scholarship has belatedly conceded that relations between the Russians and other nationalities within the tsarist empire were too variegated and complex to substantiate many of the inherited stereotypes and clichés. To attempt to generalize about the one hundred or more national minorities within the empire on the basis of just three patently unrepresentative nationalities must be indefensible for any professional historian. The experience of the Jews, for example, a chronicle of pogrom, harassment, and expulsion on a scale that was not suffered by any other minority under tsarist jurisdiction, cannot be regarded as 'typical' or 'standard' by any definition. Western historians have therefore begun to move away from their past, academically misleading, over-concentration on the Finnish, Polish, and especially Jewish experiences, and are attempting to cover a spectrum of tsarist nationalities.[5]

Study of the later tsarist empire has also benefited from promptings by broader historiographical trends in the treatment of the 'confrontation' between traditional empires and emergent nationalism. For too long the familiar scenario has been of a hopelessly incompetent tsarist regime, whose only recourse when

---

[5] A prime recent example is E. C. Thaden, *Russia's Western Borderlands 1710–1870* (Princeton, NJ, 1984), which boldly covers the Finns, Estonians, Latvians, Baltic Germans, Lithuanians, Belorussians, Poles, and right-bank Ukrainians.

challenged by a nationalist upsurge was the crudest and cruellest repression; which leaves the reader wondering how the tsarist dinosaur, large of bulk but small of brain, could have survived for so long under the onslaught of the forces of progress. Modern scholarship is inclined to regard nationalism as less 'democratic' and 'progressive' than it has traditionally been portrayed. Moreover, past historians may not have made a sufficient distinction between the passive resilience of newly discovered national identity and the practical limitations on nationalist militancy. Nationalism undeniably made enormous advances over the late nineteenth century, converting the tsarist empire from a politically inert, multi-ethnic estate into a politically charged, multinational agglomeration. But 'national awakening' was far from synonymous with 'nationalist rebellion'. While retaining a healthy respect for the defensive resources of the nation under attack, historians are now less convinced of the offensive capabilities of nationalist movements, seeing the much-vaunted nationalist 'challenge' as more élitist and less authoritative than the hindsight of the immediate post-1917 period suggested.[6]

At the same time, modern scholarship is inclined to regard the traditional Romanov, Habsburg, and even Ottoman Empires in a less unsympathetic light, reassessing the policies that were once so unanimously dismissed as inexcusably vindictive and irremediably inept. Part of a broader re-evaluation (if not quite rehabilitation) of tsarist performance is the ongoing investigation into the phenomenon of Russification. In the past, the term 'Russification' (as *obrusevanie* is conventionally rendered) has been employed carelessly, most commonly as an ironic euphemism for brutal physical subjugation. Even in academic circles, Russification has often been projected as a centrally planned, demonic imperial strategy, a tsarist blueprint for the 'savage and mindless' persecution of minorities, with little attempt to understand its purpose, dynamic, and scope.[7] Reflecting a general drift towards greater emphasis on the constraints on government intervention in nineteenth-century society, the newer line highlights the bureaucratic understaffing and especially

---

[6] e.g. A. E. Adams, 'The Awakening of the Ukraine', *Slavic Review*, 22/2 (1963), 217–18.

[7] See R. F. Leslie's very 'Polish' view in his *The History of Poland since 1863* (Cambridge, 1980), 99.

the lack of administrative centralization within the tsarist establishment *vis-à-vis* the nationalities. John Keep, for example, points out not only that 'Russian society generally never developed an elaborate, well-articulated "imperial ethos"', but also that 'the regime had no consistent policy or machinery for dealing with the "nationalities problem", whose very existence was barely recognized'.[8] The fact—perhaps surprising—that there was no top-level official responsible for the minorities in Russia until Stalin was appointed to *Narkomnats* in November 1917 has been seen as evidence of the low priority accorded to the nationalities issue, rendering untenable the concept of a tsarist 'grand design' for Russification.[9]

The investigation into Russification, especially for the last twenty-five years of tsarism, is very far from complete.[10] Some specialists make a point of differentiating between 'administrative Russification' (a process admitting the possibility of tangible material benefits) and 'cultural Russification' (a policy generally regarded as both iniquitous and counter-productive).[11] In the past, many historians used the terms 'Russification' and 'Russianization' interchangeably, as stylistically variant labels for the same phenomenon.[12] Others wish to bring a greater precision to the debate by drawing a clear distinction between 'Russification', necessarily involving a surrender of ethnic identity through forced assimilation, and 'Russianization', meaning the increased hegemony of Russian language, culture, and institutions. According to this retrospective relabelling, what has in the past generally been dubbed 'Russification' would be better named 'Russianization', especially in the light of the strengthening view that the tsarist state possessed neither the totalitarian ambition nor the

---

[8] J. L. H. Keep, 'Imperial Russia: Alexander II to the Revolution', in R. Auty and D. Obolensky (eds.), *An Introduction to Russian History* (Companion to Russian Studies, 1; London, 1976), 197, 200.

[9] S. F. Starr, 'Tsarist Government: The Imperial Dimension', in J. R. Azrael (ed.), *Soviet Nationality Policies and Practices* (New York, 1978), 3–5. This is probably the most challenging article on the imperial question in recent years.

[10] Despite its title, E. C. Thaden (ed.), *Russification in the Baltic Provinces and Finland 1855–1914* (Princeton, NJ, 1981), only really covers the nineteenth century. There is no comprehensive, authoritative study of Russification for the period 1900–17.

[11] Starr, 'Tsarist Government', pp. 22, 24; Thaden (ed.), *Russification*, p. 75.

[12] Examples include G. Vernadsky, *A History of Russia* (New Haven, 1961), 233; and J. N. Westwood, *Endurance and Endeavour: Russian History 1812–1971* (London, 1973), 45–6.

modern resources to undertake the ethnic assimilation of its minorities (other than perhaps the Ukrainians and Belorussians).[13] The trend in reassessment makes tsarism appear less organizationally monolithic and more pragmatic—discriminating as well as discriminatory—than in the past. Even so, Richard Pipes can still muddy the waters of historiography by declaring on one and the same page that: 'at no point in its history did tsarist Russia formulate a consistent policy towards its minorities', and 'the Russian government perhaps for the first time in its entire history adopted a systematic policy of Russification and minority repression'.[14]

No real consensus has been reached by historians about the dynamics of Russification, only about the identification of likely contributory components. Traditionally, the uniquely Russian context has been emphasized, with the Russian Orthodox hierarchy, particularly under the crusading twenty-four-year procuratorship of Konstantin Pobedonostsev, as a prime mover.[15] The peculiar geopolitical circumstances of the empire agitated the military: with the most nationalist minorities distributed along the vulnerable western periphery, the security of the empire from invasion from the west became a mounting preoccupation (especially after 1894, when the Franco-Russian alliance implicitly identified Germany as the future invader).[16] The Polish risings of 1830–1 and particularly 1863–4, widely interpreted within Russia as base ingratitude for tsarist gestures of goodwill, proved to be emotional catalysts in the precipitation of 'public opinion' on the nationalities question outside the immediate bounds of 'official Russia'.[17] A multinational empire in which by far the largest nationality was not automatically at the head of the hierarchy of privilege was an affront to Russian national pride

[13] V. V. Aspaturian, 'The Non-Russian Nationalities', in A. Kassof (ed.), *Prospects for Soviet Society* (New York, 1968), 158–64; H. Rogger, 'Empire at Home: The Non-Russians', ch. 9 of his *Russia in the Age of Modernisation and Revolution 1881–1917* (London, 1983), 183.

[14] R. Pipes, *The Formation of the Soviet Union: Communism and Nationalism 1917–1923*, rev. edn. (Cambridge, Mass., 1964), 6.

[15] Thaden (ed.), *Russification*, pp. 67–70; and *Conservative Nationalism in Nineteenth-Century Russia* (Seattle, 1964), 196–203; G. Stephenson, *A History of Russia 1812–1945* (London, 1969), 197–9.

[16] C. L. Lundin, 'Finland', in Thaden (ed.), *Russification*, pp. 373–81.

[17] See memorandum of Petr Valuev, dated 13 Apr. 1863, quoted in M. Raeff (ed.), *Plans for Political Reform in Imperial Russia 1730–1905* (London, 1966), 122–3.

after the mid-nineteenth century; and the inferior status of the Russians within what they increasingly regarded as their own domain became insupportable. A broader-based and more militant Russian nationalism has been discerned over the last decades of tsarism, restless with the traditional, supranational, dynastic legitimism of the Romanov Empire, and seeking to infuse the government with bolder principles along the lines of 'Russia for the Russians' and 'Russia, one and indivisible'.[18] According to this interpretation, the later tsarist regime was compelled to take account of a newer rival to 'official nationalism', making reluctant but necessary concessions to more populist policies geared to securing an empire which was 'Russian' (*russkii*), not just 'Russian-owned' (*rossiiskii*).[19]

More recently, the concept of Russification as a unique, *sui generis* phenomenon has lost ground, under pressure from the view that it was essentially a local manifestation of international trends. A drive for greater government authority and administrative uniformity was general throughout Europe; only the effort that the relatively undergoverned Russian Empire had to expend to make up the bureaucratic backlog and organizational deficiency was remarkable. In the administrative realm, therefore, 'Russification may have been synonymous with modernization'.[20] The same might be said of the shift away from crypto-federalism towards the unitary, centralized state.[21] The economic value of minority territories meant that the Romanovs were as determined to retain such industrial prizes as Finland, 'Latvia', and Poland as the Habsburgs were to keep Bohemia. The decline of the gentry across much of Europe forced many into government service, gradually introducing into official policy the conservative and xenophobic predilections of that class. According to this explanation, Russification was an almost incidental product of the crisis of the Russian gentry, in much the same way that

---

[18] Note the rise of more nationalist newspapers like *Moskovskiya vedomosti* (under Mikhail Katkov) and *Novoe vremya*, journals like *Okrainy Rossii*, and books like General A. Kuropatkin, *Rossiya dlya russkikh*, 3 vols, (St Petersburg, 1910).

[19] Seton-Watson, *Russian Empire*, pp. 485, 663–4, 673–5, 737–8.

[20] T. U. Raun, 'The Estonians', in Thaden (ed.), *Russification*, p. 287; also Starr, 'Tsarist Government', pp. 10–11, 24.

[21] Rogger, *Russia*, p. 187; M. Raeff, 'Patterns of Russian Imperial Policy towards the Nationalities', in E. Allworth (ed.), *Soviet Nationality Problems* (New York, 1971), 37–8.

Magyarization in contemporary Hungary was based upon the dispossessed Magyar gentry.[22] At the demographic level, the combination of population explosion and rising literacy sharpened Europe-wide competition for employment (and especially top appointments), making Russification almost an example of what might today be called a government-sponsored job-creation scheme.[23] At the most basic level, Russification was (like Magyarization in Hungary and Prussianization in Germany) a government counter-offensive to contain the burgeoning threat of a minority nationalism which was undermining the very existence of the state. It has even been suggested that Russification was an instance of the currently fashionable imperial 'diversion technique': 'an endeavour to utilize Great Russian national sentiments as a weapon against growing social unrest in the country'.[24]

In attempting to identify what Marc Raeff has so circumspectly termed the 'patterns of imperial policy', the fundamental point of reference must be the rationale of the tsar as 'the autocratic (*samoderzhavnyi*) and unlimited (*neogranichennyi*) monarch'.[25] At no historical juncture were concessions willingly made to anything resembling 'contractual rights', a mutually binding bargain struck between sovereign and people. The traditional emphasis —indeed, insistence—on untrammelled executive authority inhibited both official and public observance of, and respect for, legal procedures. Even tsarist initiatives like the Code of Laws in 1832 and the judicial reform of 1864 did not represent a basic change of heart regarding tsarism's low esteem for the world of the law, a conversion to a *Rechtsstaat*. To the tsarist functionary, 'legal' continued to mean (to quote clause 47 of the Fundamental Laws) 'on the firm basis of positive laws, institutions and charters established by autocratic authority'. As a consequence, tsarist government never relinquished its view of total authority over its 'subjects' (*poddannye*), implicitly scorning the notion of 'citizens' (*grazhdane*) with their inalienable 'rights' and therefore conditional loyalty.[26] Taking for granted the certainty of subjects'

---

[22] Seton-Watson, *Russian Empire*, p. 486.

[23] J. A. Armstrong, 'Mobilized Diaspora in Tsarist Russia: The Case of the Baltic Germans', in Azrael (ed.), *Soviet Nationality*, p. 84.

[24] Starr, 'Tsarist Government', p. 6; Pipes, *Formation*, p. 6.

[25] Raeff, 'Patterns', p. 22.

[26] R. Pipes, *Russia under the Old Regime* (London, 1974), 288–90; L. Schultz, 'Constitutional Law in Russia', in G. Katkov *et al.* (eds.), *Russia Enters the*

duties and obligations, the most that tsarism would entertain was the availability of 'privilege' for select groups on a class, occupational, or territorial basis. Literally operating as a kind of 'private law', privilege was the discrimination of advantage sanctioned on the understanding that it in no way compromised the autocratic powers of the tsar and could therefore be cancelled by authority at will, unilaterally, without explanation, and without legal redress. For example, tsarist apologists like K. F. Ordin argued that the special status accorded to the Grand Duchy of Finland in 1809 was not the product of a legal contract freely entered into by equal partners, but an historic—and quite revocable—gesture of autocratic magnanimity.[27] To the bitter end, tsarism expected and exacted unconditional duties from its subjects, offering in return only the possibility of group privilege. Little hope of 'contractual rights' between sovereign and citizen was extended, and no prospect of the voluntary recognition of 'natural' or 'human' rights was ever contemplated. In so far as 'rights' existed at all in Russia, they were monopolized by the tsar and his government; the most that the non-Russian population could aspire to was 'privilege'.

Given that Russification featured some common denominators among its often contradictory manifestations, a short working definition might be 'the state-sponsored transfer of privilege from the nationalities to the Russians'. The first phase was the revocation of existing *formal* privilege enjoyed by nationalities, the tsarist concession by charter, or other document of special dispensation, to a defined territory or social/national minority within the empire. A characteristically eighteenth-century phenomenon, the grant of formal privilege had been motivated by two cognate considerations: the creation of privilege to attract foreign immigrants (like those extended to the Volga Germans in the 1780s); and the confirmation of existing privilege to buy off local élites during the process of territorial aggrandizement, to sweeten the bitter pill of tsarist take-over (as with the Baltic Germans after 1721 and the Finns after 1809) or reincorporation (as with the Poles after 1815). What amounted to an exercise in the

---

Twentieth Century (London, 1973), 35, 41; Seton-Watson, *Russian Empire*, pp. 356–7, 731–3.

[27] Lundin, 'Finland', pp. 359–64; K. F. Ordin, *Pokorenie Finlandii*, 2 vols. (St Petersburg, 1889).

revocation of formal privilege continued throughout the nineteenth century. If a nationality proved obstreperous, its privileges
were revoked all the sooner (like those of the Poles in 1832 and
again after 1864). Good behaviour provided no guarantees,
however, as the loss of privileges by Bessarabia after 1828,
Armenia after 1840, the Volga Germans after 1874, and the
Finns after 1899 was to prove. Revocation of privilege became
progressively more certain; only the timing might be negotiable.
The revocation exercise marked a definitive shift away from the
crypto-federalism of acquisitive tsarism in the eighteenth century
to the unitary state ambitions of consolidating tsarism in the
nineteenth century.

The next, broadly sequential phase was the elimination of
informal privilege, that is to say, social, economic, political, or
cultural advantage not explicitly sanctioned by tsarist certification
but occurring historically through the complaisance or 'benign
neglect' of authority.[28] The campaign to achieve this ambitious
objective necessarily entailed two complementary exercises:
adverse or prejudicial discrimination against the non-Russian
minorities; and positive or affirmative discrimination in favour
of the Russians. A vital (and sometimes underrated) aspect of
imperial policy was the degree to which Russification constituted
both a levelling-down for the over-privileged nationalities and an
upgrading for the underprivileged Russians. Some half-dozen
salients in this spasmodic but protracted offensive of Russification
may be discerned.[29]

A fundamental problem for the 'Russifiers' was the criteria by
which a 'Russian' might be defined and identified. In a
nineteenth-century Europe where racialist doctrine was still in
the making, race remained a politically unconsidered factor in the
Russian Empire. With no overt racial ethos, Russification was
constrained to operate upon more concrete and 'visible' considerations.[30] The confessional criterion—the Russian Orthodox

---

[28] R. L. Rockett, *Ethnic Minorities in the Soviet Union: Sociological Perspectives
on a Historical Problem* (New York, 1981), 74.

[29] With few of the basic facts of the 'elimination of informal privilege' in dispute,
corroboration of the material in the next section may be found in such standard
accounts as Keep, 'Imperial Russia', pp. 197–208; Thaden (ed.), *Russification*,
pp. 15–88; and Rogger, *Russia*, pp. 182–207.

[30] V. Conolly, 'The Nationalities Question in the Last Phase of Tsardom', in
Katkov et al. (eds.), *Russia*, p. 54; also Starr, 'Tsarist Government', p. 19.

faith—proved to be the most convenient. What became an Orthodox 'crusade' was launched from as early as the 1840s (in the case of the Baltic provinces) to convert to the 'Russian faith' those populations of European Russia which embraced other creeds. A joint offensive against the Churches of minority nationalities was mounted by the government and the Russian Orthodox hierarchy: Roman Catholicism in Poland and 'Lithuania', Judaism in the Pale of Settlement, Lutheranism in the Baltic provinces, and Islam in the Volga and Caucasus regions all came under attack, with the abolition of the Uniate Church in Poland in 1875 and the persecution of the Gregorian Church in Armenia after 1903 providing the most extreme examples of 'religious Russification'. New cathedrals were provocatively sited in such non-Russian cities as Riga, Reval, and Warsaw to add the heaviest 'architectural symbolism' to 'Orthodoxization'.

The Russian language was the criterion for sustained 'linguistic imperialism' and the introduction of the 'shibboleth concept' into tsarist society. Russian-related 'dialects' were increasingly proscribed: publication in Belorussian and Ukrainian, for example, was specifically banned by laws of 1868 and 1876. Limitations were placed upon the currency of minority languages in such official spheres as the higher reaches of the provincial administration and judiciary: the Russian language was forced upon public institutions in the Baltic provinces after 1850 (and especially after 1885), in Poland after 1869, and in Finland after 1900. Monoglot officials of a minority language were typically granted a set period of time (often five years) to become proficient in Russian or else vacate their employment. From the mid-1880s, Alexander III insisted that all diplomatic and police business should be conducted in Russian.

Educational Russification came high up on the list of priorities. Schools became a front line for tsarist 'acculturation': for example, Russian was imposed on Polish secondary schools from 1866 and on primary schools from 1885. Universities became prime objects of suspicion as potential nationalist staff colleges, and were even harder hit. Forcible take-over became common: the Polish University of Vilna was transposed to Kiev as the Russian St Vladimir University in 1832; the Polish 'Main School' was replaced by the Russian University of Warsaw in 1869; and in 1893 the German University of Dorpat was transformed into

the Russian University of Yuriev. New universities created after
the mid-nineteenth century were all planned as Russian citadels.
Thus, the educational inferiority which had traditionally offset
the Russians' numerical superiority over such minorities as the
Poles and Germans was tackled by tsarist 'affirmative action'.
As ever, the Jews were marked out for particular adverse
discrimination. From the 1880s, government legislation imposed
limitations on Jews' access to higher education in order to eliminate what was perceived as their unhealthy over-representation in
the universities and, therefore, the professions. The *numerus
clausus* legislation of 1886–7, establishing quotas for Jewish
admission to educational establishments, represented the most
notorious instance of the strengthening official commitment to
the elimination of informal privilege retained by non-Russian
nationalities.

The tsarist administration itself was not immune. As the
'Mamelukes of the Russian Empire', the Baltic Germans enjoyed
a disproportionate (and provocatively visible) importance within
the tsarist personnel establishment: the upper reaches of the
bureaucracy (especially the Ministry of Foreign Affairs) were
bastions of Baltic German informal privilege. The notion of a
non-Russian minority administering—if not determining—the
foreign policy of Russia became intolerably offensive to Russians.
After 1870, this anomaly was reinforced by the suspicion that the
Baltic Germans might serve as a Trojan Horse for the ebullient,
newly unified Germany on Russia's western frontier. Although
no purges of personnel were ever effected, official moves to prune
German privilege within the tsarist civil service were afoot from
the time of Alexander III.

Military Russification was not neglected. Smaller, vulnerable,
and less self-conscious nationalities were drafted as an assimilation
exercise: by the late nineteenth century, recruitment into the
army was colloquially called 'becoming Russian' by the Latvian
peasantry. Larger and more self-conscious nationalities, especially
those located near the imperial frontier, might be rationed in, or
even excluded from, military conscription. Although the high
percentage of Germans in the officer corps was never eliminated,
the official trend was to reduce their entrenched informal
privilege. The separate Finnish regiment that was permitted after
1878 was abolished as a security risk in 1901: thereafter, Finns

were first liable to conscription into the imperial Russian army, and from 1905 were required to pay an annual levy in lieu of military service (to forestall the creation of a potentially disloyal nationalist army on the doorstep of the imperial capital).

A final dimension of Russification, as usual involving both adverse and positive discrimination, was territorial. The national minorities found the integrity of their homelands progressively infringed. As early as 1866, the tsarist government added insult to injury by imposing geographical nomenclature which officially converted Russian-held 'Poland' into the ten 'Vistula provinces'. Over the last years of peacetime, Poland, Finland, and even the Jewish Pale all suffered physical Russian encroachment: Kholm (Chełm) province was detached from 'Poland' in 1912 and absorbed into Russia; within the overall integration of the Grand Duchy of Finland into the Russian Empire, plans were laid in 1914 for the Russian take-over of the Finnish province of Vyborg (Viipuri); and within a Pale which was already shrinking, the number of *shtetls*—pales within the Pale—was drastically reduced. Towards the west, therefore, the territorial and coloniz-ing pressure of expanding Russia squeezed the traditional heartlands of the Poles, Finns, and Jews, compelling their fast-growing populations to consider emigration ever more seriously. Reluctant at first to abandon its traditional embargo on permanent emigration, the tsarist government made an exception for the Jews in the 1880s, then showed a green light to an expanding range of minority nationalities from the 1890s. In line with overall tsarist thinking, there was of course no 'right' to emigrate, only an administratively determined 'informal privilege' to 'escape' extended to certain nationalities when convenient to the state. As the advantages of exporting its minority problems—leaving behind a more homogenized Russian society—became apparent, the temptation to employ emigration to effect 'demo-graphic Russification' became irresistible.[31] Politically, the Russian Empire was becoming more Russian; territorially, 'Great Russia' was becoming greater.

Russification provoked a more spirited and concerted response from the national minorities after the 1890s. Instead of statutory, but essentially despairing, complaint against their treatment, the

---

[31] For a discussion of 'demographic Russification', see my *National Minorities in Eastern Europe 1848–1945* (London, 1983), 100–5.

more advanced nationalities took heart and raised their horizons of ambition, combining protests against Russification with campaigns to persuade the Tsar not so much to restore or grant privileges, but to recognize their rights. These rights might be 'absolute'—inalienable and unconditional human rights constituting a minimum standard of relations between authority and the individual acceptable to the international civilized community— or 'contractual'—rights earned by the performance of duties through a negotiated or implicit but mutually binding contract between authority and the individual. De Tocqueville's remark that 'there is nothing which elevates and sustains the human spirit more than the idea of rights' is particularly appropriate to the leading minorities in Russia over the first decade of the twentieth century. Self-confidence was boosted as the concept of rights, as against privilege, grew in currency and sophistication. Increasingly, nationalist élites were motivated by a sense of legitimate grievance, perceiving themselves neither as rebels inviting punishment nor as suppliants deserving contempt, but as legitimate claimants demanding satisfaction. Matching tsarism's reinforcement of its dynastic rationale through nationalist legitimacy came the nationalities' espousal of the legitimacy of rights.

The nationalities' growing self-assurance made no perceptible impression upon the tsarist establishment's fundamental political philosophy. The few remissions in Russification that occurred over the last years of the empire were ephemeral and incidental by-products of overwhelming extraneous events. In 1905, for example, a year of missed opportunities for the minorities, Nicholas II took care to prevent what was a very 'Russian Revolution' becoming imperial in scope by prompt and substantial concessions to the nationalities. Russification was temporarily suspended: a religious-toleration edict of April 1905 permitted reconversion from Orthodoxy and prompted a reinforcement of national identities; linguistic concessions were granted to Polish, German, Estonian, Latvian, and Ukrainian (which—just—made the official transition from a dialect to a language); the decree of 1903 initiating the drive against the Armenian Gregorian Church was rescinded; and a manifesto of November 1905 cancelled the anti-Finnish legislation that had been prosecuted since 1899. However, such concessions to the nationalities were viewed by the Emperor not as freely granted rights, but as expedient privileges extorted under revolutionary threat. Operating on the unspoken assumption that transactions under duress carried no legal or moral validity, the new tsarist administration headed by Petr Stolypin returned to Russification with a heightened sense of urgency and renewed vigour once the emergency had passed. '1905' did not prove to be the dawn of a better era for the nationalities, but the briefest respite from a Russification which soon recovered its lost ground and intensified during the remaining years of peace.[32]

Nor did the First World War prompt any change of heart on the part of a tsarist empire *in extremis*. Having forfeited all 'right' to absolute loyalty by its peacetime treatment, the tsarist government was expected by some leading nationalities to make concessions to secure their wartime conditional loyalty. Talk of the granting of genuine rights, or at least the selective reintroduction of formal privilege, momentarily raised the spirits of the minorities. The experience of the Poles was encouraging, uniquely as it turned out. Appreciating the pivotal position of Poland in the combat zone of the Eastern Front, Russia, Germany, and Austria-Hungary were gradually drawn into a political auction in their attempts to secure Polish allegiance. A manifesto from the Grand Duke Nikolai Nikolaevich in August 1914 was as prompt as it was vague in its promises of a retreat from the Russification of Poland. In August 1915, and again in July 1916, the tsarist government agreed to Polish 'autonomy', in effect a return to the formal privilege of the 1815 constitution of 'Congress Poland'. Exploiting the conspicuous shortcomings of the Russian offer, Germany and Austria-Hungary jointly promised an 'independent' Poland in November 1916. On the eve of the fall of tsarism, the Polish minority found itself in the happy political position of being offered more self-determination by both the Central and Allied powers than had been dreamed of in peacetime.[33]

Overall, however, far from another respite from Russification, the First World War saw the tsarist government actually strengthen its campaign under the plea of wartime necessity. The

---

[32] The best survey of the 'non-Russian 1905' and its aftermath remains H. Seton-Watson, *The Decline of Imperial Russia* (London, 1952), 231–45, 303–10; but see also Rockett, *Ethnic Minorities*, pp. 48–9, 53, 64–5.

[33] N. Davies, *God's Playground: A History of Poland* (London, 1981), i, 382–4.

promise of privileges to the Poles was exceptional and out of character; the withdrawal of surviving privileges remained the rule. The Korevo Commission's plans for the complete 'integration' of Finland into the empire were published in November 1914. In June 1916, Kirghiz exemption from conscription, an informal privilege enjoyed since the mid-nineteenth century, was compromised by the introduction of selective male mobilization for non-combatant rear-line duty (triggering a massive rising in Turkistan which claimed thousands of lives).[34] Adverse discrimination was intensified. The Russian military occupation of Austrian Galicia in October 1914 was accompanied by harsh treatment to root out the 'Mazeppists' and to raze the erstwhile 'Ukrainian Piedmont'; the effect of this fleeting experience of Russian rule was to alienate the local Ruthenian population irredeemably. Inevitably, the Jews suffered most of all, forced by the German advance to flee eastwards as refugees, used as scapegoats for Russian military disaster, and harassed mercilessly by the tsarist authorities. Jews who had been conscripted into the imperial army affected to believe the malicious rumour that the Tsar was considering granting full civil rights to all Jewish soldiers defending Russia who were killed in action.[35]

While the great majority of nationalities received worse treatment than in peacetime, the sole minority whose prospects improved was under no illusion: at best, the Poles might become the recipients of an expedient renewal of formal privilege. Legally, the fact that the 'Manifesto to the Poles' carried the signature of a mere grand duke (albeit the Commander-in-Chief) rather than the reigning Tsar was universally interpreted as providing the loophole for eventual disavowal. In practice, the promised privileges would be deferred until the ever more unlikely looking 'liberation' of lost Polish territories by the Russian army. Even these concessions, of course, were not so much 'earned' by Polish nationalists adroitly exploiting 'periphery politics', as 'donated' by empires conducting their self-interested superpower strategies from which Poland might become the incidental beneficiary. As in 1905, the ending of the wartime

---

[34] D. G. Kirby, *Finland in the Twentieth Century* (London, 1979), 36–9; R. A. Pierce, *Russian Central Asia 1867–1917: A Study in Colonial Rule* (Berkeley, 1960), 270–96.

[35] Keep, 'Imperial Russia', p. 204; Rogger, *Russia*, p. 186.

emergency could be expected to supply the pretext for revoking privileges deemed by tsarist authority to have been extracted under duress.[36]

Two long-term features, both historiographically undervalued, highlight Russification's paradoxical nature and impact. 'Cultural Russification' was essentially a phenomenon of the European part of the empire, and was not introduced into Russian Asia (if only because ever since 'incorporation', Russian primacy and privilege there had been uncontested). The state-sponsored colonization from the 1890s onwards of first Siberia, then Kazakhstan, and finally Turkistan with Russians, Ukrainians, and Belorussians proceeded at a pace that alarmed the indigenous Asiatic population, and, from 1909, arrangements were under way for the formal annexation of the protectorate of Bukhara. Even so, treated in much the same way as Western European empires administered their overseas colonies, Russian Asia was not only spared the excesses of 'cultural Russification', but often benefited from 'administrative Russification'. Though far from all Russians in Asia felt a conscious 'civilizing mission', the *Pax Rossica* still 'worked rather well' and did have a civilizing effect, particularly with the suppression of endemic banditry and the abolition of slavery over the last quarter of the nineteenth century.[37] Russians were thus not the only historically underprivileged nationality to benefit from the later imperial experience. A significant number of national minorities in Asia, typically falling within the official 'alien' (or *inorodtsy*) category and backward in terms of culture and economy, gained materially by their association (however involuntary) with the tsarist empire. It is not capitulation to the Soviet 'lesser evil' formula to suggest that many underpublicized and more primitive nationalities' experience of empire was an ambivalent blend of advantage and disadvantage, a close balance between profit and loss. Whether by paternalistic tsarist policy or—more commonly—through an economic and social 'tow effect', the lowest echelon of mostly Asiatic nationalities made what were sometimes quite spectacular advances at precisely the time that the highest echelon of European nationalities was being deliberately and severely handicapped.

[36] A. Polonsky in Leslie, *The History of Poland*, pp. 113, 119.
[37] Raeff, 'Patterns', pp. 22–3; and *Understanding*, p. 217; Starr, 'Tsarist Government', pp. 24–5.

The final feature to stress must surely be that no nationality gained any 'rights' from Russification. Early in the nineteenth century, the Russian mock prayer to Alexander I, 'O Tsar, bestow upon your own people what you have already granted the Poles and Finns', underlined the anomaly of the Russians' second-class status within the empire. In the era following the Great Reforms of the 1860s, the Russians collectively lost formal privileges in the reactionary *revanche*, but gained quasi-compensatory informal privileges through Russification; by contrast, the nationalities were deprived of many long-standing formal and informal privileges, but acquired no new ones. Over the last fifty years of tsarism, the nationalities saw their situation within the empire deteriorate: not only were rights denied, but even the earlier, now unacceptable privileges were effectively phased out for all but Russians. No national minority either lost or gained rights: over the nineteenth and early twentieth centuries, Russification transformed the hierarchy of privilege in favour of the Russians; but the tsarist insistence on granting privileges rather than recognizing rights was maintained, without fundamental concession or reservation, to the very end.

Religious Toleration in
Late Imperial Russia

PETER WALDRON

THE Russian Empire was multidenominational: the state's
continuous expansion had drawn into its fold people of widely
differing faiths, whilst in the Slav heartland of the empire,
schism and sectarian division had affected the Orthodox Church.
Orthodoxy was the dominant religion in the state and it
numbered some 70 per cent of the population as its adherents,[1]
but there were also numerous groups which had their roots in the
Orthodox Church although they were no longer part of it. Chief
amongst these were the Old Believers, thought to number eleven
million in the early 1900s,[2] but including many varied strands of
belief—one estimate gives over 130 different known sects.[3] Other
Christian faiths were also represented inside the empire: Roman
Catholicism dominated Poland and Lithuania, whilst Finland,
Estonia, and Latvia had populations which were overwhelmingly
Lutheran. The expansion of the empire to the south had resulted
in a substantial Muslim element being added to the population,
whilst the push into Siberia had brought eastern religions into the
state. Lastly, Poland and the western provinces of Russia itself
included significant numbers of Jews.

Religious minorities coincided to a large extent with national
minority groups, and the policies which the government adopted
towards non-Orthodox religions were often an integral part of its
attitude towards the non-Russian elements of the population.
Where religious and national minority were not coterminous,
however, the state was forced to deal with the religious group
solely on the basis of the group's religious belief and its effect on

---

[1] G. Simon, 'Church, State and Society', in G. Katkov *et al.* (eds.), *Russia Enters
the Twentieth Century* (London, 1971), 201.

[2] See A. S. Prugavin, *Staroobryadchestvo vo vtoroi polovine XIX veka* (Moscow,
1904), 7–18, for an analysis of the differing estimates.

[3] D. W. Treadgold, 'The Peasant and Religion', in W. S. Vucinich (ed.), *The
Peasant in Nineteenth-Century Russia* (Stanford, 1968), 88.

the political aims of the government. The imperial regime's dealings with the Catholic population of Poland and the Lutheran Baltic Germans, and the regulations which it imposed on the practice of their religions, were intertwined with the linguistic, educational, and political measures which it adopted towards them.[4] When the government came to deal with such groups as the Old Believers, indistinguishable from the Orthodox population in terms of their nationality, the only criterion which it had to use was that of religion. Politics and religion were inextricably linked in the state's attitude to many of the religious minorities of the empire.

This essay will consider the interaction between the overall policies of the tsarist regime in the last sixty years of its existence and the particular treatment which it meted out to the non-Orthodox elements of the empire's population. It will examine the extent to which the government was prepared to tolerate religious minorities and to allow them to practise their faiths without interference, and will deal with the reasons behind the frequent and often sudden shifts in the government's attitude to non-Orthodox groups. Religious toleration and the degree to which the state allowed its population freedom of conscience will also be considered as part of the imperial Russian government's general attitude to the provision of civil rights. Measures to extend or restrict religious freedom were often part of wider policies dealing with civil rights as a whole, and the way in which the state approached the issue of freedom of conscience can be used to illuminate its attitude towards the overall issue of civil rights.

The government was not the only institution in Russia which was concerned with religious minorities, since the Orthodox Church itself had important interests in this area. There was a triangular relationship between the government, religious minorities, and the Orthodox Church due to the Church's special position inside the empire. The legal status of the Orthodox Church was defined in Russia's Fundamental Laws as being 'pre-eminent and predominant' (*pervenstvuyushchii i gospodstvuyushchii*),[5] and it

---

[4] See A. G. Kaznacheev, 'Mezhdu strokami odnago formulyarnago spiska', *Russkaya starina*, 32 (1881), 844–5, for a description of the ties between Roman Catholicism and the Polish rebellion of 1863.

[5] *Svod zakonov Rossiiskoi imperii* (St Petersburg, 1906), i, pt. 1, art. 62.

was effectively the Established Church of the Russian Empire. The privileges which the Orthodox Church enjoyed in the middle of the nineteenth century were substantial: by law, only the Orthodox Church was allowed to proselytize and carry out missionary activities amongst the peoples of the empire, whilst it was an offence for an individual to leave the Orthodox Church and adhere to another sect or religion. The position of the Church was further strengthened by its relationship with the imperial family, since the tsar had to belong to it, as did any woman who married into the family—Nicholas II's fiancée underwent conversion shortly before her marriage in 1894. The law also provided that 'works and translations shall not be approved which contain attacks on Christian morality, the government, or religion', and printers were prohibited from producing books about the Orthodox Church without the permission of the Church's censorship committee.[6] In legal terms, therefore, the Church's position appeared assured and its power over other religious groups seemed complete.

However, the Orthodox Church was far from being an independent institution and was unable to operate policies directed at religious minorities solely on the basis of its own interests. Since the time of Peter the Great, the Church had been administered by a lay official, the Chief Procurator, who headed the Holy Synod which was comprised of clerics. The influence of the bishops who attended meetings of the Synod was severely limited, for it was the Chief Procurator who recommended to the tsar which clerics should be invited to take part in Synod sessions. Furthermore, by the late nineteenth century, the Synod had established a routine of meeting only three times a year to transact business, and the Chief Procurator and his lay officials were responsible for the general administration of the Church in the intervening periods. This responsibility was not confined to the work of the Synod in St Petersburg, but extended into each bishopric, since it was the Chief Procurator who controlled the diocesan consistories through their secretaries. In administrative matters, therefore, the Orthodox Church was subordinate to the temporal power, and this dependence was intensified in other areas. The Orthodox Church played a vital part in the provision

[6] J. S. Curtiss, *Church and State in Russia: The Last Years of the Empire* (New York, 1940), 35–6, 86.

of primary education in the Russian Empire, and over a third of all places in such schools were in church institutions, whilst the government paid a significant subsidy to support the work of the church schools.

Whilst it was the Synod which theoretically controlled the Church, in reality the Chief Procurator held the reins; he had much influence over ecclesiastical appointments and was able to move bishops from see to see at will, as well as to recommend candidates for Synod membership to the tsar. With the revival of the Council of Ministers in 1905 and the inclusion of the Chief Procurator as a member, his status could almost be described as 'Minister for the Church', for like any other minister, he had the right of access to the tsar. The spiritual power was an integral part of the Russian political system, and the Orthodox population was made aware of its responsibilities towards the state in the oath administered at the accession of a new tsar, when each individual promised to inform the authorities of anything which might be 'of detriment, harm or damage to the interests of His Imperial Majesty'.[7]

The state made direct and unashamed use of the opportunity which the Orthodox Church offered for direct contact with the population of the empire. As 70 per cent of the population was estimated to belong to the Orthodox Church, the network of over 100,000 clerics which staffed the Church provided a useful way for the government to ensure that its views were expounded to the population. Government manifestos and edicts were read from the pulpit,[8] and priests were also used to propound anti-revolutionary opinions: a Synod circular in 1902 instructed the bishops to get their priests to 'explain to their congregations the falseness, according to the word of God, of the appeals of the evil-minded who urge them to disobey the authorities established by the Tsar and to attack the property of others'.[9] Priests were also required to disclose to the police any information they had gained about plots or conspiracies against the tsar or the government, even if it had been obtained through the confessional,

---

[7] M. Szeftel, 'Church and State in Imperial Russia', in R. Nichols and T. G. Stavrou (eds.), *Russian Orthodoxy under the Old Regime* (Minneapolis, 1978), 137.

[8] The Emancipation Edict of 1861 which announced the measure to the Russian population was written by Metropolitan Filaret.

[9] Curtiss, *Church and State*, pp. 74–5.

whilst church authorities had to ensure that their villages were free of undesirable elements.[10] The government recognized that the apparatus of the Church provided it with a means of influencing the mass of the population which could not be reached in any other manner, and it utilized this apparatus to its full extent, even going so far as to use church publishing facilities to produce pamphlets explaining and supporting individual items of legislation.[11]

The position in which the Orthodox Church found itself presented it with substantial problems in asserting its own authority. Whilst religious matters were theoretically under the control of the Church, the part which the state played in the Church's administration meant that it had very great influence over the direction of church affairs. The support which the state gave to the Orthodox Church meant that it was in the Church's own interests to acquiesce in this relationship, and for much of the late nineteenth century the two institutions worked in reasonable harmony. Most noticeably, the period during which K. P. Pobedonostsev was Chief Procurator, from 1880 to 1905, saw close identification between the activities of the spiritual and temporal powers, but in the years following his departure the Church came into sharp conflict with the government over religious matters.

The occasion for dispute between Church and state was provided by the Stolypin government's proposals to extend freedom of conscience to non-Orthodox religions, and especially to the Old Believers.[12] When the Synod discussed these measures in 1906 and 1907 it stood up firmly for its own interests by declaring that such matters came within the jurisdiction of the spiritual power, since they concerned subjects which were of canonical significance.[13] The question of mixed marriages provoked the most intense dispute, and relations between the

---

[10] Szeftel, 'Church and State', p. 137.

[11] N. F. Platonov, 'Pravoslavnaya tserkov' v bor'be s revolyutsionnym dvizheniem v Rossii (1900–1917)', in *Ezhegodnik muzeya istorii religii i ateizma*, iv (Moscow, 1960), 165.

[12] The Old Believer legislation took priority in the government's plans, largely because of the sheer size of the group.

[13] Harvard University, International Legal Studies Library (hereafter HILS), Rus. 600, *Osobyi zhurnal Soveta Ministrov*, 'Po proektam: 1. polozheniya o staroobryadt-sev . . .' (5 Sept. and 13 Oct. 1906), 8.

government and the Synod became very poor, but it also raised much wider issues of the political control of spiritual matters.[14] The Chief Procurator, P. P. Izvol'skii, found himself in an impossible position, for he was torn between his responsibilities to the government of which he was a member and the interests of the body of which he was the head.[15] This exemplified the problems inherent in the Russian constitutional structure after 1905, but it also demonstrated the fragility of the relationship between Church and state under the system established by Peter the Great. The Orthodox Church retained sufficient autonomous power and influence for it to be able to confront the government if it believed that its own vital interests were being threatened.[16] The extension of religious toleration was one such area, and the persistent opposition which the Church displayed to the government's plans between 1906 and 1909 was an important reason for their eventual failure.

The position of the Church was deceptive, for by the late nineteenth century its long years of subservience to the state appeared to have eroded the status which the law afforded it. In the years after 1905 the government evidently believed that it could act to improve the conditions of non-Orthodox religions without taking the views of the Church into account, but it proved to be mistaken. The impact which the Orthodox Church had on the government's policies turned out to be far greater than the latter had anticipated: the spiritual authority which the Church possessed and the way in which it could mobilize support, especially amongst conservative groups, meant that the actual authority of the Orthodox Church was much closer to its legal position than the government liked to think.[17]

[14] The correspondence between the two bodies is in Leningrad, Tsentral'nyi gosudarstvennyi istoricheskii arkhiv SSSR (hereafter TsGIA), f. 796, op. 188, d. 7620; f. 797, op. 96, d. 188; and f. 821, op. 10, d. 693.

[15] Leningrad, Gosudarstvennaya publichnaya biblioteka im. M. E. Saltykova-Shchedrina, Rukopisnyi otdel, f. 443, d. 852, pp. 12–13, 'Dokladnaya zapiska P. P. Izvol'skago Nikolayu II-omu' [autumn 1908?].

[16] TsGIA, f. 797, op. 79, d. 549, p. 1, 'Prosheniya tsarya prichtov i prikhozhikh Podol'skoi gubernii ob otmene zakonoproekta Gosudarstvennoi Dumy . . . o svobode sovesti', is only one of a series of mass petitions addressed to Nicholas II in 1909 from Orthodox communities.

[17] The Church found right-wing support both from organizations such as the Union of the Russian People and from conservative ministers and statesmen: TsGIA, f. 796, op. 188, d. 7620, p. 295, telegram from the Tambov council of the Union of

In its dealings with religious minorities the tsarist government had a consistent aim in view—the maintenance of the autocracy. In this it was supported by the Orthodox Church. The difference between the two bodies arose over the means by which this could be most effectively achieved, and this was also the subject of disagreement inside the government itself during the last sixty years of tsarism. The attitude which the government adopted towards religious minorities altered sharply on several occasions during this period, but two main trends can be identified. The first of these was a policy of making concessions to non-Orthodox religious groups, and extending the freedoms available to them and their adherents to practise their beliefs. On the other hand, the government sometimes went to the opposite extreme, and moved to impose restrictions on religious minorities and to try to encourage their members to convert to Orthodoxy. As the ultimate responsibility for religious policy rested with the temporal power, both of these attitudes must be seen in the overall context of government policy under the last three tsars and the continuing debate over the most appropriate method for keeping the strength and authority of the autocracy as intact as possible: religious policy was only one part of the regime's general strategy.

The reform packages of the 1860s and the post-1905 era both included measures to deal with religious toleration. In the atmosphere of discontent which pervaded both periods, religious minority groups were viewed by the government as sections of the community whose support could be relatively easily assured by allowing them the freedom to practise their own faiths. This was especially true of the Old Believers, who comprised a substantial proportion of the native Russian population of the empire and whose sole reason for alienation from the regime was the disabilities which they suffered on the grounds of religion. They appeared to successive governments as a group whose support was worth endeavouring to obtain as no great cost to the state was involved. The government moved cautiously in dealing with the non-Orthodox sects, however, since it was aware of the great variety of beliefs which they espoused, and it wanted to ensure that toleration was extended only to those groups whose

the Russian People to the Holy Synod (30 Jan. 1908); *Trudy odinnadtsatago vserossiiskago s"ezda staroobryadtsev, 19–20 avgust 1910* (Moscow, 1911), 72.

reliability could be assured. From 1858 onwards measures were taken to improve the lot of the Old Believers: regulations of 1863 and 1864 gave them the right to enrol in merchant guilds, and a number of their belfries were permitted to be opened. Further minor measures were taken, but Alexander II himself did not see the need to make any wider-ranging changes to the system which restricted the Old Believers, for as he put it: 'The faults in the administration of the schismatics arise not from the system itself, but are caused by its inexact and incorrect implementation, either because of civil servants' disloyalty or else because they have an insufficient knowledge of the legislation dealing with the schism.'[18] However, in 1864 moves were made to institute a more extensive examination of the regulations which governed religious sects, and a committee was established to classify them into more and less dangerous groups, with greater rights and toleration to be extended to the latter.[19] Work on this topic proceeded slowly, and in 1875 a second commission was set up to carry on the process. Further impetus was given to this work by the attention paid by the government at the end of the 1870s to the causes of the renewed discontent demonstrated by the upsurge in terrorist activity. A special conference in 1879, chaired by P. A. Valuev, identified the Old Believers as a highly conservative force, deeply attached to Russia and its traditions, but whose continued persecution made them a potential breeding-ground for opposition to the regime. Greater tolerance by the regime, it was argued, would put a halt to this threat.[20]

The result of these two decades of deliberations was a regulation of May 1883 which aimed to provide the Old Believers with the basic conditions necessary for their religion to function: churches which had been closed could be reopened; Old Believers could hold internal passports; and they could occupy public positions. Prohibitions were to remain, however, on public manifestations of schismatic religions, such as processions or public preaching, and Old Believer ministers were not to be recognized as priests and so were to continue to be deprived

[18] K. N. Plotnikov, *Istoriya russkago raskola* (St Petersburg, 1891), 33.

[19] V. S. Markov, 'K istorii raskola-staroobryadchestva vtoroi poloviny XIX stoletiya', in *Chteniya v Imperatorskom obshchestve istorii i drevnostei Rossii*, i. *1915* (Moscow, 1914), 146–57.

[20] P. A. Zaionchkovskii, *Krizis samoderzhaviya na rubezhe 1870–1880 godov* (Moscow, 1964), 102–3.

of the privileges which the law granted to orthodox clergy.[21]

At the same time as these measures were being implemented, work was also proceeding to ameliorate the conditions of certain other minorities. The religious position in the Baltic provinces was surveyed in a report presented to the Tsar in 1864 by Count V. A. Bobrinskii which criticized some of the coercive policies pursued in the past to promote the Orthodox Church, and advocated a more conciliatory policy towards the Lutheran population. Alexander II took note of Bobrinskii's findings, and decisions taken in 1865 and 1874 allowed some 35,000 Estonians and Latvians to revert to Lutheranism.[22] Movement towards greater religious toleration was extremely slow and cautious under Alexander II, for he had no desire to be seen to yield to public pressure for greater freedom of conscience, such as that manifested by members of the Moscow duma in 1870.[23] The Tsar was content to deal with religious matters piecemeal, and whilst he was generally in favour of putting an end to persecution on religious grounds, he took few steps to reform Russia's actual legislation on the subject.

The policy of making concessions to religious minorities found little sympathy from Alexander III and his advisers, and it took further discontent and the appointment of more liberal ministers after 1900 before measures to extend religious toleration once again appeared on the government's agenda. The first decade of the twentieth century witnessed the introduction of a second major package of reforms and proposals to extend civil rights in general, including religious toleration. Two general edicts of February 1903 and December 1904 declared that the existing laws on religious toleration would be strictly observed and that the position of non-Orthodox groups would be significantly improved.[24] This was followed by the publication, on 17 April 1905, of an edict devoted specifically to religious toleration which

---

[21] *Polnoe sobranie zakonov Rossiiskoi imperii*, 3rd series (hereafter *PSZ*), iii, no. 1545, pp. 219–21.

[22] E. C. Thaden, 'The Russian Government', in E. C. Thaden (ed.), *Russification in the Baltic Provinces and Finland, 1855–1914* (Princeton, 1981), 44–5.

[23] S. N. Sukhotin, 'Iz pamyatnykh tetradei S. N. Sukhotina', *Russkii arkhiv*, 32/2 (1894), 248. Alexander II's reaction is reported in A. F. Tyutcheva, *Pri dvore dvukh imperatorov: Vospominaniya, dnevnik, 1853–1882* (Moscow, 1928–9), pt. 2, pp. 214–15.

[24] *PSZ*, xxiii, pt. 1, no. 22581, pp. 113–14; and xxiv, pt. 1, no. 25495, pp. 1196–8.

accepted that non-Orthodox Christian religions should not be
discriminated against, and made special mention of the need to
remove the restrictions which still applied to the Old Believers.[25]
Religious freedom was placed in the wider context of civil rights
in the Manifesto of 17 October 1905, which established a
legislative duma. Instead of referring merely to the toleration
(*veroterpimost'*) of religions, the term freedom of conscience
(*svoboda sovesti*) was now used and was declared to be one of the
foundations of civil liberties.[26]

These four measures provided the basis for much more
detailed legislation which, it was anticipated, would regularize
the position of religious minorities within a consistent and liberal
framework. The government was aware of the importance that
religion played in the Russian state, and it rejected the idea that
atheism could be officially recognized, as it also rejected the
introduction of civil procedures for registering births, marriages,
and deaths, and the abolition of compulsory religious instruction
in schools.[27] During Stolypin's premiership from 1906 to 1911,
however, a series of detailed measures was prepared which aimed
to put non-Orthodox religions on the same legal basis as any
other type of association.[28] The government recognized that
opposition groups might make substantial headway amongst
religious minorities if action were not taken,[29] and between
September 1906 and February 1907 a total of fourteen bills on
religious matters were submitted to the Council of Ministers. A
complete bill was devoted to the Old Believers,[30] whilst other
measures dealt with facilitating changes of religion, the extension
of the laws on blasphemy to cover approved non-Christian
religions, the extension of the right to proselytize, the removal of

[25] *PSZ*, xxv, pt. 1, no. 26126, pp. 258–62.

[26] Ibid., no. 26803, pp. 754–5.

[27] TsGIA, f. 796, op. 188, d. 7620, pp. 71–2, 'Perechen' voprosov, podlezhash-
chikh razresheniyu pri vyrabotke zakonoproekta o svobode sovesti' (Jan. 1907);
and p. 9: Ministerstvo vnutrennykh del (hereafter MVD), 'Ob izmenenii zakonopol-
ozhenii, kasayushchikhsya perekhoda iz odnago ispovedaniya v drugoe' (10 Feb.
1907).

[28] This approach excluded the Jews, to whom Nicholas II refused to make any
concessions: 'Perepiska N. A. Romanova i P. A. Stolypina', *Krasnyi arkhiv*, 5 (1924),
105.

[29] Bonch-Bruevich had recommended this approach to the second congress of the
RSDRP: B. D. Bonch-Bruevich, *Izbrannye sochineniya*, i (Moscow, 1965), 153–88.

[30] HILS, Rus. 678, MVD, 'Proekt pravil o staroobryadcheskikh obshchinakh'
(20 Feb. 1907), 1–13.

civil and political disabilities imposed by virtue of an individual's religion, as well as such family matters as mixed marriages.[31] The thrust of all these proposals was to put all non-Orthodox religions on the same basis, making a distinction only between those faiths which were seen as harmful to the state and were therefore prohibited, and those which presented no danger and were therefore to be permitted to exist without restriction.

However, these measures to implement the government's commitment to freedom of conscience met the same fate as the vast majority of Stolypin's other proposals for reform. None of the bills which the government prepared on this topic ever became law, for they all became entangled in the fierce political controversy which arose over Stolypin's overall programme. Opponents of Stolypin's plans argued that reform was, in general, unnecessary once the remnants of the 1905 disturbances had been firmly quelled, whilst specific attacks were made on the religious proposals by the Church and right-wing political parties. By 1909 the disaffected groups from whom the regime needed support had changed, and the threat to the existence of Stolypin's government now came from the right; the bills to implement full freedom of conscience were only one of the casualties of a renewed turn-away from reform.

The second strand of Russian government policy during the last decades of its existence was a belief that the way to preserve and strengthen the autocracy was to refuse to compromise its essential principles and to avoid all measures of liberal reform that could dilute the powers of the regime. This deeply conservative approach to the governing of the Russian Empire ran parallel to the reform-centred ideas which dominated the 1860s and the years after 1905, and it exerted great sway over the rulers of the state. The period between 1881 and 1905, when Alexander III and the young Nicholas II ruled Russia, saw the state attempting to retrieve the authority it had lost through the reforms of the 1860s, and religious minorities were one of the groups which felt renewed repression.

Even during the reign of Alexander II, however, there was pressure from sections of the government to strengthen the position of the Orthodox Church and to impose greater religious

---

[31] TsGIA, f. 796, op. 188, d. 7620, pp. 19–90; and f. 821, op. 10, d. 41, p. 87.

uniformity across the empire. This trend was most pronounced in the Baltic areas, even though conciliatory measures were being taken at the same time. The bishops and local administrators of the region pressed for greater financial resources to be assigned to the well-being of the Orthodox population and for action to be taken to stem the decline which the Orthodox Church was experiencing in the Baltic provinces. Support came from such conservative and Slavophile thinkers as Yurii Samarin and M. P. Pogodin, who believed that the Church in the Baltic region needed help against the overwhelmingly Lutheran nature of the area; they wanted to see Orthodoxy placed on the same footing as the Lutheran Church, despite the fact that the majority of the local population was Lutheran.[32] The action which the government took in response to these calls was mainly financial: additional sums of money were made available to build new Orthodox churches and to establish Orthodox education on a better basis in the area. The government also acted to provide land for landless Orthodox peasants in the Baltic provinces, whilst voluntary Orthodox organizations were given encouragement in their educational work in the region.[33] This promotion of the state Church, and the consequent attack on what was, in overall imperial terms, a religious minority, was being carried on at the same time as the government was moving to allow minorities more leeway in their own affairs. This contradictory policy in religious matters was symptomatic of the differing approaches to reform in general within the tsarist regime of Alexander II; with the accession of his son, however, the attitudes of the state towards religious minorities and reform became much less confused.

Under Alexander III, Russian nationalism became the regime's guiding principle in dealing with both national and religious minorities within the empire. The imposition of uniformity across the empire was seen as an effective method of strengthening the authority of the regime in St Petersburg, whilst conservative ideologists argued for the innate superiority of Russia and things Russian over other nations. The Russification policy of the 1880s and 1890s had a severe effect on religious minorities. Even

---

[32] Thaden, 'Russian Government', p. 44; and M. P. Pogodin, *Ostzeiskii vopros: Pis'mo M. P. Pogodina k professoru Shirrenu* (Moscow, 1869), 58–9.
[33] Thaden, 'Russian Government', pp. 45–6.

though new legislation to improve the conditions of the Old Believers had been issued in 1883, the authorities were loath to implement the provisions of the statute and it proved to be a dead letter in the twenty years after its enactment.[34] However, Old Believers did not suffer the direct persecution which was the fate of other minority groups during the 1880s and 1890s. The Baltic provinces and Poland were the chief targets for this work, and great emphasis was placed on work to convert people from their native religion to Orthodoxy. It is estimated that during Alexander III's reign some 37,000 Lutherans were converted to the Orthodox faith, but many of these were nominal conversions. The methods used by the Orthodox Church and its missionaries stressed the material benefits to be gained from a change of belief—such as the chance to acquire more land—and many converts became Orthodox in name only and continued to practise the Lutheran faith.[35] The campaign to increase the numbers of Orthodox believers met with very limited success in the long run; by 1904 only some 10 per cent of the population of the Baltic provinces were Orthodox Church members.

Alongside this policy of active promotion of Orthodox religion was one of action against the Lutheran Church. Prosecutions were intensified against those people who were apostates from Orthodoxy, as well as against the Lutheran ministers who held services for them; in the decade up to 1895 some 175 Lutheran ministers were prosecuted for this offence. As well as this, the Orthodox authorities were given a say in the affairs of the Lutheran Church; after 1885 all applications for the construction and repair of non-Orthodox religious buildings had to gain the approval of the local Orthodox bishop. The Lutheran Church's financial resources also came under attack when Lutheran clergy were prohibited from levying taxation upon Orthodox believers. The state itself drew up regulations for the administration of the Lutheran Church: the Ministry of the Interior demanded that the proceedings of Lutheran synods should be submitted to it in Russian, and six years later, in 1891, it was laid down that Lutheran parish registers must also be kept in Russian.[36]

[34] S. P. Mel'gunov, *Staroobryadcheskiya i sektantskiya obshchiny* (Moscow, 1907), 5; and Markov, 'K istorii', p. 158.
[35] Zaionchkovskii, *Krizis samoderzhaviya*, p. 69; and Thaden, 'Russian Government', pp. 161–2.   [36] Ibid. 163.

Individual members of the Lutheran Church also suffered from the renewed imposition of the rules governing mixed marriages involving a member of the Orthodox Church, whereby children of such a marriage had to be brought up in the Orthodox faith. Despite petitions to Alexander III from the Baltic German nobility requesting a relaxation in the government's policy, the state's pro-Orthodox policy continued unabated in the Baltic provinces.

Other regions were also victims of the policy of official Orthodoxy which was imposed from 1881 onwards. The aftermath of the Polish uprising in 1863 had seen measures to curb the influence of Roman Catholic clergy who were believed to have supported the Poles against their Russian masters,[37] but further moves were also taken to close down Catholic monasteries and to promote the purchase of land inside Poland by non-Catholics. Missionary activities by the Orthodox Church gained renewed impetus in the east and south of the empire, and were concentrated in the efforts of the All-Russian Orthodox Missionary Society which had been established in 1870. By 1894 the society reported that nearly 60,000 'heathens and Muslims' had been converted through its activities, and it made use of the visit of the future Nicholas II to Siberia in 1891 to undertake a forced mass baptism of members of the Buryat community.[38]

The policies of Russification which the government pursued included action against non-Orthodox religions as an essential part, but the renewed discontent of the years around 1905 prompted the government to make further concessions to religious minorities. The consensus for the introduction of these measures was short-lived, however, and as details of the proposals became known, opposition to them intensified. General misgivings amongst conservative politicians about the need for further reform once the disturbances of 1905 had been quelled included specific doubts as to the wisdom of allowing non-Orthodox religions the freedom of conscience which they had been promised in the general edicts of 1905. The Orthodox Church argued that the privileges which it was proposed to grant to other religions in effect disestablished the Orthodox faith. In

---

[37] Kaznacheev, 'Mezhdu strokami', outlines some of the difficulties in taking such action.
[38] Zaionchkovskii, *Krizis samoderzhaviya*, pp. 71–2.

particular, it opposed the plans to abolish the legal penalties for apostasy from Orthodoxy and to give non-Orthodox religions the right to proselytize, for the Holy Synod believed that if these provisions were brought into force the Orthodox Church could no longer be said to be dominant inside the empire.[39] By implication, any attack on the Orthodox Church was an attack on the most fundamental institutions of the empire, and was seen by the Synod and its supporters as being akin to an assault on the autocracy itself. An address from the Kiev branch of the *Russkoe sobranie* to the Synod in January 1908 congratulated the Synod on its stand against the government's bills, declaring that the proposals were based not on Russian traditions, but on West European models.[40]

The influence which the Church and its allies were able to exert on the Tsar and the highest reaches of Russian government helped to bring about the downfall of Stolypin's plans to extend freedom of conscience. By the beginning of 1909 the government was ready to make substantial concessions to the Church over its religious bills, as it was toning down or abandoning its reform proposals overall as a result of strong opposition from the right. When Stolypin spoke to the Duma in the spring of 1909 he emphasized his own change of heart on the question of religious reform and his recognition that the Tsar would never approve legislation which appeared to be anti-Orthodox: 'The monarch, according to our law, is the defender of the Orthodox Church and the custodian of its dogmas . . . [and] these religious laws will operate in the Russian state and will be confirmed by the Russian Tsar, who for more than one hundred million people was, is and will be an Orthodox Tsar.'[41] In the autumn of 1909 the government withdrew its most contentious religious bills from further consideration by the legislative institutions, and Stolypin wrote to the Chief Procurator admitting the government's capitulation, 'so that [the bills] can be made to correspond to the canon law of the Orthodox Church and to its position as the established Church of the state, as provided by the Fundamental

---

[39] TsGIA, f. 796, op. 188, d. 7620, pp. 287–9, 'Mnenie Sinoda, 15 dekabr' 1907, po zakonoproektam, kasayushchimsya osushchestvleniya svobody sovesti'.

[40] Ibid. 296.

[41] *Gosudarstvennaya Duma: Stenograficheskii otchet*, Third Duma, session 2 (St Petersburg), iv, col. 1764.

Laws'.[42] At the same time, new measures were prepared by the government to limit the activities of non-Orthodox religions. In March 1910 rules were issued to restrict the number and scope of congresses which could be held by non-Orthodox groups,[43] and later in the year, controls were instituted over all meetings held by such groups. Gatherings specifically for religious worship were permitted, but any other sort of assembly had to be authorized by the local governor.[44]

The debate inside the Russian regime about the most effective method of dealing with religious minorities, and indeed, about the best way to maintain the authority of the autocratic regime, had finally been settled in favour of the promotion of the Orthodox Church as a spiritual buttress to the political structure of the state. To the Church and conservatives in general, it appeared that the policy of making concessions to religious minorities had opened the way to the expression of yet more discontent rather than restored the authority of the state.

For the imperial Russian government, religious toleration was only a part of its overall political strategy. At those times when the regime was intent on making concessions to sectors of the population, and introduced reforms as a means of attempting to enhance its own authority, non-Orthodox groups benefited and found themselves able to practise their religions more freely. When reform as a whole disappeared from the government's agenda, any chance of freedom of conscience being extended also disappeared. Legislation to extend civil rights was seen not so much as desirable for its own sake, but as a means of removing some of the causes of discontent which appeared to threaten the stability of the Russian state.

Attempts to provide greater freedom of conscience for the Russian people foundered partly because of the ambivalent attitude to reform inside the Russian regime during the last

[42] TsGIA, f. 796, op. 188, d. 7620, pp. 306–10, P. A. Stolypin to S. M. Luk'yanov (10 Oct. 1909).
[43] 'Rasporyazheniya pravitel'stva o poryadke ustroistva posledovatelyami sektantskikh verouchenii veroispovednykh s"ezdov' (31 Mar. 1910), Tserkovnyya vedomosti, 1 May 1910, 146–8.
[44] 'Tsirkulyar' MVD, 4 oktyabr' 1910, gubernatoram, nachal'nikam oblastei i gradonachal'nikam po voprosu o bogosluzhebnykh i molitvennykh sobraniyakh sektantov', ibid., 26 Feb. 1911, 42.

decades of its existence, but also because the question of religious rights brought the government up against the Orthodox Church. Any increase in the privileges of religious minorities meant a concomitant loss of authority for Orthodoxy, and this prospect aroused displeasure both from the Church itself and from its conservative supporters. Although it had been subordinated to the temporal power since the early eighteenth century, the size of the Orthodox Church and the spiritual authority which it possessed meant that it was still able to display some degree of independence. Furthermore, the special links which existed between the Church and the whole system of autocratic government meant that the Church and its supporters could portray proposals to increase the status of non-Orthodox religions as attacks on the fabric of the Russian state itself.

It was this tie between Orthodoxy and autocracy which gave such force to the Church's protests about the extension of toleration to other religions. The Church gained automatic support from right-wing politicians and ideologists, and it was these sections of society which proved to be the most influential in directing the course of the Russian state under the last three tsars. Orthodox tsars had little inclination to promote the development of religions inimical to Orthodoxy itself. Plans to extend freedom of conscience were doubly doomed therefore; the very notion of reform in any sphere was regarded with deep mistrust by the last rulers of imperial Russia, and of all areas of reform, that of religion struck deepest at the roots of their dogmas.

The Concept of 'Jewish Emancipation' in a Russian Context

JOHN D. KLIER

We find that the Jews do not have any right to register in the *kupechestvo* in interior Russia's towns and ports and only by Our *ukaz* are they permitted to exercise the right of citizenship and [to enrol in] the *meshchanstvo* in Belorussia.

Decree of Catherine II; 23 December 1791

Jews, who are Russian subjects, fall under the general statutes in all situations where special rules are not promulgated.

Decree of Nicholas I; 13 April 1835

As members of European society gradually began to secure varying degrees of 'civil rights' in the modern period, the Jewish population was seldom included. Historians have therefore treated the Jews as a special case, and have used the expression 'Jewish emancipation' to describe the accumulation of civil and political rights by European Jewry in the eighteenth and nineteenth centuries. However, Jacob Katz has shown that the expression was not commonly employed by contemporaries of the process until the late 1820s. At first it was designed to describe a specific phenomenon, like its predecessors 'naturaliz-ation' and 'civic betterment'. 'Emancipation' itself had initially been used by those who sought to remove the legal, religious, and political disabilities imposed upon Irish Catholics under British rule, and was extended to the Jews only by analogy. Katz demonstrates how the meaning of the term gradually shifted in

* Preparation of this essay was assisted by participation in the International Research and Exchanges Board's academic exchange programme with the Soviet Union; through grants from the Graduate Research Committee at Fort Hays State University and the Kennan Institute of the Woodrow Wilson Center; and through participation in the University of Illinois' Summer Research Laboratory. I would like to acknowledge Professor George Yaney of the University of Maryland, who first suggested the topic of this essay to me.

the light of changing circumstances. When the most onerous examples of legal and religious restrictions were lifted from Catholics and Jews at the end of the eighteenth century, 'emancipation' became the slogan of the struggle for full political equality.[1]

The opponents of extended rights for European Jewry were fully aware of the expanded connotations of the phrase 'Jewish emancipation', and opposed it. H. E. G. Paulus, for example, protested against its use on linguistic grounds: it implied liberation from the power of another (as in its original Roman usage), whereas Jews were protected under German law with the status of *Schützburger*. Prerogatives which the Jews now claimed—state service and political rights—could not legitimately be covered by the term. Paulus was more than a linguistic purist, of course. He recognized that 'emancipation' had become a powerful emotional catchword. As he complained: 'This foreign word—emancipation—with which most people are incapable of connoting anything distinct, has already been misused in the case of the poor people of Ireland. . . . Such words are meant to shine, to blind, but when one observes them closely, they turn out to be not a star, but a shooting star.'[2]

Katz's biography of the catchwords 'Jewish emancipation', with their shifting meanings and differing functions, can serve historians of Russian Jewry as a cautionary tale. The expression appears frequently in our works, and is, admittedly, useful shorthand for complex historical phenomena. But what exact meaning can 'Jewish emancipation' have in a Russian context? This essay seeks to answer this question.

In the Russian language, the term 'emancipation' was usually tied to western concepts such as the 'emancipation of women'.[3] For Russian conditions such as the emancipation of the serfs, the term *osvobozhdenie* was employed. The various official committees which dealt with the 'Jewish question' invariably saw the transformation of the legal status of the Jews as dependent upon changes in the Jews themselves rather than upon changes in

---

[1] J. Katz, 'The Term "Jewish Emancipation": Its Origins and Historical Impact', reprinted in *Emancipation and Assimilation: Studies in Modern Jewish History* (Farnborough, 1972), 38–9.

[2] Ibid. 39–40.

[3] See V. Dal', *Tolkovyi slovar' zhivogo velikorusskago yazyka*, 3rd edn. (St Petersburg and Moscow, 1909), iv. 1535.

the law. Therefore they bore such titles as: 'The Committee to Extend the Well-Being of the Jews' (1802); 'The Committee for Radical Transformation of the Jews' (1840); or 'The Committee for the Reorganization of Jewish Life' (1872). Jewish publicists throughout the nineteenth century generally avoided the use of 'emancipation' to describe the desiderata of Russian Jewry; but they used the expression continually when referring to the Jews of Western Europe. Perhaps this restricted use was a recognition of the fact that conditions in Russia and Western Europe were not sufficiently analogous. As the author of a legal survey in the inaugural issue of the Russian-language Jewish newspaper *Razsvet* observed in 1860: 'Our kin (*edinoplemenniki*) in a large part of the states of Europe have for a long time pursued the path leading to this goal [civil rights]. Longer than others have we enviously watched as along the wide road, cheerfully and joyfully, advanced our kin in Western Europe.'[4] (In that same issue it was noted that Austrian Jewry sought 'complete emancipation'.)

As a consequence, Jewish objectives in Russia usually focused on gradual changes in specific, harmful restrictions, such as the onerous residence restrictions constituting the Jewish Pale of Settlement. Only in the late nineteenth century did Jewish activists begin to describe their goals as 'emancipation', and to understand the term in its most developed European sense as 'civil equality and equal submission to general laws . . . as conscientious citizens of a modern state'.[5] It is appropriate that this latter declaration came only in 1905, because prior to the revolution of that year—and to a certain extent thereafter—Russia was far from being a modern state on the European model, nor was there any possibility of emancipation in the European sense. Indeed, the history of the legal status of Russian Jewry, a discrete system lasting from 1772 to 1917, is a useful reference tool for the study of the evolution of the Russian legal and social system itself.

The most distinctive feature of Russian society in 1772—when the first partition of Poland introduced a legally tolerated Jewish

[4] 'Obzor peremen, proizshedshikh v polozhenii russkikh evreev s 1855 po 1860 god', *Razsvet*, 1 (27 May 1860).
[5] S. W. Baron, *The Russian Jew Under Tsars and Soviets*, 2nd edn. (New York and London, 1976), 59.

community into the Russian Empire for the first time—was the system of *sosloviya*, or estates. While there were many exceptions, the Russian *soslovie* system divided all of society into four categories: the nobility (*dvoryanstvo*); the clergy (*dukhovenstvo*); enserfed peasantry (*krest'yanstvo*); and the two urban estates of the merchants (*kupechestvo*) and the townspeople (*meshchanstvo*). Russian society lacked the well-developed western concepts of 'natural rights' or 'civil rights'. Moreover, it would be misleading to equate the Russian *sosloviya* with the estates of the medieval West. The Russian *soslovie* was devised more as a vehicle for exploitation by the state than as a repository of organized rights, prerogatives, and privileges. The Russian nobility, for example, had been moulded by the state into a service class in which social status depended upon service to the state. Class obligations were explicit until 1762, and implicit thereafter. The systems of local autonomy and class government granted to various *sosloviya* were intended to serve the administrative needs of the state rather than to acknowledge class rights. Small wonder that the members of these estates were often slow to avail themselves of their electoral-administrative 'privileges', or—with the possible exception of the clergy[6]—to develop any feeling of 'class consciousness'. To be included in a *soslovie* meant, in essence, to be equal in inequality.

None the less, for the Russian Empire's new Jewish subjects, inclusion in a *soslovie* was an improvement in their status compared with most of Europe. Throughout Europe, Jews were treated as aliens, regardless of the circumstances of their birth or residency. Consequently, the first phase of European emancipation was 'naturalization', the extension of basic rights of residence and citizenship, however restricted.[7] In Russia in 1772, on the other hand, Jews were at once recognized as Russian subjects and were *not* regarded as foreigners or aliens. They were promised the same legal protection as all other residents of the newly annexed lands, and, more than this, they were permitted (along with the Gentile population) to retain for the moment any

---

[6] See G. L. Freeze, *The Russian Levites: Parish Clergy in the Eighteenth Century* (Cambridge, Mass., 1977). See also Freeze's examination of the *soslovie* paradigm as a tool for the study of Russian social history, in 'The *Soslovie* (Estate) Paradigm and Russian Social History', *The American Historical Review*, 91/1 (Feb. 1986), 11–36.

[7] Katz, 'Jewish Emancipation', pp. 28–32.

prerogatives and privileges which they had enjoyed under Polish rule. For Jews this meant the retention of their elaborate system of autonomous communal self-government, the *kahal* (or *kehillah* in its Hebrew form).[8]

During this initial period the Russian state also defined for itself exactly what a 'Jew' was. As evidenced by statutes offering special privileges to Jews who would convert to Christianity, a Jew was an adherent of the religious system of Judaism. Conversion to Christianity, through the formal act of baptism, made one cease to be a Jew. Converts enjoyed a period of special, privileged status, during which they were granted tax exemptions and received gratuities in money or land, and then they were subsumed into one of the *sosloviya*. For most imperial bureaucrats, conversion remained the preferred, if unanticipated, method for the resolution of the Jewish question until the late 1880s. At that time, due to ever greater disabilities and the weakening bonds of the traditional Jewish community, more and more pragmatic conversions took place. The government grew suspicious of converts, and began to place restrictions and quotas on Jews and 'persons of Jewish descent'.[9]

It should be noted that the Russian state was somewhat discriminating in its objections to Judaism. In 1794 the state doubled the rate of taxation on Jews as a revenue-producing measure. At the behest of Count Platon Zubov, the Governor-General of New Russia, a Jewish sect of the area known as the Karaites was granted exemption from this. Through this action, as well as through subsequent state-sponsored ethnographical studies of the Jews and the Karaites, it was shown that the state objected to the Talmud as an object of study and as a source of Jewish legal and moral precepts. (The Karaites claimed not to use the Talmud.) The Karaites retained their privileged status *vis-à-vis* Talmudic Jews until the demise of the monarchy, although various other reform movements in Judaism, some of which specifically rejected the Talmud, were unable to secure similar rights, perhaps because their rejection of Talmudic Judaism was viewed as insincere.[10]

[8] For the annexation decree, see *Polnoe sobranie zakonov Rossiiskoi imperii*, 1st series (hereafter *PSZ* 1) (St Petersburg, 1830–43), xix, no. 13865 (13 Sept. 1772).

[9] H. Rogger, 'The Jewish Policy of Late Tsarism: A Reappraisal', *The Wiener Library Bulletin*, 25/1–2, NS 22–3 (1971), 48–9.

[10] For the tax exemptions of the Karaites, see *PSZ* 1, xxiii, no. 17340 (8 June

Despite half-hearted conversionary efforts, the position of Jews in the Russian state after the first partition continued to improve. In 1780 the Jews were permitted to enrol in the urban estates, thus establishing their position in Russian society. In 1785 they were specifically included under the provisions of the Charter to the Towns of that year. They were guaranteed full participation in the mechanics of urban self-government, which operated through the *sosloviya* of the merchants and the townspeople. Jews began to be appointed as electors and officials of town governments. It would not be an exaggeration to say that if the rights they had been promised had in fact been delivered, Russian Jewry would have been the most equal subjects in Europe, 'emancipated' before the existence of the term.

A number of factors underlay this governmental action. The regime of Catherine II was endeavouring to strengthen and expand Russia's urban centres, which necessitated an increase in the numbers of merchants and townspeople. The Jews were an extensive urban element in those areas of Belorussia absorbed by the first partition, and they came to be seen by the Empress and her servitors as the raw material of urban development. For this reason the decree of 1780 ordered all Jews to enrol in the urban estates in the nearest municipality.

Although Jews hastened to participate in the municipal institutions, the system quickly broke down. Christian townspeople, long accustomed to looking at the Jews as social inferiors as well as economic competitors, protested vigorously against the action of the Russian government, and even used force to bar Jews from electoral assemblies.[11] In addition, municipalities added to the empire after 1793 had been guaranteed the rights which they had exercised under Polish rule, which included the system of Magdeburg law for municipal self-government. As applied to Polish cities, this law code specifically excluded Jews from any electoral participation.[12] Provincial authorities began

---

1795); for a typical ethnographic account, see 'Evrei-Karaimy', *Zhurnal Ministerstva vnutrennikh del*, 1 (Jan. 1843), 263–84. The most famous example of a Jewish sect seeking an improvement in the legal status of its membership was the so-called Spiritual-Biblical Brotherhood. See 'K istorii Dukhovno-bibleiskago bratstva', *Perezhitoe*, 1 (St Petersburg, 1909), 38–41.

[11] Yu. I. Gessen, *Evrei v Rossii* (St Petersburg, 1906), 209–10.

[12] S. A. Bershadskii, 'Polozhenie o evreyakh 1804 goda', *Voskhod*, 15 (June 1895), 55–61.

unilaterally to restrict Jewish electoral rights, even those to which they were entitled, in order to keep the peace. Moreover, as they became better acquainted with Jewish life, Russian administrators realized that while all Jews were enrolled in the urban estates, they often lived in rural areas—in villages and *shtetls*—and pursued professions like tavern-keeping and distilling, occupations which were not associated with the urban estates. The apparent hopelessness of Jewish–Gentile co-operation in municipal government, coupled with shifting evaluations of the nature of Jewish life and economic activity, brought an end to the experimental period of civic equality for the Jews of the Russian Empire.

As the regime began to view the Jews with a more jaundiced eye, restrictions and disabilities began to replace privileges. The most notorious restriction on Russian Jewry, the Pale of Settlement, had its genesis under Catherine (although the nature of the Pale and the motives underlying it at its inception were far from being as hostile as they subsequently became). In 1790 Jewish merchants petitioned the Empress for the right to enrol in the merchant guilds of Moscow and Smolensk. Catherine, intent on defending the economic well-being of established merchant groups, declined. This was a violation of the Charter to the Towns of 1785, which had offered merchants residential rights in any urban centre. The Empress justified her decision by noting that whatever rights Jews enjoyed in the empire had been granted by specific imperial decrees.[13] Historians have made much of this formula, with its implication that the Jews lacked any rights except for those specifically designated for them. Yet, as Richard Pipes and Isabel de Madariaga have both pointed out, this was the legal norm for *all* estates in the empire.[14] According to Pipes:

no estate in eighteenth-century Russia (the post-1785 nobility again excepted) possessed any generalized freedoms or rights: these are notions derived from a feudal tradition of which Russia knew nothing. . . . In the patrimonial regime of Russia, which was still entrenched in the eighteenth century, nothing was permitted that was not permitted

---

[13] *PSZ* 1, xxiii, no. 17006 (23 Dec. 1791).
[14] I. de Madariaga, *Russia in the Age of Catherine the Great* (New Haven and London, 1981).

explicitly; or, to put it another way, whatever was not specifically allowed was deemed forbidden.[15]

In retrospect, however, this formula proved more advantageous for the Jews than the subsequent declaration in 1835 that they were permitted whatever was not specifically forbidden.

In the reigns of Catherine II and her son Paul, questions involving the Jews had increasingly been resolved by administrative decisions. Not surprisingly, the reform-minded Tsar, Alexander I, resolved to eliminate the resultant legal ambiguities and discrepancies through the promulgation of a new, comprehensive law code for Russian Jewry. In 1802 he appointed a high-level committee which produced the Jewish Statute of 1804. The code was a strange blend of contradictions. It encouraged the Jews to pursue cultural assimilation by opening all Russian schools to them, and by insisting that rabbis and communal officials use European languages in their activities; but at the same time, the law retained the autonomous Jewish *kahal*, the most reliable defence of the Jews against the temptations, dangers, and opportunities offered by integration and assimilation. By ignoring the question of Jewish electoral rights, the new code left them completely exposed to the caprices of provincial governor-generals and the implementation of inconsistent systems which merely reflected the needs of the moment.

The primary concern of the drafters of the Statute of 1804— and the code's chief legacy to the future—was the perceived economic and social damage caused by the Jews to the Christian population among whom they lived. Reflecting the findings of government officialdom in the 1790s, the central government concluded that the Jewish pursuit of petty trade, money-lending, and manufacture and trade in alcohol harmed the local population and the national economy as well.[16] The new law attempted to deter such activities, largely by turning the Jews to new undertakings such as agriculture and small-scale industry. To this end, the code created new legal categories—a sort of quasi-

---

[15] R. Pipes, 'Catherine II and the Jews: The Origins of the Pale of Settlement', *Soviet Jewish Affairs*, 5/2 (1975), 14.

[16] Bershadskii, 'Polozhenie', *Voskhod*, 15 (Jan. 1895), 82–104; ibid. (Mar. 1895), 69–96.

soslovie—of agricultural colonists and 'manufacturers'.[17] The new classes, with their special rights and prerogatives, never amounted to much, since most Jews continued to occupy themselves with trade, handicrafts, and petty-bourgeois activity. The Statute of 1804 did set the tone for the rest of the nineteenth century, however: the Jews continued to be viewed as a harmful or retrograde community. The solution of the Jewish question, therefore, had to take the form not of granting more or equal rights to the Jews, but of 'rendering them harmless', so that any additional rights they might receive could not be used to threaten the well-being of the rest of the population. Jewish harmfulness was perceived to lie in their exclusivity and clannishness, buttressed by the dictates of the Talmud, and in economically retrograde or exploitative activities. These became the special targets of Russian legislation.

To suggest that Tsar Nicholas I—almost universally reviled in Russian-Jewish historiography as the Russian Haman—was a partisan of Jewish emancipation might at first glance seem to be a perversion of the very words. None the less, the methods which Nicholas's government employed sought to resolve the Jewish question by breaking down important legal distinctions between Jews and Gentiles. Thus the Jews, most of whom were enrolled in the *meshchanstvo* estate, were made eligible for personal military service, as were Christian members of the estate. The system of Jewish autonomous self-government, the *kahal*, was abolished. An elaborate system of schools was created to provide both religious and secular instruction in Western European languages rather than in Yiddish or Hebrew. Moreover, a legislative committee produced a Jewish statute in 1835 which devised a new legal formula for the Jews: everything was now permitted unless it was specifically forbidden by law.[18]

In fact, these measures proved to be a parody of emancipation; they saddled the Jews with civic responsibilities, and removed their existing prerogatives, without providing any corresponding rights or privileges. This was an example of 'equality in inequality' at its worst: given the hundreds of special statutes and rulings (especially those limiting Jewish mobility) which remained

[17] *PSZ* 1, xxviii, no. 21547 (9 Dec. 1804).
[18] *Polnoe sobranie zakonov Rossiiskoi imperii*, 2nd series (hereafter *PSZ* 2) (St Petersburg, 1830–56), x, no. 8054 (13 Apr. 1835), art. 1.

on the books, it was meaningless to declare that the Jews could do anything unless it was specifically denied to them.

Military service in the Russian Empire—from which all Jews had hitherto been able to purchase a collective exemption—was notorious for its length and its brutal conditions. Military life was especially onerous for religiously devout Jews, with their special dietary laws and taboos against sabbath work. Their lot was not made any easier by an implicit governmental policy of attempting to convert Jewish soldiers to Christianity. The government imposed much harsher disciplinary measures on Jews who balked at military service than it did on non-Jews. Huge fines were levied upon communities where draft-evaders were registered, communal officials were themselves drafted to make up shortfalls, and the infamous cantonist system—whereby underaged children were drafted into service—was employed. It is not surprising that the system of autonomous self-government forced to enforce these draconian measures began to disintegrate under the strain.[19]

In any event, the days of the autonomous *kahal* were also numbered. In 1844 the system was abolished, although the government did retain separate Jewish officials to bring in the taxes and recruits for which the Jews were still collectively responsible. The Jews received nothing in return: they were restricted to setting quotas for participation in municipal government, and limits were placed on the offices which they could hold and on the electors they could select for municipal elections.[20]

Finally, Russian Jews viewed the new school system, correctly or incorrectly, as an attempt to subvert the religious foundations of Judaism. Influential members of the community avoided sending their children to these schools, and when the government demanded the attendance of Jewish students, children of the communal poor were dragooned to the school benches. Despite the fact that the Jewish community displayed no enthusiasm or support for the schools, it was still forced to pay the entire cost through a special system of taxes.[21]

[19] M. Stanislawski, *Tsar Nicholas I and the Jews: The Transformation of Jewish Society in Russia, 1825–1855* (Philadelphia, 1983), 123–54.

[20] S. Dubnow, *History of the Jews in Russia and Poland*, ii (Philadelphia, 1918), 41.

[21] For an official report on the Jewish school system, see A. I. Georgievskii,

The Nicholine years introduced one further innovation in the legal treatment of Jews. As noted above, the attempt of the Statute of 1804 to direct Jews into new professions and new social classes was a failure, and most Jews remained enrolled in the urban *meshchanstvo* even though they often lived in the country. In the 1840s, Nicholas's bureaucrats devised a plan to encourage movement into the ranks of the agricultural colonist and the manufacturer by taking punitive action against the rural Jewish *meshchanstvo*. All Jews were to be divided into categories of 'useful' and 'non-useful', and the latter, the self-same rural *meshchanstvo*, were to be sternly punished if at the end of five years they had not entered a 'useful' occupation and left the countryside.[22] Fortunately for the Jews, even Nicholas's administrators paused before the daunting task of classification and removal, and its execution was lost in the turmoil of the Crimean War. The concept of dividing Jews into 'good' and 'bad' was not lost, however, and it resurfaced in the next reign, albeit with a totally different emphasis.

One final problem involving the legal status of the Jews can be traced to the reign of Nicholas I. This period witnessed the first comprehensive codification of laws for the modern Russian Empire, the *Svod zakonov*, published in 1835. Volume 10 of this code, an explication of the legal standing of each of Russia's four estates, introduced a legal definition of the Jews which has been noted by most observers but never satisfactorily explained.[23] Yet this innovation bears directly on the long-standing debate as to whether Russia's legal treatment of the Jews was or was not anomalous. The first scholars of the problem emphasized the anomaly of legal treatment of the Jews, pointing to a host of special restrictions and unique enactments.[24] In his recent study of the reign of Nicholas I, Michael Stanislawski has rejected this characterization. He argues that 'at no time in this period did policy toward the Jews depart from the framework and pattern of overall governmental activity'. For Stanislawski, the departure

Doklad po voprosu o merakh otnositel'no obrazovaniya evreev (St Petersburg, n.d.), a report prepared for the Pahlen Commission.

[22] Stanislawski, *Nicholas I and the Jews*, pp. 155–60.

[23] *Svod zakonov Rossiiskoi imperii*, x. *Zakony o sostoyaniyakh* (St Petersburg, 1835), pt. 6, ch. 1, art. 713.

[24] I. G. Orshanskii, *Russkoe zakonodatel'stvo o evreyakh* (St Petersburg, 1877), 1–5.

from general norms occurred 'only one generation later, when the rules that had determined the governing of the empire for several centuries ceased to apply, and the caprices of prejudice—and violence—filled the vacuum'.[25] In the main, Stanislawski is correct, but he neglects an important piece of contrary evidence, namely, the classification of the Jews as 'aliens' (*inorodtsy*) in the 1835 *Svod*, where it remained through each successive revision of the code.

In popular parlance, an *inorodets* was any non-Slavic Russian subject, such as a Finn, a German, an Armenian, etc. In the first half of the nineteenth century, however, a very precise legal definition was established. As Russia began to penetrate and colonize Siberia and Central Asia, she brought under her control small and scattered groups of native peoples, such as the Kalmucks, the Kirghiz, and the Samoyeds. These people were often migratory or even nomadic, and were adherents of various animistic-shamanistic religions. As Russians began to encroach on the hunting-grounds and areas of settlement of these groups, central government saw the need to extend to them special legal protection, since their style of life made much of the fundamental law of the empire inappropriate for them. As early as 1822 all *inorodtsy* were divided into three categories of settled, migratory, and nomadic, and these divisions served as guidelines for their subordination to Russian administration and civil law. The anomaly of the Jews' inclusion in this legal category, which occurred in 1835, is obvious. Indeed, it would be accurate to call the Jews an anomaly among the *inorodtsy*, so thoroughly did they fail to conform to the general characteristics of this group.

This latter point may be affirmed through a survey of the legal position of the *inorodtsy*. By definition, it was a status conferred by race, since *inorodtsy* who converted from paganism to Christianity, with their subsequent alienation from their community, retained all their rights and privileges as *inorodtsy*. The Jew who converted to Christianity, however, ceased to be a Jew in any legal sense; he received a temporary status loaded with special privileges, and he was eventually subsumed into the *soslovie* of his choice.

The most important privileges of the *inorodtsy* involved

---

[25] Stanislawski, *Nicholas I and the Jews*, p. 5.

extensive self-government through their tribal chieftains. In addition, migratory and nomadic *inorodtsy* were freed from military service, since their cultural level was too low and their style of life was too remote from the requirements of military discipline.[26] Jews, on the contrary, had recently been deprived of their special prerogatives of self-government, and the government was fighting a vigorous battle to ensure that they served in the army in equal measure to the rest of the population. Even in their place of residence, Jews were divided from all other *inorodtsy*. There were no other *inorodtsy* within the Pale, except for a few in the Caucasus, and Jews were generally forbidden to live in those areas of Siberia and Central Asia where most other *inorodtsy* were to be found.

In short, nothing was to be gained, from a legal point of view, by including the Jews in a category for which they were quite inappropriate. We are left to guess at the underlying motives for this move. It is possible that the Jews were thought of as *inorodtsy* because of their particular status as a group placed in a special position by rank (*sostoyanie*) and administration, this being the basic legal definition of the *inorodtsy*. But their inclusion occurred at the very moment when the Russian state was attempting to remove this special status through the promotion of 'merging'. Perhaps their inclusion with people 'of a low cultural level' was a studied insult, akin to the legal classification of Judaism as a 'false religion'.[27] Certainly the Russian government scorned the Jewish masses, seeing them as isolated and fanatical. Nevertheless, this curious categorization did little to clarify—and much to obscure—the intended position of Jews within the ranks of Russian society. But it was maintained. Journals of the Council of Ministers indicate that the intricacies of the Jewish question were discussed side by side with resettlement programmes for migratory Kirghiz, land rights for Bashkirs, and the tax responsibilities of the Yukagirs.[28]

The closest Russia ever came to 'Jewish emancipation' in either a European or even a Russian sense was in the reign of Alexander

---

[26] *Novyi entsiklopedicheskii slovar'*, xiii (St Petersburg, 1911), 484–8; A. D. Gradovskii, *Sobranie sochinenii*, vii (St Petersburg, 1907), 355–62.

[27] *Obzor nyne deistvuyushchikh isklyuchitel'nykh zakonov o evreyakh* (St Petersburg, 1883), 1.

[28] Komitet Ministrov, *Istoricheskii obzor deyatel'nosti Komiteta Ministrov*, v (St Petersburg, 1902), 74–6.

II (1855–81). This was the 'era of the great reforms', when the revisionary impulse touched all sides of Russian life, including the Jewish question. The agenda for reform in the status of the Jews was set forth in a charge given by the Tsar to a committee headed by Count P. D. Kiselev: to 'review all the existing resolutions concerning the Jews with the objective of bringing them into agreement with the general views of merging [*sliyanie*] this people with the native population, insofar as the moral position of the Jews may permit it . . .'.[29] Only in part did this declaration represent a new course, for it preserved, although with a different emphasis, the Nicholine 'assortment' of the Jews. The essential difference was that instead of punishing 'harmful' Jews, the new regime attempted to reward 'good' Jews. This inaugurated the period which the great Russian-Jewish historian Simon Dubnow sarcastically called 'homoeopathic emancipation'.[30]

Despite Dubnow's scorn, the Jewish reforms of Alexander II were significant. Almost at once, the ruthless military recruitment was relaxed. More important in the long run was the relaxation of the Pale restrictions for a widening circle of 'productive' Jews. Jewish members of the first merchant guild were granted free settlement in 1859, a privilege which was progressively extended to Jews with a university degree (1861), and to Jewish craftsmen, mechanics, and craft-guild members (1865).[31] This latter measure, which took place only after long and heated debate, was of great potential significance. While it did not touch the vast mass of Jews, it none the less offered an escape for a significant minority. It thus remains one of the great unanswered questions of Russian-Jewish history why more eligible Jews did not avail themselves of the privilege. Contemporaries were certainly aware that no great movement took place, and Judaeophobes even used it as an argument against any further widening of the Pale. Jews were reluctant to leave the Pale, they claimed, because it was so easy to exploit the Christian population within it, and because departure would disrupt Jewish clannishness and isolation. Partisans of the Jews, on the other hand, emphasized the

---

[29] Yu. I. Gessen, 'Aleksandr I', *Evreiskaya entsiklopediya*, i (St Petersburg, 1913), 812.

[30] Dubnow, *History*, ii. 157.

[31] *PSZ* 2, xxxiv, no. 34248 (16 Mar. 1859); xxxvi, no. 37684 (27 Nov. 1861); xl, no. 42264 (28 June 1865).

obstacles placed in their path by those local administrators and corrupt police who had to register the passport of a departing Jew.[32]

Among other reforms, Polish Jews were permitted free transit into the Russian Pale, from which they had hitherto been loosely barred. Of greater significance still, the Russian Crown assented to a true emancipation within the wider empire: the granting of civil and political rights to Polish Jewry in 1862 by the ill-fated reform movement of the Marquis Aleksander Wielopolski.[33] Even when the rights of the Poles themselves were curtailed in the aftermath of the Polish revolt of 1863, the Jews of Poland retained theirs. While measures in Russia proper did not go as far as this, in 1861 Jews with a university degree were permitted to enter state service.[34] Restrictions on Jewish electoral participation in municipal self-government had been retained since the days of Nicholas, but when the *zemstvo* system of local government was implemented in 1864, no restrictions whatsoever were placed on Jewish participation. (It should be noted, however, that the *zemstvo* system was not originally extended to most of the provinces which constituted the Pale, for fear that they would be dominated by Polish landlords. Thus, few Jews lived in areas that were served by *zemstva*.) While these reforms applied largely to élites within the Jewish population, they were significant in that as Russia evolved more modern political institutions, Jews were increasingly permitted to participate in them. Modernization and emancipation appeared to go hand in hand, as in the classic European model.

Even the semi-emancipation of the 1860s provoked a backlash, and it was never completed; some restrictions either remained or were introduced. Thus, Jews were briefly permitted to own or to lease rural land within the Pale, but in the aftermath of the Polish revolt, this right was rescinded.[35] (The motive of this measure was political: the Russian government attempted to Russify the Russo-Polish borderlands by gradually removing the existing Polish landowning class. The Jews were regarded as the

[32] For an editorial discussion of this problem, see *Den': Organ russkikh evreev*, 22 (29 May 1870).
[33] See A. Eisenbach, *Kwestia rownouprawnienia Zydow w Krolestwie Polskim* (Warsaw, 1972).
[34] *PSZ* 2, xxxvi, no. 37684 (27 Nov. 1861).
[35] Ibid. xxxix, no. 40656 (5 Mar. 1864).

economic allies of the Poles in the workings of the semi-feudal
economy.) In 1870, when a new municipal statute was drafted,
the old restrictions confining Jews to no more than one-third of
the total number of aldermen, and barring them completely from
the post of mayor, were retained, to prevent the Russian element
falling 'under the domination of Judaism'.[36] No special Jewish
provisions were included when the law governing universal
military service was implemented in 1874, but as the regime
became convinced that the Jews were evading service, a wide
variety of punitive measures were introduced.[37] The extensions of
rights to Jews, however limited, was increasingly condemned by
the emergent periodical press, led by the Slavophile publications
of Ivan Aksakov, and the provincial newspapers *Kievlyanin*
(Kiev), *Vilenskii vestnik* (Vilna), and *Novorossiiskii telegraf*
(Odessa).[38]

The reign of Alexander III (1881–94) has been called the 'era
of the counter-reforms' because of the leadership's ideological
commitment to undoing the liberal reforms of Alexander II. The
Jews shared the effects of this anti-liberal trend, although in their
case the motivation was not merely ideological but pragmatic as
well. Within two months of the assassination of Alexander II by
the terrorists of *Narodnaya volya*, the Pale of Settlement was
rocked by the outbreak of a terrifying wave of pogroms. The
violence engulfed major urban centres like Kiev and Odessa, as
well as more than a hundred villages, *shtetls*, and agricultural
colonies. The pogroms horrified the new regime, especially because they were thought at first to be the work of revolutionaries.
Subsequent investigations failed to reveal a significant terrorist
role, and the government, led by the Minister of the Interior,
N. P. Ignat'ev, sought other causes. Eventually the blame was
placed on the Jews themselves; their 'exploitation' of the native
population had finally produced a violent retribution. This was a
charge which had been gestating in public opinion since the 1860s
and which now provided a plausible and integral explanation for

---

[36] Dubnow, *History*, ii. 198–9.

[37] See Y. Slutsky, 'The Russian Military Service Act (1874) and the Jews',
Heaver, 21 (1975), 3–19 (in Hebrew).

[38] J. D. Klier, 'The Jewish Question in the Reform-Era Russian Press, 1855–
1865', *Russian Review*, 29/3 (July 1980), 301–20; id., '*Kievlianin* and the Jews: A
Decade of Disillusionment, 1864–1873', *Harvard Ukrainian Studies*, 1 (Mar. 1981),
81–101.

confusing events, as well as an agenda for preventive measures. Instead of 'merging' the Jews with the wider Christian community, the state must endeavour to protect Gentiles from the myriad forms of Jewish exploitation. Such a goal was best secured by isolating and restricting the Jews, and by undoing the hesitant moves towards emancipation that had been made in the previous reign.

Ignat'ev made the Jewish question his own, and launched a variety of initiatives. On 22 August 1881 he secured the Tsar's authorization to convoke commissions in all the provinces of the Pale; their aim was to identify the harmful economic activities of the Jews and to suggest measures for control. Even before the commissions had met and had made any recommendations to the central government, Ignat'ev was at work on restrictive legislation. He operated through a committee which was appointed on 19 October 1881 to review the reports of the provincial commissions, but he ordered it to draft restrictive legislation even before the reports had been received. The committee, headed by the Deputy Minister of the Interior, D. V. Gotovtsev, proposed legislation which encompassed virtually every restrictive measure devised by Judaeophobe publicists over the previous two decades. Its most important provisions would have stopped all movement of Jews from the Pale to the Russian interior, even if they possessed the necessary qualifications; those resident outside the Pale, but not, in the opinion of the local administration, pursuing their legitimate occupation, were to be returned to the Pale; local communities were to be authorized to expel Jews whom they considered 'harmful'. In addition, restrictions were to be placed on Jewish professional rights, on trade and commerce, and on the lease and purchase of land within the Pale. Special norms were to be set for Jewish participation in municipal self-government, *zemstvo* assemblies, and lower and middle schools.

Some of Gotovtsev's proposals were temporary administrative measures, while others envisaged fundamental revisions in the existing legal system for Jews. For the moment, Ignat'ev distilled four temporary rules which he wished to introduce immediately in order to reduce the friction between Christians and Jews which might lead to pogroms: Jews would not be allowed to live anywhere in the Pale except in the towns and *shtetls*, a measure which implied the resettlement of thousands of Jews from their rural homes; Jews were to be forbidden to lease or buy land, or to build homes outside the towns and *shtetls* of the Pale; Jews were to be banned from trading in alcohol in the countryside.[39]

Whatever the effect of these measures in preventing pogroms, they promised economic ruination for many Jews. The Council of Ministers recognized this fact and severely criticized Ignat'ev's proposal when it was introduced for discussion. Ignat'ev's programme was reduced to a prohibition against further settlement of Jews outside the towns and *shtetls* of the Pale, thus creating a 'Pale within the Pale', and Jews in the Pale were forbidden to purchase—but not to lease—land outside the towns and *shtetls*. Restrictions were placed on trade by Jews on Sundays and on Christian holidays. As is evident, the resultant compromise, while restrictive, nowhere near approached the disabilities envisaged by Ignat'ev.[40] The proposals were not submitted to the State Council for incorporation into statutory law, but instead were promulgated as 'Provisional Regulations' on 3 May 1882, becoming known universally as the 'May Laws'. The May Laws were designed to reduce the immediate risk of pogroms, and to operate only until a more comprehensive legal codex for the Jews was devised. A new code was to be made by the High Commission for the Revision of the Existing Laws Pertaining to the Jews, created by the Council of Ministers on 4 February 1883, and ultimately chaired by the former Minister of Justice, K. I. Pahlen. It was to this body that the reports of the provincial commissions, plus countless other papers, both solicited and unsolicited, were submitted during the five years of its deliberations.[41]

Despite the unpromising conditions of political reaction in which the Pahlen Commission was created and operated, some specialists have suggested that it might actually have accomplished something like the emancipation of Russian Jewry, especially through the relaxation of the Pale of Settlement.[42] The provincial commissions invariably had minorities—and sometimes even majorities—in favour of abolishing the Pale; members of the

---

[39] Yu. I Gessen, 'Graf N. P. Ignat'ev i "Vremennyya pravila" o evreyakh 3 maya 1882 goda', *Pravo*, 30 (1908), cols. 1631–7.

[40] Ibid. 31 (1908), cols. 1679–84.

[41] Ibid., col. 1685.

[42] I. M. Aronson, 'The Prospects for the Emancipation of Russian Jewry during the 1880s', *Slavonic and East European Review*, 60/3 (July 1977), 348–69.

Pahlen Commission itself, as well as a number of state officials, argued for this and other reforms.[43] By the time the report of the Pahlen Commission was completed, however, a thoroughly Judaeophobic spirit possessed the government, and its recommendations were totally ignored.

As a consequence, no comprehensive code ever replaced the provisional regulations, which endured to the end of the tsarist regime. They were soon joined by a plethora of other restrictions, accomplishing piecemeal what Gotovtsev had sought to achieve in one fell swoop. Administrative decrees, many of them promulgated through secret circulars, became the accepted method for dealing with the Jews, an obvious retreat from previous attempts to devise a body of integral and coherent law. Caprice now replaced precedent and legal tradition.

It should be noted, however, that the Judaeophobic administrative policies under Alexander III were only part of a wider political reaction. The imposition of quotas, the *numerus clausus*, on Jewish pupils in secondary schools and universities occurred alongside the efforts of the Ministry of Education to discourage schooling for the 'wrong sort' of people, exemplified by I. D. Delyanov's notorious 'circular on cooks' children'.[44] Similarly, restrictions on the admission of Jews to the Russian Bar, implemented in 1889, were part of a wider interdiction on non-Christian attorneys in general. The new *zemstvo* law of 1890 which denied Jews any participation in these organizations was primarily designed to destroy the vestiges of *zemstvo* independence. Some measures, none the less, were directed specifically against the Jews, especially the imposition (through secret circulars) of still greater residence restrictions within and without the Pale. The most celebrated example of this was the expulsion of most of the Jewish population of Moscow on the first day of Passover 1891.[45]

The reign of Nicholas II (1894–1917) began on the same reactionary path that had been mapped out by his father, and was highlighted by the new Tsar's attack on the 'senseless dreams' of

[43] I. M. Aronson, 'Russian Bureaucratic Attitudes toward Jews, 1881–1894', Ph.D. thesis (Northwestern University, 1973).

[44] P. L. Alston, *Education and the State in Tsarist Russia* (Stanford, 1969), 130–9.

[45] See the special issue of *Heaver*, 18 (1971), devoted to this subject.

would-be political reformers. The initial decade of Nicholas's rule was free of dramatic legal innovations regarding the Jews; the restrictive provisions of the May Laws and supplementary administrative measures were found to be sufficient. In all other respects the position of the Jews deteriorated, a situation exemplified by the outbreak of lethal pogroms in Kishinev and Gomel in 1903.

The Revolution of 1905 seemed to promise an improvement in the Jews' legal position, but this ultimately proved to be a false emancipation. In a sense, the assurances inherent in the Imperial Manifesto of 17 October 1905, wrung from the Tsar by revolutionary events, should have equalized the legal situation of the Jews with the rest of the population. It committed the government 'to grant the population the unshakeable foundations of civic freedom based on the principles of real personal inviolability, freedom of conscience, speech, assembly, and union'. Also speaking to the Jews was the report of Count Sergei Witte, sanctioned by the Tsar on the same day, which called for 'the work of equalizing all the Russian citizens, without distinction of religion and nationality, before the law', and a 'firm tendency toward the elimination of extraordinary regulations'.[46] One of the first political acts of the new constitutional monarchy also augured well for the Jews: they were permitted unrestricted participation in elections to the new State Duma, and in fact managed to elect twelve co-religionists to the First Duma.[47]

Under these new conditions the aspirations of Russian Jewry began to change as well; they rejected both piecemeal reform and the emancipation of privileged élites within the Jewish population. Even before the October Manifesto, six thousand Jews signed the Declaration of Jewish Citizens, which said, in part:

We expect to secure civil equality not because it would make the Jews more useful citizens and benefit others. Nor do we look forward to equality as a reward for the blood our brothers are shedding on the Manchurian fields, just as our brothers had shed their blood in former

[46] Both these documents are reprinted in translation in H. D. Mehlinger and J. W. Thompson, *Count Witte and the Tsarist Government in the 1905 Revolution* (Bloomington and London, 1972), 331–5.

[47] S. Harcave, 'The Jews and the First Russian National Election', *American Slavic and East European Review*, 9/1 (1950), 33–41.

wars. We do not even demand civil equality because of our centuries-old residence in lands which now form part of the Russian Empire. We demand civil equality and equal submission to general laws as men who, despite everything, are conscious of their human dignity, and as conscientious citizens of a modern state. We do not expect these rights to be bestowed upon us as an act of grace and magnanimity or because of some political expediency, but rather as a matter of honor and justice.[48]

Already, in March 1905, a League for the Attainment of Full Rights for the Jewish People of Russia had been founded in Vilna. It called for 'the realization in full measure of civil, political and national rights for the Jewish people'.[49] The call for national rights made this programme broader still, and revealed the significant growth of a Jewish national consciousness within the Russian Empire, exemplified by the strength of various forms of Zionism. But not only Jews benefited from the emergence of organized political life in Russia. Right-wing groups began to appear as well, and Judaeophobia became an integral ideological component of such organizations as the Union of the Russian People.

Just as the First Duma proved a disappointment to those liberals who had seen it as a 'Russian Estates-General' which would soon turn into a constituent assembly, or at least an equal partner of the tsar in the operation of a true constitutional monarchy, so too its activities proved disillusioning for partisans of the final emancipation of Russian Jewry. The First Duma was dominated by the Constitutional Democrats, for whom a radical revision of the Jewish question was a well-publicized electoral plank. Interpellations to the government from its members on the responsibility of local officials for recent pogroms were one factor in the Tsar's decision to abrogate the Duma after only seventy days.[50] The Second Duma, equally truculent, also failed to advance the agenda of Jewish rights. The Third and Fourth Dumas, the result of a revised electoral system, were dominated by centrist–right coalitions, which had no commitment to improving the lot of the Jews. Even the Constitutional Democrats,

[48] Baron, *Russian Jew*, p. 59.
[49] Harcave, 'Jews and National Election', pp. 33–4.
[50] Baron, *Russian Jew*, p. 60.

in the changed political surroundings, proved that their loyalty to emancipation was questionable.[51]

The most energetic intervention for the Jews during the Duma monarchy ultimately came from the state bureaucracy, in the person of the Chairman of the Council of Ministers, P. A. Stolypin. In correspondence with the Tsar, Stolypin conceded that the Jews could claim full civil rights purely on the basis of the October Manifesto. The Duma had not accomplished this through legislation, and the government might be able to forestall complete equality by making partial improvements in Jewish rights. Stolypin's proposed reform of 1906, therefore, was a cautious and incomplete one. It failed significantly to enlarge the Pale, and maintained the restriction on Jews' purchase of land in rural areas of the Pale. It largely comprised the relaxation of numerous petty restrictions on Jewish trade and commerce. Even this half-hearted effort failed, rejected by the Tsar at the urging of an 'inner voice'.[52] Jewish disabilities actually increased under Stolypin through their exclusion from wider reforms. When the zemstvo system of local government was finally extended to the western provinces which made up most of the Pale, Jews were specifically excluded from any participation.[53]

The outbreak of the war in 1914 led eventually to the de facto abolition of the Pale as thousands of Jews were evacuated to the east from combat areas within it. This measure was carried out with extreme reluctance, and was accompanied by rhetoric impugning the loyalty and patriotism of Russian Jews.[54] In any event, by this time the days of the Judaeophobic tsarist regime were numbered: Nicholas II abdicated on 2 March 1917, in the face of revolutionary unrest. Established in the aftermath of his abdication, the Provisional Government moved quickly to destroy the old order. On 9 March 1917 the Minister of Justice was designated to devise a bill abolishing all national and

---

[51] See M. F. Hamm, 'Liberalism and the Jewish Question: The Progressive Bloc', Russian Review, 31/2 (Apr. 1972), 163–72.

[52] M. S. Conroy, Peter Arkad'evich Stolypin: Practical Politics in Late Tsarist Russia (Boulder, 1976), 48–51.

[53] G. A. Hosking, The Russian Constitutional Experiment: Government and Duma, 1907–1914 (Cambridge, 1973), 122.

[54] H. Rogger, 'Government, Jews, Peasants and Land in Post-Emancipation Russia', Cahiers du monde russe et soviétique, 17/1 (1976), 5–6.

religious restrictions.[55] The appropriate measure—in effect, the bill of emancipation for Russian Jewry—was promulgated on 20 March 1917. Essentially it abolished all restrictive legislation based on adherence to a particular religious denomination or sect, or nationality. Thus, however one chose to regard the Jews—as adherents of a religious confession, Judaism, or as members of a distinct national group—they were included. Since the Provisional Government had also committed itself to the dismantling of the *soslovie* system, this ensured the equality of Jews with all other Russian citizens.[56] As a final epitaph for Jewish disabilities, the government published a supplement to the law of 20 March, a list of 140 distinct laws which had applied to the Jews at the end of the old regime.[57]

Complete Jewish emancipation, on the model of Western Europe, was attainable in Russia only with the modernization of the Russian state itself, and was accomplished only with the total collapse of the old regime. The dilemmas of Jewish existence in the Russian state were not instantaneously resolved on 20 March 1917; basic questions tied up with emergent Jewish nationalism remained to be confronted. But liberals, socialists, and Zionists alike could relish the freedom which they now enjoyed—if only for the moment—to mould their own particular visions of the Jewish future in Russia.

Efforts have been made by virtually all historians of the legal status of Russian Jewry to identify a small number of basic principles, such as religious antipathy or economic pragmatism, upon which Russian legislation was based. As this survey has suggested, the actual circumstances giving rise to legal dicta were much more complex, and cannot be removed from a broader social-political context. It would not be inappropriate to apply to Russia the observation frequently made apropos of Europe by Jewish publicists in the nineteenth century, that the treatment of the Jews in a given country was a reflection of that nation's cultural level. Russian monarchs intent on internal reform and 'modernization' in all its guises—Catherine II, Alexander I, and

[55] R. P. Browder and A. F. Kerensky (eds.), *The Russian Provisional Government, 1917: Documents* (Stanford, 1961), i. 210.
[56] Ibid. 215.
[57] A. A. Gol'denveizer, 'Pravovoe polozhenie evreev v Rossii', *Kniga o russkom evreistve* (New York, 1960), 111.

Alexander II—initially brought the Jews under the rubric of reform, and embarked upon experiments to integrate them more fully into the Russian state system, from both a social and a legal point of view. These well-intentioned experiments invariably failed, because they derived from abstract views of the Jews as 'urban commercial elements', or 'unproductive exploiters', or as a dichotomous group of 'good and bad subjects'. These views were as much the result of wishful thinking or prejudice as they were of objective reality. Reforms rooted in such caricatures could not but fail, and failure produced disillusionment and counter-reform. Conservative and reactionary rulers such as Nicholas I, Alexander III, and Nicholas II also responded to stereotypes, but as a justification for repression, not reform. Repression, however, proved no better a remedy for the intricacies of the Jewish question than reformist optimism had done. In short, the legislative treatment of Russian Jewry by tsarism was a consistent failure, with serious implications for the fate of a multinational, multi-ethnic state.

Workers and Civil Rights in Tsarist Russia, 1899–1917

S. A. SMITH

I T is customary in western historiography to portray the Russian working class under the tsarist regime as one with little time for the niceties of civil liberties; a class more concerned with bread-and-butter issues than with issues of political rights; a class more interested in the rights of workers as a collective than with the rights of the individual citizen; a class which equated the rule of law with rule by the privileged classes; a class which preferred 'soviet' democracy to 'bourgeois' democracy. There is an important element of truth in this stereotype, and it is not the purpose of this essay to try to overturn it, but rather to challenge it as being too monolithic and undifferentiated. The essay sets out firstly to show that Russian workers regularly raised demands for civil and political rights after 1899, especially during the 1905 Revolution, making a not insignificant contribution to the battle for civil and political rights in tsarist Russia. Secondly, it seeks to explore how workers perceived the issue of civil and political rights in relation to their wider struggles and aspirations, and, without attempting a comprehensive account of the changing dimensions of labour protest, to show how concern for civil rights fitted into the evolving configuration of working-class consciousness. Thirdly, it tries to point to certain limitations inherent in working-class conceptions of civil rights, in the hope of shedding some light on why the Bolsheviks were so quick to dismantle the frail structure of civil rights established after the February Revolution.

In the West, we tend to associate concern for civil and political rights with liberal political movements. By the turn of the

* I wish to thank Linda Edmondson, Chris Ward, and Reginald Zelnik for their valuable comments on an earlier draft of this essay. I also wish to thank participants in the conference on civil rights in Russia before 1917 for their comments and suggestions.

century, Russian liberalism had developed into a robust force on
the radical wing of politics, but one conspicuous for its failure to
create a significant constituency among the popular masses.[1]
Despite limited co-operation between labour and the liberation
movement between 1903 and 1905, the workers' movement
which emerged from the 1905 Revolution was, to a large extent,
insulated from liberal influence—colonized by socialists of
various hues. Paradoxically, it was Marxists who were chiefly
responsible for fostering an awareness of civil liberties within the
nascent labour movement.[2]

Marx himself had recognized the importance of both the rights
of political participation and the corporate civil rights of labour
(the right to strike, to form trade unions, etc.). He was, however,
implacably hostile to the 'rights of man', which he saw as
intrinsically individualistic, separating person from person and
the individual from the community,[3] or, to use the felicitous
phrase of Andrzej Walicki, as 'boundary markers which separate
competing egos'.[4] Marx's ideal of freedom was not the 'negative'
one of classical western liberalism, but rather a positive ideal
which saw freedom as residing in man's ability to exercise
conscious rational control over the natural and social environment.[5] Yet Marx's own thinking was not to become the
orthodoxy of the Second International. Neither Kautsky nor
Hilferding, for example, believed that socialism would destroy
the individual rights embodied in the democratic institutions of
bourgeois society,[6] and civil rights demands became well

---

[1] G. Fischer, *Russian Liberalism from Gentry to Intelligentsia* (Cambridge,
Mass., 1958); K. Fröhlich, *The Emergence of Russian Constitutionalism, 1900–04*
(The Hague, 1981), 239.

[2] Marxists were, of course, by no means the first among the intelligentsia to raise
issues of civil liberties. The Slavophiles, for example, whilst eschewing political rights
and upholding autocracy, nevertheless advocated freedom of conscience, speech, and
the press as being essential to 'freedom of the spirit'. And later, *Narodnaya volya*
raised the standard of civil rights whilst pursuing its programme of terror. See N. V.
Riasanovsky, *Russia and the West in the Teachings of the Slavophiles* (Cambridge,
Mass., 1952), 141; F. Venturi, *Roots of Revolution* (Chicago, 1960), 677–8.

[3] K. Marx, 'On the Jewish Question', in *Karl Marx: Early Writings*, ed. T.
Bottomore (London, 1963), 26.

[4] A. Walicki, 'Marx and Freedom', *New York Review of Books*, 30/18 (24 Nov.
1983).

[5] I. Berlin, 'Two Concepts of Liberty', in *Four Essays on Liberty* (Oxford, 1964).

[6] L. Kolakowski, 'Marxism and Human Rights', *Daedalus*, 12/4 (1983), 81–92;
S. Lukes, 'Can a Marxist Believe in Human Rights?', *Praxis International*, 1/4
(1983), 335.

entrenched in the minimum programmes of the major parties affiliated to the International. The SPD in Germany, for example, fought valiantly for civil and political rights and equality before the law, though not always without a certain ambivalence.[7]

The Russian Social Democrats (SDs) considered the achievement of civil and political rights to be the main feature of the bourgeois revolution which Russia was fated to undergo before she was ready for socialism. As is well known, after 1903 the Menshevik and Bolshevik factions differed in their prognoses regarding the bourgeois revolution. The Mensheviks believed that the struggle for civil rights and a democratic republic provided a real basis for unity with the liberals during the first phase of the revolution, whereas the Bolsheviks judged the liberals to have neither the will nor the strength to carry through the overthrow of the autocracy; this could come about only via an alliance of the proletariat and the peasantry. Both factions, however, tended to the view that civil and political rights were not so much ends in themselves as means necessary to the proletariat to wage the struggle for socialism.[8] At the second congress of the SDs in 1903, V. E. Mandel'burg, later a Menshevik deputy to the Second Duma, argued forcefully that 'all democratic principles must be subordinate to the exclusive advantage of our party'.[9] And G. Plekhanov concurred in the following famous lines:

Every democratic principle must be considered not by itself, abstractly, but in relation to what may be called the fundamental principle of democracy, namely *salus populi suprema lex*. Translated into the language of the revolutionary, this means that the success of the revolution is the highest law. And if the success of the revolution demanded a temporary limitation of the working of this or that democratic principle, then it would be criminal to refrain from such a limitation.[10]

---

[7] G. Roth, *The Social Democrats in Imperial Germany* (Totowa, NJ, 1963), 129–35; A. Hall, *Scandal, Sensation and Social Democracy: The SPD Press and Wilhelmine Germany, 1890–1914* (Cambridge, 1977), ch. 2.

[8] J. L. H. Keep, *The Rise of Social Democracy in Russia* (Oxford, 1963), 22.

[9] *Vtoroi s"ezd RSDRP* (Moscow, 1959), 181.

[10] Ibid. 181–2. Cf. Herzen: 'All those maxims such as "Salus populi suprema lex, pereat mundus et fiat justitia" have about them the strong smell of burnt flesh, blood,

At this stage, there were not many SDs who did not believe that socialism would guarantee, and even extend, 'bourgeois' freedoms, but it is salutary to recall how short a time it took after the overthrow of the autocracy before first Kerenskii and then Lenin invoked the 'salvation of the revolution' as the justification for the suppression of civil liberties.[11]

Among the early SDs, there was no unanimity concerning the tactical appropriateness of raising demands for civil and political rights within the workers' milieu. During the 'agitation period' of the mid-1890s, the SDs concentrated on workers' economic struggles and avoided raising political demands, but by the late 1890s, there is evidence that some circles had come to the conclusion that even modest economic improvements were impossible without the securing of basic political freedoms.[12] From 1897, May Day celebrations became the main occasion on which SDs raised demands for civil and political rights.[13] In that year the Union of Russian Social Democrats put out a leaflet which spelt out the importance of civil rights in a straightforward fashion:

Freedom of speech and assembly, so that we have the possibility publicly and collectively to discuss our affairs; freedom to strike so that we are not subject to every kind of persecution, arrest or exile for demanding higher wages; freedom of coalition so that we can form mutual-aid funds in the event of strikes, collectively resolve various

inquisition, torture, and of the "triumph of order".' (A. I. Gertsen, 'S togo berega', in *Sobranie sochinenii v tridtsati tomakh*, vi (Moscow, 1955), 140.

[11] Unfortunately, space does not permit a consideration of the contribution of the Socialist Revolutionaries (SRs) towards shaping working-class perceptions of civil rights. Judging from their first congress in January 1906, the SRs showed themselves more committed to the absolute value of civil and political liberties than the SDs did. Roslavlev declared: 'We must put the demands for political freedoms at the very beginning of our programme. This is required by our world-view, in which freedom of the person plays an absolutely essential role. Without this freedom we cannot conceive of a socialist system.' *Protokoly pervogo s"ezda partii sotsialistov-revolyutsionerov, 1905–06*, ed. M. Perrie (Millwood, NY, 1983), 163–4. See also M. Hildermeier, *Die Sozialrevolutionäre Partei Russlands: Agrarsozialismus und Modernisierung im Zarenreich, 1900–14* (Cologne, 1978), 101.

[12] The Social Democrats did not, of course, suddenly 'discover' the importance of political freedoms. Back in 1885, for example, D. G. Blagoev's Marxist study circle in St Petersburg had emphasized the importance of this issue: *Rabochee dvizhenie v Rossii v XIX veke*, iii. *1890–4*, pt. 2 (Moscow, 1952), 393–4.

[13] V. Nevskii, 'Materialy k istorii Pervogo maya v Rossii', *Krasnaya letopis'*, 4 (1922), 261.

problems concerning working life, and settle disputes with the employers.[14]

The following year a small group of workers took part in a demonstration organized by the St Petersburg Union of Struggle for the Emancipation of the Working Class, whose leaflet called for: freedom to strike; freedom of speech, the press, assembly, and association; freedom of conscience and religion; equal rights for all nationalities; an elected parliament; and a statutory eight-hour day.[15] In 1899, however, the same organization dropped all political demands from its May Day propaganda, whereas socialist circles in Ekaterinoslav and Kiev declared the struggle for civil rights to be the 'chief aim' of the working class.[16]

It is difficult to estimate the effect of this propaganda upon workers as a whole.[17] An examination of strikes shows that their demands were overwhelmingly 'economic', concerned with the amelioration of immediate working conditions. It was quite exceptional for strikers to demand the right to strike and freedom of assembly, as they did at the Pal' and Maxwell cotton-mills in the capital in December 1898.[18] Yet whilst the vast majority of strikes displayed an indifference to political issues, one should remember that individual strikes were hardly an appropriate vehicle for the accomplishment of political objectives. Strikers tend to demand what they believe they can get from their employers, and there was little that an individual Russian employer could do in the 1890s to effect a democratization of the political order.

It was not until 1900 that there was a celebration of May Day on anything like a national scale. In the capital, eighteen 'workers' circles' issued a leaflet which proclaimed 'Down with the Autocracy!' and demanded 'the right to form unions and to hold meetings; the right to believe and think as we wish, and to

---

[14] *Rabochee dvizhenie v Rossii v XIX veke*, iv. *1895–97*, pt. 1 (Moscow, 1961), 526–30.

[15] Ibid. iv. *1898–1900*, pt. 2 (Moscow, 1963), 52.

[16] Ibid. 343, 375–6.

[17] Cf. R. Pipes, *Social Democracy and the St Petersburg Labour Movement, 1885–1897* (Cambridge, Mass., 1963); and A. Wildman, *The Making of a Workers' Revolution* (Chicago, 1967).

[18] D. Kol'tsov, 'Rabochee dvizhenie v 1890–1904 gg.', in *Obshchestvennoe dvizhenie v Rossii v nachale XX-ago veka*, i (St Petersburg, 1909), 203.

speak and write as we think; an eight-hour day'.[19] In 1901 workers and students joined forces in several cities, and on May Day of the following year, ten thousand took to the streets of Baku, resulting in many arrests. The *maevki* of 1903, which took place in a record twelve industrial centres, called for a democratic republic and full civil liberties; but the radicalism of the slogans belied the numerical weakness of the movement.[20] Between 1901 and 1904—the so-called 'demonstration period'—as many as half a million workers may have gone on strike, but most remained unaffected by the antipathy to the government which gripped the political layer.[21] Even among the latter, not all those who called loudly for civil and political rights believed that this necessitated the violent demise of the autocracy.

By the autumn of 1904 there were huge strikes in Poland, the Baltic, and the Caucasus which coincided with the burgeoning of the liberation movement with its objectives of a constitutional regime, a constituent assembly, and universal suffrage—to be achieved by 'pressure from below'.[22] In Odessa, Nizhnii Novgorod, Saratov, Smolensk, Kharkov, and Ekaterinoslav, workers responded to the liberation movement by calling for an end to the Russo-Japanese war, and for political representation and an amnesty for political prisoners.[23] The biggest disturbances were once again in Baku, where strikers clashed with police in December, but gained a nine-hour day, wage increases, and a representative committee.[24] For a time, the liberation movement emerged as a united front of all the politically active strata of Russian society, something akin to the broad coalition envisaged by political thinkers as diverse as P. Struve and B. P. Aksel'rod.

It is hard to gauge how prevalent an awareness of the

---

[19] *Rabochee dvizhenie*, iv, pt. 2, p. 474.

[20] *Rabochii klass Rossii ot zarozhdeniya do nachala XX veka* (Moscow, 1983); J. Schneiderman, *Sergei Zubatov and Revolutionary Marxism* (Ithaca, NY, 1976), ch. 13).

[21] Yu. I. Kir'yanov, 'Statistika stachechnykh vystuplenii rabochikh Rossii nakanune revolyutsii 1905–07 gg.', in *Rabochii klass v period burzhuaznoi demokraticheskoi revolyutsii* (Moscow, 1978), 43.

[22] Fischer, *Russian Liberalism*, p. 122; S. Galai, *The Liberation Movement in Russia, 1900–05* (Cambridge, 1973), 180–90, discusses the Liberationists' awareness of the urgency of major social and economic reforms to alleviate the lot of the peasants and workers.

[23] *Rabochii klass v pervoi rossiiskoi revolyutsii, 1905–07 gg.* (Moscow, 1981), 76.

[24] Ibid. 77; W. Sablinsky, *The Road to Bloody Sunday: Father Gapon and the St Petersburg Massacre of 1905* (Princeton, 1976), 141–2.

significance of civil and political rights was among workers on the eve of 1905. Only a minority of workers was politically conscious, but a broader layer did possess a rudimentary class consciousness and a propensity for militant collective action. The 'grey masses', in contrast, lacked all class awareness, and remained loyal to God and the tsar.[25] In Russian conditions, however, class consciousness did not develop in a unilinear fashion: it tended to 'explode' in moments of sharp class conflict which affected even 'backward' workers.[26] After all, they too suffered not only from the low wages, long working hours, and brutalizing working conditions, but also from the *proizvol* ('arbitrariness') of foremen and supervisors, who subjected them to abuse and violence, fines and searches, and who denied them all opportunity to redress their grievances. There is evidence that dissatisfaction with the general condition of *bespravie* ('absence of rights') was widespread, and in this context, calls for civil and political rights may have resonated among wide circles of workers whose political awareness was otherwise very limited. An index of this dissatisfaction can perhaps be seen in the growing number of complaints to the Factory Inspectorate about 'bad treatment' (*durnoe obrashchenie*), which rose from 2,136 to 21,873 between 1901 and 1913.[27] Such protests were not 'political', of course, since a demand for better treatment does not necessarily imply a transformation of power relations,[28] but they do testify to a growing sense of dignity and self-respect among workers, making them more receptive to arguments linking *bespravie* in the work-place to *bespravie* in society at large.

The autocratic character of the Russian factory regime made it easy for workers to make connections between their work situation and the political situation. Such a linkage was facilitated, for example, by the frequency with which the forces of law and order intervened in industrial disputes. In these circumstances,

[25] Yu. I. Kir'yanov, 'Ob oblike rabochego klassa Rossii', in *Rossiiskii proletariat: Oblik, bor'ba, gegemoniya* (Moscow, 1970), 121.

[26] R. Zelnik, 'Russian Workers and the Revolutionary Movement', *Journal of Social History*, 6/2 (1972–3), 217–22. See also M. Mann, *Consciousness and Action among the Western Working Class* (London, 1973), ch. 6.

[27] K. A. Pazhitnov, *Polozhenie rabochego klassa v Rossii*, iii (Leningrad, 1924), 130; O. Crisp, 'Labour and Industrialization in Russia', *Cambridge Economic History of Europe*, vii (Cambridge, 1978), pt. 2, p. 382.

[28] B. Moore, *Injustice: The Social Bases of Obedience and Revolt* (London, 1978), 207–8.

socialist arguments that the government defended capitalist interests and that political rights were essential if workers were to achieve material betterment found a ready audience. Just how rapidly workers could latch on to ideas of civil and political rights is revealed by a contemporary description of the situation in Kharkov in 1900. Apparently, local SDs dropped the demand for freedom of assembly from a leaflet which they were putting out to railway workers, on the grounds that 'unconscious' workers disliked outsiders trying to foist politics upon them. However, after a lively May Day demonstration in the city, it was reported that some workers 'learnt for the first time, and with astonishment, that they were deprived of the rights of assembly and association'; when a factory inspector asked a crowd at the steam-engine plant what their most urgent request was, to a man they yelled: 'a constitution!'. The writer commented: 'Political rights are becoming something absolutely necessary for their daily lives—for the daily struggle for existence and for the future. These rights have ceased to be something completely alien or incomprehensible, or at best, some abstract good which is acknowledged only by that minority which can read about them in the legal press.'[29]

The petition which was presented to the Tsar on 9 January 1905 demonstrates the belief of workers in the capital that their lack of rights was the key cause of their servitude to capital and a corrupt state:

The present position of the working class in Russia is totally unsecured by law or by those free rights of individuality which would enable workers independently to defend their interests. Workers, like all Russian citizens, are deprived of freedom of speech, conscience, the press and assembly. . . . In the light of the complete absence of personal rights and the support given by the police and governmental authorities to capitalist interests—which extends from arrest and exile to the encouragement by the security police of spying and provocation—and in the light of the unquestioned power which the capitalists wield, thanks to their advantage over labour on a world-wide scale, an advantage which is enhanced by the protection they receive from officials and by the legal defencelessness of the toilers, the workers

[29] *Rabochee dvizhenie*, iv, pt. 2, pp. 624–5.

are, in the full sense, serfs (*krepostnymi rabami*) of the factory owners.[30]

The reception which the bearers of this petition received at the hands of government troops caused half a million workers—with metalworkers in the van—to go on strike. The strikes of the spring months raised mainly 'economic' demands, but noteworthy was the demand for worker representation. This was not a new demand—indeed, in 1903 the government had introduced a law on *starosty* ('elders') designed to stifle the growing pressure for elected worker deputies—but now it took on a new urgency. Taking their cue from the liberation movement, whose shibboleth was a 'constitution', workers called for a 'constitutional' factory, by which they meant a factory regime in which workers had the right to elect permanent representatives to negotiate with the administration on a wide range of matters, such as hiring and firing, the fixing of wage rates, and the rules of internal order.[31] This enthusiasm for representation was given a focus in early February by the elections to the Shidlovskii Commission, which took place in 208 enterprises in St Petersburg.[32] Workers at the Nevskii shipbuilding and engineering works called on their seven electors to clarify the powers of the commission, and noted: 'It is necessary to establish guarantees and determine the rights of deputies in relation to the factory administration. Undoubtedly, the work of the commission can only be successful if the worker-deputies have the right to meet and speak freely and are guaranteed inviolability of the person.'[33] Other factories expressed the wish for their electors to become the nucleus of permanent representation in the work-place, and 'factory commissions' were established in many enterprises in the capital in the course of the spring.[34]

It is possible that throughout 1905 most workers remained

---

[30] *Nachalo pervoi russkoi revolyutsii, yanvar'-mart 1905 g.*, ed. N. S. Trusovaya (Moscow, 1955), 16–18, 28–31. An English translation of the final version of the petition is in Sablinsky, *Road to Bloody Sunday*, pp. 344–9.

[31] D. Kol'tsov, 'Rabochie v 1905–07 gg.', in *Obshchestvennoe dvizhenie v Rossii*, ii (St Petersburg, 1910), 193; K. Dmitriev, 'Professional'nye soyuzy v Moskve', *Pravda*, Jan. 1906.

[32] Sablinsky, *Road to Bloody Sunday*, p. 285.

[33] *Pravda*, Mar. 1905, 317.

[34] V. E. Bonnell, *Roots of Rebellion: Workers' Politics and Organizations in St Petersburg and Moscow, 1900–14* (Berkeley, 1983), 115–16.

principally concerned with work-related issues, even though the incomplete data of the Factory Inspectorate suggest that the percentage of 'political' strikers outweighed the percentage of 'economic' strikers in most months (January, April, May, June, August, October, November, and December).[35] The springtime strike demands and resolutions of workers in the provinces reveal a lower level of political awareness than in the metropolis, with the most popular demands being for an eight-hour day and higher wages, followed at some distance by the demand for the right to form trade unions and for protective labour legislation.[36] In Moscow, there were fewer strikes than in St Petersburg and their aims were mainly 'economic', although some instances of workers demanding the right to elect deputies and form trade unions are recorded (e.g. in the railway workshops).[37] By September the election of deputies was common in Moscow, and in Kharkov, Baku, Kostroma, Ivanovo, and elsewhere, 'factory commissions' and local councils of work-place deputies had been set up.[38] Only in a few major regions, such as Poland, the Baltic, and the Donbass, is there evidence prior to October of sizeable numbers of workers calling for full civil and political rights and a democratic republic.[39]

The general strike of October marked the apogee of the 1905 Revolution, with possibly as many as two million workers and employees joining it. Calls for the abolition of autocracy, a constituent assembly, and democratic rights enjoyed wide currency.[40] The First All-Russian Congress of Railway Employees, for example, called for a constituent assembly, civil liberties, an amnesty for political prisoners, an end to martial law and the death penalty, and an eight-hour day.[41] On 17 October Nicholas II capitulated, promising a parliament and full civil liberties, but the newly formed St Petersburg soviet rejected his concessions as being too little and too late. Workers felt that they

---

[35] *Rabochii klass v pervoi rossiiskoi revolyutsii*, pp. 95, 125, 184, 187, 200.

[36] B. Nevskii, 'Yanvarskie dni v 1905 g. v provintsii', II, *Krasnaya letopis'*, 5 (1923), 111.

[37] B. Nevskii, 'Yanvarskie zabastovki 1905 g. v Moskve', ibid. 2–3 (1922), 14, 23.

[38] L. Engelstein, *Moscow, 1905* (Stanford, 1982), 80; *Materialy po istorii professional'nogo dvizheniya v Rossii*, ii (Moscow, 1925).

[39] Nevskii, 'Yanvarskie dni', p. 111.

[40] *Rabochii klass v pervoi rossiiskoi revolyutsii*, p. 161.

[41] *Revolyutsiya 1905–07 gg. Dokumenty, materialy: Vserossiiskaya politicheskaya stachka v oktyabre 1905 g.*, i, ed. L. M. Ivanov (Moscow, 1955), 205–6.

were better off relying on their own resources—the soviets, the trade unions, and the factory commissions—rather than on promises extracted from a reluctant government. In practice, the freedom to strike, to associate, and to assemble had already been won, just as in some enterprises workers had unilaterally enforced (*yavochnym poryadkom*) an eight-hour day.

The far-reaching concessions to 'the public' (*obshchestvo*) contained in the October Manifesto largely served to conciliate the liberal opposition, but cut little ice with the workers. The government's pursuit of a policy of vigorous repression in the face of continuing popular disorder served to harden working-class opposition to it. The St Petersburg metalworkers proved irreconcilable. In November the Possel' workers declared their readiness to go into 'decisive battle for freedom' at the first signal from the soviet; and the Old Lessner workers proclaimed: 'we shall fight until the last drop of blood . . . to defend the rights of man and of the citizen'.[42] However, the arrest of the St Petersburg soviet on 2 December revealed that the workers' movement in the capital had run out of steam. The baton passed to Moscow, where the arrest of that city's soviet caused an electrical fitter to comment: 'All these liberties which the proletariat has wrenched from the claws of the autocracy are now being destroyed; the proletariat must respond to this challenge from the government. Without freedom of the press and assembly, and freedom to strike, the proletariat cannot exist. There is only one way out: either victory or death with honour.'[43] In the event, the couple of thousand workers and Bolshevik activists who rushed to the barricades of Krasnaya Presnya were quickly bludgeoned into surrender.[44]

The dominant discourse of the labour movement in 1905 was focused on 'liberty' (*svoboda*) rather than 'socialism'. By 1905 workers were painfully aware of their *bespravie*, often likening themselves to 'slaves' or 'serfs': 'We have no rights, we are slaves', declared the 'Bloody Sunday' petition. 'We are not recognized as people but are regarded as things which can be thrown out at any moment.' Even the most benighted workers in the bakery trade

[42] Ibid. 396, 399.

[43] *Vysshii pod"em revolyutsii 1905–07 gg. i. Noyabr'–dekabr' 1905*, ed. A. L. Sidorov (Moscow, 1955), 409.

[44] Engelstein, *Moscow, 1905*, pp. 197–221.

began to cry 'we, too, are people'.[45] The claiming of 'rights' was thus rooted in an experience of subordination and oppression, and their achievement was seen to be the means of realizing liberty and human dignity.

From one angle, the labour movement in 1905 can be seen as almost wholly concerned with 'rights'. It is true that the principal strike demands—an eight-hour day and higher wages—were 'economic', but even these can be reformulated in terms of 'rights': the right to free time and the right to a decent existence (which comprised not only demands for better wages and conditions, but also demands for the abolition of searches and the corporal punishment of workers). As far as civil rights were concerned, the most popular demands were for class-related civil rights, i.e. to form trade unions, elect representatives, and withdraw labour. These were the rights which the SDs had most assiduously popularized, and the ones which cropped up most often in strike demands. Without these corporate civil rights, workers recognized that they would be unable to improve their material conditions or their status as a class. In this sense, then, their perception of civil rights was similar to that of the SDs: such rights were valued not so much as goods in themselves but as the means necessary to workers to promote their class interests.

However, it would be wrong to infer from this that workers were only concerned with their corporate rights as workers, or that they viewed rights solely in instrumental terms. They also appreciated the significance of broader, non-class-specific civil rights, such as freedom of speech and conscience, and the inviolability of the person; indeed, it was common for the nascent trade unions to incorporate such demands into their programmes. The St Petersburg printers' union, for example, the first to emerge in the capital, called not only for a series of measures to enable workers to 'escape from our present economic slavery', but also for laws which would 'guarantee the free and full development of all the spiritual forces of the individual personality'.[46] Workers, in fact, do not seem to have made any clear distinctions between economic or social rights (e.g. the rights to social

[45] B. Ivanov, *Po stupen'yam bor'by: Zapiski starogo bol'shevika* (Moscow, 1934), 67.

[46] Kol'tsov, 'Rabochie v 1905–07 gg.', p. 202.

insurance, education, or labour protection) and civil or political rights: they viewed them as all of a piece, all interconnected. Together they added up to 'liberty'. Freedom was indivisible.

The discourse within which claims for 'rights' were located merits further examination. Singularly absent from this discourse were Lockian themes emphasizing the rights to life, liberty, and property, or Painite appeals to reason, conscience, self-interest, or 'self-evident truths'.[47] In the Anglo-American tradition, which traced its lineage from Locke through the American Declaration of Independence, rights had been grounded in a conception of the individual as essentially the proprietor of his own person or capacities, owing nothing to society for them.[48] In Russia in 1905, however, it was not the 'individual' which functioned as the organizing concept of workers' discourse, but rather the 'toiling people' (*trudovoi narod*) or the 'working class', which was seen as having various pressing entitlements. Moreover, it was to the state that workers looked to promote their rights—albeit a state genuinely representative of the toilers. In this respect, paradoxically, proletarian discourse may have been the bastard child of the very political traditions against which it was rebelling, for the very etiolated conception of the individual and the correspondingly hypertrophied conception of the state within Russian political culture may have disabled workers from thinking of the individual as having rights against the state or the collective. Whereas the western liberal tradition construed rights as essentially restrictive of state power and as defining a private sphere into which the state might not legitimately interfere, the Russian tradition identified the state with the person of the tsar, and thus never sought explicitly to limit the competence of the state by law.[49] In 1905, even as workers sought to shuck off this tradition, their perceptions continued to be shaped by it at a subliminal level; they thought in terms of what a putative workers' state should do, rather than what it should not do.

In other respects, workers' discourse in 1905 bore certain

[47] M. Cranston, 'Are there any Human Rights?', *Daedalus*, 12/4 (1983), 1–17.

[48] C. B. Macpherson, *The Political Theory of Possessive Individualism* (Oxford, 1962), 3. From the last quarter of the eighteenth century, Locke's labour theory of property was increasingly utilized within English radical discourse—a fact which suggests a revision of the view of Locke as archetypal theorist of bourgeois rights. See G. Stedman Jones, *Languages of Class* (Cambridge, 1983), 138.

[49] B. H. Sumner, *Survey of Russian History* (London, 1944), 80.

hallmarks of the western tradition, most noticeably in the
frequency with which rights were linked to 'citizenship' (*grazh-
danstvo*). In a brief but illuminating discussion, Victoria Bonnell
has argued that in 1905 workers had a dualistic conception of
rights, demanding on the one hand the rights of citizenship, and
on the other, the rights of 'worker control', by which she means
the rights to elect work-place representatives, to participate in
decisions affecting conditions of employment, and—perhaps by
extension—to control the direction of government, as with the
soviet.[50] This distinction clearly identifies an antinomy within
workers' discourse (albeit one that was potential rather than
actual) between rights deemed to belong to all members of the
polity, and those deemed to be exclusive to one class, that of the
wealth-producers. Closer examination shows, however, that even
'citizenship' was perceived in strongly class terms, as appertaining
not so much to the rights and duties of each member of the *polis*,
as to the status of workers as a class. A typical invocation of
'citizenship' comes in the inaugural manifesto of the St Petersburg Union of Tavern Employees, which, on 9 November 1905,
declared: 'Our condition is difficult and demeaning. At present
all the labouring classes of Russia are united in defence of their
rights. The toilers of all Russia are struggling to obtain
satisfaction of their basic economic needs and their needs as
citizens.'[51] Here, citizenship implied raising workers as a group
to a position of equality with the rest of society; and whilst this
was deemed to entail the realization of certain individual
liberties, it was through the *collective* upgrading of workers that
true citizenship would be achieved.[52] This necessarily required
not only the reform of the political system, but also the
transformation of socio-economic structures. In an ascriptive
society such as tsarist Russia, therefore, appeals to 'citizenship'
had a subversive, egalitarian thrust, and the attainment of
citizenship was closely identified with the creation of a society of
liberty and equality.[53] Thus, the discursive conditions existed for
the subsumption of citizenship within a discourse of socialism.
This is evident in the following extract from a speech by
the President of the St Petersburg Union of Watchmakers on

---

[50] Bonnell, *Roots of Rebellion*, p. 190.   [51] Cited in ibid. 171.
[52] T. H. Marshall, *Citizenship and Social Class* (Cambridge, 1950).
[53] R. Bendix, *Nation-Building and Citizenship* (New York, 1964), 98–107.

27 November 1905, in which the invocation of citizenship leads directly into a denunciation of capitalist exploitation: 'With the help of the union, after we have developed self-consciousness and raised our legal, intellectual, and moral level, we shall be transformed into free citizens. Not as pathetic and dispersed cowards, but as brave men proud of our solidarity, fully armed with justice and truth, we shall present our demands before the insatiable sharks who are our employers.'[54]

If, during the heady 'days of freedom', a militant minority saw socialism as the logical consummation of citizenship, the objectives of the great majority of workers were not yet so intrinsically revolutionary as to have made their realization impossible within a democratic capitalist order. This is not to say that workers perceived capitalism as a desirable framework for the achievement of citizenship (it is, indeed, hard to find legitimacy of any kind being accorded to capitalism by Russian workers), but the October Manifesto did create a potential for reformism within the labour movement, and, had there been a gradual amelioration in the condition of workers, this might well have produced a narrowing of the conception of citizenship and a less sweeping vision of *svoboda*.

Despite its brutal suppression of the workers' movement at the end of 1905, the autocracy did proceed to implement a series of reforms which conceded many of the demands of organized labour, and substantially altered the framework of industrial relations.[55] The Provisional Regulations of 2 December 1905 permitted strikes that were economic in character, that were not accompanied by violence or intimidation, and that did not occur in 'socially necessary' establishments. On 4 March 1906 provisional regulations were introduced which legalized non-political trade unions and workers' clubs so long as they were authorized by the police, and permitted public meetings if they were deemed not to damage the public or state interest.[56] Workers were quick to take advantage of these concessions, and nowhere more so than in the creation of trade unions. By 1907, 71 trade unions existed legally in St Petersburg and 111 in Moscow.[57]

[54] Cited by Bonnell, *Roots of Rebellion*, p. 152.
[55] See the excellent discussion in ibid., ch. 5.
[56] *Rabochii klass Rossii 1907–fevral' 1917 g.* (Moscow, 1982), 110–11.
[57] V. Bonnell, 'Trade Unions, Parties and the State in Tsarist Russia', *Politics and Society*, 9/3 (1980), 303–4.

The Stolypin 'coup' of 3 June 1907 gave the signal for an assault on the labour movement. During the next five years, organized labour fell into the doldrums: the trade unions began to disintegrate under renewed pressure from the police; and economic recession led to a slump in the number of strikes. Developments during the 'years of reaction', however, paved the way for a renewed upsurge of labour militancy after 1912.[58] Firstly, the ubiquitous violations of civil rights by the authorities —between 1907 and March 1912, for example, no fewer than 600 unions were refused registration[59]—served to harden workers in their conviction that only by the overthrow of tsarism could their rights be guaranteed. Secondly, the break-up of the liberation movement, and the drift of some liberal elements towards appeasement of the regime, confirmed the more militant workers' distrust of their erstwhile allies. Thirdly, after the chastening experience of 1905, the employers began to develop their own class organizations, and, though they remained too riven to act as a coherent force in the national arena, they began to co-ordinate resistance to labour by experimenting with lock-outs, blacklists, fines for strikers, work rationalization, etc. This not only amplified worker hostility to the employers, but also identified them even more closely with the *vlast'* ('state power') on which they continued to rely in the event of disorders.

During the 'years of reaction', the Menshevik *praktiki* ('practical workers') who led the battered remnants of the trade unions clung to the project of building a mass labour movement, comprising unions, clubs, insurance funds, etc. This fitted with their commitment to 'Europeanizing' the working class, and to co-operating with the middle classes to carry through the bourgeois revolution. Some Bolsheviks also devoted themselves to keeping afloat the labour movement, but many within the party considered this to be a stultifying endeavour. Instead they tried to preserve their underground organization, and vainly sought to whip up working-class support for the armed overthrow of the regime.[60] Against the background of this conflict over

---

[58] L. Haimson, 'The Problem of Social Stability in Urban Russia, 1905–17', I, II, *Slavic Review*, 23/4 (1964), and 24/1 (1965).

[59] G. Swain, *Russian Social Democracy and the Legal Labour Movement, 1906–14* (London, 1983), 31.

[60] L. Schapiro, *The Communist Party of the Soviet Union* (London, 1963), 104–20.

strategy, the issue of civil and political rights took on a changed significance. For the Mensheviks, the issue of civil rights continued to be perceived as it had been in 1905, as the essential pre-condition for developing a mass labour movement: an issue which, when linked to the demand for democracy in the political sphere, could serve to unite the labour movement with other progressive strata in a common battle against the autocracy. For the Bolsheviks, the much-vaunted liberties of the October Manifesto had proved to be a smoke-screen designed to conceal the basically unchanged character of the autocracy. Whilst they continued to believe that civil rights were necessary to the creation of a fighting labour movement, they now tended to demote the issue of civil rights in favour of an unequivocal call for the overthrow of the autocracy and the establishment of a democratic republic.[61] The tacit abandonment by the Bolsheviks of a clear-cut two-stage model of revolution facilitated this tactical demotion of the civil rights issue. To many militant workers after 1912 the Bolshevik tactics seemed to be based on a realistic assessment of the political situation, whereas the Mensheviks' continued faith in the viability of a legal labour movement seemed faintly ludicrous, even treacherous.

The massacre of workers in the Lena gold-fields in April 1912 triggered a nation-wide wave of labour protest. As many as 360,000 workers—mainly metalworkers in St Petersburg, the Caucasus, the Urals, and the north-western region—went on strike, and the year as a whole witnessed a surge of political strikes, many with a distinctively 'bolshevik' *élan*.[62] At the time of the elections to the Fourth Duma in October 1912, the *Putilovtsy* struck 'in protest at the violation of our electoral rights. We declare that only with the overthrow of tsarism and the achievement of a democratic republic can workers be guaranteed the right of truly free elections.'[63] A pungent *ouvriériste* note entered the discourse of the more radical layers. In May 1912 some workers at the Franco-Russian works in St Petersburg condemned the laying-off of night-shift workers and the imposition of overtime working, and pledged 'to fight our oppressors for the

[61] Keep, *Rise of Social Democracy*, pp. 292–3.

[62] G. A. Arutyunov, *Rabochee dvizhenie v Rossii v period mirnogo revolyutsionnogo pod"ema, 1910–14 gg.* (Moscow, 1975), 133, 136–7.

[63] Ibid. 20.

freedom to form unions for old-age and invalidity pensions, and for equal rights for all citizens'. They concluded: 'Comrades, what do we see at the Franco-Russian works? Servility [*raboleptsvo*], the debasement of our dignity, the swaying [*kachanie*] of our foremen, the bowing and scraping to the lackeys [*kholopami*] of capital, who understand nothing of our work and who serve only as informers and heartless slave-drivers.'[64]

The political strike movement continued at the same level in 1913, but the number of economic strikes increased compared to the previous year. This radical mood was translated into growing support for the Bolsheviks within the renascent labour movement. Demands for civil rights were less common than they had been in 1905, and where they were raised, it was invariably alongside an expression of mistrust of the government. A group of 'organized workers' from Kiev, for example, proposed that the SD deputies should introduce a bill on press freedom to the Duma: 'We do not have any illusions in the Third of June regime and are fully aware that complete freedom of the press can be realized only through a radical transformation of the existing political system.'[65]

According to the conservative estimates of the Factory Inspectorate, 1.2 million workers went on strike in the first half of 1914—two-thirds of them for political ends—but the outbreak of war in July quickly terminated the unrest.[66] On 24 July the government issued an *ukaz* forbidding all meetings and demonstrations, incitement to strike, the distribution of revolutionary literature, and the singing of revolutionary songs. Sweeping arrests were made of socialists, including the Bolshevik Duma deputies in November; *Pravda* and other newspapers were shut down; trade unions were banned and their organizers rounded up. Petrograd was effectively placed under martial law, although much-discussed plans to 'militarize' labour failed to get on to the statute book.[67] After a hiatus in the second half of 1914, the strike movement slowly began to pick up. Throughout the war, strikes remained overwhelmingly 'economic', but there were widespread political stoppages in the autumn of 1915 and 1916. These were

[64] *Rabochee dvizhenie v Petrograde v 1912–17: Dokumenty i materialy* (Leningrad, 1958), 47–8.

[65] *Rabochee dvizhenie na Ukraine v gody novogo revolyutsionnogo pod"ema 1910–14 gg.* (Kiev, 1959), 502.

[66] *Rabochii klass Rossii 1907–fevral' 1917 g.*, pp. 226–30.

[67] Ibid. 274–5.

dominated by the metalworkers of Petrograd, in particular of Vyborg district, who on numerous occasions debouched on to the streets of the capital bearing red flags and banners, and calling for a constituent assembly, a democratic republic, and an end to the war. Typical of the views of these workers is a resolution passed on 25 September 1915 by the Old Lessner work-force: 'We will stand up for our fatherland when we are given complete freedom to form labour organizations, complete freedom of speech and the press, freedom to strike, full equal rights for all nations of Russia, an eight-hour day, and when the landlords' lands are handed over to the poor peasants.'[68] An Okhrana official explained the pugnacity of such workers as follows:

The ban on workers' meetings, the closure of trade unions, the arrests of active members of the medical funds, the closure of the labour press, etc. have forced the working masses, who are led in their actions and sympathies by the most conscious, even revolutionary elements, into a sharply negative attitude to the government and into protest of every kind against the further continuance of the war.[69]

Not all 'conscious' workers were as extreme in their views as the Petrograd metalworkers. Menshevik labour leaders met with a modicum of success in their efforts to set up workers' groups attached to the War Industries Committees, especially in smaller industrial centres. By February 1917, 54 of the 182 War-Industries Committees had established workers' groups which strove to unite workers with the *obshchestvo* behind the war effort, to establish *starosty* in the factories, and to restore civil and political rights.[70] In Taganrog, for example, the workers' group called for an amnesty for religious and political prisoners; a ministry responsible to the Duma; a Duma elected by universal suffrage; freedom of the press, association, and assembly; an eight-hour day; and a guaranteed minimum wage.[71] The Menshevik Defencists and Progressive Bloc could thus command some working-class support for a package of political reforms

[68] *Rabochee dvizhenie v Petrograde*, p. 355.
[69] Ibid. 484.
[70] *Rabochii klass Rossii 1907–fevral' 1917 g.*, p. 312.
[71] Yu. I. Kir'yanov, *Rabochie yuga Rossii 1914–fevral' 1917 g.* (Moscow, 1971), 172.

which did not entail root-and-branch opposition to the war and the regime.

The toppling of the Romanov dynasty in February 1917 and the installation of the Provisional Government largely resolved the question of civil rights as far as most workers were concerned. With justification, Lenin in April could call Russia 'the freest of all the belligerent countries in the world'.[72] The issue of civil and political rights remained a vital one only for those categories whose status as political subjects had not yet been clarified, such as women workers, young workers, and workers belonging to the national minorities. At the militant Cable works in Petrograd, for example, the factory committee called on the Provisional Government to withdraw eighteen-year-olds from the Front until it allowed them voting rights.[73] And women at the Siemens-Schuckert works in the capital refused to support the Liberty Loan, arguing: 'We women have reviewed our position and now recognize that for a long time we have been totally enslaved. The capitalist regards us as slaves and considers us as worthless objects. At present we are working in the mills and factories in place of our menfolk. We therefore demand civil rights and immediate wage increases equal to those of men.'[74] As in the pre-revolutionary period, this resolution testifies to the fact that *svoboda* was perceived to be a multidimensional condition in which political rights were inextricably tied up with economic and social betterment.

The granting of full civil and political rights to everyone over the age of twenty, together with the establishment of the 'constitutional' factory—in the shape of factory committees, conciliation chambers, and trade unions recognized by the employers and the law—meant that civil rights faded from the agenda of the labour movement in the late spring of 1917. It resurfaced only in the wake of the July Days, after the Kerenskii government closed down *Pravda* and arrested leading Bolsheviks. A meeting of young workers at Putilov denounced the government as the 'ministry for the resurrection of counter-revolution', and

---

[72] V. I. Lenin, 'The Tasks of the Proletariat in the Present Revolution', *Collected Works*, 4th edn., xxiv (Moscow, 1964), 22.

[73] A. N. Atsarkhin, *Pod bol'shevistskoe znamya: Soyuzy rabochei molodezhi v Petrograde v 1917 g.* (Leningrad, 1958), 76–7.

[74] *Rabotnitsa*, 1–2 (1917), 13.

warned it against tampering with hard-won civil liberties.[75] The workers' section of the Petrograd soviet voiced widespread disaffection in the labour movement when it demanded either the immediate release of those arrested or their open trial.[76]

The restrictions on *Pravda* touched on the civil liberties issue which was perhaps most salient for the labour movement in 1917: freedom of the press. In 1905 this issue had been of vital concern, particularly to the unions of printers and bookshop employees, who had sought to achieve press freedom by boycotting all publishing concerns that continued to submit material to the censor in advance of publication.[77] In that year, too, printers had wrestled with the problem of whether or not press freedom could ever legitimately be restricted, since many of them were troubled when called upon to print blatantly reactionary material. There were instances of printers refusing to do so, for example in Saratov, but the general policy was to print such material but to demand a right of reply (e.g. the Kushner works printers in Moscow).[78] The printers' concern for freedom of the press reflected not only their level of education, their closeness to the intelligentsia, their developed civic sense, and their Menshevik sympathies, but also their economic interest in job security and employment opportunities (press censorship not only restricted the range of permitted publications, it also led to the closure of publishing houses and consequent unemployment for those who worked in them).

After the temporary closure of *Pravda* in July 1917, the Central Bureau of Trade Unions and the Central Council of Factory Committees rejected any infringement of press freedom as a matter of principle, and argued that the correct tactic in dealing with the openly counter-revolutionary press, such as *Malen'kaya gazeta*, was to launch a workers' boycott but not to try to close it down.[79] Nevertheless, on 26 July printers at the *Sel'skii vestnik* works refused (by 113 votes to 47) to print a Bolshevik leaflet, and during the Kornilov rebellion the Bolshevik-controlled Vyborg district soviet banned the sale of bourgeois

---

[75] *Putilovets v trekh revolyutsiyakh*, ed. I. I. Gaza (Leningrad, 1933), 363–4.

[76] *Novaya zhizn'*, 95 (8 Aug. 1917), 3.

[77] *Pravda*, Dec. 1905, 234–6; Engelstein, *Moscow, 1905*, p. 174.

[78] *Pravda*, Dec. 1905, 239.

[79] *Delo naroda*, 99 (13 July 1917), 4.

newspapers (though it was criticized for doing so by the Executive Committee of the city soviet).[80] Of course, the biggest attack on press freedom came with the Bolshevik seizure of power, when the Milrevkom and the Red Guards closed down several bourgeois newspapers, supposedly as an emergency measure.[81] A side-effect of this was to cause nearly 2,000 printers in Petrograd to lose their jobs, a fact which contributed to their passionate opposition to the new government.[82] Printers in the capital condemned attempts to 'stifle the free word, which we consider the greatest benefit of a free people', and in December 1,200 workers at the Trubochnyi works echoed this sentiment.[83] In Moscow, printers at the large Levenson works complained that not even Nicholas II had dared to attack the press as brazenly as the Bolsheviks had done since October. However, it is not the purpose of this essay to extend the examination of workers' relation to civil rights into the Soviet period. Suffice it to say that the civil rights for which many workers had fought for a decade and a half had barely had chance to take root before they once more came under attack from the state.

This essay has endeavoured to show that Russian workers displayed considerable concern for civil and political rights from around 1899 to 1917, and that the Russian labour movement was therefore no exception to Eric Hobsbawm's generalization that 'labour movements being concerned with people who have cause to demand a lot of rights . . . have played a very large role in the development of human rights'.[84] We have seen that the SDs were the chief disseminators of ideas of civil and political rights within the labour movement, though they had no monopoly on such ideas. Concern for civil and political rights ran right across the political spectrum of the labour movement—from the Zubatovists, to the Union of Unions, to Menshevik *praktiki*, to Bolshevik

[80] *Pechatnoe delo*, 7 (1917), 14; *Rabochaya gazeta*, 152 (5 Sept. 1917), 4.

[81] M. Liebman, *Leninism under Lenin* (London, 1975), 258–61; P. Kenez, 'Lenin and the Freedom of the Press', in A. Gleason, P. Kenez, and R. Stites (eds.), *Bolshevik Culture* (Bloomington, Ind., 1985), 131–50.

[82] *Novaya zhizn'*, 176 (9 Nov. 1917), 3.

[83] S. Volin, *Deyatel'nost' men'shevikov v profsoyuzakh pri sovetskoi vlasti* (New York, 1962), 31.

[84] E. J. Hobsbawm, 'Labour and Human Rights', in *Worlds of Labour* (London, 1984), 284.

militants—yet it never provided sufficient basis for united action. Given the record of the Bolshevik government after 1917, however, can we seriously suggest that the commitment of Russian workers to civil and political rights was ever more than skin-deep?

In his seminal article of 1964, Leopold Haimson argued that after 1905 the labour movement assumed a more sharply etched class character, and came to define itself increasingly in opposition to the *obshchestvo* as well as to the state.[85] Expanding on this thesis with characteristic acumen, Reginald Zelnik has suggested that in this period working-class culture came to be typified by:

an acutely felt class particularism that increasingly closed the minds of multitudes of workers to the possibility of collaboration with the more privileged classes of society for the purpose of creating a liberal polity based on equal citizenship. Universalistic social values came to be meaningful to Russian workers only as embedded in their own special context of class identification and pride, which reconciled a universalistic vision with their particularistic, even exclusionary emotional world.[86]

The examination of civil rights largely bears out this perspective. Even in 1905 workers perceived 'citizenship' largely in class terms, even though the battle for civil and political rights temporarily harnessed the liberation movement and labour movement in tandem. By 1914 many workers had become alienated from the liberal opposition and disillusioned with the possibility of any substantial change short of a frontal assault on the existing social order. The tone of workers' resolutions and proclamations had become hard-edged: the talk of *svoboda* had not disappeared, but it was infused with a visceral hatred of the state and the privileged classes, and associated with an explicit commitment to overthrow tsarism by force of arms rather than to transform it by force of public opinion. Class analysis, though not necessarily Marxist class analysis, was to the fore.

If Haimson and Zelnik have correctly pin-pointed a major shift in working-class culture, one should nevertheless beware of

---

[85] Haimson, 'Problem of Social Stability', I. 629–30.

[86] R. Zelnik, 'Passivity and Protest in Germany and Russia: Barrington Moore's Conception of Working-Class Responses to Injustice', *Journal of Social History*, 15/3 (1982), 497.

construing that culture as monolithic. It goes without saying, for example, that there was a minority of workers whose political attitudes were straightforwardly reactionary (the supporters of the Union of the Russian People) or conservative (e.g. those St Petersburg workers who sent a letter to right-wing deputies in the Fourth Duma asking them 'to protect those who wish to engage in honourable labour from the *proizvol* of members of that illegal and criminal organization, the RSDRP').[87] More importantly, from our point of view, if the dominant tendency within working-class culture was towards a sense of exclusion from, and opposition to, the *obshchestvo*, there were still contradictory impulses at play which strove for unity with it against the *vlast'*—less powerful than in 1905, to be sure, but by no means negligible even in 1917. These seem to have been particularly evident outside Petrograd (in Moscow, for example). Yet even if one takes into account the variation in, and contradictoriness of, working-class culture, it would still appear to be the case that the dominant tendency was towards class particularism. After 1905, among the ranks of the most militant layers, the ideal of 'citizenship' was gradually being displaced by a vision of a dictatorship of the proletariat.

What were the implications of this for the future of civil rights in Soviet Russia? Did the increasingly class-based perspective which workers brought to the issue of rights lead inevitably to the exclusion of certain categories of citizens from the enjoyment of rights, and thus to the denial of civil liberties in any meaningful sense? Possibly. It is important to remember, however, that ideologies do not determine historical outcomes: they are selectively appropriated by historical actors who pursue their goals within intractable objective circumstances and against historical contingencies, and it is all of these things which combine to produce specific outcomes. Nevertheless, ideologies do play a crucial role in defining the agenda of historical actors, in foregrounding certain issues and in foreclosing others. In this limited sense, the proletarian discourse of *svoboda* may have facilitated the ultimate suppression of civil rights, by linking rights too tightly to class interests and by failing to consider how they might constrain the treatment of people in the here and now,

[87] P. E. Lyubarov and A. S. Rud', 'Proletariat i Gosudarstvennaya Duma', in *Rossiiskii proletariat: Oblik, bor'ba, gegemoniya*, p. 184.

as opposed to some idealized future.[88] We have suggested, for example, that Russian workers' discourse inherited from the indigenous political culture a certain blindness to the possible conflicts of interest which may arise between the individual and the state or the individual and the collective. Similarly, the SDs may have imparted to that discourse their own principled distrust of the individualism, legalism, absolutism, and moralism immanent in the rights tradition of the West.[89] Combined with the bitter experience of the working class, these biases and blindnesses may have led some to value civil rights not as goods in themselves to be incorporated into all the goals of political action, but as expedient, and thus expendable, means to the greater end of socialism, which would, they imagined, realize a liberty immeasurably superior to that of bourgeois democracy. One can hazard that such workers would not have been unduly troubled after 1917 by the way in which the 'salvation of the revolution' was rapidly deemed to require the suppression of 'bourgeois' freedoms, especially since the vast majority of the population had never been in a position to enjoy them anyway. And yet the historical record prior to October 1917 does not warrant so unilateral a reading: if the evidence suggests that some workers were hazily aware that the pursuit of their class goals might require the sacrifice of civil rights, it also suggests that the majority were content to inhabit that tension between what Bonnell terms the 'rights of citizenship' and the 'rights of worker control' without resolving it. These workers continued to regard rights of all kinds (civil, political, social, and economic) as desirable in themselves, as constituent elements of *svoboda*, socialism, or whatever other name they gave to the good society. It was only in the bleak circumstances that pertained after 1917 that a beleaguered Bolshevik government ironed out the ambivalences of workers' conceptions of rights, and spelt out in ruthless fashion some of the implications of a class-based vision of citizenship.

[88] See S. Lukes, *Marxism and Morality* (Oxford, 1985), 67.
[89] See T. Campbell, *The Left and Rights: A Conceptual Analysis of the Idea of Socialist Rights* (London, 1983), ch. 1.

Freedom of Association and the Trade Unions, 1906–14

G. R. SWAIN

THERE was no law guaranteeing freedom of association for the trade unions in tsarist Russia. However, the labour unrest of 1905 persuaded the authorities to issue the 'Provisional Regulations for Professional Societies of People Employed in Trade and Industrial Enterprises or the Owners of such Enterprises' on 4 March 1906. On the basis of this law, trade unions operated legally until 1914.

From the start, the rights guaranteed by this law were dependent on how real, or otherwise, the revolutionary threat was perceived to be by the tsarist government. Work on drafting a law on the trade unions had begun in May 1905, after the Shidlovskii Commission had finished its work, when the task was entrusted to F. V. Fomin, an official of the Central Office for Factory Affairs. That initial draft referred to the right to 'defend' workers' interests in order to improve working conditions, and explicitly mentioned the possibility of collecting funds for striking workers. It also allowed unions to form a federation, and made it clear that questions concerning the registration or closure of a union would be the concern of the courts.

Peace in the Far East, the transfer of loyal troops to Moscow, and the crushing of the Moscow uprising in December 1905 radically changed the political climate. The labour movement was suddenly on the defensive, and late in 1905 the State Council narrowed the scope of the proposed law in four crucial ways. Firstly, there was no longer any mention of 'defending' workers' interests; the trade unions were permitted only to 'seek means of eliminating, by means of agreements, or by submitting to arbitration, the misunderstandings that arise over conditions in labour contracts between employers and employees'. Secondly, despite the fact that strikes in defence of existing conditions had been legalized for employees of private companies (except those engaged on certain state contracts) by a law of 2 December 1905, the provisional regulations avoided all mention of strike funds. Thirdly, 'in view of the serious danger to social peace and order', no two trade unions could join together to form a united body, even by means of elected deputies. While this did not prevent the establishment of subordinate branch organizations at district level, so long as they did not have separate governing bodies, it did proscribe the creation of 'All-Russian' unions, or a trade-union confederation.

The fourth change, however, was the most far-reaching. The courts were no longer to supervise the affairs of the trade unions. Instead, the governor or city captain would decide on such questions as the registration or closure of a union, acting on the instructions of the newly created Office for Trade-Union Affairs. These existed at city level in St Petersburg, Moscow, Odessa, Kronstadt, Nikolaev, Kerch, Sevastopol, and Rostov-on-Don, and at provincial level elsewhere. The members of this new office were either bureaucrats or local duma officials: in St Petersburg, they included the police chief, the provincial marshal of nobility, the director of the Treasury, the procurator of the district court, a representative of the Ministry of the Interior, the president of the provincial *zemstvo*, the city mayor, the president of the city duma, a member of the city duma, and the senior factory inspector.

Thus, the process of registration was hidden from public scrutiny, allowing a bureaucratic body to interpret any vagueness in the law. And, indeed, the law was unclear on many points: political activities and those threatening the social order were explicitly banned, while the unions were specifically called on to (*a*) elucidate wage scales and other conditions of labour; (*b*) provide material benefits for members; (*c*) establish funeral and mutual aid funds; (*d*) establish libraries and reading-rooms; (*e*) help members obtain reasonably priced tools and assist in the search for work; and (*f*) provide legal aid for members. Just how the unions were to go about any of these tasks, however, was left unclear. The only details given in the legislation were concerned with union registration.

The sponsors of a proposed union had to apply to the district factory inspector, giving two weeks' notice and legal proof of the authenticity of their signatures. They also had to provide a copy of the proposed union's charter; but again, little guidance was given as to what should be included in the charter. The provisional regulations were only specific about such bureaucratic concerns as the full name, rank, and address of the sponsors, the conditions for admission, the method of electing the managing board, the method of book-keeping, the organization of general meetings, and the organization of branches.

The factory inspector would then pass the charter to the city captain, who passed it to the Office for Trade-Union Affairs, which was to report back to the city captain within a month. The city captain would then sign, or reject, the registration document, making the union's charter, once registered, a legal document; for a union to break its own rules meant certain closure. After registration, a trade union had to inform the factory inspector of the addresses of all board members, keeping him up to date on any changes that might occur. The factory inspector also had to be informed of any alterations to the union's charter or to the organization of the union, and was obliged to pass on all this information to the city captain, and ultimately to the police. Unions had to get advance police permission to hold a general meeting, and the police would then be in attendance. Board meetings, on the other hand, required no such authorization and took place without the police being present.[1]

The provisional regulations were an improvement on the law of 10 June 1903 which had established factory 'elders', since the 'elders' were selected by the factory owners while the unions were run by the workers themselves. However, the list of explicitly sanctioned union activities was scarcely an improvement on the existing mutual aid societies, and when delegates to the Second Conference of Trade Unions gathered in St Petersburg from 24 to 28 February 1906, there was understandably much angry debate as to whether or not the provisional regulations should be boycotted.[2] After heated discussion, the conference decided to

[1] This summary of the provisional regulations has been compiled from my own *Russian Social Democracy and the Legal Labour Movement* (London, 1983), 4–6; the Ph.D. thesis on which that book was based, 'Political Developments within the Organized Working Class: St Petersburg, 1906–14' (London, 1979), 9–14; and V. E. Bonnell, *Roots of Rebellion: Workers' Politics and Organizations in St Petersburg and Moscow, 1900–14* (Berkeley, 1983), 195–202. The provisional regulations are reproduced in A. Kats and Yu. Milonov, *1905 v professional'nom dvizhenii* (Moscow, 1925).

[2] The press had leaked the terms of the regulations well before their enactment, so when the trade-unionists met in February they were well aware of what to expect. The

register under them because of the 'exceptional circumstances', and to seek to turn them 'from a weapon for the enslavement of the working class, to a point of departure for a new, more stubborn struggle to win the rights of strike and association'.[3]

For both government and unions, therefore, the provisional regulations were exactly that, provisional. The unions saw them as the starting-point for future struggle, accepting as dogma the Social Democratic view that only a democratic republic could give genuine trade-union freedom, while the government had already shown its determination to narrow the scope of trade-union activity as soon as it felt strong enough to do so.

By mid-May 1907 a total of 245,555 workers had joined trade unions—3.5 per cent of the work-force.[4] In the country as a whole, 904 unions were registered between March 1906 and December 1907.[5] This process was far from easy. Although work began on organizing the St Petersburg metalworkers' union in May 1906, it was not until 15 May 1907 that the union was formally registered with the authorities. The St Petersburg print-workers' union was not registered until April 1907, and the textile-workers' union had to wait until September 1907.[6]

During the era of the First and Second State Dumas, struggle to extend the scope of the law in accordance with the Second Conference resolution was most evident in the way trade-unionists ignored those sections of the provisional regulations which prevented the formation of All-Russian unions or a trade-union confederation. The Central Bureau of St Petersburg Trade Unions, an illegal organization, had been instrumental in

First Conference of Trade Unions took place in Moscow during the general strike of October 1905. It began as an open meeting of workers' organizations, and only during the course of the deliberations did it constitute itself a trade-union conference and resolve to call a trade-union congress. The Moscow uprising meant that plans for a congress were abandoned and a Second Conference was held instead. For the proceedings of the First and Second Conferences, see Kats and Milonov, *1905 v professional'nom dvizhenii*; S. Rappoport and P. Kolokol'nikov, *1905–7 v professional'nom dvizhenii* (Moscow, 1925), 343–50; V. Grinevich, *Professional'noe dvizhenie rabochikh v Rossii* (St Petersburg, 1908), 98; P. Kolokol'nikov, 'Otryvki iz vospominanii', *Materialy po istorii professional'nogo dvizheniya* (hereafter *Materialy*), iv (Moscow, 1925), 274.

[3] I. L. Borshchenko, *Profsoyuzy SSSR: Dokumenty i materialy*, i (Moscow, 1963), 104; Kolokol'nikov, 'Otryvki', p. 274.

[4] A. Elnitskii, *Istoriya rabochego dvizheniya v Rossii* (Moscow, 1925), 282–3.

[5] Bonnell, *Roots of Rebellion*, p. 202 and app. 2.

[6] *Rabochii po metallu*, 15 (13 June 1907).

arranging the Second Conference, and, like its Moscow counter-part, continued to play an active role throughout 1906 and the first half of 1907. The St Petersburg Bureau saw one of its main functions as helping trade unions to register under the law, and hired lawyers to help with this complex process.[7] It sought to mediate in inter-union disputes,[8] and helped found the metal-workers' union.[9]

Nor did the St Petersburg metalworkers' union, once established, ignore its fellow unions outside the capital: two delegates attended the Moscow Regional Conference of Metalworkers' Unions in February 1907.[10] The print-workers were even more successful in flouting the provisional regulations; in April 1907 they organized a national conference in Helsingfors (Helsinki), and established a Central Council of Print-Workers' Unions.[11] The textile-workers also held conferences in February and May 1907, but the effectiveness of these was hampered by the need for secrecy; a meeting in a night-watchman's hut on the Ryazan–Moscow railway was hardly the same as the printers' grand gathering in Helsingfors.[12]

Undeterred by such problems, the Organizing Commission for a Trade-Union Congress, established by the Second Conference of Trade Unions, stuck to its timetable of trying to hold a congress, or at least a third conference, by the summer of 1907. When the commission met on 15–17 April 1907 to discuss progress, however, the sheer practicalities of organizing such an illegal gathering overwhelmed the members. The commission expressed the pious hope that, despite the law, the government might allow the congress to take place under the guise of an assembly of workers' representatives; a congress of workers, as

---

[7] Grinevich, *Professional'noe dvizhenie*, p. 67.

[8] 'Otchet o zasedanii tsentral'nago byuro', *Professional'nyi vestnik*, 2 (20 Jan. 1907).

[9] Swain, 'Political Developments', pp. 19–25.

[10] 'Moskovskaya konferentsiya', *Rabochii po metallu*, 9 (17 Feb. 1907); V. Tomskii-Kopp, 'Konferentsiya soyuzov rabochikh po metallu', *Professional'nyi vestnik*, 4–5 (10 Mar. 1907).

[11] S. Ainzaft, 'Popytka vserossiiskoi tsentralizatsii soyuzov pechatnikov', *Materialy*, i. 29; I. S. Orlov, 'Pervaya vserossisskaya konferentsiya pechatnikov', *Professional'nyi vestnik*, 6 (10 May 1907).

[12] M. Zayats, *Tekstil'shchiki v gody pervoi revolyutsii* (Moscow, 1925), 216; id., 'Oblastnaya stachka tekstil'shchikov v Moskovskom promyshlennom raione', *Materialy*, iii. 174.

opposed to a congress of trade unions, was not actually prohibited under the law.[13]

That meeting of the Organizing Commission was held in rooms provided by the Social Democratic faction of the Duma,[14] and relations between the Central Bureau of St Petersburg Trade Unions and the Social Democratic deputies to the Second Duma were particularly close. The deputies at once set up a Commission on the Workers' Question, which included a member of the St Petersburg Central Bureau.[15] Although this led to some disquiet among certain Central Bureau members when the deputies proposed a general law on freedom of association rather than one specifically guaranteeing trade-union freedom,[16] for the most part the two bodies co-operated amicably, and in May 1907 the deputies questioned the government in the Duma about the St Petersburg city captain's closure of some of the capital's smaller trade unions.[17] Such a close association, of course, brought trade-unionists, if not trade unions, into active politics, which the provisional regulations specifically forbade. The authorities cannot have been unaware that K. Dmitriev (P. Kolokol'nikov) was a member of both the Organizing Commission and the Central Committee of the Social Democratic Party.

The authorities' first moves against the trade unions came with the dissolution of the First State Duma in the summer of 1906. On 28 July the leaders of the St Petersburg metalworkers' union were arrested, and the union was informed that it was closed.[18] This swoop also included the leaders of all the other main St Petersburg unions, and was something of a pre-emptive strike. A week earlier, the textile-workers' union had elected delegates to the re-formed Soviet of Workers' Deputies set up in response to

---

[13] Rappoport and Kolokol'nikov, *1905–7 v prof. dvizhenii*, pp. 543–4, 655; P. Kolokol'nikov (signed K. Dmitriev), 'K remeslennomu s"ezdu', *Pechatnoe delo*, 25 (5 Oct. 1910).

[14] 'Predstoyashchii vserossiiskii s"ezd profsoyuzov', *Professional'nyi vestnik*, 7 (10 May 1907).

[15] Grinevich, *Professional'noe dvizhenie*, p. 29.

[16] 'Nuzhen li osobyi zakon o profsoyuzakh?', *Professional'noe delo*, 28 (Moscow, 2 June 1907); 'Pravo soyuzov i stachek', *Rabochii po metallu*, 16 (27 June 1907); P. Kolokol'nikov, 'Nuzhen li seichas v Rossii osobyi zakon o profsoyuzakh?', *Professional'nyi vestnik*, 10 (15 July 1907).

[17] 'Okolo dumy', *Professional'nyi vestnik*, 7 (10 May 1907).

[18] 'Chto delat'', *Rabochii po metallu*, 1 (30 Aug. 1906).

the Duma dissolution, and a second Soviet was something the authorities could not allow.[19]

By the spring of 1907 the government had developed an alternative strategy to that of widespread and arbitrary arrests. At the same time as preparations were under way for the 3 June coup and the arrest of the Social Democratic deputies on charges of sedition, the police were busy compiling evidence of 'extremist' penetration of the trade unions. Their investigation revealed that of the 34 major trade unions in St Petersburg, 18 were controlled by the Social Democrats and 9 by the Socialist Revolutionaries.[20] It was on the basis of this information that the government issued the first of its 'explanations' (raz″yasneniya) to city captains and governors on how they should interpret the provisional regulations. In future, any link between the trade unions and the Social Democrats would be interpreted as a threat to social peace, and would be considered legitimate grounds for non-registration or closure.[21]

Thus, the dissolution of the Second Duma coincided with a thorough purge of the trade unions, which was to continue in subsequent years. In 1907, 159 unions were closed down, in 1908 the figure was 101, then 96 and 88 in 1909 and 1910 respectively. During the years 1907–11, 604 unions were refused legal registration and 206 trade-union activists were either imprisoned or exiled.[22] In those unions which survived there was a catastrophic decline in membership. By 1909 the number of trade unions in St Petersburg and Moscow had been halved, and membership had fallen even more sharply; in Moscow, 14 per cent of the 1907 figure remained in the unions, while in St Petersburg, the figure was nearer 10 per cent.[23] Clearly the trade unions had lost the first round of their battle to extend the scope of the provisional regulations.

The weapon chosen by the government to narrow still further their own provisional regulations was the 'explanation'. The first

[19] 'Izvlecheniya iz protokolov zasedanii pravleniya', Tkach, 5 (19 Aug. 1906).

[20] D. Antoshkin, Professional'noe dvizhenie v Rossii (Moscow, 1924), 179; Bonnell, Roots of Rebellion, p. 252.

[21] Grinevich, Professional'noe dvizhenie, p. 85.

[22] Elnitskii, Istoriya, p. 285; D. Antoshkin, Kratkii ocherk professional'nogo dvizheniya v Rossii (Moscow, 1928), 42.

[23] M. S. Balabanov, Ot 1905 k 1917: Massovoe rabochee dvizhenie (Moscow, 1927), 108.

of these provided legal grounds for the widespread repression of the trade unions after June 1907, but there were other 'explanations' which equally sought to circumscribe legitimate trade-union activity, depriving them of any real ability to confront the employers. Shortly after the St Petersburg metal-workers' union had registered its rules in May 1907, the board was informed that the election of a delegate council was not allowed. This was an important ruling. As we have seen, the provisional regulations prohibited the coming-together of two trade unions, even by means of elected deputies; branch organizations were permitted, but they could not have separate governing bodies. The idea of an elected delegate council clearly involved a grey area; it was elective—something banned—but served to link branches—something permitted. The 'explanation' that an elected delegate council was illegal meant that the St Petersburg metalworkers' union, the only union to retain important influence throughout the Stolypin years, was deprived of the right to hold elections at local level; as a result, links between the board and the factories were often tenuous.[24]

A further 'explanation' of 1907 made it clear that unions did not have the right to organize public meetings, only meetings of their own members.[25] Just how broad the authorities' definition of 'public' was became clear in December 1908 when the St Petersburg metalworkers' union asked the city captain for permission to hold a special meeting of trade-union members to discuss the government's proposed social insurance legislation: the meeting would be addressed by the Social Democratic deputies to the Third Duma. After due consideration the city captain decided to ban the meeting, on the grounds that the public nature of the matter to be discussed made this private meeting of trade-union members into public activity on the part of the union.[26] Then, in August 1909, the St Petersburg print-workers' union fell foul of the authorities when it, too, was warned against getting involved in public activity, in this case an inquiry into the sanitary conditions in which members worked.

[24] F. A. Bulkin (Semenov), *Na zare profdvizheniya* (Moscow, 1924), 206. Elections to the renamed 'delegate meeting' continued to be held, but they had to be clandestine.

[25] Grinevich, *Professional'noe dvizhenie*, p. 93.

[26] F. A. Bulkin (Semenov), 'Soyuz metallistov i departament politsii', *Krasnaya letopis'*, 8 (1923), 223.

After discussion with the city captain, it was agreed that the union's Sanitary Commission could resume its work so long as only trade-union members sat on it, thus excluding outside experts.[27]

The ban on public activity became increasingly important during the Stolypin years, when one of the few areas of activity open to the trade unions was to participate in the series of legal congresses which took place from 1908 to 1911. The first such congress, the Congress of Representatives from Societies of People's Universities, took place in January 1908. Since one of the legitimate activities of the unions was to educate their members, the Central Bureau of St Petersburg Trade Unions had already (in 1907) come to an understanding with the People's Universities about organizing courses; thus it was logical for trade-union representatives to attend the congress. While trade-union representatives had no similar justification for attending the Congress of Co-operative Societies in Moscow in April 1908, links between these two wings of the labour movement were strong, and many trade-unionists did attend as individuals. Equally, the First All-Russian Women's Congress in December 1908 provided the St Petersburg textile-workers' union with an ideal opportunity to put the case for equal employment legislation.[28]

However, the degree of organization displayed by the workers' group at the Women's Congress—seen by Trotskii's *Pravda* as the first sign of recovery in the labour movement[29]—alerted the authorities to the potential danger of allowing the unions to attend such events. At the Women's Congress, the government's proposals for social insurance legislation were subjected to particularly severe criticism; criticism which was more than repeated at the All-Russian Congress of Factory Panel Doctors in April 1909, in preparation for which the St Petersburg Bureau had drawn up some 'Theses on Insurance'. These were adopted by the workers' group at that congress, and formed the basis for their activities.[30]

---

[27] *Pechatnoe delo*, 9 (Aug. 1909); 12 (Oct. 1909).

[28] These first legal congresses are discussed more fully in Swain, *Russian Social Democracy*, ch. 1.

[29] 'Pravda svoim chitatelem', *Pravda*, 1 (3 Oct. 1908).

[30] K. and R., 'Tsentral'noe byuro v osveshchenii tsarskoi okhranki', *Materialy*, v. 158.

The workers' group at the Congress of Factory Panel Doctors
was composed of more than forty-three trade-unionists, and
although the Organizing Commission had played no part in
assembling the group, its members did attend the congress and
did attempt to arrange a meeting to re-establish links with the
provinces. Equally disturbing for the government was the
presence among the group of the Social Democrat deputy, I. P.
Pokrovskii. When he tried to read out the Theses on Insurance,
he was prevented from doing so by the police; this provoked a
small scandal, and thirty doctors joined the workers' group which
walked out in protest.[31]

When trade-unionists began to arrange representation at the
First All-Russian Congress on the Struggle against Alcoholism in
December 1909–January 1910, the authorities decided to intervene. The St Petersburg metalworkers' union was already under
investigation by the police for its decision to send a delegation[32]
when the St Petersburg city captain informed trade-union boards
that attendance at the congress would be considered public
activity.[33] Although some trade-unionists did manage to attend
the congress as individuals, usually delegated by various workers'
clubs, this marked the end of organized trade-union participation
at such assemblies; twenty of those who did attend were arrested,
including the leading lights of the St Petersburg Central Bureau.
No St Petersburg trade-unionists were prepared to risk attending
the Congress on the Struggle against Prostitution and its Causes
which took place in Moscow in April 1910; only three unions
were allowed to send delegates to the Congress of Handicraft-
Trade Workers in January 1911 (the St Petersburg metalworkers'
union took legal advice before sending its representative);[34] and
the overwhelming majority of union representatives to the
Second Congress of Factory Panel Doctors in April 1911 were
arrested.[35]

In issuing the 'explanations', the government was in part
responding to pressure from the employers. In late 1907 Russian
industry entered a severe recession. Lay-offs became a regular

[31] The Congress of Factory Panel Doctors is discussed in Swain, *Russian Social
Democracy*, ch. 2.
[32] *Edinstvo*, 7 (10 July 1909).
[33] *Vozrozhdenie*, 1 (1910).
[34] *Nash put'*, 13 (10 Feb. 1911).
[35] For these legal congresses, see Swain, *Russian Social Democracy*, ch. 3.

feature of life for metalworkers; in 1909 the giant Baltic works sacked over 1,000 men and temporarily ceased production.[36] In the Moscow area, textile-workers regularly worked a four-day week,[37] while hardly any industry escaped the scourge of unemployment which affected 17 per cent of the capital's print-workers.[38] Employers, especially those in metalworking trades, responded by introducing the so-called American system of productivity payments,[39] or (notably in the printing industry) by obtaining exemption for their plant from the requirement to maintain the standards demanded by the Factory Inspectorate.[40]

However, the employers still felt threatened by the existence of the trade unions. In 1909 the Duma spokesman for the St Petersburg Society of Factory- and Mill-Owners criticized the Provisional Regulations of 1906. They had been drawn up in exceptional, revolutionary conditions, he said, and because they were unclear on certain points, they were now being interpreted by each in his own way; industry did not need trade unions.[41] By the end of 1909 the employers were holding secret discussions with the Ministry of the Interior about a possible revision of the provisional regulations.[42]

Not surprisingly, the Ministry of the Interior welcomed this initiative. Since early 1908 one of its officials, a certain Blazhchuk, had been looking at the provisional regulations with a view to their possible revision. The Blazhchuk Report did not recommend abolishing the freedom to form trade unions, but it did favour a radical revision of the law to make it harder for revolutionaries to penetrate them. Thus, according to Blazhchuk, it should be the Ministry of the Interior that drew up the union's charter, approved all the elected officers, and limited union activity to co-operation with the employers.[43]

New legislation of this type, however, would be controversial

---

[36] 'Iz zhizni i deyatel'nosti soyuza', *Edinstvo*, 3 (19 Mar. 1909); 6 (15 June 1909); Balabanov, *Ot 1905 k 1917*, p. 100.

[37] Ibid.

[38] Bonnell, *Roots of Rebellion*, p. 319, n. 3.

[39] 'Iz zhizni i deyatel'nosti soyuza', *Vestnik rabochikh po obrabotke metalla*, 1 (15 May 1908).

[40] *Pechatnoe delo*, 13 (24 Nov. 1909).

[41] Balabanov, *Ot 1905 k 1917*, p. 46.

[42] *Pechatnoe delo*, 13 (24 Nov. 1909).

[43] Bonnell, *Roots of Rebellion*, pp. 276–8; see also Antoshkin, *Professional'noe dvizhenie*, p. 179.

and its passage through the Duma would be time-consuming. Yet for the employers the situation was beginning to be urgent. State orders for the navy after the humiliation of the Bosnia–Herzegovina crisis meant that by 1910 the slump was over, and an upturn in the economy was under way. The organizational weakness of the unions had to be exploited before market forces began to favour the workers again and they tried to regain what had so recently been lost.

When they met with the Ministry of the Interior in late 1909 and early 1910, the employers raised one particular complaint: the lack of any precise definition of the phrase in the provisional regulations, to 'clarify the size of wage settlements'; did this mean the unions could organize strikes over pay?[44] The question of strikes had always been unclear, for the government's laws relating to the matter fell either side of the Moscow uprising. On 2 December 1905 the government had legalized certain categories of economic strikes in private industry; but by the time the provisional regulations were introduced in March 1906 all references to strike activity had been removed.

In 1907 the St Petersburg print-workers' union had been closed down for paying strike benefit to non-members after a Senate 'explanation' dated 30 November 1907,[45] but supporting members on strike was tolerated during 1908 and 1909. By 1910, however, the print-workers' union had become increasingly involved in economic struggle. While in 1908 under 5 per cent of the union's income had been spent on economic struggle, in 1909 this had risen to 20 per cent, and in 1910 to 25 per cent, 15 per cent of which was in the form of strike pay.[46] At a general meeting in November 1910, the board proposed increasing the amount given in strike pay by lifting the rule that stated that a member had to have been in the union for three months before becoming eligible for strike pay.[47]

Official concern at these developments became clear as early as February 1909, when the police attended a board meeting of the union.[48] On 7 October 1910 the police searched the union offices,

---

[44] Balabanov, *Ot 1905 k 1917*, p. 221.   [45] *Pechatnoe delo*, 3 (27 Jan. 1909).
[46] G. Chigarev, 'Obshchestvo rabochikh graficheskikh iskusstv v 1910', ibid. 25 (5 Oct. 1910).
[47] 'Izvlechenie iz zhurnala zasedanii', ibid. 27 (15 Dec. 1910).
[48] Ibid. 4 (21 Feb. 1909).

and, although the union tried to protest to the city captain at such gross interference in its operations, the union was closed down on 14 December 1910. The reasons given for the closure included simple support for the strike: it was not suggested that benefit had been paid to non-members, simply that the union's typewriter had been used by the strike committee, something that the union denied. Another reason given was that non-members had attended a delegate meeting, although the union insisted that they were new members waiting to join.[49]

This *de facto* limitation on the right to strike was quickly followed by an attack on the St Petersburg metalworkers' union on similar grounds. During 1910 the industrial recovery also enabled the metalworkers' union to intervene on the industrial scene, although to a more limited extent. In June it supported a three-week strike at the small Svet plant and won recognition for a workers' factory commission.[50] More importantly, much of the year was spent discussing a long-running dispute at Pintsh, another small plant. Matters came to a head on 18 January 1911 when the workers unanimously rejected revised work-schedules which extended shift times by half an hour per day, and went on strike. The union immediately offered its support; the board was told by the police not to support strikers, and when 200 roubles were donated to the strikers in February, the union was instructed to cease operations.

This incident became a minor *cause célèbre*, for the union appealed to the Office for Trade-Union Affairs, and, after talks with the board on 22–4 February, the office overruled the city captain's decision and lifted the closure of the union.[51] The official reason given for the closure was that 7 of the 207 who had attended a branch meeting were non-members, therefore the union had organized an illegal public meeting. The question of support for the strike was not raised because of continuing confusion about when a strike was, or was not, legal: strikes in the private sector to defend existing working conditions, which had been the case at Pintsh, were legal according to the December 1905 legislation.[52]

[49] Ibid. 28 (5 Jan. 1911); 'V mire truda', *Zvezda*, 6 (22 Jan. 1911).
[50] 'Iz zhizni i deyatel'nosti obshchestva', *Nash put'*, 4 (15 July 1910).
[51] Ibid. 14 (4 Mar. 1911).
[52] Ibid.; Bulkin, *Na zare*, p. 209.

In closing the print-workers' union and moving against the
metalworkers' union, the Ministry of the Interior was not so
much ignoring the law as jumping the gun and acting before its
revision could take legal effect. Early in 1911 the Senate issued an
'explanation' seeking to make clear what was, and what was not, a
defensive strike. It did so in the context of discussions which took
place throughout 1910 on the innocuous sounding 'Law on Certain
Changes in the Law relating to Conditions of Employment'. To
the unions this was a 'law on the freedom of lock-outs',
empowering employers faced by a strike, even in just one section
of their plant, to sack the entire work-force.[53]

Under existing legislation, the fact that workers were paid two
weeks in advance and two weeks in arrears meant that employers
had to give two weeks' notice of any changes in working
conditions. Employers found this irksome enough, but it also
meant that a striker could not be sacked on the spot unless he was
paid two weeks' wages. The Senate's 'explanation' neatly turned
these provisions on their head. If a worker went on strike without
giving two weeks' warning to the employer, he was breaking his
terms of employment, something contrary to rule 51 of the Law
on Conditions of Employment, which stated that any worker
leaving a factory 'without good cause' was liable to arrest. This
clause had been introduced before 1905, during a period of
labour shortage when workers were continually changing their
jobs without giving formal notice. Now the phrase 'without good
cause' was to apply to any economic strike, other than one
prompted by an employer's refusal to pay wages or by a decision
drastically to reduce wages without due notice. Any other strike
activity left the striker open to prosecution.[54]

The legislative process to revise the law in line with the
Senate's 'explanation' was not easy—the print-workers' journal
talked of 'long and passionate debates'—but it was eventually
accepted by the State Council and came into force on 1 January
1912. Its impact was immediate. When, on 26 February 1912,
the refounded St Petersburg print-workers' union agreed to
support strikers at the Yablonskii works, the police present at the
meeting duly reported the fact, and on 29 February the union

[53] 'Zakonoproekt o svobode lokautov', *Edinstvo*, 14 (16 Feb. 1910).
[54] 'Novoe raz"yasnenie senata', *Nash put'*, 13 (10 Feb. 1911); 'Senat raz"yasnyaet',
Pechatnoe delo, 31 (22 Feb. 1911); 'Novyi rabochii zakon', ibid. 2 (1 Feb. 1912).

was closed.[55] Similarly, late in 1911, when the St Petersburg metalworkers' union drew up plans to rationalize its strike-support activities by concentrating on small, winnable factories, the police did not hesitate to act. On 4 February 1912 a board meeting was raided by the police, and on 15 March the union was closed down.[56]

The closure of the print-workers' union in 1910 for supporting strikes was not only a turning-point for the employers and the government, marking as it did the start of a renewed offensive to narrow the scope of the provisional regulations, it also represented the start of a counter-offensive by the unions. The closure of the print-workers' union that year saw the start of a campaign by the unions for the introduction of a genuine law on freedom of association. The key to such a campaign was the relationship between the trade unions and the Social Democratic deputies to the Third Duma.

One of the first moves by the Social Democratic deputies had been to question the government about the reasons for the clamp-down on trade unions in the second half of 1907. Because of the Duma majority's decision that this question was not urgent, the issue was not debated in the Duma until 28 October and 4 November 1909. Then, the Deputy Minister of the Interior, Kruglov, simply quoted from the police report of 1907 (referred to above), which showed that of the 35 trade unions in the capital, 18 were run by the Social Democrats and 9 by the Socialist Revolutionaries. He added that by 1909 the situation had become even worse; at a time when the mass of ordinary workers were leaving the unions, the Social Democrats remained behind. Thus, while in 1907 one-third of union members were committed Social Democrats, by 1909 the figure had risen to almost one-half.[57] The trade unions would continue to be closed whenever the presence of Social Democrats posed a threat to social peace, he said.

In practical terms, then, the deputies' question achieved little. It did mean that whereas before 1907 many governors had simply ignored the law and closed unions at whim, once the question had

[55] Ibid. 4 (21 Mar. 1912).
[56] 'Chto delat'', *Metallist*, 4 (10 Nov. 1911); 5 (26 Nov. 1911); 'Iz zhizni i deyatel'nosti obshchestva', ibid. 7 (30 Dec. 1911); 11 (23 Feb. 1912).
[57] Antoshkin, *Professional'noe dvizhenie*, pp. 174–7.

been put to the Duma, the letter of the law was observed.[58] Also, and more importantly, work on the issue did bring together the deputies and the Central Bureau of St Petersburg Trade Unions. Co-operation between these two organizations was at first hesitant; in 1908, for example, the deputies took no part in the Congress of People's Universities, or the Congress of Co-operative Societies, or the Women's Congress. But the Congress of Factory Panel Doctors—and the key question of social insurance legislation to be debated at it—inevitably brought the two organizations together. While there was some caution about maintaining contacts with an illegal organization like the Central Bureau (at the end of 1907 the authorities had prevented the deputies from meeting representatives of the St Petersburg metalworkers' union, a legal organization, to discuss the insurance question[59]), the deputies' proposed Worker Commission began operations in February 1909 and included on it representatives of the Central Bureau.[60]

As we have seen, Duma deputy Pokrovskii attended the Congress of Factory Panel Doctors; he was succeeded by A. I. Predkal'n, who attended the Congress on the Struggle against Alcoholism, and Pokrovskii was joined by G. S. Kuznetsov at the Congress of Handicraft-Trade Workers. In March 1910 the loyal deputies questioned the government after the arrest of twenty worker delegates to the Congress on Alcoholism, and linked this to a protest against the proposal to revise the Law on Conditions of Employment then being discussed by the Duma. As with their previous question, the matter was not ruled urgent and disappeared into the 'vermicelli' of Duma procedure.[61]

At all the legal congresses, the workers' delegations had called for a new law guaranteeing genuine freedom of association, but it was only in January 1911, when the deputies' commitment to the unions was clear and the government's intention of removing the right to strike was there for all to see, that the unions initiated an organized campaign on this issue. The campaign was launched at a meeting of members of the workers' delegation to the

[58] *Vestnik truda*, 2 (Moscow, 12 Dec. 1909).

[59] Bulkin, *Na zare*, p. 208.

[60] P. V. Barchugov, *Revolyutsionnaya rabota bol'shevikov v legal'nykh rabochikh organizatsiyakh, 1907–11* (Rostov-on-Don, 1963), 21; 'Pis'mo iz Peterburga', *Proletarii*, 26 (13 Nov. 1908).

[61] *Edinstvo*, 16 (1 Apr. 1910).

Handicraft Workers' Congress. The original concept was for a 'petition campaign': when the novelist L. N. Tolstoi had died in 1910, several workers had spontaneously petitioned the Duma, urging it to debate the issue of the death penalty, which Tolstoi had consistently opposed. In a similar manner, the unions now hoped to encourage workers to petition the Duma to debate the closure of the print-workers' union and the threatened closure of the metalworkers' union. Such a campaign would also neatly coincide with the fifth anniversary of the Provisional Regulations of March 1906.[62]

The idea did not meet with much success; partly because of disagreements among Social Democrats as to whether petitioning the Duma meant recognizing its validity as a legislative body, and partly because it was clear that the Duma would ignore the petitions. However, the campaign for freedom of association grew from strength to strength. Petitions could be ignored by the Duma, but the Social Democrat deputies could not. At the October 1911 general meeting of the St Petersburg metalworkers' union (the one which also resolved to continue supporting strikes), it was decided to call on the deputies to introduce their own 'Law on the Freedom of Association', which would include a guarantee of the right to strike. This the deputies did in December 1911, after receiving petitions to this effect signed by over 14,000 workers.[63]

The proposed law was endorsed by the Bolshevik weekly, *Zvezda*, as well as by the trade-union press.[64] A similar bill was introduced into the Fourth Duma in the spring of 1914 which Lenin's 'orthodox Marxist' deputies agreed to support even though the sponsors were Mensheviks.[65] The freedom of association campaign was non-factional, and for the Leninists to disassociate themselves from it would have spelt disaster.[66] After the mass shooting of peaceful strikers in a legal dispute about the

---

[62] Swain, *Russian Social Democracy*, p. 119.

[63] 'Iz zhizni i deyatel'nosti obshchestva', *Metallist*, 4 (19 Nov. 1911); N. M. Dobrotvor, *Rabochie deputaty v III Gosudarstvennoi Dume* (Gor'kii, 1957), 163; G. Kuznetsov, 'Rabochie i politicheskaya zhizn'', *Zhivoe delo*, 6 (24 Feb. 1912); 'Rabochee dvizhenie', *Zvezda*, 29 (12 Nov. 1911).

[64] For a discussion of *Zvezda* and the party groups that supported it, see Swain, *Russian Social Democracy*, pp. 117–23.

[65] *Metallist*, 7 (8 May 1914).

[66] V. Sher, 'Nashe profdvizhenie za dva poslednikh goda', *Bor'ba*, 4 (28 Apr. 1914).

non-payment of wages on the Lena gold-fields, freedom of association became the principal slogan of the labour unrest that rocked Russia on the eve of the First World War. At every opportunity, with every strike prompted by the shootings and the subsequent discussion in the Duma, the slogan was repeated.[67] Similarly, once the government's social insurance legislation had been passed in the late spring of 1912, the campaign to elect worker representatives to insurance councils, which lasted throughout 1913 and into 1914, provided endless meetings at which the slogan could be invoked, especially since the authorities were at such pains to exclude the unions from any influence over the insurance councils.[68]

The fate of the metalworkers' union is particularly instructive in this context. The union which was closed in March 1912 was succeeded by a 'bogus' union, registered since 1908 and complete with fictitious membership reports. That was closed in August 1912, and it was not until 2 March 1913 that the refounded metalworkers' union was registered again.[69] The new union could not (a) improve the intellectual or spiritual life of members; (b) organize a hostel; (c) open a café; (d) organize excursions; (e) open a library; (f) organize legal aid; (g) open an employment office; (h) ask non-members for advice; (i) open trade sections or elect delegates; (j) include the unemployed as members; (k) aid the unemployed; (l) accept subscriptions for less than one full year; (m) organize fund-raising concerts; (n) appoint subscription-collecting factory representatives; or (o) transfer its property to a similar union in the event of closure. Several of these activities were specifically sanctioned by the provisional regulations.[70]

Given this long list of prohibitions, it is not surprising that the union was closed down in March 1914.[71] The reasons given were that the chairman had not signed all the minutes of the meetings; that members of the former metalworkers' union had been

---

[67] 'Lena i proletariat', *Zhivoe delo*, 14 (20 Apr. 1912).

[68] The government tried hard to ensure that sympathetic workers were elected to insurance groups rather than those supported by the unions. Trade-union meetings on the question of insurance continued to be banned. See Swain, *Russian Social Democracy*, ch. 6.

[69] Bulkin, 'Soyuz metallistov', pp. 125–33.

[70] 'Raz"yasnenie prava na professional'nuyu organizatsiyu', *Metallist*, 24 (14 Dec. 1912).

[71] Ibid. 3 (40) (15 Mar. 1914).

improperly transferred to the new union; that the budget had not been confirmed by the general meeting; and that the union was subsidizing the journal *Metallist*.[72] Such justifications for the closure were fairly transparent: the real reason was the dramatic wave of strikes that continued to shake Russia, and St Petersburg in particular. The problem for the authorities was that, even under Bolshevik leadership, the metalworkers' union observed the letter of the law. When the police tried to close the union in August 1913, the Office for Trade-Union Affairs could find no reason to justify the closure, as in February 1911, and it resumed its activities.[73] As Manfred Hagen has shown, the Lena shootings resulted in widespread opposition at all levels of society to an increasingly introverted regime. Even as bureaucratic a body as the Office for Trade-Union Affairs could not ignore public opinion, and apparently insisted on acting in accordance with the rule of law and not the arbitrary demands of the Ministry of the Interior.[74]

The Ministry of the Interior, however, was acting in the knowledge that further changes to the provisional regulations were in the air. The government's plans for a revised trade-union law were well advanced by 1914. As the trade-union press reported that April, the new law drafted by the Ministry of the Interior would narrow the scope of union activity still further. Apart from relatively minor changes, like lengthening the time the Office for Trade-Union Affairs took to consider union rules from one month to six weeks, the new law struck at the heart of one specific feature of the urban unrest on the eve of the First World War. All commentators were struck by the youth of the new labour activists, the 'raw recruits' from the villages who were apparently responsible for 'Bolshevizing' the trade unions.[75] The proposed new law restricted membership to those over twenty-one who had been employed in the same factory for at least one year; and union officers had to be at least twenty-five.

A further provision sought to subdivide the unions into weaker units by insisting that a union could only be formed in one

[72] Antoshkin, *Professional'noe dvizhenie*, p. 227.
[73] Bonnell, *Roots of Rebellion*, p. 375.
[74] M. Hagen, '"Obshchestvennost'": Formative Changes in Russian Society before 1917', *Sbornik*, 10 (1984).
[75] See Swain, *Russian Social Democracy*, p. 179.

factory, or of one trade, thus forcing fitters and turners into
separate unions. Police surveillance of union affairs would also
increase. In future, the police could attend more than general
meetings, and unions had to show membership lists to the
authorities. However, the final change was the most significant:
the city captain or governor was empowered to close down a
union on his own authority, thus removing the limited ability of
the Office for Trade-Union Affairs to prevent arbitrary closure.[76]
The revised law, which would clearly have extended government
control and surveillance over the trade-union movement, was put
to the Council of Ministers in May 1914, but it was abandoned
with the outbreak of war.

Clearly, as war approached, the government was just as
determined to narrow the scope of the provisional regulations as
the trade unions were to expand them. The tussle between
government and union, which had begun with the issuing of the
provisional regulations, and had passed through the union
closures of 1907 and the 1911 changes in the conditions of
employment, was likely to reach its zenith when the 1914 revised
legislation was confronted by the unions' 'freedom of association'
campaign.

The tsarist government, then, was in no way committed to the
principle of freedom of association, but it did seek to act within
the framework of the law in its handling of the unions. The
provisional regulations were never repealed, only interpreted;
even the 1914 legislation would have retained labour organizations
of a sort. In the climate of growing labour unrest and public
disquiet which characterized Russia in 1914, the government was
still cautious about returning to overt arbitrariness and abandoning the belief that, after 1905, autocratic powers were wielded
only according to the law.

---

[76] 'Svoboda soyuzov, sobranii', *Nashe pechatnoe delo*, 10 (3 Apr. 1914); Bonnell,
Roots of Rebellion, p. 377.

Freedom of the Press under the Old Regime, 1905–1914

CASPAR FERENCZI

THE constitutional reforms of 1905 and 1906 changed not only Russia's political institutions, but also her style of government and her political culture. Through the establishment of a parliament, the authorization of political parties, and the easing of censorship laws, public opinion gained a significance that it had not hitherto possessed. Along with the Duma and the political parties, the press was the main institution through which public opinion expressed itself between 1905 and 1914. Thanks to the repeal of preliminary censorship, journalism in general experienced a remarkable upswing: discussion and criticism in the press developed more vigorously than before into an independent political force. Despite continuing repression, which was further intensified in 1907, public opinion succeeded in acquiring and maintaining a new breadth, and in increasing its influence over governmental decisions.[1]

The increasing importance of the press is traceable in part to the rapid growth in literacy which occurred at the turn of the century among the lower strata of society, including the peasants.

* For comments and criticism, I am greatly indebted to other participants at the conference on civil rights in Russia, held in London in July 1985, especially Olga Crisp, Linda Edmondson, Geoffrey Hosking, John Klier, John Morison, and Marlene and Richard Wortman. I also want to thank Helmut Neubauer of the University of Heidelberg for his advice. This essay is based primarily on materials from the periodical press (newspapers, journals, magazines, etc.). Its observations and conclusions, however, hold true for the non-periodical press, which before 1905 already enjoyed more relative freedom than the periodical press. It should be noted that military and ecclesiastical censorship is excluded from consideration here.

[1] On the Duma period, see G. A. Hosking, *The Russian Constitutional Experiment: Government and Duma, 1907–1914* (Cambridge, 1973); L. H. Haimson (ed.), *The Politics of Rural Russia, 1905–1914* (Bloomington, 1979); T. Emmons, *The Formation of Political Parties and the First National Elections in Russia* (Cambridge, Mass., 1983); H. Rogger, *Russia in the Age of Modernisation 1881–1917* (London, 1983), 208–50; A. Ya. Avrekh, *Stolypin i Tret'ya Duma* (Moscow, 1968); id., *Tsarizm i IV Duma 1912–1914 gg.* (Moscow, 1981).

Although the illiteracy rate remained relatively high, the press was no longer of interest only to the educated. According to new calculations based on a comparison between circulation and numbers of inhabitants, over a third of the entire population prior to the First World War had a steady contact with newspapers, and in the large cities, even a majority of all adults.[2]

The press was able to play this special role within public opinion principally because it was much less subject to judicial, administrative, and political restrictions than the Duma and the parties. Even contemporary observers recognized the special significance of the press in the political life of pre-revolutionary Russia, and saw in the relatively free press the chief 'refuge' (*pribezhishche*) of public opinion. They went so far as to designate the press as the substitute for defective parliamentary institutions.[3] The daily press in particular proved to be an irreplaceable link between the government and politically conscious members of society. More than the parliament, it was felt to be a kind of 'counter-power' to the autocratic and bureaucratic government. On major political questions, the government for its part often attached more importance to contact with the press than to agreement with the Duma.

In order to understand the role of public opinion in the Russian political system prior to 1914, the following factors must also be taken into consideration:

1. The ruling class's need of legitimization and its wish for prestige grew considerably during the constitutional experiment. The imponderables of reform politics increased its desire for ideological agreement with society at large. The leadership was forced to recognize that traditional means of integration (like Orthodox piety or the charismatic element of tsarist autocracy) had lost their meaning in a rapidly changing society. Because of the composition and restricted authority of the newly established Duma, it could not adequately perform an integrating function;

[2] M. Hagen, *Die Entfaltung politischer Öffentlichkeit in Russland 1906–1914* (Wiesbaden, 1982), 144–8. On reading-public and public opinion, see J. Walkin, *The Rise of Democracy in Pre-Revolutionary Russia* (New York, 1962); W. M. Todd (ed.), *Literature and Society in Imperial Russia, 1800–1914* (Stanford, 1979); G. Guroff and S. F. Starr, 'A Note on Urban Literacy in Russia, 1890–1914', *Jahrbücher für Geschichte Osteuropas*, 19 (1971), 520–31; B. V. Bank, *Izuchenie chitatelei v Rossii XIX v.* (Moscow, 1969).

[3] V. L'vov-Rogachevskii, *Pechat' i tsenzura* (Moscow, 1906), 52.

instead, the press became almost indispensable to the government in this role, and proved itself to be a valuable index of the support that the government enjoyed in society. It could also be used as an indicator of a social consensus which, even if it did not correspond to the actual state of things, could be made to appear as if it did. This function of the press may well account for the personal trust which individual journalists enjoyed with ministers and high officials.

2. The influence of the press, however, did not rest only on its mirroring of the different opinions in the country at large, but also on its mirroring of political differences and conflicts within the leadership itself. The 'united government' was not a monolith of like-minded friends; liberal conservative, moderate conservative, and reactionary views clashed with each other in the cabinet. If ministers could use the power of the press to push through their views in the government, they could also be compromised by articles in the papers. In the personal quarrels among the different 'spheres' in the leadership and the disputes between departments, reference to public opinion and the press was a frequently used and often weighty argument. Journalists often received their information from competing groups within the leadership who believed that their views would have a better chance of realization with public support. St Petersburg newspapers above all enjoyed very close contact with the government and bureaucracy. This was especially true of conservative papers, but liberal newspapers also had their informants in the ministries. Thus, almost no important proceedings within the state apparatus could remain hidden from the public for long—a situation which frequently had embarrassing consequences for the government.

The manifold and close relations between government and bureaucracy on the one hand, and press on the other, should at least partly explain why the authorities had a basic respect for freedom of the press, even though large national newspapers expressed opinions that not infrequently exerted pressure on them. With respect to the developments in Russia after 1917, it is also worth remembering that for a short period before the First World War, it was possible to attack and criticize the government openly and legally—and sometimes with a radicalism that placed even the fundamental principles of the state in question. This gives the study of the Russian press between 1905 and 1914 an interest and significance that it would not otherwise possess.

After western scholars' long neglect of the significance of public opinion and the press in pre-revolutionary Russia, there are now signs of change. West German scholars have recently published a series of studies on the function of public opinion and the press in a semi-autocratic regime;[4] and English and American historians have also shown growing interest in similar subjects.[5] Soviet historiography, on the other hand, has long given the study of the Russian press considerable attention. First there appeared extremely useful newspaper bibliographies[6] and numerous works on the Bolshevik press.[7] Further Soviet research concerned itself with press legislation, censorship, and tsarist policy towards public information.[8] Since the middle of the 1970s there has been a boom in Soviet historical studies of the press; and recently several works on the Russian 'bourgeois' press have been published.[9]

Yet despite the increased interest of scholars in public opinion and the press, there remain serious gaps in our knowledge. There is still no new comprehensive history of the Russian press before

[4] Hagen, *Entfaltung*; C. Ferenczi, *Aussenpolitik und Öffentlichkeit in Russland, 1906–1912* (Husum, 1982); R. Rexheuser, *Dumawahlen und lokale Gesellschaft* (Cologne, 1980); C. Ferenczi, 'Funktion und Bedeutung der Presse in Russland vor 1914', *Jahrbücher für Geschichte Osteuropas*, 30 (1982), 362–98.

[5] D. R. Costello, 'Novoe Vremia and the Conservative Dilemma 1911–1914', *Russian Review*, 37 (1978), 30–50; W. E. Mosse, 'Imperial Favourite: V. P. Meshcherskiy and the Grazhdanin', *Slavonic and East European Review*, 59 (1981), 529–47; see also D. C. B. Lieven, *Russia and the Origins of the First World War* (London, 1983), 118–19, 129–38.

[6] The most important of the newspaper bibliographies is *Bibliografiya periodicheskikh izdanii Rossii 1901–1916*, i–iv (Leningrad, 1958–61).

[7] e.g. *Bol'shevistskaya pechat' i rabochii klass Rossii v gody revolyutsionnogo pod"ema 1910–1914 gg.* (Moscow, 1965); L. P. Strel'tsina and V. V. Shvedov, *Bol'shevistskaya legal'naya pechat' v gody pervoi revolyutsii v Rossii* (Leningrad, 1967).

[8] A. F. Berezhnoi, *Tsarskaya tsenzura i bor'ba bol'shevikov za svobodu pechati* (Leningrad, 1967); id., *Russkaya legal'naya pechat' v gody pervoi mirovoi voiny* (Leningrad, 1975); B. I. Esin, *Russkaya dorevolyutsionnaya gazeta* (Moscow, 1971); id., *Russkaya gazeta vtoroi poloviny XIX v.* (Moscow, 1973); id., *Russkaya gazeta i gazetnoe delo v Rossii* (Moscow, 1981).

[9] N. A. Balashova, *Rossiiskii liberalizm nachala XX veka (bankrotstvo idei 'Moskovskogo ezhenedel'nika')* (Moscow, 1981); S. V. Smirnov, *Legal'naya pechat' v gody pervoi russkoi revolyutsii* (Leningrad, 1981); A. N. Bokhanov, *Burzhuaznaya pressa Rossii i krupnyi kapital: Konets XIX v.–1914 g.* (Moscow, 1984); see also B. P. Baluev, *Lenin polemiziruet s burzhuaznoi pressoi* (Moscow, 1977).

1917, nor are there any individual studies of chief press organs and opinion-makers (e.g. Men'shikov). Moreover, the economic and financial aspects of the Russian press, as well as the question of ownership and of press monopolies, have been only inadequately investigated. Unlike the situation of the press in the large cities, where it possessed considerable freedom, the provincial press has scarcely been studied. This neglect extends to the foreign-language newspapers in Russia, which have been almost completely ignored by Soviet historians; the most important of these were the German newspapers in St Petersburg (*St. Petersburger Zeitung*, *St. Petersburger Herold*) and in Moscow (*Moskauer Zeitung*), and the French *Journal de Saint-Pétersbourg*.[10] Even the contemporary discussion of freedom of the press, which is particularly instructive for the development of civil rights and a legal order in tsarist Russia, remains untapped.[11]

This essay attempts to sketch the development of the Russian press between 1905 and 1914, and pays special attention to questions concerning freedom of the press. Central points of interest are censorship laws and practice, government policy towards the press, the rapid expansion of the periodical press after 1905, and the relationship of political parties and press. The presentation concentrates on the St Petersburg and Moscow press, for it was these political and cultural centres that dominated the public life of Russia.

Censorship: Laws and Practice

Although the reforms of 1905–6 sparked off a press boom, government controls and bureaucratic repression continued. It is true that the newly enacted press law abolished preliminary censorship and the administrative punishment of publishers and

---

[10] With certain reservations, this observation is also true for the newspapers published in Polish in the Russian territories of the empire, e.g. for the St Petersburg *Kraj*. For further information on the Polish press in tsarist Russia, see Z. Kmiecik, 'Prasa polska w zaborze rosyjskim w latach 1905–1915', in *Prasa polska w latach 1864–1918* (Warsaw, 1976), 58–113.

[11] *Svoboda pechati pri obnovlennom stroe* (St Petersburg, 1912); N. Ol'minskii, *Svoboda pechati* (St Petersburg, 1906); V. Rozenberg, *Letopis' russkoi pechati (1905–1914)* (Moscow, 1914). For the contemporary discussion of civil rights in Russia, see Linda Edmondson's essay in this volume.

journalists,[12] and that article 79 of the new Fundamental Laws of 23 April 1906 established the basic right of free expression: 'Everyone may, within the limits prescribed by law, express his ideas orally and in writing and may also disseminate them by means of the press or by other methods.'[13] But at the same time, criminal regulations concerning the press were considerably stiffened. Further, the new 'provisional' press law (*vremennye pravila*) applied only to periodicals published in the cities. The previous regulations remained in force for the provincial press, so that a newspaper or magazine could be started only with the permission of the Minister of the Interior. Similarly, preliminary censorship of articles about religious and ecclesiastical questions, as well as about court and military affairs and many other topics, was retained. Censorship committees in large cities were renamed 'Committees for Press Affairs', but censorship continued in a reduced and concealed form.[14]

Compared with pre-constitutional conditions, the new press law represented undeniable progress: starting a publication no longer required official permission. Confiscation of printed matter, punishment of publishers and editors, and suspension (temporary or permanent) of magazines and newspapers were no longer exclusively a matter for the administrative authorities, but lay within the jurisdiction of the courts. Yet despite these improvements, the government still had a means of control whose effect as a deterrent significantly infringed upon the freedom of the press. On publication, a specified number of copies of every issue of a newspaper or magazine had to be submitted to the appropriate committee or official for 'press affairs'. If the authorities found that their content violated the criminal code, they could confiscate individual issues of a

---

[12] J. Walkin, 'Government Controls over the Press in Russia, 1905–1914', *Russian Review*, 13 (1954), 203–9. For censorship policy before 1906, see D. Balmuth, *Censorship in Russia, 1865–1905* (Washington, DC, 1979); C. Ruud, *Fighting Words: Imperial Censorship and the Russian Press, 1804–1906* (Toronto, 1982).

[13] G. Vernadsky (ed.), *A Source Book for Russian History from Early Times to 1917*, iii (New Haven, 1973), 772–3; M. Szeftel, *The Russian Constitution of April 23, 1906: Political Institutions of the Duma Monarchy* (Brussels, 1967), 88–9, 148–50. For background information on concepts of individual rights and civil liberties in Russia, see W. E. Butler's and R. Wortman's essays in this volume.

[14] I. V. Novozhilova, 'Politika tsarskogo pravitel'stva v oblasti zakonodatel'stva o pechati 1905–1914 gg.', *avtoreferat* of the unpublished diss. (Leningrad, 1971), 5–6; Hagen, *Entfaltung*, pp. 102–13.

newspaper or prohibit its further publication. At the same time, officials were required to notify the court whose responsibility it was either to withdraw the confiscation or to initiate criminal proceedings against the 'responsible' editor. While the number of confiscations was relatively high, and the court's privileges were often passed over, the press regarded these measures more as a nuisance than as an effective deterrent. Criminal prosecution of publishers, editors, and authors, however, was a more substantial means of curbing freedom of the press.[15]

Although the new freedoms of 1905–6 were weakened by a series of accompanying regulations, official supervision of the press did not have the hoped-for effect. The government developed a new form of administrative punishment, therefore, which became its most effective and its most feared weapon. As a result of the state of emergency declared in June 1907, the governor or governor-general of a province was empowered to punish violations of the press law with fines of up to 3,000 roubles and imprisonment for up to three months. These emergency regulations partially restored the arbitrary administrative controls that had been repealed in 1905. Especially in the case of recurrent violations, the fines often caused financial difficulties for small newspapers and forced them to close.[16]

In 1907 official repression of the press reached its zenith: between 1907 and 1909 a total of 341 editors were sentenced to imprisonment, more than half of them (175) in 1907 (1908: 101; 1909: 65). In the same period, official decrees temporarily suspended 519 newspapers, 413 of which suspensions (*priostanovlenie*) occurred in 1907 alone (1908: 72; 1909: 34). The bulk of these punishments (over 80 per cent) were initiated by the administration and not by the courts. The same was true of fines. In 1907, 291 fines, with a sum total of roughly 170,000 roubles, were imposed: 265 by the administration (163,950 roubles), and only 26 by the courts (5,378 roubles).[17]

Yet despite the renewed pressure exerted against newspapers and magazines after 1907, the government never succeeded in

[15] Walkin, 'Government Controls', pp. 207–8.
[16] Berezhnoi, *Tsarskaya tsenzura*, pp. 204–5; 'Repressii', *Ezhegodnik Rech' na 1912 g.* (St Petersburg, 1913), 516–23; ibid., . . . *na 1913 g.* (St Petersburg, 1914), 33–40; ibid., . . . *na 1914 g.* (St Petersburg, 1915), 36–50.
[17] *Gosudarstvennaya Duma: Stenograficheskii otchet*, Third Duma, session 5 (St Petersburg, 1912), ii, col. 310; Novozhilova, 'Politika', pp. 10–11.

stopping the relatively free development of the press. After 1905 the rapid expansion of the press (including the rise of a tabloid press), the ever-increasing volume of printed matter, the diversification of society, the discovery of legal loopholes, and last but not least, inadequate money and staffing for supervisory organizations rendered a restoration of earlier checks on the press impracticable. The total number of periodicals rose from 1,002 in 1900 to 2,391 in 1910, and had reached 3,111 at the outbreak of the First World War. Of these, 1,293 were dailies (1912: 1,132), and the rest—1,818—were weeklies and monthlies.[18] The sheer quantity of publications impeded administrative control, while even mild forms of supervision, like any kind of censorship, only inspired the press to devise legal methods of evasion.

Through the adroit exploitation of legal possibilities and strict self-censorship, newspapers could dodge most of the administration's repressive measures. Two methods of legal evasion in particular were thorns in the side of the press committees. One was the 'language of Aesop'; the other was the elaboration of 'genealogy'. The 'language of Aesop', already a well-known technique of evasion in nineteenth-century Russia, continued to serve after 1905 as a form of coded communication between journalist and reading public.[19] Proscribed words and expressions were replaced by harmless-sounding formulations. For example, it was not permitted to mention the Russian Social Democratic Workers' Party, so the Bolshevik *Pravda* spoke instead of the 'underground', of 'consistent democrats', or 'consistent Marxists'. The reader understood perfectly well what these expressions meant— and so, apparently, did the censor. Another common trick was to 'camouflage' 'explosive' news, e.g. about strikes or workers' uprisings in Russia, as reports from the foreign press.[20] The

---

[18]   B. Rigberg, 'The Efficacy of Tsarist Censorship Operations', *Jahrbücher für Geschichte Osteuropas*, 14 (1966), 327–46. Soviet historians offer the opinion that only about one-fifth of the periodicals issued possessed political and social significance. Though this is certainly a considerable understatement, there is no doubt that even such a reduced amount was beyond the reading capacities of the press authorities. See M. S.Cherepakhov and E. M. Fingerit (comps. and eds.), *Russkaya periodicheskaya pechat': Spravochnik* (Moscow, 1957), 8.

[19]   Rigberg, 'Efficacy', pp. 336–9; W. Bassow, 'The Pre-Revolutionary Pravda and Tsarist Censorship', *The American Slavic and East European Review*, 13 (1954), 47–65; T. Riha, 'Riech': A Portrait of a Russian Newspaper', *Slavic Review*, 22 (1963), 663–82.

[20]   Bassow, 'Pre-Revolutionary Pravda', p. 50.

other method, 'genealogy', presented the censor with a virtually insoluble problem. After being banned by the authorities, a paper could ensure its continued publication by a mere change of name, leaving the editorial format otherwise the same. There were innumerable cases of newspapers and magazines dodging the official regulations in this way. The metamorphosis of opposition papers could be charted in a whole series of genealogical tables.[21]

An adroit publisher could also evade criminal prosecution by substituting for the real editor a so-called 'responsible' or 'sitting' editor, 'a comical figure in the annals of the Russian press' who then went to gaol for the violation of the law.[22] The more outspoken papers customarily hired a straw-man, usually a peasant or worker, to serve as the 'responsible' editor, and, if necessary, to go to gaol.[23] Confiscation and banning could also be avoided by another method: copies had to be sent to the censorship committees only after they had been printed and distribution had begun, so that even if the committee reacted swiftly, no more than 10 or 20 per cent of the general circulation (usually less) could be confiscated. Still another trick was ingeniously to delay delivery of copies to the committees. Often, too, periodicals, pamphlets, and books were printed without official permission, surreptitiously spirited from the printers and distributed before the censor had ever laid eyes on them.[24]

Use of these methods of evasion, particularly by the opposition (left liberal and socialist) press, undoubtedly overtaxed and partially paralysed the machinery of censorship. The under-manned and underfinanced press offices could not keep up with the tumultuous journalistic expansion, or, more precisely, the tsarist government did not attempt correspondingly to expand and consolidate them. As Benjamin Rigberg has shown, the Ministry of the Interior's reported expenditure for censorship offices remained approximately the same between 1882 and 1917. During those forty-five years, the total number of censors

[21] Rigberg, 'Efficacy', pp. 337-8.
[22] Walkin, 'Government Controls', p. 204.
[23] Ibid.; Hagen, *Entfaltung*, pp. 113-22.
[24] E. G. Golomb and E. M. Fingerit, *Rasprostranenie pechati v dorevolyutsionnoi Rossii i v Sovetskom Soyuze* (Moscow, 1967), 44-7; A. I. Merkulov and A. V. Man'kov, *Bol'shevistskaya podpol'naya pechat' v gody reaktsii* (Moscow, 1980), 11-21.

increased only negligibly, from 44 in 1882 to 46 in 1917. Even if one includes the provincial governors upon whom devolved the supervision of the press in their provinces, the total number of officials charged with censorship probably amounted to less than one hundred. In 1914, for example, this 'staff' found itself faced with the enormous task of inspecting 32,338 books and pamphlets and over 3,000 periodicals in more than fifty languages.[25]

These statistics indicate the relative harmlessness of a censorship machinery confronted with an immense flood of publications. Correspondingly, the evident inadequacy of the censor reflects an advance in freedom for the press. The inefficacy of the censorship machinery and censorship laws explains, at least in part, 'a major paradox' which has long puzzled historians of the old regime, namely, 'the existence of a flourishing press alongside a narrow and repressive censorship'.[26]

To balance this assessment, however, some peculiarities of the official censorship policy should be kept in mind: censorship regulations were applied selectively; the censor took more drastic action against small 'revolutionary' papers than against large 'moderate' ones; provincial papers and those of national minorities were more strictly controlled than the big city press; and the reporting of domestic politics was more rigorously censored than foreign-policy commentary.

The files of the Chief Administration for the Affairs of the Press (*Glavnoe upravlenie po delam pechati*) show that critical discussion of the following topics was particularly risky: the situation of factory workers, strikes, demonstrations, political prisoners (e.g. *katorga*), suppression of the socialist movement, emancipation of women, the Jewish question and anti-Semitism, as well as problems of nationality in general. In addition, penalties were frequently imposed for critical articles on religious and ecclesiastical questions, on the affairs of the Court (particularly those concerning Rasputin), and on armament policy and the state of the army. The fact that most of these penalties were imposed on workers' newspapers and tabloids reveals the socially defensive character of tsarist censorship policy. It was directed primarily against the urban lower classes and their political organizations. But it also operated against the provincial population

[25] Rigberg, 'Efficacy', pp. 331–41.
[26] Ibid. 343.

and non-Russian minorities. Polish newspapers in particular suffered disproportionately under censorship regulations.[27] For all that, the tsarist government made no serious attempt to muzzle the press during the constitutional period. It did not yield to the constant pressure from reactionary parties and sections of the bureaucracy for a new, restrictive press law, and it withdrew the press bill of 1913–14 following massive public protest. As the debates over the bill show, the Duma proved to be an important protector of freedom of the press.[28]

The conduct of the government towards the press corresponded to the main features of its conduct towards the political parties. In neither case did the government exhaust the judicial and administrative means of control at its disposal. An exception to this rule was its conduct towards the extreme left of the journalistic spectrum. While moderate (conservative and liberal) newspapers also complained about censorship regulations, official repression was primarily directed against small 'revolutionary' papers, which, unlike the larger papers, lacked the financial wherewithal to offset fines and other penalties. Although at the start of 1906 it appeared as if official efforts to bring the press under control again were a hopeless enterprise, by the autumn of that year the bureaucracy and the police had the situation so far in hand that it was impossible for Social Democratic and Socialist Revolutionary papers to publish. By contrast, the moderate liberal, conservative, and reactionary press enjoyed a relatively unhindered development. None of the large 'moderate' newspapers was plagued by confiscation and criminal prosecution to such an extent that it felt its existence endangered. The conduct of the government towards the press thus indicated its readiness to co-operate with 'moderate public opinion'. For its part, the press exploited the possibilities of this situation to enlarge its scope extensively. In general, although the half-hearted censorship after 1905 still exerted an irritating influence on the free development of the press, police methods were no longer the main means of implementing official press policy.

[27] Tsentral'nyi gosudarstvennyi istoricheskii arkhiv (hereafter TsGIA), f. 776 (Glavnoe upravlenie po delam pechati), op. 10, d. 630–5. These observations agree with those of G. R. Swain, W. G. Wagner, S. A. Smith, R. Pearson, P. Waldron, and J. D. Klier in this volume.

[28] I. V. Shestakova, 'K istorii zakonoproekta o pechati ot 26 aprelya 1914 goda', Voprosy istorii SSSR XIX–XX vv. (Leningrad, 1971), 129–44.

Official Press Policy

With the decline of direct repression, indirect methods of control and influence gained increasing importance. Although the Tsar and many of his ministers continued to regard journalistic criticism as destructive, and the authorities often complained about the 'insolence of newspaper scribblers', the government did not hesitate to exploit the possibilities of a free press to propagate its political views. After the abolition of preliminary censorship, the government in general, and various departments in particular, rapidly developed flexible and graduated means of influencing the press and public opinion. These means ranged from the control of information via government-owned papers and semi-official news agencies, through behind-the-scenes conversations and the 'inspiration' of important journalists, to surreptitious subsidies for publishers and direct bribes to individual journalists.[29] But the press policy of the government was not a one-sided affair; it coincided to a large extent with the actual interest of the press—authentic information about official policies. It is against this background that the manifold informal relations between state apparatus and press should be understood.

By the beginning of 1905 it had already become clear to some tsarist ministers that the government must do something about the growing 'harmful' influence of the opposition press. Since the existing official organs of the ministries and the government gazettes (*Pravitel'stvennyi vestnik* and *Russkoe gosudarstvo*) could not counterbalance the independent press, the government founded a new semi-official organ, *Rossiya*, in November 1905. Although *Rossiya* was no match in quality and influence for the large St Petersburg and Moscow papers, it did win a certain respect in its early years for its relative independence. After it was placed under stricter government control in 1910, it lost its good reputation, and in April 1914 it had finally to be shut down.[30]

Semi-official news agencies offered much better opportunities

---

[29] E. V. Letenkov, 'Iz istorii politiki russkogo tsarizma v oblasti pechati', unpublished diss. (Leningrad, 1974); Hagen, *Entfaltung*, pp. 122–6.

[30] S. I. Stykalin, 'Russkoe samoderzhavie i legal'naya pechat' 1905 goda (k voprosu o proektakh sozdaniya ofitsioznoi pressy)', in B. I. Esin (ed.), *Iz istorii russkoi zhurnalistiki kontsa XIX–nachala XX v.* (Moscow, 1973), 67–98.

for controlling information than official and semi-official papers. Owing to the underdeveloped system of communications, especially in the provinces, many newspapers depended on the services of these agencies. The most important of these semi-official distributors of information were the St Petersburg Telegraph Agency (*Sankt-Peterburgskoe telegrafnoe agentstvo*), the Information Bureau of the Chief Administration for the Affairs of the Press (*Osvedomitel'noe byuro pri Glavnom upravlenii po delam pechati*), and the Bureau of Russian Journalists (*Byuro russkikh zhurnalistov*).[31]

The emphasis of official information policy plainly lay on the St Petersburg Telegraph Agency. It was charged with circulating political, financial, economic, commercial, and other news 'of public interest' at home and abroad.[32] By contrast, the Information Bureau and the Bureau of Russian Journalists had comparatively limited tasks. The former, established in 1906 by the Chief Administration for the Affairs of the Press, was charged with informing the press about the aims and the activity of the government through 'confidential' bulletins. The latter, founded in November 1912 as a counterweight to the growing oppositional mood, concerned itself primarily with the provincial press. All three news agencies were more or less dependent on state allocations. All in all, they did not pay for their upkeep. Because of their bureaucratic indolence and one-sided reporting, they could not compete with the independent press. The tsarist government never succeeded in turning these agencies into efficient instruments of its information policy, despite various organizational reforms which continued into the period of the First World War.[33] After 1905 a function comparable to that of the semi-official news agencies was performed by press bureaux attached to individual ministries.[34]

Another common method of influencing the press was the

---

[31] E. V. Letenkov, 'K istorii pravitel'stvennykh informatsionnykh tsentrov v Rossii (1906–1917 gg.)', *Vestnik Leningradskogo universiteta*, 2 (1973), 80–8; on the activities of the agencies, see TsGIA, f. 776, op. 34, d. 18; f. 1358 ('Sankt-Peterburgskoe telegrafnoe agentstvo'), op. 1, d. 24, 375, 841, 1255–7, 1917.

[32] Polozhenie Soveta Ministrov o Sankt-Peterburgskom telegrafnom agentstve (3 Dec. 1909), in *Sobranie uzakonenii i rasporyazhenii pravitel'stva, izdavaemoe pri Pravitel'stvuyushchem senate*, 10 (1910), 95–8.

[33] Letenkov, 'K istorii', pp. 80–4.

[34] Such information centres existed in the Ministries of the Interior, Foreign Affairs, Finance, War, and Commerce.

direct and indirect subsidizing of certain papers. Those that profited from direct allocations were mainly reactionary papers like *Russkoe znamya*, *Zemshchina*, and *Moskovskiya vedomosti*, which, despite their financial dependence on the government, numbered among its sharpest critics. The group of newspapers that received indirect financial support (e.g. through the placing of state announcements and the publication of decrees) was much wider: moderate conservative and Octobrist papers also received such 'state commissions', and only the Kadet and socialist press went away empty-handed.[35]

The direct effect of this method was probably negligible. The public was too vigilant for large newspapers to be able to afford to be 'bought' in this way—an assumption that seems to be borne out by the steady criticism which precisely these conservative papers directed against the government. Apart from that, large national papers were generally so well provided for financially that they could easily do without government subsidies.

As well as both secret and open subsidies, the government frequently applied subtler methods to influence the press. Not only 'liberal' ministers used confidential conversations to 'inspire' the editors of certain newspapers to express opinions similar to their own. Occasionally these inspirations were heightened by monetary gifts.[36]

Since the government had only inadequate means to bring its views before a larger public, it was thrown back on influential independent newspapers. Hence it was no accident that ministers preferred to 'inspire' journalists attached to well-known moderate conservative and liberal papers. The inferior quality and limited influence of the official, semi-official, and government-subsidized right-wing press made it impossible for it to perform the same function as the influential independent papers.

The importance of these indirect methods and informal contacts in official efforts to influence the press means that their success cannot be precisely evaluated. In domestic politics the government usually supported the right wing of the journalistic

---

[35] E. V. Letenkov, 'Iz istorii reptil'nogo fonda Glavnogo upravleniya po delam pechati', *Vestnik Leningradskogo universiteta*, 14 (1973), 137–9; A. Chernovskii (ed.), *Soyuz russkogo naroda* (Moscow, 1929), 32, 38–40, 42, 56, 75–6; V. N. Kokovtsov, *Iz moego proshlogo*, ii (Paris, 1933), 111–24.

[36] Ferenczi, *Aussenpolitik*, pp. 70–5.

spectrum (i.e. reactionary, conservative, and Octobrist papers), while in foreign policy it also supported Progressist and Kadet papers; in this way, the impression could be created that a broad public approved its policies. But this impression was not so much the work of the official press policy as a reflection of the existing power relations in Russia.

The Press Boom

With the relaxation of censorship laws, the Russian daily press expanded rapidly. The number of dailies climbed from 125 in 1900 to 856 in 1913. In the same period they tripled their daily total circulation from one million to over three million.[37] The Moscow daily *Russkoe slovo*, which was also widely read in central Russia, reached a circulation of over 600,000 copies in 1914, making it the largest Russian daily. (At the turn of the century its circulation had been 13,000; in 1905, already 250,000.) The second largest Moscow paper, *Russkiya vedomosti*, also had a circulation of more than 100,000.[38]

Among the largest St Petersburg newspapers were *Novoe vremya* (published by the 'Press Tsar', Aleksei Suvorin), with a circulation of over 200,000 (1905: 60,000); the financial newspaper *Birzhevyya vedomosti*, with a morning and an evening edition of 170,000 copies (morning edition, 1907: 37,000); the tabloid *Gazeta-kopeika*, which in 1909 already had a circulation of 250,000; and *Vechernee vremya* (founded in 1911 and also published by Suvorin), with about 140,000 copies. In addition, there were several smaller papers with circulations of between 20,000 and 100,000 copies.[39]

A striking characteristic of the press boom was that tabloids—with their extensive advertising sections, proportionately little text, and short, simply written articles—achieved the highest

[37] Walkin, 'Government Controls', pp. 204–6; Cherepakhov and Fingerit, *Russkaya periodicheskaya pechat'*, pp. 20–2, 45–8, 83–6, 132–6; Bokhanov, *Burzhuaznaya pressa*, pp. 28–43.

[38] The figures are taken from newspaper bibliographies: *Bibliografiya*, i–iv; Cherepakhov and Fingerit, *Russkaya periodicheskaya pechat'*; A. G. Dement'ev (ed.), *Russkaya periodicheskaya pechat' (1702–1894): Spravochnik* (Moscow, 1959).

[39] Cherepakhov and Fingerit, *Russkaya periodicheskaya pechat'*, pp. 17–20; Bokhanov, *Burzhuaznaya pressa*, p. 37.

circulation. In this category belong *Gazeta-kopeika*, *Vechernee vremya*, and, with certain qualifications, *Birzhevyya vedomosti* and *Russkoe slovo*. Their influence on the shaping of public opinion, however, was probably slight, since they stood on the margin of Russian journalistic discussion. Public discussion was dominated by the newspapers of parties and movements. Apart from *Novoe vremya* and *Russkiya vedomosti*, these had a relatively low circulation, usually between 20,000 and 60,000 copies. For example, the Kadet organ, *Rech'*, never exceeded a peak circulation of 40,000 (average circulation was only 17,000). The Progressist paper, *Utro Rossii* (founded in 1909), published on average barely 40,000 copies daily. The circulation of other party or party-sympathetic newspapers like *Golos Moskvy*, *Slovo*, *Svet*, *Moskovskiya vedomosti*, and others, was probably in the same range.[40] By contrast, the papers of the Black Hundreds never exceeded a circulation of 10,000 copies daily (1915: *Russkoe znamya*, 3,000; *Zemshchina*, 6,000).[41] The circulation of the semi-official *Rossiya* swung between 9,000 and 32,000 copies.[42] The legal Bolshevik newspaper *Pravda* was published between 1912 and 1914 with an average circulation of 30,000, at times reaching approximately 60,000. The Menshevik *Luch*, published between 1912 and 1913, had a circulation of between 9,000 and 12,000.[43]

The bulk of a paper's circulation was at the place of publication; supraregional distribution was confined mainly to *Novoe vremya*, *Russkoe slovo*, *Russkiya vedomosti*, and—despite its low circulation—the Kadet *Rech'*. On the other hand, the financially and editorially less well-equipped provincial papers regularly reprinted articles from big city papers, and adopted the views of metropolitan opinion-makers.

Among the periodicals (including weeklies and monthlies) that dominated the shaping of public opinion belonged principally *Novoe vremya*, *Rech'*, *Slovo*, *Rossiya*, and, to a lesser degree, *Birzhevyya vedomosti*, *Rus' (Novaya Rus')*, *St. Petersburger Zeitung*, *Svet*, *Sankt-Peterburgskiya vedomosti*, *Russkoe znamya*, *Zemshchina*, and *Grazhdanin* (all of St Petersburg), as well as

[40] Bokhanov, *Burzhuaznaya pressa*, p. 37; N. S. Vertinskii, *Gazeta v Rossii i SSSR XVII–XX vv.* (Moscow, 1931), 127–34.
[41] *Bibliografiya*, i. 650; iii. 95.   [42] Ibid. iii. 46.
[43] Ibid. ii. 286, 629; Esin, *Russkaya dorevolyutsionnaya gazeta*, pp. 73–4.

the Moscow papers, *Russkiya vedomosti*, *Golos Moskvy*, *Utro Rossii*, *Russkoe slovo*, *Moskovskiya vedomosti*, the weekly magazine *Moskovskii ezhenedel'nik*, and the monthly journals *Russkaya mysl'*, *Vestnik Evropy*, and *Russkoe bogatstvo*. The journalistic spectrum sketched above represents to some extent the opinion-market in which all the important political questions of the day were discussed. These periodicals dominated journalistic discussion; they quoted and referred to each other, and conducted countless controversies among themselves which decisively shaped the political life of pre-war Russia. Thus the Russian press scene was dominated by St Petersburg and Moscow newspapers. With few exceptions, the provincial papers were ignored in the main cities. The Moscow and provincial papers generally featured news of domestic politics, while the St Petersburg papers paid more attention to foreign affairs.

The quality and editorial staffs of the newspapers differed widely. Owing to their extensive knowledge in the areas of politics, society, economy, and culture, *Slovo*, *Novoe vremya*, *Russkiya vedomosti*, *Rus'*, *Rech'*, *Utro Rossii*, and, with qualifications, *Moskovskiya vedomosti* stood far above the other papers. They also had more pages than the others, seldom less than eight and frequently twice or three times that number at weekends (plus an illustrated supplement). Finally, these moderate conservative and liberal papers were better equipped financially and editorially. They had large editorial staffs, a wide-flung net of correspondents both in and out of Russia, and numerous contributors from every field of public life. Not only leading parliamentarians, but also other 'public figures' (*obshchestvennye deyateli*) like university professors, writers, artists, and even diplomats and high officials (using pseudonyms) wrote for the large national newspapers.[44]

Parties and Press

On the whole, the Russian press of the pre-war decade offers a faithful mirror of the country's political and cultural trends. After

---

[44] H. W. Williams, *Russia of the Russians* (London, 1914), 99–125, provides a useful survey on the press after 1905; see E. E. Kluge, *Die russische revolutionäre Presse in der zweiten Hälfte des neunzehnten Jahrhunderts, 1855–1905* (Zürich, 1948), for the situation before 1905.

1905 the common feature of journalistic criticism was its front against autocracy and bureaucracy, as well as the demand for more democratic participation at all levels. But this polarization soon broke down. In the press a wide spectrum of opinion was formed: reactionary, conservative, liberal, and even socialist voices were heard.[45]

The journalistic spectrum of the pre-war period was dominated by papers that represented either a particular political party or at least a definite political trend. The countless professional and political organizations established in 1905 and 1906 promptly founded their own periodicals, though many of these proved to be ephemera and swiftly vanished from the scene. Even independent newspapers almost always declared themselves in favour of the programme of a parliamentary party or of a certain (seldom more than one) political trend. Except for the moderate right, all parliamentary groups owned their own periodicals. Contact between party and press was especially close among the Kadets and the extreme right. In the case of the Union of the Russian People, the party organization usually consisted of nothing more than the publication of a periodical financed by state and private donations. Typically, only those groups with the least organizational coherence (the moderate right and the Nationalists) had no real party newspaper.

The close connection between party and press resulted partly from the retarded development of Russian parliamentarianism. Whereas in the Duma the parties usually had to exercise caution and reserve, in their papers they could propagate their views fairly freely.

The political physiognomy of the Russian press as it was formed in 1905–6 remained largely the same until 1914. Radical changes of policy almost never occurred, though sometimes a periodical slightly modified its political point of view. The reverse side of this situation was that established papers reacted only slowly to shifts in political opinion, and new political movements and groupings were thus forced to found their own papers.

The political viewpoints of the Russian press before 1914 may be divided into five groups: liberal, Octobrist, conservative,

---

[45] For further information on the connections between political parties and press, see Ferenczi, 'Funktion', pp. 382–98.

reactionary, and socialist. Although the liberal press did not have the highest circulation, it nevertheless played a key role in the journalistic spectrum. The St Petersburg daily *Rech'*, edited by Milyukov and I. V. Hessen (Gessen), was the main organ of the Kadet party, but it was not the only one. Between 1906 and 1908 (and later again in 1917–18) the party published the weekly journal *Vestnik partii narodnoi svobody* as its theoretical organ. In addition, the Kadets maintained a small news agency in St Petersburg. The organ of the Moscow Kadets was the illustrious professorial paper, *Russkiya vedomosti*. From December 1912 until August 1913 the right wing of the party around P. B. Struve and V. A. Maklakov published its own paper, *Russkaya molva*, which was soon ruined by official fines. There was also a series of independent liberal papers, of which the main ones were *Birzhevyya vedomosti*, *Rus'*, *Sovremennoe slovo*, *Stolichnaya pochta* (all of St Petersburg), and *Russkoe slovo* (of Moscow). The papers of the Party of Peaceful Renewal/Progressists also betrayed a liberal slant: *Slovo* (St Petersburg; shut down in 1909), and *Utro Rossii* (Moscow; founded 1909).

A few liberal weeklies and monthlies played a special role among the liberal press, constituting the main journalistic forum for the progressive intelligentsia. These included *Polyarnaya zvezda* (1905–6; editor, Struve) and *Moskovskii ezhenedel'nik* (1906–10; editors, E. N. and G. N. Trubetskoi), and the highly respected old learned journals, the so-called 'thick journals' (*tolstye zhurnaly*), *Russkaya mysl'*, *Russkoe bogatstvo*, and *Vestnik Evropy*.[46]

Compared with Kadet and Progressist papers, those of the Octobrists were of less importance. The main Octobrist paper, *Golos Moskvy* (published by the party president, A. I. Guchkov), was never really able to cast off its provincial-newspaper manner. The small *Golos pravdy* (1905–10) was for a time regarded as the organ of the St Petersburg Octobrists, but it could never have survived without the bribes of the German embassy.[47] However, the underrepresentation of Octobrist papers in the press was

---

[46] Riha, 'Riech'', pp. 663–5; U. Liszkowski, *Zwischen Liberalismus und Imperialismus* (Stuttgart, 1974), 57–9; Bokhanov, *Burzhuaznaya pressa*, pp. 64–71, 75–9.
[47] Politisches Archiv, Auswärtiges Amt, Bonn, Russland 74 secr., i (Die russische Presse).

redressed by the fact that Octobrist voices were frequently heard
in right-wing Kadet, Progressist, and conservative papers.
Nevertheless, the journalistic influence of the Octobrists was in
no way comparable to that of the liberal and conservative
papers.[48]

None of the liberal papers, however, equalled Suvorin's *Novoe
vremya* in quality and influence. Apart from some high-
circulation tabloids, this was the largest and most influential
Russian newspaper. For its undisputed leading role the 'Russian
Times' had to thank its astonishing adaptability. With remarkable
skill, it accommodated itself at all times to precisely the dominant
trends in society and bureaucracy; which was why contemporaries
called it the 'Russian weathervane'. *Novoe vremya* enjoyed close
contact with the government and bureaucracy, and was frequently
regarded outside Russia as a government organ. The paper owed
much of its prestige to its *feuilleton* section, which was
considered to be the best in Russia. Its political range extended
from liberal to reactionary, although its editorials followed
mainly a moderate conservative course. *Novoe vremya* liked to
regard itself as a suprapartisan paper, but in fact it can be seen as
the journalistic representative of the moderate right and the
Nationalists in the Duma.[49] Other important papers that
belonged to the conservative camp were *Svet* and the *Sankt-
Peterburgskiya vedomosti*.

Unlike the conservative camp, connections between party and
press among the reactionaries were close. *Russkoe znamya* and
Zemshchina were the official organs of the Black Hundreds, and
the main reactionary newspaper, *Moskovskiya vedomosti*, considered itself the press representative of all monarchistic organizations. The militant Kiev rightist paper, *Kievlyanin*, is also to be
seen against this background.[50]

Among the opinion-makers of the (extreme) right, the two
'élitist free spirits' should be mentioned: Prince V. P. Meshcherskii and M. O. Men'shikov, who numbered among the most important ideologists of the *ancien régime* in Russia. Meshcherskii's

---

[48] Bokhanov, *Burzhuaznaya pressa*, pp. 74–5.

[49] Costello, 'Novoe Vremia'; E. Ambler, *Russian Journalism and Politics 1861–
1881: The Career of Aleksei Suvorin* (Detroit, 1972), 176–82; N. Ya. Abramovich,
Novoe vremya: Istoricheskii ocherk (Petrograd, 1916); A. S. Suvorin, *Dnevnik*
(Moscow, 1923).

[50] Ferenczi, 'Funktion', pp. 392–4.

journal, *Grazhdanin*, discussed the political questions of the day with wit and mischief. Men'shikov, the *enfant terrible* of Russian journalists, played a similar role in his permanent special column in *Novoe vremya*, where he took positions on all important political and cultural questions. Expressive of his extreme, but at the same time undogmatic, conservatism, Men'shikov's brilliant, original, and often cynical style made his articles into a kind of journalistic institution.[51]

Unlike the newspapers of the extreme right, whose small influence can be fairly precisely evaluated, it is harder to judge the impact of the extreme leftist press. Like the 'bourgeois' press, the 'revolutionary' press also experienced an immense upswing in 1905. In the main cities in the provinces, numerous Social Democratic and Socialist Revolutionary papers were founded, and their average circulation (between 10,000 and 30,000 copies) is an indication of considerable public influence. Many of them soon vanished, however, because of official repression and financial problems. The last legal Bolshevik paper, *Nashe ekho* of St Petersburg, had to shut down in April 1907 (though Social Democratic newspapers printed outside Russia, like *Proletarii* and *Sotsial-demokrat*, continued to be distributed by the underground).[52] The resulting gaps were partly filled by such left liberal newspapers as *Tovarishch* and *Sovremennoe slovo*.

Only the changed political situation in Russia some years later allowed Bolshevik and Menshevik newspapers a return to legality: from 1910 until April 1912 the Bolshevik paper *Zvezda* was legally published in St Petersburg. But of its total of 60 issues, 30 were confiscated, and on 22 April 1912 the authorities banned it 'for ever'. Its successor, *Pravda* (founded 22 April 1912), was able to hold its ground better. Although 190 of the 646 issues printed up to 1914 were confiscated and its editors were repeatedly subjected to criminal prosecution, *Pravda* was able to remain in existence under different names until the outbreak of the First World War. On 8 July 1914 it was shut down and the staff were gaoled. Not until after the fall of the tsarist regime could *Pravda* begin publishing again in March 1917 as the organ of the Central Committee of the RSDRP.[53]

[51] Ibid. 394–6; on Meshcherskii and his *Grazhdanin*, see Mosse, 'Imperial Favourite'.   [52] Esin, *Russkaya dorevolyutsionnaya gazeta*, pp. 69–70.
[53] Bassow, 'Pre-Revolutionary Pravda'.

By 1912 the Mensheviks also possessed once again a legal press organ in Russia. But the St Petersburg daily *Luch*, the descendant of the exile paper *Golos sotsial-demokrata* which had been suspended in 1911, was itself banned at the beginning of July 1913. Its successors fared no better: *Zhivaya zhizn'* appeared from 11 July till 1 August 1913; and *Novaya rabochaya gazeta* from 8 August 1913 till 23 January 1914. The main Menshevik paper never achieved even a third of the Bolshevik *Pravda*'s average circulation.[54]

The legal newspapers of the Socialist Revolutionaries had little success: *Trudovoi golos* and *Zhivaya mysl'* (both of St Petersburg) lasted only a short time—from 17 February till 23 July 1913, and from 17 August till 6 September 1913 respectively. Of both papers' total of thirty issues, twenty were confiscated—apparently less because of their 'revolutionary zeal' than their 'unbridled language'.[55]

The Social Democratic and Socialist Revolutionary press was largely ignored by the 'bourgeois' press. At most, Kadet newspapers showed occasional interest in the internal battles of the Social Democrats. Speeches of Social Democratic representatives in the Duma received much more notice, and were frequently reprinted at full length by liberal papers.

Conclusion

Compared with other freedoms in pre-revolutionary Russia, freedom of the press was already considerable before 1905; but the constitutional reforms of 1905–6, in particular the repeal of preliminary censorship and the guarantee of further human rights, substantially enlarged the scope of the press. This resulted in a press boom; the number of newspapers, magazines, and journals, as well as their circulation, rose immensely. The main characteristics of this development were the irrepressible rise of the tabloid press, the considerably increased importance of liberal papers of all shades (to the cost of the conservative

---

[54] 'Pamyatnaya zapiska o rabochikh gazetakh v Peterburge', *Krasnyi arkhiv*, 10 (1925), 286–99.
[55] Ibid.

papers), and the growing economic support for the press, especially from the banks.

Thanks to its relative freedom, the press succeeded in partly compensating for the limited possibilities of the parliament and the political parties. If a piece of information seemed too risky to print, journalists often asked deputies to discuss the issue in the Duma. Since the authorities respected parliamentary privileges, not only the liberal opposition but even the revolutionary parties could express their views fairly freely in the Duma, while the press could disseminate reports of the discussion throughout the entire country. Press and Duma often helped one another: newspapers reported on Duma affairs in detail (but not on the State Council), and the Duma fought for freedom of the press. Thus, to a certain extent, the skilfully organized co-operation between press and parliament balanced the deficiencies of the political system. Similarly, parties and press working together could often get around restrictions on the freedom of assembly. In order to elude a police ban, political parties would bar the public from their meetings but would admit the press; next day the interested reader could find a report of the proceedings in his newspaper.

But Russia in 1905–14 was far from being a liberal democracy. In large parts of the empire, the civil rights that had been guaranteed in 1905 were restricted by emergency regulations. Particularly in the provinces, the government resorted to drastic measures and succeeded in almost completely suppressing the opposition press and parties. The main advances in freedom of the press were the removal of the press from exclusive administrative control, its protection by regulations defined by law, and its subjection to the jurisdiction of the courts. This decisively improved its situation; but at the same time the government retained the power to impose heavy fines and imprisonment, which seriously infringed upon full freedom of expression. As other articles in this volume show, the main problem was the lack of absolute legal guarantees. Arbitrary acts of the authorities against the press were still possible and did take place.

The main goal of censorship was to maintain political, social, and intellectual barriers among the population. Censorship regulations drew a clear distinction between reading matter intended for the learned, and reading matter destined for the general populace. The penal code was also applied unequally, depending upon whether one belonged to the educated or to the uneducated, the upper or the lower classes.

Nevertheless, the government never succeeded in bringing the press under the same degree of control as existed before 1905. This can be traced to a number of factors, of which the most important were: the immense growth of the press, which made efficient supervision nearly impossible; the government's decision not to enlarge the censorship machinery accordingly; and last but not least, the overtaxing of the press authorities through the common practice (especially by opposition papers) of legal evasion.

Still, the effect of official repression showed itself not only in the provinces, but also among the liberal and socialist papers in the large cities. Thus no Social Democratic or Socialist Revolutionary paper could be published legally from the end of 1906 to the end of 1910. On the other hand, thanks to their prestige and affluence, large moderate newspapers could develop relatively freely. These newspapers constituted what in Russia could be understood as a journalistic 'counter-power'.

In sum, although censorship continued to exert an irritating influence on the free development of the press, between 1905 and 1914 Russia possessed a relatively free press of high quality, which in its freedom of criticism was not substantially different from the western press.

Crime and Punishment in the House of the Dead

ALAN WOOD

DOSTOEVSKII's novel *Crime and Punishment* (1866),[1] which concludes with Raskolnikov's banishment to Siberia for the murder of a parasitical old crone, was written only a few years after the author's own return from a spell of penal servitude and military service in Siberia, where he was exiled in 1849 for his participation in the Petrashevskii affair.[2] Shortly after his release he began to immortalize his own experiences and observations of human beings *in extremis* in his thinly fictionalized *Memoirs from the House of the Dead* (1861), which has become one of the classic pieces of the long, gloomy repertoire of Russian prison and exile literature.[3]

It is partly due to this grim, but moving, literary tradition that Siberia has become fixed in the popular imagination as little more than a vast frozen wasteland inhabited by the shackled victims of Russian authoritarianism. Despite this notoriety, however, the legal and social history of the Siberian exile system under the tsars has not until recently been the subject of any serious scholarship in the West.[4] Unfortunately, if understandably,

---

[1] F. M. Dostoevskii, *Polnoe sobranie sochinenii v tridtsati tomakh* (Leningrad, 1972–), vi. *Prestuplenie i nakazanie* (1973).

[2] On the *Petrashevtsy*, see J. L. Evans, *The Petraševskij Circle, 1845–1849* (The Hague and Paris, 1974); P. E. Shegolev (ed.), *Petrashevtsy v vospominaniyakh sovremennikov*, 3 vols. (Moscow and Leningrad, 1926); and on Dostoevskii's involvement, see ibid. i. 6–9; and J. Frank, *Dostoevsky: The Seeds of Revolt, 1821– 1849* (Princeton and London, 1977), 239–91.

[3] Dostoevskii, *Polnoe sobranie*, iv. *Zapiski iz mertvogo doma* (1972) (hereafter Dostoevskii, *Zapiski*); see also the new English translation by D. McDuff, *The House of the Dead by Fyodor Dostoyevsky* (Harmondsworth, 1985).

[4] The last major western work to deal with Siberian exile in any detail was that of the American journalist, G. Kennan, *Siberia and the Exile System*, 2 vols. (New York, 1891). For a brief historical outline, see A. Wood, 'The Siberian Exile System in Tsarist Russia', *History Today*, 30 (Sept. 1980), 19–24. In Russian the literature is plentiful: see esp. the report of the official government inquiry into the system, published as *Ssylka v Sibir': Ocherk eya istorii i sovremennago polozheniya*

political considerations have ensured that most investigations
into the abuse of Russian penal practice have focused on the post-
revolutionary and particularly the Stalinist period; the implication
—or even the explicit assumption—being that before the
revolution, exile to Siberia was a comparatively soft option, or
indeed, not really a punishment at all.[5] A detailed examination of
the historical record does not support such a complacent
judgement, however, and the heavily Dostoevskian title of the
present essay has been deliberately chosen to underline the
purgatorial quality of the punishment suffered by hundreds of
thousands of criminals in the living death of Siberian exile—the
very quality, in fact, which led Dostoevskii to adopt the funereal
title of his work. Should this be thought unnecessarily melo-
dramatic, it is worth remembering that the tsarist authorities
themselves recognized the terminal nature of some categories of
exile by officially regarding the condemned victims as legally
dead, in the sense that they were stripped of all personal, civil,
and property rights pertaining to their social class, children could
'inherit' their goods, and remaining spouses were free to remarry.
Indeed, after the *de facto* abolition of capital punishment in
Russia during the reign of Empress Elizabeth, it was replaced by
the practice of 'civil execution' (*grazhdanskaya kazn'*) and the
concept of 'political death' (*politicheskaya smert'*).[6] Bereft of the

---

(St Petersburg, 1900); also I. Ya. Foinitskii, *Uchenie o nakazanii v svyazi s
tyur'movedeniem* (St Petersburg, 1889), 196–306; N. M. Yadrintsev, *Sibir' kak
koloniya* (St Petersburg, 1882), 164–222; S. V. Maksimov, *Sibir' i katorga*, 3rd edn.
(St Petersburg, 1900). More recently, the researches of Soviet historians working in
both central and regional archives have produced much new valuable material: see
e.g. V. N. Dvoryanov, '*V sibirskoi dal'nei storone . . .': Ocherk istorii tsarskoi katorgi i
ssylki, 60-e gody XVIII v.–1917 g.*, 2nd edn. (Minsk, 1985); L. M. Goryushkin (ed.),
Ssylka i katorga v Sibiri (XVIII–nachalo XX v.) (Novosibirsk, 1975); id. (ed.),
Ssylka i obshchestvenno-politicheskaya zhizn' v Sibiri, XVIII–nachalo XX v.
(Novosibirsk, 1978); id. (ed.), *Politicheskie ssyl'nye v Sibiri (XVIII–nachalo XX v.)*
(Novosibirsk, 1983); E. A. Skripelev (ed.), *Gosudarstvenno-pravovye instituty
samoderzhaviya v Sibiri* (Irkutsk, 1982); and the series *Ssyl'nye revolyutsionery v
Sibiri*, ed. N. N. Shcherbakov, i–viii (Irkutsk, 1973–83, continuing).

[5] Solzhenitsyn is particularly dismissive of the agonies of the pre-revolutionary
exile system. See e.g. A. Solzhenitsyn, *Arkhipelag GULag*, iii (Paris, 1975), 351–6;
and for a critical view of his account, see A. Wood, 'Solzhenitsyn and the Tsarist Exile
System: A Historical Comment', *Journal of Russian Studies*, 42 (1981), 39–43.

[6] *Ukaz* of 25 May 1753, *Polnoe sobranie zakonov Rossiiskoi imperii* (*PSZ*), xv, no.
10101; and 30 Sept. 1754, no. 10306. The latter reads in part: 'Those condemned to
political death are to be flogged with the knout, have their nostrils torn out, be
chained in fetters, and sent to Rogervik and other places.'

original barbarous tortures and mutilations, the macabre public ritual of civil execution continued to be performed well into the nineteenth century.[7] While the victims were not actually killed, and continued to carry out their natural bodily functions and their unnatural enforced labours in exile, they were, to all other intents and purposes, dead men.

Dostoevskii, of course, was more concerned with the psychological, moral, and spiritual dimensions of crime and punishment in 'the House of the Dead', whereas the less elevated purpose of this essay is to trace the penological history and social consequences of the exile system as it affected both common and political criminals. Attention will also be drawn to the ways in which Siberia's traditional role as a vast penal colony was inconsistent with the civic development of Siberian society and the rights and freedom of its inhabitants. Finally, a brief assessment will be made of the arguments for and against the retention of Siberian exile as the central feature of Russian penal practice.

Before proceeding, however, it is necessary to clarify the actual meaning, both theoretical and historical, of 'exile' (*ssylka*). Brockhaus and Efron's encyclopaedia defines it as follows: 'The forcible removal by the state authorities of its own citizens or aliens to remote regions on the periphery of the state or its colonies either for life or a limited period of residence.'[8] The aims of exile are usually to punish criminals (judicial exile); to rid the metropolitan society of what are considered by the state or the community to be harmful or subversive elements (political or administrative exile); to populate underdeveloped territories (enforced settlement); or a combination of any two or all three of these.

The ancient Middle Eastern civilizations, the Greek city states, and Roman law all practised different forms of banishment, ostracism, deportation, and transportation, and the nation states of early modern Europe regularly dispatched condemned criminals

---

[7] The best-known victim of this humiliating ordeal was N. G. Chernyshevskii, condemned to *katorga* and exile for his political activities in 1864. For a discussion of the many eyewitness accounts of the degrading ceremony on Mytnaya Square, St Petersburg, 19 May 1864, see M. N. Gernet, *Istoriya tsarskoi tyur'my*, 3rd edn., ii (Moscow, 1961), 285–9.

[8] *Entsiklopedicheskii slovar' Brokganz–Efron* (St Petersburg, 1890–1907), lxi (1900), 372.

to their overseas possessions in the Americas, Africa, and the Antipodes. Russia initiated the practice on an irregular and often *ad hominem* basis with the conquest of Siberia in the late sixteenth and early seventeenth centuries, though according to the nineteenth-century Russian criminologist, Foinitskii, the system owed nothing to foreign example and developed 'entirely on the basis of Russian needs and Russian conditions'.[9] However this may be, there is a common factor between Russian and other practices which deserves to be underlined, and that is the distinction between *banishment* and *exile*. In whatever historical or linguistic context, banishment involves the expulsion of someone *from* a specific locality to which they are forbidden, either permanently or temporarily, to return; exile, on the other hand, consists of dispatching someone *to* a specific, desired location beyond the territorial limits of which he is forbidden to move. In the Russian context, the nineteenth-century writer, Feldstein, adds a further refinement by drawing a distinction between expulsion, banishment, and exile (*izgnanie*, *vysylka*, and *ssylka*). In his definition, *vysylka* (which he translates into Latin as *deportatio*) is a kind of transition stage between simple *izgnanie* (literally 'driving-out') and *ssylka* proper. In other words, *vysylka* does represent banishment to a specified locality, but with no other restrictions attached apart from those on movement, whereas *ssylka* in the narrowest sense involves 'the subjection of the criminal to a specific regimen incorporating measures which are designed to achieve certain desired objectives'.[10] In the case of Siberia, the 'specific regimen' included the deliberate curtailment of personal rights, and the imposition of an elaborate set of rules and procedures governing the everyday conduct, obligations, activities, movement, domicile, occupation, financial, and even marital affairs of those exiled. The transition from simple banishment to full-scale exile occurred in the West at a time when the overseas empires of the European powers were expanding; in Russia, it was the territorial aggrandizement of Muscovy beyond the Urals and the acquisition of Siberia's huge, thinly populated expanses which rapidly led to the consolidation of exile (along with corporal punishment) as the central and most

[9] I. Y. Foinitskii, *Uchenie*, p. 260.
[10] G. Fel'dshtein, *Ssylka: Ocherki eya genezisa, znacheniya, istorii i sovremennago sostoyaniya* (Moscow, 1893), 2–3.

characteristic feature of the tsarist penal system. It had not always been so, however.

In the oldest Russian legal codes, most penalties were subsumed under the general and untranslatable term *potok*.[11] This could take multifarious forms from capital punishment to simple fines, and included primitive forms of banishment. Corporal punishment, however, was largely unknown in Russia until the Mongol occupation, when it was introduced on a wide scale, thereafter turning Russia into what Foinitskii described as 'the classical land of corporal punishments'.[12] Until the seventeenth century, therefore, the punitive measures most commonly practised were, in descending order of severity: first, the death penalty, which could be either simple or aggravated, i.e. either by the use of swift and immediate means of execution, or else by more protracted and excruciating methods which it would be unnecessarily distasteful to enumerate. Next came corporal punishment, which consisted of varying degrees and types of flagellation and physical mutilation, the former involving the use of different types of flogging instruments, the latter including such barbaric practices as breaking or amputation of the limbs, severing external organs and extremities, gouging out the eyes, branding, and castration.[13] Finally, for less serious offences there was a range of fines and financial compensations payable either to the authorities or to the injured parties. In this early period, imprisonment or other forms of deprivation of liberty were seldom used, except as a preventive, rather than a strictly punitive, measure.

During the course of the seventeenth century, three interrelated factors served to foster and finally to establish Siberian exile as a major new component of Russian penal procedure. These were: firstly, the conquest of Siberia itself; and next, the implementation of the two separate, but complementary, concepts of clemency and conscription. The Muscovite rulers were quick to realize that the simple acquisition of their new trans-Uralian territories by merchant adventurers and Cossacks required more physical back-up in order to consolidate their gains and exploit the country's valuable resources. Both economic and political imperatives therefore encouraged the authorities to conscript the manpower

---

[11] Foinitskii, *Uchenie*, p. 79.
[12] Ibid. 158.   [13] Ibid. 135–7 and 158–62.

and service personnel they needed by the expedient of com-
muting sentences of death to exile in Siberia. Tsar Alexei's Code
of Laws, the *Ulozhenie* of 1649, contains ten explicit references
to exile as a penalty for a variety of offences ranging from homi-
cide to hooliganism, though Siberia as the specific destination is
only mentioned once.[14] But it was still treated as an additional or
supplementary penalty to some other punishment—imprisonment, flogging, or mutilation—already inflicted. Thieves, for
instance, had their left ear sliced off, while snuff-takers had the
septum ripped from between their nostrils. It would be wrong,
however, to conclude that Siberia was treated simply as a vast
dumping-ground for criminals and other undesirables who had
already been crippled or maimed by the public executioner. As
far as possible, the government tried to press the exiled
manpower into some form of service useful to the needs of the
state—usually urban or agricultural settlement, or else some
other kind of military, civil, or ecclesiastical service.

The ever more common recourse to exile as a means of
punishment, and the increasing use of Siberia as the destination,
is demonstrated by the fact that by the time of the first official
census of the territory in 1662, exiles already counted for 8,000
out of a total population of 70,000, i.e. more than 11 per cent.[15]
Despite the barbaric preliminaries, and despite the punitive
conditions prevailing in the region, most authorities tend to look
on Siberian exile in the seventeenth century as a positive
phenomenon which both fulfilled its penological purposes and
made a beneficial contribution to the settlement of the territory
and to the overall interests of the state.

Making use of criminals for the service of the state was taken
one stage further by Peter the Great, who introduced the massive
use of forced labour with the institution of *katorga*. At first
applied only to the work of convict oarsmen on the galleys of
Peter's new navy, the term soon began to be extended to other

[14] *Pamyatniki russkogo prava*, ed. K. A. Sofronenko, vi. *Sobornoe ulozhenie
tsarya Alekseya Mikhailovicha, 1649 goda* (Mosow, 1957), arts. x. 129, 198; xix. 13;
xxi. 9, 10, 11, 15, 16; xxv. 3, 16. The direct reference to Siberia occurs in xix. 13,
where it states that certain law-breakers should be flogged and 'exiled to the river Lena
in Siberia' (*ssylati v Sibir' na zhit'e na Lenu*); otherwise, only general directions are
given (e.g. *ssylati v dal'nye gorody, gde Gosudar' ukazhet*).

[15] P. N. Butsinskii, *Zaselenie Sibiri i byt eya pervykh nasel'nikov* (Kharkov,
1889), 184–295.

forms of penal servitude on his colossal military and civilian construction projects, and was retained, after Elizabeth's abolition of the death penalty, as the harshest form of punishment in the tsarist Criminal Code right until the Revolution of 1917 when it was abolished by the Provisional Government. The widespread use of *katorga* in European Russia in the early eighteenth century caused a reduction in the numbers exiled to Siberia, though the pace quickened considerably during the reign of Catherine the Great, who confirmed her predecessor's decree of December 1760 empowering noble landowners and others to hand over their recalcitrant and subordinate serfs to the state authorities for exile to Siberia.[16] Although this was an extrajudicial procedure, and therefore not strictly a part of the criminal law, it nevertheless added a significant quantitative dimension to Russian penal practices.

An extra, qualitative dimension was introduced by Catherine in 1785, when her Charter to the Nobility granted the Russian *dvoryanstvo*, among other things, immunity to corporal punishment. This 'enlightened' concession introduced the legal principle, as well as the practice, of punishment not according to the crime, but according to the social class of the criminal. This principle—that all are unequal before the law—was later officially enshrined in the new Penal Code of 1845 and the complex scale of punishments (*Lestnitsa nakazanii*) which remained in force right up to 1917. Despite Catherine's familiarity with such Enlightenment theories of crime and punishment as those contained in Beccaria's *Dei delitti e delle pene* and Montesquieu's *L'Esprit des lois*, and apart from the social distinctions just mentioned, no significant changes in punitive practice were introduced during her reign.[17]

However, her grandson, Alexander I, was responsible for some minor acts of legislation which helped to attenuate some of the crueller aspects of criminal procedure. Torture was officially abolished, as was the use of the word *neshchadno* ('mercilessly') in sentences of corporal punishment. In 1818 the practice of

[16] *PSZ*, xv, no. 11166.

[17] Exile to Siberia was in fact temporarily abandoned in 1773, though this was almost certainly not due to any principled objection, but because of practical obstacles created by the Pugachev rebellion. At any rate, it was reinstated in 1755 after the suppression of the revolt. On Catherine's legislative activity in general, see I. de Madariaga, *Russia in the Age of Catherine the Great* (London, 1981).

facial disfigurement by slitting the nostrils was abandoned, but not so branding, which was retained well into the nineteenth century. The knout, too, was preserved as the severest instrument of flagellation until it was abolished in 1845, when it was replaced by the three-thonged lash or *plet'*. (It was this humanitarian gesture of Nicholas I's which provoked Belinskii's withering scorn in his famous *Letter to Gogol*.[18])

It was also during Alexander's reign that the first attempt was made by Count Mikhail Speranskii to bring some kind of order and efficiency into the chaotic state of the exile system when he introduced his Exile and Convoy Regulations of 1822, which, with some later amendments, were to govern the transport, distribution, settlement, and also punishment of the exile population until the end of the nineteenth century.[19] Ten years later, the same bureaucrat's Code of Laws (*Svod zakonov*) sought to regularize the rest of Russia's penal system, and served as the basis of Count Bludov's more sophisticated Penal Code (*Ulozhenie o nakazaniyakh*) of 1845. According to their provisions, all punishments were divided into so-called 'criminal punishments' (*nakazaniya ugolovnye*) and 'correctional punishments' (*nakazaniya ispravitel'nye*). Criminal punishments were reserved for the most serious crimes, and were divided into four grades, all of which were accompanied by complete loss of the personal rights pertaining to one's social rank. The first was the death penalty, but this could only be pronounced on the authority of special supreme tribunals, and was only implemented under extraordinary circumstances. Next came exile to *katorga*, which was further subdivided into different lengths of sentence, ranging from four to six years to life. ('Life' in practice usually meant twenty years, but whatever the stretch, *katorga* was always followed by perpetual exile.) Next came 'exile for settlement in Siberia' (*ssylka na poselenie v Sibir'*), either to the 'most remote' (*otdalenneishie*) or the 'not so remote' (*ne stol' otdalennie*) places of Siberia. Fourthly came 'exile for settlement in the Transcaucasus' (*ssylka na posslenie v Zakavkaz'e*), which was mainly reserved

---

[18] V. G. Belinskii, *Polnoe sobranie sochinenii* (Moscow, 1953–6), x. 'Pis'mo k Gogol'yu' (1956), 212–20.

[19] 'Ustav o ssyl'nykh', and 'Ustav ob etapakh sibirskikh', *PSZ*, xxxviii, nos. 29, 128, 129. For an analysis of the latter, see S. V. Kodan, 'Ustav ob etapakh 1822 goda', in Skripelev (ed.), *Gos.-pravovye instituty*, pp. 24–39.

for religious offences. Despite the fact that these criminal punishments were supposed to be inflicted for only the most serious offences, such as murder, arson, robbery, and rape, or else only on hardened criminals or recidivists, *katorga* and *ssylka* were nevertheless prescribed for the vast majority of crimes. Foinitskii calculates that forced labour and exile were specified for 206 types of crime, while the other penalties available, such as prison, workhouses, confinement in a fortress, houses of correction, and convict gangs, accounted for only 54 (i.e. excluding the death penalty).[20] These figures demonstrate quite clearly not only the central position which Siberian exile occupied in the tsarist penal system, but also the very high level of serious crime in nineteenth-century Russia.[21] The fact that so many major crimes and often violent criminals were punished in this way was to have very serious repercussions on the social fabric and historical development of Siberia, as will be further explained.

The correctional punishments, imposed for less serious offences committed by people for whom there was some genuine hope of reform, were further subdivided by class into those for the privileged members of society and those for the non-privileged. The privileged, who were exempt from corporal punishment, included the nobility, the clergy, honorary citizens, and merchants of the first and second guilds. For these a new category of 'exile for residence' (*ssylka na zhit'e*) was introduced in 1845, the conditions of which, compared to other types of exile, were not too onerous (more like *vysylka* in Feldstein's definition). The equivalent grades of punishment for the non-privileged were various terms of commitment to 'correctional convict detachments' (*ispravitel'nye arestantskie otdeleniya*). Thereafter, for members of all classes and for more trivial misdemeanours, there followed a variety of terms of confinement and arrest, admonitions and fines.[22] There were, of course, further additions, emendations, and alterations to these statutes later in the century, most notably during the judicial reforms of the 1860s, the softening of the laws

---

[20] Foinitskii, *Uchenie*, pp. 283–4.
[21] For details of Russia's criminal statistics in the second quarter of the nineteenth century, see the tables compiled by E. N. Anuchin, *Izsledovaniya o protsente soslannykh v Sibir' v period 1827–1846 gg.* (St Petersburg, 1873), 17–22.
[22] A convenient exposition of the official 'Scale of Punishments' is to be found with accompanying tables under 'Lestnitsa nakazanii', in *Ents. slovar' Brokgauz–Efron*, xxxv. 177–82.

governing corporal punishment in 1863, and the revised Criminal
Code of 1884, but the overall pattern of the tsarist penal system,
with exile to settlement and hard labour in Siberia at its core, was
to remain more or less fixed for as long as the tsarist social and
political order prevailed.

Regulations for the punishment of exiles already undergoing
sentence and resident in Siberia were contained *not* in the civilian
Penal Code, but in the Exile Regulations (*Ustav o ssyl'nykh*),
which provided for a special and extremely severe system of punishments to which the rest of the civilian population was no longer
subject. Mostly these took the form of ferocious beatings, extension
of the length of sentence, demotion into a harsher form of *katorga*,
or transfer to more remote areas, including the island of Sakhalin,
which had a particularly grim reputation as the most dreadful of
the tsarist penal colonies.[23] Before the reform law of 1871, forced
labourers and exiles in Siberia could be sentenced to up to six
thousand strokes of the rods.[24] In 1871, however, the use of the
rods was abolished, and thereafter the most severe form of
physical chastisement was up to one hundred lashes with the
plet', which could nevertheless be fatal in its effects and up to
1893 was applied indiscriminately to both sexes. Apart from the
plet', the law also provided for the chaining of exile prisoners to a
wheelbarrow for anything up to three years, a bread and water
diet, solitary confinement, and birching. Most of these sentences
could be passed and executed by the local authorities, the exile
administration, and police officials without recourse to the
courts. The 'official brutality' of this particularly Draconian
regime was both a reflection of, and in some ways a contributory
factor to, the extremely high level of criminality among the exile
population in Siberia, which in its turn was one of the major
obstacles not merely to the system's success, but even to its
manageable operation.

The most obvious reason why Speranskii's efforts to put the exile
system on a more 'orderly and businesslike' foundation failed was
the sheer weight of numbers involved. His regulations were

---

[23] Foinitskii, *Uchenie*, pp. 161–2. On conditions on Sakhalin, see A. P. Chekhov,
Polnoe sobranie sochinenii i pisem v tridtsati tomakh (Moscow, 1974–), xiv–xv.
'Ostrov Sakhalin' (1978), 39–372.

[24] Foinitskii, *Uchenie*, p. 85.

drawn up on the expectancy of an annual rate of exiles of around three thousand—which was about right for the first quarter of the century. However, for a variety of reasons the rate soon shot up alarmingly, and by the 1860s and 1870s anything from ten to twenty thousand convicts and forced settlers per year were making the agonizing journey along the *etap* route to prison, hard labour, and exile.[25] The organizational problems of providing adequate facilities and maintaining satisfactory supervision for this miserable mass of uprooted humanity were almost insurmountable, and given the intolerable conditions both on the exile journey and in the places of settlement, and also that the majority were of a criminal disposition or social misfits of one sort or another, it is not surprising that so many responded to their unfortunate situation by escaping from their appointed destination and reverting to a life of vagabondage and violent crime.[26] The vitiating circumstances of the exile environment were obviously far more conducive to recidivism than to remorse and rehabilitation. Dostoevskii observed this truth from dire personal experience, and was later to write of it in his *House of the Dead* as follows:

Prison and forced labour do not, of course, reform the criminal; they only punish him and secure society against his further attempts on its peace. In the criminal himself, prison and the most strenuous forms of hard labour develop only hatred, a thirst for forbidden pleasures, and terrible irresponsibility. . . . It sucks the living sap out of a man, wears down his spirit, weakens it, terrifies it, and then presents the morally shrivelled, half-demented mummy as a pattern of repentance and reform.[27]

Dostoevskii was, of course, basing his comments on his experiences at the military prison at Omsk, but they also hold good for the generally debilitating and demoralizing effects on its victims of the exile system as a whole.

In one respect, however, part of Dostoevskii's remarks do need some qualification, in that Siberian exile, while it certainly

[25] *Ssylka v Sibir'*, app. 1, pp. 1–2. See also A. D. Margolis, 'O chislennosti i razmeshchenii ssyl'nykh v Sibiri v kontse XIX v.', in L. M. Goryushkin (ed.), *Ssylka i katorga v Sibiri* (Novosibirsk, 1975), 223–37.

[26] On levels of criminality among the exile population, see A. Wood, 'Sex and Violence in Siberia: Aspects of the Tsarist Exile System', in J. M. Stewart and A. Wood, *Siberia: Two Historical Perspectives* (London, 1984), 23–42.

[27] Dostoevskii, *Zapiski*, p. 15.

punished the criminal, did very little in the way of 'securing society from his further attempts on its peace'. European Russia, it is true, was to some extent able to purge itself of its malefactors and miscreants, but only at the ruinous cost of Siberia's own consequential suffering. The exile population lived in a curious social and legal limbo between the free inhabitants on the one hand, and the incarcerated *katorzhane* on the other, enjoying neither such civil liberties as appertained to the former, nor enduring the total constraints and *durance vile* of the latter. This ambiguous situation had deleterious effects, both direct and indirect, on the human rights and collective aspirations of the free population of Siberia.

This was because, despite the very low ratio of the exile to the free population, the former was overwhelmingly responsible for the exceedingly high incidence in Siberia of such distressing phenomena as vagabondage (*brodyazhestvo*), mass mendicity, serious crimes against persons and property, casual violence, and sexually transmitted disease—particularly syphilis, which in some areas reached epidemic proportions.[28] The citizens of the Siberian towns and countryside lived under constant threat of arson, murder, abduction, rape, and pillage committed by the regiments of absconded rogues and vagabonds popularly referred to as 'General Cuckoo's army'.[29] These roving outlaws were in turn regularly hunted down and slaughtered in acts of communal vengeance and reprisal carried out by the free population, both Russian and native. Siberian newspapers in the late nineteenth century were full of grisly details and descriptions of crimes of quite horrific and gratuitous brutality which, by comparison, make the atrocities of their British contemporary, Jack the Ripper, seem like the amateurish peccadilloes of an apprentice thug. In 1900 a government report had this to say on the subject:

It would be possible to adduce a wealth of official information and accounts of crimes committed by the exile population which are remarkable for their astonishing cunning, their bloodcurdling cruelty, and complete fearlessness of punishment. . . . Almost all these crimes, if

---

[28] Wood, 'Sex and Violence', p. 41.
[29] A Wood, ' "General Cuckoo's Army": Siberian Brigands and *Brodyagi*', *Britain–USSR*, 65 (Sept. 1983), 5–9.

they had been committed in European Russia, would have caused a national sensation and been the talk of the reading public for a very long time, but in Siberia, they are lost among the welter of similar 'events' and go completely unnoticed. . . . The unavenged corpses [of the victims] do not and cannot disturb anyone's conscience: they are simply the fruits of the deeply imbued poison of Siberian exile, and against this the local authorities are powerless.[30]

This is an aspect of the tsarist exile system which does touch quite plainly, though not immediately obviously, on the subject of civil rights, in so far as the average Siberian citizen's expectation of individual security, freedom from fear, and communal well-being were permanently threatened by the depredations of the exile fraternity. Moreover, the local authorities, both police and administrative, were so preoccupied by the attendant problems that insufficient time, energy, or resources were left to devote to the guardianship of a sound, responsible, and prosperous society with the full range of civic, cultural, and economic amenities which it both required and increasingly insistently demanded. The abolition of the exile system, therefore, was the most urgent and uncompromising demand of those, like the Siberian regionalists (*oblastniki*), for whom the territory's welfare was their most cherished concern. It was their contention that only when the exile system was finally dismantled could Siberia begin to throw off its quasi-colonial status and develop peacefully and with dignity into a mature and civically responsible society.[31]

If the judicial and administrative exile of thousands of common criminals rotted the fabric of Siberian society, then it is no less true that greater recourse to the administrative banishment of political activists and malcontents—rather than the neutralization of their influence—only helped to swell the ranks and to broaden

[30] *Ssylka v Sibir'*, pp. 304–5.
[31] On Siberian *oblastnichestvo*, see W. Faust, *Russlands goldener Boden: Der sibirische Regionalismus in der zweiten Hälfte des 19. Jahrhunderts* (Cologne, 1980); M. G. Sesyunina, *G. N. Potanin i N. M. Yadrintsev: Ideologi sibirskogo oblastnichestva. K voprosu o klassovoi sushchnosti sibirskogo oblastnichestva vtoroi poloviny XIX v.* (Tomsk, 1974); A. Wood, 'Chernyshevskii, Siberian Exile and *Oblastnichestvo*', in R. Bartlett (ed.), *Russian Thought and Society 1800–1917: Essays in Honour of Eugene Lampert* (University of Keele, 1984), 42–66.

the social and geographical base of political opposition to tsarism, a fact which, ironically, was perfectly well known to those functionaries whose job it was to administer the system. Warning about the counter-productive effects of administrative political exile, and arguing for its abolition, the Governor-General of eastern Siberia, Kutaisov, wrote to the Minister of the Interior, von Plehve, in 1903 as follows:

Your High Excellency knows better than anyone how deeply the contagion of propaganda has spread its roots here; and the investigations of political crimes which have been instituted against the indigenous inhabitants of Siberia, against workers dwelling here, and even against both male and female students of the most diverse types of educational institution, serve as the best evidence that Siberia is already far from being a region of order and tranquillity.[32]

Despite these warnings, the government continued to resort to the administrative exile of revolutionaries, student leaders, striking workers, revolting peasants, nationalist agitators, and other subversives in ever-increasing numbers until the tsarist political and legal order, of which the exile system was part, itself collapsed. It seems inappropriate, therefore, not to make some general remarks about the lot of those many thousands of people condemned for crimes against the state (*gosudarstvennye prestupniki*) or considered to be politically untrustworthy (*neblagonadezhnye*) who shared a similar fate—sometimes better, sometimes worse—to that of the common criminals.

Political exile to Siberia is as old as the history of the system itself, and dates back to the late sixteenth century. Over the following two hundred years, from the reign of Boris Godunov onwards, most of those involved were victims of the personal vengeance or caprice of individual rulers,[33] though numbers were considerably swelled by the mass expulsion of religious dissenters after the great schism in the Russian Orthodox Church in the second half of the seventeenth century. It was really only after

---

[32] Quoted in A. D. Margolis, 'Zakonodatel'stvo ob administrativnoi politicheskoi ssylke v Rossii kontsa XIX veka', in Skripelev (ed.), *Gos.-pravovye instituty*, pp. 59–60.

[33] Maksimov, *Sibir'i katorga*, pp. 367–89; F. G. Safronov, 'Ssylka v vostochnuyu Sibir' v pervoi polovine XVIII v.', in Goryushkin (ed.), *Ssylka i katorga*, pp. 15–37.

the Decembrist uprising of 1825 that Siberian exile for crimes against the state (rather than plots against an individual monarch) became an entrenched feature of the Russian political scene. Despite their notoriety, however, the number of political exiles was never particularly large (excluding the Polish rebels of 1830 and 1863, who were counted in tens of thousands), and even at the times of greatest political reaction only accounted for just over 1 per cent of the total exile population.[34]

Despite the relative smallness of the numbers, political exiles were nevertheless totally at the mercy of the vindictiveness and caprice of the police and civil authorities in whose locality they were forced to reside. Before 1882 their situation was in many ways anomalous, and in some cases less satisfactory than that of a condemned criminal, who at least was aware of the precise nature of the charge against him, knew the length of his sentence, and to some extent had a certain number of rights as a prisoner or exile. In contrast, the treatment of administratively banished political exiles was totally inconsistent and contradictory. Some were allowed to find employment, others were not; some were given limited freedom of movement, others were confined in virtual house arrest; some corresponded freely, others' letters were censored and withheld.[35] In the wave of repression that followed the assassination of Alexander II, however, the newly promulgated Statute on Police Surveillance (March 1882) set out precise instructions which in theory standardized the reception, imbursement, behaviour, movement, correspondence, occupations, supervision, and punishment of all persons officially under police surveillance (*podnadzornye*), the majority of whom were in administrative banishment throughout Siberia.[36] The actual conditions in which they lived varied in practice from the relatively comfortable to the downright intolerable. In the 1880s, for instance, the American journalist, George Kennan, met small communities of political exiles living in rather Spartan surroundings but managing to maintain a reasonable level of cultural awareness and physical well-being.[37] Lenin, exiled in 1897, spent a rather healthy and productive three years with his wife, Krupskaya, at the village of Shushenskoe in southern Siberia,

---

[34] Margolis, 'O chislennosti', pp. 232–6.   [35] Kennan, *Siberia*, ii. 31–2.
[36] Ibid. 29–59; Margolis, 'Zakonodatel'stvo', pp. 50–62.
[37] Kennan, *Siberia*, i. 168–87, 227–41.

exercising, hunting, reading, and writing among other things *The Development of Capitalism in Russia*.[38] Less fortunate individuals, however, found themselves banished to solitary exile in the far-flung wastelands of Yakutia, forced to live in vermin-infested huts, with no communication with the outside world, no common language with the indigenous tribesmen, and with no possessions of their own.[39]

On arrival at the specified destination, the exile's first duty was to report to the local police, who would issue him or her with a copy of the surveillance regulations and a residence permit (*vid na zhitel'stvo*). Having, in the face of much hostility, managed to secure lodgings among the suspicious local population, the exile's next task was to find some means of subsistence and employment. However, as most of the political exiles at this time were from the educated and professional classes of Russian society, the very terms of the regulations directly precluded this possibility. Exiles were expressly forbidden to engage in teaching, medicine, law, pharmacy, theatrical performances, printing, photography, and librarianship. Without special permission from the Minister of the Interior they were also barred from holding public office, entering higher education, belonging to private societies or companies, or engaging in 'any business which the governor of the province, at his own discretion, feels may enable an exile to attain illegal ends or render him a menace to the public peace and order'.[40] This effectively excluded the exiles from any gainful or useful occupation for which they were suited or trained, or indeed, which the local population needed. As many of them had no other trade or craft, were unused to manual labour, and were unable to engage in agriculture because of unavailability of land, the effect of the regulation was to reduce them to hardship, penury, and near-starvation levels of subsistence, always with the threat of their administrative sentences being extended or their conditions worsened for the slightest infringement of the regulations.

It would be possible to give many harrowing examples of the atrocious treatment of political prisoners and exiles in Siberia as

---

[38] On Lenin's early political activities, see the excellent monograph by R. Service, *Lenin: A Political Life*, i (London, 1985).

[39] Kennan, *Siberia*, ii. 19–25.   [40] Ibid. 35.

evidence of the degradation, humiliation, insensitivity, and physical brutality to which many, like the common criminals, were subjected.[41] It seems otiose to rehearse them at this juncture, however. Suffice it to say that as the horrors of the system became more widely publicized towards the end of the century, the clamour of public protest from within Siberian society and from progressive opinion inside the judicial and legal establishment, and mounting pressure from abroad, finally impelled the government to subject the entire exile operation to more detailed scrutiny with an eye to introducing some measure of reform.[42]

Particularly urgent in the view of many was the question of *non-political* administrative exile (*ssylka v administrativnom poryadke*), which posed an especially large and awkward problem. However, as this subject has been dealt with in some detail elsewhere, only a few words need to be said in the present context.[43] Since the eighteenth century, peasant and other communities had exercised the right of handing over to the civilian authorities for administrative disposal to Siberia those of their members who were collectively judged to be guilty of unsociable behaviour or otherwise unacceptable (though not necessarily criminal) conduct. This practice had the unfortunate effect of condemning to Siberian exile—sometimes for life—individuals whose activities, however reprehensible, were not of such a felonious nature as to warrant their appearance before the courts. In this way, adulterers, drunkards, debtors, and other petty ne'er-do-wells could suffer the same dire punishment as convicted murderers and other violent criminals. Similarly inequitable was the practice of refusing to readmit into the commune convicted criminals who had already served a custodial or some other sentence, but who, despite having 'discharged their debt to society', found themselves ostracized from the commune and banished by administrative process to Siberia. This, of course, amounted to double punishment for the one offence, an offence which had not been judged to be so grave as to warrant

[41] Ibid. 191–277; L. Deutsch, *Sixteen Years in Siberia: Some Experiences of a Russian Revolutionist* (London, 1903).

[42] *Ssylka v Sibir'*.

[43] A. Wood, 'The Use and Abuse of Administrative Exile to Siberia', *Irish Slavonic Studies*, 6 (1985), 65–81.

that particular penalty in the first place. In the late nineteenth century this form of banishment accounted for more than half of all the cases of exile by administrative order, and indeed, administrative exiles as a whole made up just over 50 per cent of the entire exile population.[44] It was therefore quite understandable that among the debates, arguments, and reports which surrounded the whole question of the abolition of the exile system, the peculiar problem of administrative exile occupied an especially prominent place.

To those who defended the continuance of the system on the grounds of its flexibility, its deterrent effect, its attractiveness as an alternative to both capital punishment and imprisonment, its alleged success in securing the safety of metropolitan society, and its contribution to the population and manpower requirements of Siberia, its opponents raised sound practical, as well as moral and penological, objections. Firstly, despite Siberia's enormous size, there was the problem of finding suitable locations which were both underpopulated and yet congenial to human habitation. Secondly, there was the difficulty of forcibly settling unwilling and manifestly ill-equipped human material on the land, or else finding sufficient useful employment to keep it occupied. Thirdly, there was the question of transportation—a costly and ruinous business in both financial and human terms, fraught with the problems of supervision, supply, corruption, and the endemic violence of a close-packed criminal community. Also, and this has already been pointed out, the existence of a penal colony not only impeded the cultural and civic development of a chosen region, but also set its stamp on the civilian administration of the area, thus affecting the rights and expectations of the free, local community. This unsatisfactory situation was, in its turn, aggravated by the debilitating effects of the marauding gangs of disease-ridden murderers, rapists, and thieves whose activities artificially inseminated Siberia with the agents and seeds of mass social distemper. Finally, of course, there was the fundamental problem underpinning all other objections, namely, the basic incompatibility between the aims of punishment and the aims of colonization, the former involving the deprivation of those personal rights and liberties which are essential for the successful achievement of the latter.

[44] Margolis, 'O chislennosti', p. 226, table 1.

Although the exile reform law of 12 June 1900 went some way towards meeting some of these criticisms, it did little to alter or ameliorate the system's intrinsic drawbacks and deficiencies.[45] *Ssylka* remained at the heart of the tsarist penal system until tsarism itself was destroyed. For a brief period, the revolutions of 1917 created the political conditions and the social and intellectual atmosphere in which the new Provisional Government was able to abolish the last remaining categories of punitive exile,[46] and thereby promise to bring to an end the agony and untold human misery with which the charnel house of Siberian exile—the 'House of the Dead'—had always been suffused. In the present context it would be an act of supererogation to comment on what was to happen in the years to follow.

[45] A. D. Margolis, 'Sistema sibirskoi ssylki i zakon ot 12 iyunya 1900 goda', in L. M. Goryushkin (ed.), *Ssylka i obshchestvenno-politicheskaya zhizn' v Sibiri* (Novosibirsk, 1978), 126–40.

[46] *Sbornik ukazov i postanovlenii Vremennago pravitel'stva* (Petrograd, 1917–18), 26 Apr. 1917.

The Security Police, Civil Rights, and the Fate of the Russian Empire, 1855–1917

D. C. B. LIEVEN

OF all the enemies of civil rights in imperial Russia, none was more important than the officers of the security police and the senior officials who controlled them. Indeed, unless one studies police operations and mentalities it is impossible to understand the uphill struggle and eventual failure of the civil rights movement. The aim of this essay is to look first at the functions of the Russian security services, and then to study the techniques they used to carry out these functions. I will move on to investigate the personnel of the security services, concentrating in particular on their mentality and level of competence, before turning to the ways in which police operations infringed on civil rights. Finally, I will seek to put the struggle between the security police and civil rights into the broader context both of the modernization of Russian society and of the fate of the Russian Empire. Of course, such a vast topic cannot be covered definitively in one essay, especially since my sources have largely been confined to what is available in the United Kingdom.[1]

[1] The main sources for this paper are *Katorga i ssylka* (hereafter *KS*), 115 vols. (Moscow, 1921–35); the records of the interrogation of former members of the imperial security services and administration in *Padenie tsarskogo rezhima* (hereafter *PTR*), 7 vols. (Leningrad, 1925); the speeches by former senior officials of the Ministry of the Interior contained in *Gosudarstvennyi Sovet: Stenograficheskii otchet* (hereafter *GSSO*), 12 sessions (St Petersburg, 1906–17); V. K. Agafonov, *Zagranichnaya okhranka* (Petrograd, 1918), which contains many police documents; and the numerous memoirs of officials of the security services. Some archival material from Tsentral'nyi gosudarstvennyi arkhiv Okt'yabr'skoi revolyutsii (hereafter TsGAOR), and Otdel rukopisei Biblioteki imeni Lenina (hereafter RO) was also of use. Among secondary sources, E. E. Smith, *The Okhrana* (Stanford, 1967), provides a useful bibliographical basis for study of the imperial security services, but there is no adequate general history of the security police from 1855 to 1917. Recent works on the security police include R. J. Johnson, '"Zagranichnaya agentura": The Tsarist Political Police in Europe', *Journal of Contemporary History*, 7 (1972), 221–42;

Nevertheless, these sources do provide a detailed insight into the nature of the Russian security services, and enable one to come to some firm conclusions about the impact of the police both on civil rights and on Russia's political development in the last decades of the empire.

Before attempting to tackle my theme, however, it is important to define the words 'security services' and 'security police'. I use these terms interchangeably to describe both the institutions set up in 1826 by Nicholas I to guarantee state security, and the heirs to these institutions which emerged between 1880 and 1917. In the wake of the Decembrist rising, Nicholas I established both the Third Section of His Imperial Majesty's Own Chancellery and the Corps of Gendarmes. The former was to be the brain of the imperial security police, the latter its eyes, ears, and arms.[2] As the official historian of the Third Section himself acknowledged, the new security police was little tested in the first thirty-five years of its existence, since the overwhelming majority of the population was loyal or at least quiescent.[3] When in the 1870s a revolutionary underground did come into existence, the failings of the security police became alarmingly apparent. As a result, the Third Section was abolished in 1880, and its functions were transferred to the new Police Department of the Ministry of the Interior. Together with a new central headquarters, the security services also acquired in this year new institutions 'in the field'. So-called security sections (*okhrannye otdeleniya*), usually known in the West as the Okhrana, were set up first in St Petersburg, Moscow, and Warsaw, and after 1902 in many other cities as well. Though there was some overlap between the tasks of the Okhrana and those of the provincial Gendarme Administrations

R. Pipes, *Russia Under the Old Regime* (London, 1974), ch. 11; N. Schleifman, 'The Internal Agency: Linchpin of the Political Police in Russia', *Cahiers du monde russe et soviétique*, 24 (1983), 152–72; F. S. Zuckerman, 'The Russian Political Police at Home and Abroad (1880–1917): Its Structure, Functions, and Methods', Ph.D. thesis (New York, 1973), esp. chs. 1–4.

[2] On the security services under Nicholas I, see P. S. Squire, *The Third Department: The Political Police in the Russia of Nicholas I* (Cambridge, 1968); and S. Monas, *The Third Section: Police and Society in Russia under Nicholas I* (Harvard, 1961).

[3] 'Obzor deyatel'nosti Tret'ego otdeleniya Sobstvennoi vashego imperatorskago velichestva kantselyarii za 50 let', in V. Bogucharskii, 'Tret'e otdelenie Sobstvennoi ego imperatorskago velichestva kantselyarii o sebe samom', *Vestnik Evropy*, 3 (1917), 85–125, esp. p. 94.

(which existed from Nicholas I's reign until 1917), in practice it was usually the former which uncovered, penetrated, and destroyed revolutionary organizations. The Gendarme Administrations, while sharing with the Okhrana the tasks of discovering revolutionaries and monitoring public opinion, came increasingly to concentrate on the preparation of cases against arrested revolutionaries. In this latter function, Gendarme officers were supervised by 'procurators' (*prokurory*), who were officials of the Ministry of Justice. The job of the *prokurory* was both to ensure that the Gendarmerie acted legally in its preparation of cases, and to act as state prosecutors should these cases come to trial. Between them, the procurators and the gendarmes decided whether the evidence available was sufficient to bring arrested revolutionaries before the courts, or whether on the contrary recourse should be had to the system of administrative exile. Whereas the Okhrana had almost no say in this matter, the Procuracy had even less control over Okhrana intelligence-gathering operations. Although the shifting relationship between the various institutions involved in state security was at times both confused and confusing, the key point to bear in mind is that the Okhrana was infinitely more effective than the great majority of Gendarme Administrations. For this reason all the key figures in the Ministry of the Interior, namely, the minister, the director of the Police Department, the provincial governors, and the city police chiefs, came to regard the Okhrana as the main bulwark of state security.[4]

In any society the main function of a security police is to protect the existing legal order from subversion. The definition of subversion, however, differs greatly from one society to another, as does, correspondingly, the scale and scope of the legitimate activities of the security police. In some European countries even

---

[4] There is no easy guide to the division of functions between the various institutions involved in state security. Therefore one must return to the memoir material, reading it with a clear eye for political and departmental bias. The best place to start is A. A. Lopukhin, *Iz itogov sluzhebnago opyta: Nastoyashchee i budushchee russkoi politsii* (Moscow, 1907). Lopukhin, a former procurator and head of the Police Department, became disillusioned and passed important information to the revolutionaries. Of the Okhrana memoirs, the most valuable are: A. P. Martynov, *Moya sluzhba v otdel'nom korpuse zhandarmov* (Stanford, 1972); A. I. Spiridovich, *Zapiski zhandarma* (Kharkov, n.d.); and P. P. Zavarzin, *Rabota tainoi politsii* (Paris, 1924).

before 1914 it was reasonable to hope that major political, economic, and social changes could be achieved peacefully through parliamentary institutions. It was not considered subversive either to advocate such changes or to mobilize opinion in their support. In Russia, on the other hand, especially before 1905, not only the monarchy itself but also its absolute powers were considered sacrosanct. Though considerable freedom was allowed to scholarly debate on economic and social issues, the open advocacy of socialism was generally regarded as subversive. So, too, was any attempt to mobilize public support behind political or even socio-economic goals, a prohibition which extended not only to workers and peasants, but even to members of the aristocracy and gentry.[5] It is true that after 1905 much greater freedom was allowed for political debate, but the definition of subversion, and consequently the activities of the security police, still remained very broad compared to most of the rest of Europe. On the other hand, by the twentieth century Russia's rulers did indeed face a revolutionary movement which enjoyed great potential public support. This movement threatened the destruction not only of the old regime, but also of most of the economic, cultural, and social pillars of European bourgeois civilization. Whereas in 1855 subversion had been a fear, by 1914 it was a reality.

The key functions of the Russian security police can be divided into two halves, the first more narrowly technical and professional, the second more broadly political. In the first section came the campaign by the police to deter, uncover, and destroy revolutionary organizations. Inevitably, deterrence, discovery, and destruction were closely linked, since a security police capable of systematically destroying revolutionary groups almost at birth was likely to deter all but the most self-sacrificing and self-confident of citizens from the seemingly impossible task of fighting an invulnerable and all-seeing state. In the second, broader category of security police functions came the duty to keep the government informed about public moods, to analyse

---

[5] Even when petitions were sent to the monarch from legally constituted noble or *zemstvo* assemblies. See T. Emmons, *The Russian Gentry and the Peasant Emancipation of 1861* (Cambridge, 1968), and compare the pre-1905 situation depicted in G. M. Hamburg, *Politics of the Russian Nobility 1881–1905* (Rutgers, 1984), with the creation of gentry pressure groups after 1905, for which see R. T. Manning, *The Crisis of the Old Order in Russia* (Princeton, 1982).

these moods from the point of view of state security, and in addition to ensure that overall governmental policy, both domestic and foreign, was conceived with due attention to the interests of state security and the regime's need to survive the struggle against revolution. Apart from these major functions, however, the security police, especially before 1880, played other subsidiary roles. Under Nicholas I the Gendarmerie was given almost a general commission to ensure that justice, efficiency, and honesty reigned in the Russian Empire.[6] Armed with this commission, the Gendarmerie watched and intervened in almost any aspect of social life, concentrating in particular on issues such as master–serf relations which might conceivably threaten state security at some point. Owing to the awful inadequacies of the Russian legal system, the security police became an arbitrary, but basically well-meaning, court of arbitration to which ordinary citizens brought their griefs and problems. The police gloried in their self-image of omnipotent and benevolent paternalism, and even amidst the struggle with the revolutionary underground in the 1870s still retained their role as, for example, the chief arbitrator between husbands, wives, and children on the breakdown of marriages.[7]

Although before 1880 the security police had a broad and, to modern eyes, sometimes bizarre set of functions, it is significant also to note that some of the roles performed by the security services in other societies remained unknown in Russia. After the judicial reforms of 1864, and definitively after 1881, the security police had no judicial or punitive functions. Revolutionaries were either tried by the courts or, in the case of administrative exile, by a joint board of senior officials of the Ministries of the Interior and Justice.[8] The security police did not run the gaols nor, on the rare occasions when capital punishment was enforced, did they

---

[6] See the works cited in n. 2 above. Also Bogucharskii, *Tret'e otdelenie*, pp. 90–1. The legend of the handkerchief given by Nicholas to Benckendorff provides an insight into the Gendarmerie's own self-image and view of its functions.

[7] Bogucharskii, *Tret'e otdelenie*, pp. 116, 118–21; B. Bukhshtab, 'Posle vystrela Karakozova', *KS*, lxxviii (1931), 50–88.

[8] As regards the regulations covering administrative exile, see *Polnoe sobranie zakonov Rossiiskoi imperii* (hereafter *PSZ*), 3rd series (St Petersburg, 1885), no. 350 (14 Aug. 1881), section 5, arts. 33–6; and no. 383 (4 Sept. 1881), arts. 2, 4. Also W. Santoni, 'P. N. Durnovo as Minister of Internal Affairs in the Witte Cabinet', Ph.D. thesis (Kansas, 1968), 428–36.

have anything to do with executions.[9] Nor, of course, did the police control such vast economic empires or armed forces as either Himmler's SS or Stalin's NKVD did. And it is important to note that the security police did not even carry responsibility for defending the state from outbreaks of public disorder. Even in 1914 there were fewer than 15,000 gendarmes throughout the empire, and much of this force was deployed to maintain law and order on the railways. In the face of any major disturbances, not only in the countryside but also in the cities, both the very small Gendarme detachments and the relatively small regular police were quickly swamped. Although many improvements in the ordinary police were introduced in 1902–6, financial stringency ensured that their numbers remained far too low. Even after 1906, and even in St Petersburg itself, large-scale demonstrations or rioting always forced the government to bring in the army.[10]

Military involvement in matters of internal security was a disaster from every point of view, however. In the first place the generals believed, correctly, that using the army in this role weakened regiments' training, cohesion, and morale, and in addition undermined the army's prestige in society.[11] Moreover, soldiers had no training in crowd control, which tended to make their intervention either ineffective or lethal. This was particularly true of the infantry, who had no other means to disperse crowds but the use of firearms.[12] Leaving aside humanitarian consider-ations, the use of firearms was likely to create martyrs, alienate wide groups in society, and sink the regime's prestige both at home and abroad.[13] If Bloody Sunday in January 1905 illustrates

[9] On this, see Zavarzin, *Rabota*, pp. 10–14; A. T. Vassilyev, *The Ochrana* (London, 1930), 37–40.

[10] On the inadequacies of the police, see Santoni, 'Durnovo', pp. 397 ff.; and N. B. Weissman, *Reform in Tsarist Russia: The State Bureaucracy and Local Government 1900–1914* (Rutgers, 1981), 205–20 esp. For Durnovo's own analysis, see *GSSO*, session 3 (24 May 1908), cols. 1288–90. On 26 Jan. 1912 (ibid., session 7, cols. 1260–1), he returned to this theme, underlining the many weaknesses of the police and asking rhetorically: 'Let any of us ask himself if order is guaranteed under the present extremely weak police force.'

[11] See A. N. Kuropatkin, *Dnevnik A. N. Kuropatkina* (Nizhnii Novgorod, 1924), 14. Also Santoni, 'Durnovo', pp. 361–90.

[12] P. G. Kurlov, the Deputy Minister of the Interior, wrote in his memoirs that he had always been a strong opponent of using infantry against crowds, since heavy casualties were inevitable. *Konets tsarizma* (Moscow and Petrograd, 1923), 28.

[13] Even Sir Charles Hardinge, an experienced administrator who was by no means hostile to the Russian government, wrote: 'it is difficult to explain the callous

the awful consequences of using the army against demonstrators, the run-up to 9 January shows how incompetent police chiefs and inadequate numbers of regular policemen allowed the Gapon movement to get so out of control as to make military intervention almost inevitable.[14] Finally, in using soldiers against crowds, the regime ran the risk of mutiny on the part of the ordinary conscripts. By 1916 the security services were very uncertain about the political reliability of the armed forces;[15] not only did they have no control over troop discipline or deployment, but in addition their sources of information about moods in the ranks were limited.[16] It is indicative of the values of the rulers of imperial Russia that the penetration of the armed forces by police spies so offended their sense of military honour, pride, and discipline that it was expressly forbidden by V. F. Dzhunkovskii, the Deputy Minister of the Interior, on 13 March 1913.[17]

In moving from the functions of the security services to their techniques, one is shifting from a study of strategy to a study of tactics. The efficient operation of the security services depended on three factors: firstly, the gathering of intelligence; secondly, the storage of this information in such a way that it could easily be cross-referenced and utilized at national level; thirdly, the

---

indifference of the Russian military authorities in the taking of the lives of quiet and orderly workmen, who were unarmed and showed no signs of aggressive action.' Hardinge to Lansdowne, 23 Jan. 1905 (n. 5), *British Documents on Foreign Affairs: Reports and Papers from the Foreign Office Confidential Print* (hereafter *BD*), iii, pt. 1, series A, Russia 1859–1914, pp. 7–8.

[14] On this, see Madhavan K. Palat, *Police Socialism and the Mutation of Autocracy in Tsarist Russia* (New Delhi, 1983), 161–74; W. Sablinsky, *The Road to Bloody Sunday: Father Gapon and the St Petersburg Massacre of 1905* (Princeton, 1976).

[15] See a report by A. T. Vasil'ev, the Director of the Police Department, of 30 Oct. 1916, in Tsentrarkhiv, *1917 god v dokumentakh i materialakh: Burzhuaziya nakanune Fevral'skoi revolyutsii* (Moscow, 1927), no. 58, p. 137. Also P. P. Zavarzin, *Zhandarmy i revolyutsionery* (Paris, 1930), 234–8.

[16] Zavarzin, *Zhandarmy*, pp. 235–6; Martynov, *Moya sluzhba*, pp. 291–2.

[17] Dzhunkovskii's memorandum is cited by Agafonov, *Okhranka*, p. 215. See also Kurlov, *Konets*, p. 136; Zavarzin, *Rabota*, pp. 20, 120–4; and id., *Zhandarmy*, p. 20; 'Dopros S. P. Beletskogo', 12 May 1917, *PTR*, 270, 274–5. Commander Grenfell, the British naval attaché, reported on the outcome of the Okhrana activity in the fleet, which resulted in naval officers accusing the police of fabricating evidence, an accusation supported in Prince V. P. Meshcherskii's *Grazhdanin*. Nicholas II pardoned the arrested sailors: *BD*, vi, 3 Sept. 1913 (n.s.), 333–4, Grenfell to O'Beirne. On 20 May 1916 Klimovich ordered the restoration of the 'internal agency' among garrison troops: 'Dopros S. P. Beletskogo', 15 May 1917, pp. 329–30.

existence of security police officers who were capable not only of waging war against the revolutionary underground, but also of seeing this struggle within the broader context of Russia's modernization and the regime's overall political strategy. Until 1880 the security services were deficient in all respects, but in particular as regards the techniques of counter-revolutionary operations. From about 1880 major improvements occurred. By the last decade of the old regime, revolutionaries were faced by a security police which, although still weakened by internal conflict, was a professional and formidable body.

The overall improvement of the security services was reflected in its methods of storing information. As with so many other aspects of security police activity, the creation of an effective records system was linked in part with the role of S. V. Zubatov as head of the Moscow Okhrana.[18] The systematic registration of all information on political suspects—achieved in Moscow by the turn of the century—was extended to the St Petersburg brain of the entire security police by M. I. Trusevich between 1906 and 1909. As a result the security police was able to utilize the intelligence collected by all its branches on a co-ordinated national scale—a central registration system described by Zuckerman as huge, sophisticated, and efficient. In addition, the Police Department could now keep a closer check on the activities of Okhrana bureaux and provincial Gendarme Administrations than had previously been possible.[19]

As regards gathering information and keeping checks on the population, the security services were aided by the passport system and by the requirement to register a change of residence with the police. In the rural areas, as the narodniks found to their cost, it was very difficult for an outsider to pass unnoticed. Starosty, priests, 'kulaks', or simply neighbours were all likely sources of information about suspicious arrivals in a village.[20] In the big cities, where much of the population lived in large blocks of flats, the dvornik ('concierge') usually acted as the eyes and

[18] Zavarzin, Rabota, pp. 68–9; J. Schneiderman, Sergei Zubatov and Revolutionary Marxism (Cornell, 1970), 51–5.
[19] 'Dopros S. P. Beletskogo', 15 May 1917, pp. 329–30; 'Dopros M. I. Trusevicha', 4 May 1917, PTR, iii. 213; Martynov, Moya sluzhba, pp. 90–2; Zuckerman, 'Russian Political Police', pp. 62–4.
[20] On this, see M. Frolenko, 'Nachalo "narodovol'chestva"', KS, xxiv (1926), esp. p. 19.

ears of the police.[21] Moreover, ordinary Russians, whether as loyal subjects, simple busybodies, or, most often, from motives of personal jealousy and hatred, were frequently inclined towards the denunciation of their fellow subjects to the police.[22]

The systematic gathering of intelligence by the security services was achieved by four main methods. The first of these was through the so-called 'external agency', the plain clothes police agents who served Okhrana and Gendarme administrations. The functions of these agents included watching suspected dwellings, shadowing revolutionaries' movements and noting whom they met, questioning and suborning neighbours, and many other basic techniques of detection. These policemen, of whom there were never more than a thousand within Russia and forty under the External Agency in Paris, were for the most part ex-NCOs of the armed forces. According to Zavarzin, it took two years adequately to train these agents in the techniques of their trade, and their work required commitment, quick wits, and considerable physical hardihood and courage. As one would expect, in time these agents developed a sixth sense as regards suspicious behaviour, and the memoirs of security police officers are filled with examples of their exploits. The systematic training of new agents was introduced at the turn of the century by a subordinate of Zubatov and former regular police officer, E. P. Mednikov.[23]

The second major source of intelligence was so-called 'perlustration', in other words, intercepted mail. Although this had long been carried out in Russia on occasion, the procedure was extended and systematized under Alexander III, who wanted information not only on revolutionaries but also on court, official, and aristocratic society, behind whose veneer of flattery and obedience he wished to penetrate.[24] Between 1881 and 1914,

---

[21] For examples of *dvorniki* aiding the police, see P. S. Ivanovskaya, 'Pervye tipografii Narodnoi voli', ibid., esp. p. 54. See also Zavarzin, *Zhandarmy*, p. 47.

[22] e.g. the waves of denunciations after the Karakozov affair and the assassination of Alexander II: Bukhshtab, 'Posle vystrela Karakozova', pp. 50–88; I. I. Rakitnikov, 'Otgoloski 1 Marta 1881', in *Trudy kruzhka narodovol'tsev pri o-ve politkatorzhan i ssyl'noposelentsev, 1 Marta 1881 goda* (Moscow, 1933), 89–120.

[23] On the External Agency, see Martynov, *Moya sluzhba*, pp. 64–6; Zavarzin, *Rabota*, pp. 33–41; Johnson, 'Zagranichnaya', pp. 227–30; Spiridovich, *Zapiski*, pp. 52–4; Vassilyev, *Ochrana*, pp. 41–52.

[24] 'Dopros S. P. Beletskogo', 12 May 1917, pp. 293–5; Spiridovich, *Zapiski*, pp. 59–61.

so-called 'black offices' existed in seven towns, at a cost of 200,000 roubles a year by 1913.[25] The government derived two major benefits from perlustration. In the first place, awareness that the post was subject to interception greatly hampered communication between revolutionaries. In a country of Russia's vast size, in which the co-ordination of revolutionary activity was both difficult and vital for success, perlustration played an important role in isolating and weakening underground groups. In addition, careless use of the mail led to the uncovering of revolutionaries.[26] It was perlustration, for instance, that caused the downfall of the plot to assassinate Alexander III for which Aleksandr Ul'yanov, among others, was hanged in 1887.[27] Although the revolutionaries developed codes and invisible inks, the police had the resources to stay ahead of them in this sphere, and, as one would expect in Russia, they could draw on outstanding cryptographic talent.[28]

The third route through which information was gathered was the interrogation of arrested revolutionaries. In imperial Russia, even after 1881, interrogating officers did operate under some constraints.[29] The law did not allow the indefinite detention of suspects without trial, and unless sufficient evidence could be produced to satisfy a court of law of a revolutionary's guilt, the most a prisoner could be threatened with was five years' administrative exile. Although some examples of the physical mistreatment or even torture of arrested revolutionaries are cited, these were undoubtedly highly exceptional.[30] Nor—again unlike

[25] R. Kantor, 'K istorii chernykh kabinetov', *KS*, xxxvii (1927), 90–100.

[26] See e.g. Zavarzin, *Rabota*, pp. 42–5.

[27] See E. I. Yakovenko, 'Protsess 1 Marta 1887', *Narodnaya volya pered tsarskim sudom* (Moscow, 1931), 97.

[28] Kantor, 'K istorii', p. 92; I. Zybim, the leading cryptographer, continued to serve under the Bolsheviks: Vassilyev, *Ochrana*, pp. 93–5.

[29] Lopukhin, *Iz itogov*, pp. 22–7, discusses the limited constraints put on the Gendarmerie by the Procuracy in the 1870s, and stresses the effect of the 1881 decrees in liberating the security services from this control. Spiridovich, however, asserts that even after 1881 'the arrest of each person, even under the Okhrana's rights, had to have serious causes', and that the arrest in particular of an *intelligent* or a student would lead to immediate telephone calls from the Procuracy asking for reasons; in the event of a prolonged period of detention under arrest, the Procuracy would press hard for the suspect's release, though in general it could only seek to make life difficult for the security police and was not able to order suspects' release: *Zapiski*, pp. 75–6; Martynov, *Moya sluzhba*, p. 52.

[30] See e.g. Fülöp-Miller's introduction (p. 26) to Vassilyev's *Ochrana*. Also Bogucharskii, 'Tret'e otdelenie', pp. 123–5; 'Zhandarmskie otkroveniya', *KS*, liv (1929), 96–105. The latter contains the confessions of Colonel I. P. Vasil'ev, the last

under Stalin—could pressure be brought to bear on suspects by threatening their families. Nevertheless, the interrogator had many advantages, the most important of which was the promise of immunity or better treatment for those who turned state's evidence. Most revolutionaries spurned such offers and remained silent under interrogation, but enough of them talked to yield a vast amount of information about the revolutionary underground.[31] To elicit maximum information, the skilled interrogator became something of a psychiatrist. He sought to understand the personality of the arrested suspect, often to win his or her confidence and to exploit whatever weakness there might be in his or her 'revolutionary armour'. Thus, interrogators used the worker Sukennik's resentment against his intelligentsia comrades, quickly grasped that Romon Malinovskii was more of a vain egoist than a true socialist, and, in the person of V. K. Plehve, exploited the basic cowardice, need for sympathy, and lack of convictions of Okladskii.[32] On occasions, very skilled interrogators, such as S. V. Zubatov and G. P. Sudeikin, even succeeded in persuading revolutionary activists of the error of their ways and in winning (though not always permanently) their willing collaboration.[33]

The fourth means of gathering intelligence was described by the security police as the 'internal agency' and by most of the rest of society as 'provocation'. Police agents penetrated revolutionary organizations, worked within them, and passed on all their secrets to the government. In some cases these agents were genuine adherents of the regime, or they were simply apolitical types who enjoyed the adventure.[34] Both groups, and in particular the former, were much more reliable than the average secret agent, an ex-revolutionary 'turned' by the police, sometimes by bribery but most often under the threat of imprisonment or

head of the Special Section of the Police Department, written in 1917 and clearly designed to win the favour of his captors by denouncing former colleagues. Some of his accusations may nevertheless be true.

[31] Zavarzin, *Rabota*, p. 53; Spiridovich, *Zapiski*, p. 77, says that the Socialist Revolutionaries were less inclined to talk under interrogation than the Social Democrats.

[32] 'Okladskii, kak predatel', i ego provedenie na sude', *KS*, xv (1925), 139–47.

[33] Schneiderman, *Zubatov*, pp. 78–82; V. I. Sukhomlin, 'Protsess dvadsati odnogo', *Narodnaya volya*, pp. 34–69.

[34] The 'genuine adherent' most often cited in police memoirs is Zinaida Zhuchenko (née Gerngross). See e.g. Spiridovich, *Zapiski*, pp. 45–7; Martynov, *Moya sluzhba*, p. 228; Zavarzin, *Zhandarmy*, pp. 73–5, for examples of agents loving adventure.

exile.[35] These ex-revolutionary double agents lived under tremendous nervous pressure. If they were discovered by their comrades they were either likely to be murdered or induced to exculpate their guilt by killing their police minders. In addition, the strain of living a double life and betraying one's comrades, without in most cases the support of feeling that one was acting in a good cause, often told.[36] Zubatov, once again an expert in this field, told security police officers that they must treat their secret agents like a much-loved but neurotic, and potentially homicidal, mistress.[37] Here more than ever the effective security policeman had to have some grasp of the human psyche. He needed to inspire trust without feeling it; to use information without disclosing his sources; to cross-check information received from different agents; and to keep a close eye on his agents' emotional balance.

If the problems of the internal agency were great, however, so also were its rewards, for it was undoubtedly the most devastating weapon that the government possessed in its war against the revolutionary underground.[38] Just as the regime's failure to defeat terrorism in the 1870s was owed above all to the security forces' lack of an 'internal agency', so the eventual crushing of *Narodnaya volya* in the early 1880s stemmed from the establishment of such an agency by G. P. Sudeikin and V. K. Plehve.[39] Under Zubatov in the early twentieth century the 'internal agency' was spread across Russia and played a decisive role in smashing the revolutionary underground between 1906 and 1914. Okhrana penetration of the Bolshevik, Menshevik, Socialist Revolutionary, and even Kadet parties reached almost comic

---

[35] e.g. Zavarzin, *Rabota*, pp. 16–18.

[36] All the security policemen's memoirs have long sections devoted to the internal agency. See e.g. Zavarzin, *Rabota*, pp. 16–31; Martynov, *Moya sluzhba*, esp. pp. 169–79, 225–30; Vassilyev, *Ochrana*, most of chs. 2, 3, 4; Spiridovich, *Zapiski*, pp. 193–7. Interrogations of security policemen in *PTR* also centre around the internal agency.

[37] See e.g. Spiridovich, *Zapiski*, p. 50.

[38] See M. I. Trusevich's statement of 10 Feb. 1907 (Agafonov, *Okhranka*, p. 187), that the internal agency was the key to successful counter-revolutionary operations.

[39] See e.g. L. Deich's comment about G. P. Sudeikin: 'for the first time he began to introduce spies and provocateurs into the ranks of the revolutionaries'. *KS*, liv (1929), 7–43 (here p. 36). Deich records the devastating effect of Sudeikin's methods compared to those of his predecessor, Baron Heyking. Beletskii claims Plehve was the man who regularized the internal agency: 'Dopros S. P. Beletskogo', 12 May 1917, p. 276.

proportions; virtually nothing that related to these parties remained a secret from the government.[40] Knowledge that secret agents were everywhere sowed havoc and distrust in revolutionary ranks, as the SRs' reactions to the disclosure of Azev's treachery make clear.[41] By 1912, according to Agafonov, police penetration and manipulation of the Social Democratic party had reached such levels that the Police Department was able to avert the threatened reunification of the Menshevik and Bolshevik factions by carefully arresting only 'moderate' delegates to the SDs' congress.[42] Yet, for all its triumphs, the internal agency also had its price. Leaving aside the general issue of the broad political consequences of the government's arbitrary methods of struggle with revolution, the regime's involvement in the murky world of double agents did nothing for its prestige at home or abroad. Moreover, although accusations of 'provocation' were vastly exaggerated, on some occasions, especially before 1908, police officers did encourage or even create revolutionary 'cells' in order to claim the credit for their discovery.[43] Finally, in order for the internal agency to function effectively, some sort of revolutionary underground had to be allowed to exist. The police argued, correctly, that it was better to have a few revolutionary cells operating under the government's eye than to sweep up all known revolutionaries and risk new movements emerging outside the security services' surveillance. However, existing cells had to be allowed some leeway to conduct their propaganda. Similarly, the fact that Malinovskii was a police agent did not reduce the impact of his speeches from the Duma tribune.

The intelligence-gathering techniques used by the security police were of service not only in the struggle against the revolutionary underground, but also as a means of studying shifts in public opinion. Even the provincial Gendarme Administrations were of some use in this role. The latter's officers were often well

---

[40] For examples of this, see the immensely detailed report by Eremin on the SRs dated 28 Mar. 1912; Agafonov, *Okhranka*, pp. 140 ff.; or some of Martynov's equally circumstantial reports on the KDs: e.g. no. 2, 4 Nov. 1914, or no. 4, 28 June 1915 (reports to the Police Department), in Tsentrarkhiv, *Burzhuaziya*, pp. 2–4, 6–11.

[41] Agafonov, *Okhranka*, pp. 139–40; Martynov, *Moya sluzhba*, p. 179.

[42] Agafonov, *Okhranka*, pp. 205–6.

[43] Russian society tended to call all operations by the internal agency provocation. Police memoirs, while stressing that provocation was rare, nevertheless cite some examples: see Vassilyev, *Ochrana*, pp. 62–7. On the other side, see Agafonov, *Okhranka*, pp. 190–9.

informed about the moods of the upper levels of provincial society, and kept a close, and frequently objective, eye on leading figures in the province.[44] In addition, they were the recipients of a good many whispers and denunciations. In the early 1860s, for instance, Gendarme Administrations seem on occasion to have been quite capable of picking up information about unfair treatment of peasants by peace arbitrators, and of relaying this to St Petersburg.[45] Given the fact that at the turn of the century the average province contained only nine to twelve gendarmes and hundreds of thousands, indeed often millions, of peasants, the Administrations' ability to know what was going on beneath the surface in the villages was inevitably limited, however. When information was required about specific villages, the Gendarmerie usually had to appeal to the ordinary police.[46] The 8,400 ordinary police sergeants and constables who served in the Russian countryside at the turn of the century were a drop in the ninety-million-peasant ocean, but at least until the twentieth century they (together with the priests) were the closest the imperial government came to having a regular presence in peasant society.[47] After 1881 the Okhrana added greatly to the government's knowledge about public moods, even though it concentrated on revolutionary and opposition circles and never had any role in the countryside. Nevertheless, the Okhrana's ability to penetrate to the very centre both of revolutionary parties and opposition-minded public organizations yielded an astonishingly detailed and accurate picture of the tactics, internal conflicts, and hopes of vital groups in society.[48] Moreover, if security service reporting in the First World War is anything to go by, the observations of the police were accurate and hard-hitting. On

[44] Bukhshtab, 'Posle vystrela Karakozova', pp. 50–88, is good on the Gendarme Administrations; see esp. pp. 51, 60. See also V. Bochkarev on the Yaroslavl security services: 'Ocherki po istorii revolyutsionnogo dvizheniya i bor'ba s nim v Yaroslavskom krae 1860–1917 gg.', *KS*, v (1922). It is interesting to compare the Gendarme Administration's views on leading Yaroslavl figures in the 1860s and 1870s with those of V. V. Wahl, at that time Vice-Governor of the province and subsequently a member of the State Council (see TsGAOR, f. 542, op. 1, ed. khr. 352, pp. 39–62, 270–82). The Gendarmerie reports seem well informed, intelligent, and fair.

[45] Bogucharskii, 'Tret'e otdelenie', pp. 109, 113–14.

[46] Martynov, *Moya sluzhba*, p. 21.

[47] Weissman, *Reform*, pp. 10–11. He states that a regular rural policeman in 1900 could have a 'beat' of 1,800 square miles and 50–100,000 people.

[48] See n. 40 above.

more than one occasion, for instance, the police reported bitter popular hostility towards the monarch, based on the masses' conviction that he personally was responsible for their, and Russia's, ills.[49]

The only remaining question in this review of the security service's functions and techniques concerns the level of police chiefs' political sophistication, and their ability to see the struggle against revolution within the context of a broader grasp of overall government strategy. It seems clear that political sophistication was not a hallmark of the average Gendarme officer. Thus in 1880–1, when Loris-Melikov demanded a more intelligent analysis of local political, social, and economic currents from provincial Gendarme Administrations, one Gendarme colonel was so alarmed that he asked I. I. Petrunkevich, supposedly a dangerous liberal under police surveillance, to write the report for him.[50] Political illiteracy of this sort in the middle ranks of the Gendarmerie was serious but not disastrous; it was at the top level of the security service and Ministry of the Interior that political sophistication was truly vital. The senior officials responsible for internal security had to understand the nature and sources of the revolutionary threat; they had to be able to communicate this understanding to the Committee of Ministers and the Emperor; but above all, they themselves had to grasp the broad political problems posed by Russia's rapid modernization, and not simply become encased in the techniques of police repression. It seems clear from the example of the Ministry of the Interior in 1902–4 that those ultimately responsible for domestic security did not always achieve the requisite level of political understanding. General V. V. Wahl, who controlled the Gendarmerie in this period, was a conscientious but rather brutal 'man of the fist', with a narrow military mentality and antediluvian political conceptions.[51] The Minister of the Interior, Plehve,

---

[49] See the reports of A. P. Martynov on 29 Feb. 1916, and A. T. Vasil'yev on 30 Oct. 1916, in Tsentrarkhiv, *Burzhuaziya*, pp. 75–81 and 136–9.

[50] J. Walkin, *The Rise of Democracy in Pre-Revolutionary Russia* (London, 1963), 60.

[51] My comments on Wahl are based on his unpublished memoirs and extensive private papers in TsGAOR, f. 542. See also my 'Stereotyping an Elite: The Appointed Members of the State Council 1894–1914', *Slavonic and East European Review*, 63/2 (1985) 244–72. In Sept. 1902 A. A. Kireev wrote that 'Wahl is a man of the fist and no more', RO, f. 126, k. 13, p. 170.

seems to have assumed that he could repeat the triumph he had achieved over *Narodnaya volya* twenty years earlier through effective use of police techniques of repression. Despite the sources of information at his disposal, the extent to which, in the interim, revolution had acquired a much broader base seems to have eluded Plehve, who believed, even in April 1904, that in the unlikely 'event of things going to extremes the government will find support in the peasantry and *meshchanstvo*'.[52]

Nevertheless, on many occasions the reports of senior security officials reveal considerable political insight. Thus in 1861 a Third Section memorandum to Alexander II stressed that internal security rested not only on 'crushing the criminal plans of rebels', but also on the government doing all in its power 'to retain in its own hands the standard of the progressive movement which it itself has started'.[53] Eight years later, the Third Section submitted to the monarch an intelligent and balanced appreciation of the causes of the radicalization of Russian youth and in particular of the higher educational institutions. Stressing the very different social position of Russian students from their counterparts' in the rest of Europe, the report emphasized that abject poverty was the basic cause of students' radicalization. It underlined that the setting-up of loan and assistance funds, of cheaper access to books and other teaching aids, and of non-profit-making canteens for students would do much to calm student opinion. If at the same time the Third Section reported that student-run self-help organizations might be taken over by revolutionaries for political purposes, this was little more than the truth. Moreover, the police showed themselves prescient in warning that city workers would be the likeliest and most vulnerable targets in the revolutionary intelligentsia's campaign to acquire a mass base.[54] When a sizeable and volatile working class did emerge in the 1890s, the security services were, according to Madhavan Palat, quick to realize that it could not be tamed by police repression.[55] It was from the ranks of the

---

[52] The quote is from Kireev's diary, entry for 2 Apr. 1904, RO, f. 126, k. 13, p. 312. The diary is a useful source on Plehve's views and inadequacies. See also Spiridovich, *Zapiski*, p. 110.

[53] Bogucharskii, 'Tret'e otdelenie', p. 109.

[54] '"Revolyutsionnoe i studencheskoe dvizhenie 1869 g. v otsenke Tret'ego otdeleniya", soobshchil V. P. Alekseev', *KS*, x (1924), 106–21.

[55] Palat, *Police Socialism*, pp. 12–16.

security police that the famous Zubatov policy for mastering the working-class threat emerged. Though this is not the place to debate the virtues and prospects of Zubatov's schemes, it would be hard to deny that his was an exceptionally imaginative and radical programme which went far beyond the narrow realm of police repression and was designed to retain for the state its ability to arbitrate between conflicting groups in a rapidly modernizing society.[56] In the last decade of the empire, P. N. Durnovo, who headed the Police Department in 1884–93 and the Ministry of the Interior in 1905–6, was one of the key figures in Russian politics. His famous memorandum of February 1914, warning that the war with Germany would lead to radical social revolution, was probably the most impressive document produced by an imperial official in the last years of the old regime, and embodied the ability both to understand the domestic security situation and to link this understanding with exceptional prescience as regards diplomatic, military, and financial affairs.[57] In the light of the tendency, perhaps slightly less strong now than ten years ago, to dismiss all conservative officials as reactionary idiots, it is worth citing the response of Fedor Dan, the Menshevik leader, to Durnovo's memorandum: 'However para-doxical it sounds,' wrote Dan, 'the extreme reactionaries in the Tsarist bureaucracy grasped the movement of forces and the social content of this coming revolution far sooner and better than all the Russian "professional revolutionaries", and particu-larly the Russian Marxist Social Democrats.'[58]

Discussion of the political literacy or otherwise of senior police officials acts as a useful link between the study on the one hand of the security services' functions and operations, and on the other, of their personnel. Generalizations about the latter are made more difficult if one bears in mind firstly that the quality of personnel changed considerably between 1855 and 1917, and secondly that the 'struggle against subversion' drew its officials from a number of very distinct sources.

[56] See esp. ibid.; Schneiderman, *Zubatov*; A. P. Korelin, 'Krakh ideologii "politseiskogo sotsializma"', *Istoricheskie zapiski*, 92 (1973).
[57] F. Golder, *Documents on Russian History 1914–1917* (New York, 1927), has a translation of Durnovo's memorandum. See also D. Lieven, 'Bureaucratic Authoritarianism in Late Imperial Russia: The Personality, Career and Opinions of P. N. Durnovo', *The Historical Journal* (Cambridge), 26/2 (1983), 391–402.
[58] T. Dan, *The Origins of Bolshevism* (New York, 1970), 399.

At the centre of 'counter-subversion' stood the officers of the Gendarmerie. They ran the provincial Gendarme Administrations and most Okhrana sections as well. Because the regime placed unique trust in the political and moral reliability of its army officers, all of the commissioned posts in the Gendarmerie were filled from this source.[59] Unfortunately, army officers' education in patriotism, courage, uprightness, and corporate spirit often made them unsuitable for security police operations,[60] for which most Gendarme officers lacked the political sophistication, the grasp of techniques of detection and intelligence-gathering, and the stomach. Moreover, even when courses for officers transferring into the Gendarmerie were set up, these taught gendarmes a good deal about the railways (where most officers were to be deployed for most of their careers), something about the law, and nothing whatsoever about either the revolutionary movement or police techniques.[61] This bias reflected the attitude of the Gendarme headquarters staff, which was responsible for the internal life of the corps, including all promotions and appointments save those in the Okhrana. Most Gendarme officers, and in particular the older and more senior ones, regarded themselves as soldiers; they took pride in the good order and the spit and polish that the Gendarmerie maintained on the railways, and thoroughly disliked police work and in particular the murky world of the underground war against subversion. The Gendarmerie was run as a gentlemen's club—for the comfort and convenience of its members, most of whom had joined the corps in the first place because of the extra pay and better conditions it offered compared to regular army service. State interests were of distinctly secondary importance. The incompetent were protected by comradely spirit and old-boy connections, vigorous efforts were made to regulate promotion by seniority alone, and posts (including those in the provincial Administrations) were filled with much more concern for the officer's rights and the Gendarme staff's convenience than for the candidate's suitability for the job. As a result, the security police of the 1870s was dominated by 'brave fellows of Nicholas's

---

[59] This had been true since the Corps's foundation. For an example of the principles behind 'recruitment' in Nicholas's era, see Squire, *Third Department*, p. 83.

[60] See Lieven, 'Stereotyping an Elite', nn. 59–62.

[61] Spiridovich, *Zapiski*, pp. 37–8.

era, patriarchal gendarmes of the pre-Sudeikin type',[62] who, though no doubt more pleasant than the average security policeman, nevertheless did dreadful damage to the state through their incompetence.[63] In contrast even to the twentieth-century Gendarme officer, the small minority of officers who entered the Okhrana were far more professional security policemen. To volunteer for the Okhrana suggested a certain enthusiasm for the work. In any case, Okhrana sifting procedures were more rigorous, and training on the job by seniors was much more professional than was the case in the Gendarmerie as a whole. It was above all the highly competent Okhrana officers trained in the school of S. V. Zubatov who dominated the struggle against subversion in the twentieth century.[64]

The second major group involved in 'counter-subversion' was the Procuracy. As has already been mentioned, procurators were officials of the Ministry of Justice, one of whose functions was to ensure that the administration operated in accordance with the law. Every Gendarme and Okhrana agency had a procurator attached to it, and senior positions in the Police Department, including almost invariably the directorship, were held by former procurators.[65] Procurators were far better educated, had more

[62] Bukhshtab, 'Posle vystrela Karakozova', pp. 50–1.

[63] There is a considerable consensus on the inadequacies of the Gendarmerie. See e.g. Lopukhin, *Iz itogov*, pp. 31–3; Martynov, *Moya sluzhba*, passim, but esp. pp. 31, 74, 118–19, 145, 202; Spiridovich, *Zapiski*, pp. 38–40, 51, 111; Zavarzin, *Zhandarmy*, pp. 43, 51, 62. Some of the revolutionary memoirs from the 1870s bring out the gendarmes' bewilderment when faced by actual subversion, especially as embodied by young well-educated women: e.g. 'Revolyutsionnaya Odessa 1877–78 g.', *KS*, vi (1923), 50–1; and N. Golovina, 'Moi vospominaniya', ibid. 34.

[64] There is a large, but often not very distinguished, bibliography on the Okhrana (see Smith, *Okhrana*). Zavarzin, *Zhandarmy*, pp. 54–7, recalls Zubatov's role (in his case, only short-term) as a teacher. Spiridovich, *Zapiski*, p. 112, recalls the domination of the new Okhrana agencies in the twentieth century by former pupils of Zubatov. Among the incentives for successful Okhrana officers were much more rapid promotion and much better pay than in the regular army. Gerasimov was promoted to general after only two years as a colonel instead of the normal ten, for foiling a plot to kill Nicholas II: A. V. Gerasimov, *Tsarisme et terrorisme* (Paris, 1934), 174. As the colonel in command of the Moscow Okhrana, Martynov not only wielded far more power than his military equivalents, but earned as much (12,300 roubles and free accommodation, light, and heating) as some members of the State Council: Martynov, *Moya sluzhba*, p. 216.

[65] S. P. Beletskii said that all heads of the Police Department (until him), most deputy ministers, and many ministers and other top officials in the Ministry of the Interior were 'people with a judicial baggage': 'Dopros S. P. Beletskogo', 12 May 1917, p. 273.

analytical minds, and were politically much more literate than the
average Gendarme officer.[66] In their dealings with the Okhrana,
however, they suffered from their lack of first-hand experience in
intelligence-gathering and detection work.[67] As regards their
position *vis-à-vis* legality, it is important to note the shift in
procurators' attitudes between 1864 and 1917. In the immediate
post-1864 reform era many judicial officials, including procurators,
felt a crusading commitment to the establishment of a full legal
order in Russia. Over the decades, however, some of this
commitment withered, and procurators began to share the
normal preoccupations and priorities of other state officials.[68] In
addition, whereas in the nineteenth century the Ministry of
Justice had tended strongly to defend its separateness, under
I. G. Shcheglovitov after 1905 procurators realized that the route
to promotion—whether in their own ministry or *a fortiori* in the
Police Department—lay through collaboration with the security
services.[69] Finally, whereas in the 1860s and even 1870s the law
itself had empowered the Procuracy to intervene forcibly in
defence of the civil rights of suspected or arrested revolutionaries,
the legislation of 1871–81 had greatly reduced the obligation,
right, and means to do this.[70] Procurators who took senior
positions in the Police Department did not usually lose their
formal respect for the letter of the law, but they accepted the fact
that the struggle against revolution required infringements of
civil rights and a wide exercise of discretionary administrative
power. Thus M. I. Trusevich, under interrogation by the
Provisional Government, claimed that survival was the first law
for any political organism, that tsarism had been forced to use
police powers and administrative discretion 'to defend its
existence' against revolution, and that any political system faced
by the same situation would have had recourse to similar
measures.[71]

---

[66] See the section on judicial officials in Lieven, 'Stereotyping an Elite', pp. 260–3.
[67] Martynov, *Moya sluzhba*, p. 90.   [68] See n. 66 above.
[69] 'Dopros S. P. Beletskogo', 17 May 1917, pp. 372–3.
[70] Lopukhin, *Iz itogov*, pp. 21–31.
[71] 'Dopros M. E. Trusevicha', pp. 213–15, 218. P. N. Durnovo's cavalier attitude
towards the law, and some of his comments on the subject as Director of the Police
Department are of interest: A. I. Ivanchin-Pisarev, 'Vospominaniya o P. N.
Durnovo', *KS*, lxviii (1930), 42, 57; and A. V. Gedeonovskii, 'Yaroslavskii
revolyutsionnyi kruzhok 1881–1886 gg.', ibid. xxiv (1926), 95–109.

Apart from gendarmes and procurators, the officials in charge of 'counter-subversion' were drawn from a number of other sources. In some cases, people who had been involved (to a greater or lesser extent) in revolutionary circles were recruited into the Okhrana and Police Department as regular officials.[72] When such collaborators could be trusted, they brought to the security services, especially in the nineteenth century, a welcome knowledge of both revolutionary politics and intelligence-gathering techniques. The Police Department also recruited some of its officials from the general public or, as with S. P. Beletskii, from other parts of the administration.[73] Inevitably, some officials, whatever their source of origin, were unable to resist using the considerable powers possessed by state security organs to further their own interests. Agafonov cites the case of A. I. Litvin, for instance, who before 1914 ran the British section of the Okhrana's External Agency in Paris. Although denounced on a number of occasions for cheating agents of their pay and using his power to extort money, Litvin secured himself against dismissal by threatening to disclose secret information to the press or to the revolutionaries.[74] Figures like Litvin, of whom there were known to be quite a few among police officials, helped to blacken the security service's reputation in society. In 1911, denouncing the vileness of Okhrana methods, the ultra-conservative Prince V. P. Meshcherskii wrote that at least the revolutionaries' abominations were the product of a commitment to ideals, while those who used unscrupulous tactics against them were motivated by nothing but desire for power, money, and the perquisites of office.[75] Such opinions, widespread among the court and aristocratic circles to which Meshcherskii belonged, had an impact on security service operations because of their influence on Nicholas II[76] and on some senior officials of aristocratic origin

---

[72] Agafonov, *Okhranka*, pp. 15–16, gives an example of this.

[73] Beletskii was a former official from Kovno, where P. A. Stolypin had got to know him: 'Dopros S. P. Beletskogo', 12 May 1917, pp. 255–6.

[74] Agafonov, *Okhranka*, pp. 124–5. The threat to reveal all to the press or to the revolutionaries was a constant thorn in the side of the police, esp. as regards agents of the External Agency with easy access both to the foreign newspapers and to V. I. Burtsev, a one-man revolutionary agency for 'blowing' Okhrana agents and operations. See ibid. 160–9.   [75] *Grazhdanin*, 37 (25 Sept. 1911), 12–15.

[76] See n. 17 above, for Nicholas's seeming acceptance of the possibility that the Okhrana may have 'provoked' sailors into revolutionary activity. It was of course more comforting for the Emperor to believe this.

in the Ministry of the Interior.[77] Thus, for instance, although Count D. A. Tolstoi used G. P. Sudeikin's skills to crush *Narodnaya volya* in the 1880s, he apparently made little secret of his dislike for the man and his methods, and failed to reward him properly. In retaliation, the ambitious and unscrupulous Sudeikin began to withhold information from Tolstoi and started an intrigue against him which ended only with Sudeikin's murder by one of his own agents.[78] In fact, violent conflicts between institutions and individuals were a hallmark of the Russian security services, and by 1914 they were probably their major failing. The Okhrana, for instance, fought the Gendarmerie, and both at times clashed with the Procuracy. As in the classic conflict between P. I. Rachkovskii and L. A. Rataev for control of the External Agency,[79] individuals struggled for power and its rewards, as well as sometimes out of mere jealousy and personal dislike. If, for reasons I have explained elsewhere, factional struggles were endemic in the Russian civil service,[80] they reached their apogee in the security police, whose frequently unscrupulous and ambitious officers struggled both with revolutionaries and colleagues in a black underworld impenetrable not only to publicity, but also often to their own superiors.

From what has already been said in this essay about police functions, techniques, and personnel, it will come as no surprise that the security services seriously infringed the population's civil rights. In the broadest sense, of course, the police were the main shield of a regime which, where it deemed it necessary, was prepared to override any civil right. In more specific terms, however, security police operations themselves made deep inroads into civil rights. In their intelligence-gathering operations, whether run by the Okhrana or by the Police Department's 'perlustrators', the security services operated unchecked by any law. If pressure was exerted to force collaboration with the police, or if arrests were made on the basis of false information, indeed

---

[77] See Martynov, *Moya sluzhba*, pp. 234–5, 255–6, 286–7.

[78] Sukhomlin, 'Protsess', pp. 36–8.

[79] For this, see Agafonov, *Okhranka*, pp. 53–73. The battle affected the two men's protégés, and was ultimately decided by the rise and fall of their patrons at Court and in the Committee of Ministers.

[80] D. Lieven, 'Russian Senior Officialdom Under Nicholas II: Careers and Mentalities', *Jahrbücher für Geschichte Osteuropas*, 32/2 (1984), 199–223, here pp. 211–17.

virtually whatever the Okhrana did, the citizen still had no legal come-back.[81] Even the security services' powers of arrest and preliminary investigation could only be supervised very inadequately by the Procuracy.[82] Finally, evidence that administrative exile was, by the standards of many other secret police forces, a mild sentence, and the joint Interior–Justice board, by the same standards, a model of decency and fairness does not alter the fact that both were major infringements of due process. Why, then, did the security services make these inroads into civil rights?

In the first place, there was Russia's political and administrative tradition. The tsars, and therefore by extension their officials, had always been guided solely by their will, conscience, and judgement. In comparison with this age-old tradition, the attempt to impose legal constraints on officials could really be dated only from 1864.[83] In addition, many Russian officials would have agreed with the view expressed by Julius Nyerere, the present leader of Tanzania, that effective executive action was already quite sufficiently constrained by the size of the country, the nature of its peasant society, poor communications, incompetent officials, and even such extraneous factors as the climate: the last thing required were additional artificial checks and constraints. For two reasons such views were held particularly strongly in the Ministry of the Interior. In the first place, the head of this department presided over a uniquely long hierarchy, stretching down ultimately to the unimpressive lower ranks of the police force.[84] To galvanize the lower echelons of this hierarchy

---

[81] *Grazhdanin*, see n. 75 above. See also Ivanchin-Pisarev, 'Vospominaniya o P. N. Durnovo', pp. 43–7, for an example of such pressure.

[82] Lopukhin, *Iz itogov*, pp. 21–6; *Svod zakonov Rossiiskoi imperii*, xv (Petrograd, 1916), arts. 91–166, pp. 22–37, lists the regulations concerning states of emergency, martial law, police surveillance, and administrative exile.

[83] The papers of V. V. Wahl bring out the reactions of a traditional military, police, and gubernatorial official to the attempt to enforce legal constraints. He vigorously defends governors' use of administrative power in many instances, given the delay and ineffectiveness of legal remedies (e.g. in the sphere of public health): 'The slowness inevitable in the legal process can threaten real danger—one cannot sacrifice human lives in the name of the famous "*fiat iustitia*"': TsGAOR, f. 542, op. 1, ed. khr. 334, here p. 8, but the whole memorandum (dated 27 Sept. 1898) is of interest.

[84] Even in St Petersburg in 1881 the ordinary police notion of vigilance was e.g. to arrest a man in army uniform wearing spectacles on the grounds that no one looking so studious could possibly be a genuine officer. A newspaper spoke of 'the clumsiness of the lower ranks of the police force' in the capital: N. V. Narbekov, 'Vokrug 1 Marta', in *Trudy kruzhka narodovol'tsev*, pp. 60–75 (here p. 65). Also H. S. Vasudevan,

258   D. LIEVEN

into action was seen as impossible if its members were threatened
with legal responsibility for their activities, protected by laws or
regulations behind which they could find excuses for inaction, or
confused by any but a simple line of command to their ministerial
chief.[85] Secondly, the Ministry of the Interior inherited the
traditional Russian obsession with public control and order
which presumably derived in part from the immense difficulty of
governing a scattered population in a huge area. This obsession
was reinforced by the fact that a westernized élite was governing a
far more numerous peasant mass whose mentality they did not
understand, whose hostility to many of the élite's values and
interests they suspected, and whose potential for anarchy they
deeply feared. A. N. Kulomzin's comment in 1881 that the
peasantry was liable to explode at the slightest rumour amply
illustrates these fears and suspicions.[86]

Given these attitudes, the emergence of a revolutionary and
terrorist threat was likely to pose great dangers for the fragile
legal system created in 1864. Already in 1869, stressing the
danger of published socialist propaganda, the Third Section
stated that the 'laws are helpless against it, as is seen from a few
trials regarding press affairs'.[87] The trials of revolutionaries in the
1870s, in particular the famous cases of 'the 193'[88] and of Vera
Zasulich, further undermined the affection of the security police
for the courts. Even, indeed, after 1881 when the security
services became far more effective, they still faced major
difficulties in working within the law. Perlustration and blanket
indemnity for those double agents participating in crimes in
order to protect their cover were difficult to square with the legal
codes. Moreover, whereas in ordinary cases definite crimes had
been committed and concrete evidence was to hand, political
offenders usually had to be charged with vague offences such as

'Origins of the Russian Revolution of 1905: Local Government Politicians and
Professionals, 1893–1900', The Calcutta Historical Journal, 5/2 (1981), 75–6.

[85] These were all major themes of P. N. Durnovo's speeches in the State Council:
see esp. GSSO, session 2, cols. 400–18; session 8, cols. 1291–4. See also N. A.
Maklakov's speech of 6 June 1916, in ibid., session 12, cols. 1566–82. Also Lieven,
'Bureaucratic Authoritarianism', pp. 398–9.

[86] See his memoirs in RO, f. 178, k. 9803, ed. khr. 5, p. 38.

[87] 'Revolyutsionnoe i studencheskoe dvizhenie', p. 121.

[88] 'Bol'shoi protsess, ili protsess 193-kh o revolyutsionnoi propagande v imperii',
KS, xxxvii (1927), 7–31.

sedition and conspiracy.[89] Not merely were such crimes harder to prove, but the character of the double agents who were key witnesses to them was open to question, while in any event the last thing the security police wished to do was to reveal its informers.

Undoubtedly, however, the key reason why civil rights were so massively infringed in the period 1870–81 was because the security police were too incompetent to deal with the terrorist threat within the confines of a legal order. Tikhomirov's comment that 'it would be difficult to imagine a more worthless political police than that which existed at that time' is the precise truth.[90] The government's initial response to the terrorist threat was martial law, administered with a flourish by politically naïve but energetic generals. Their round-ups left the terrorist circles unaffected, but greatly increased disaffection among educated society and thereby augmented the number of those willing to aid or condone revolution.[91] In Odessa under General E. I. Todleben 'everyone began to fear for his son, brother, husband, wife, who could be seized at will, removed without any trial, just by the slander of a traitor or a spy'.[92] When Loris-Melikov became dictator in 1880 he quickly saw the idiocy of such activities and abolished them, stressing to the police that more intelligent methods were required. For this, however, the government paid a price. Vera Figner recalls that under 'the dictatorship of the heart' in 'Petersburg itself, propaganda, agitation, and organization were carried on on a broad scale. The lack of police-nagging and of round-ups by the Gendarmerie in this period was very favourable to work among the students and the workers.'[93] One explanation for this is provided by A. N. Kulomzin, who wrote about Loris-Melikov that: 'by his constant demands that it [i.e. the police] should always act legally in all its undertakings, one can with truth say that he caused its collapse; this is a strange statement but it's true; our police never knew anything about laws and when threatened with responsibility for infringing the law it becomes lost and prefers to sit and do nothing'.[94] The

[89] Lopukhin, *Iz itogov*, pp. 25–6.   [90] *Krasnyi arkhiv*, 6 (1924), 155.
[91] R. M. Kantor, 'K istorii revolyutsionnogo dvizheniya 1870–1880 godov: neizdannaya zapiska L'va Tikhomirova', *KS*, xxiv (1926), 119–22.
[92] Frolenko, 'Nachalo "narodovol'stva"', pp. 19–20.
[93] V. Figner, *Zapechatlennyi trud* (Moscow, 1921), i. 174.
[94] RO, f. 178, k. 9803, ed. khr. 5, p. 23.

degree of Gendarme incompetence is shown by their reaction to the arrest of a revolutionary who had a plan of the Winter Palace on which the Tsar's dining-room was marked in red. Even the Gendarmerie surmised that this might signify a bomb attack, but despite noisy searches of the Winter Palace, they never bothered to look under the bed of Stepan Khalturin, a palace servant who was living in a room below the dining-room, where they would have found a large store of explosives.[95] The key to breaking *Narodnaya volya* lay in effective intelligence-gathering, but not only did the police fail to do this, they allowed a revolutionary agent, N. V. Kletochnikov, to penetrate their own headquarters and to reveal all their operations to his comrades. Fortunately for the government, the regular city police were not fully under the control of security police headquarters, and it was they who ultimately made the key arrest of A. D. Mikhailov, though they did so too late to save either Alexander II or the civil rights which went with him into the grave.[96]

By the twentieth century it was no longer possible to blame police incompetence for the infringement of civil rights. By then the security services could claim with some justice that it was impossible to subdue the revolutionary movement by wholly legal means, that there was a real risk of revolution, and that the law of survival had precedence over any civil rights.[97] Certainly in 1900–17 Russian society was much more difficult to hold together, and the government's position was far more vulnerable, than had been the case in the 1870s. Rapid modernization, the tempo of which was largely dictated by the need to survive as an independent power in an imperialist era, combined with the expense of the contemporary arms race, put heavy burdens on the population. The ugliness and the naked injustices of early capitalism, whose mores offended many traditional Russian values, increased social tensions. Modernization weakened the regime's social base, namely, the gentry and the conservative, patriarchal peasantry, while increasing potential support in

---

[95] L. Tikhomirov, 'Teni proshlogo', *KS*, xxv (1926), 88–90.

[96] A. I. Popov, 'Aresty pered 1 Marta 1881 g. i arest S. L. Perovskoi', in *Trudy kruzhka narodovol'tsev*, pp. 53–7.

[97] General A. V. Gerasimov, the former chief of the St Petersburg Okhrana, subsequently said of the revolutionaries in 1905, 'they almost crushed us then': 'Dopros A. V. Gerasimova', 26 Apr. 1917, *PTR*, iii. 3. I share his view about the narrowness by which the regime survived the 1905 Revolution.

society for revolution. Attempts to reintegrate society through the use of Russian nationalism or the pursuit of prestige in foreign policy merely alienated non-Russians and increased the risks of involvement in war. Although the regime was always linked above all to Russia's westernized élite, in 1861–1905 it retained a certain distance from this élite and a certain degree of legitimacy and support among the peasantry. The events of 1905–7, however, threw the regime and the westernized élite into each other's arms. But it was far more difficult to maintain the property and status of the landowners and industrialists of early twentieth-century Russia than it was in much richer countries such as Britain, France, or Germany. A far smaller percentage of the overall Russian population shared the élite's values or its material interest in the preservation of the existing society. If Russia's landowners and industrialists were to maintain their own property, lifestyle, and status, while transferring most of the costs of modernization on to the masses, they were unlikely to achieve this goal through a political system embodying respect for civil rights. Moreover, although both the government and the élites could certainly have made more concessions than they did to popular demands, their own weakness, both political and economic, greatly reduced their room for compromise and threw them back on the use of coercion as the only available means to secure their position. The comparison between Russia and early twentieth-century Spain, also in Europe but not wholly of it, torn apart by regional particularism, and threatened by every kind of extreme political movement, is of interest. Certainly, it is relevant that, partly through the massive use of violence, the Spanish élites initially created a European-style bourgeois society, before feeling that the granting of civil rights was compatible with the preservation of their own interests.

Early twentieth-century Russia was not therefore a hospitable nursery for civil rights. Prominent figures in the government, though admittedly by no means all of them, did not believe that contemporary Russian society could be preserved if the security services were constrained by civil rights and the rule of law.[98]

---

[98] By concentrating on the security services and their chiefs, one is inevitably seeing the government at its most hardline. I have tried to give a more all-round view in my article 'Stereotyping an Elite', while my 'Bureaucratic Liberalism in Late Imperial Russia: The Personality, Career and Opinions of A. N. Kulomzin', *Slavonic*

Moreover, intelligent contemporaries were right to fear that not only the revolutionary parties, but also the bulk of the peasantry were in practice even less likely to be reliable guardians of civil rights than the westernized and often legally trained officials who ran the imperial government.[99] In my view, whoever won the political struggle that racked early twentieth-century Russia, the outcome was unlikely to be a political system incorporating firmly entrenched civil rights. Probably the most that could be hoped for was that Russia's rulers would operate with a certain sense of self-restraint, maybe derived in part from a respect for law, but above all dependent on moral and political considerations. Certainly, the chances of self-restraint depended enormously on Russia's ability to survive the process of modernization without a breakdown of political authority. The closer this breakdown approached, the more the élites would throw all constraints overboard in the struggle for survival.[100] If total collapse did occur, civil rights would be ignored not only in the inevitable struggle for power between conflicting political tendencies, but also in the restoration of authority and economic development in the midst of anarchy. Finally, the prospects of civil rights were linked to the survival of a civil society, in other words, of a society which was not wholly dependent on the state. Whatever the theoretical possibilities of civil rights flourishing in a state-controlled economy, in Russian practice the state take-over in 1918–32 of both the economy and almost all social institutions enormously increased the control of political authority over the ordinary subject, greatly weakening that individual autonomy which is at the root of all conceptions of civil rights.

and East European Review, 60/3 (1982), 413–32, is devoted to the biography of a distinctly 'soft' member of the ruling élite.

[99] M. O. Gershenzon's famous outburst in Vekhi that the westernized elements in Russian society must fear the masses 'more than all the government's executions, and we must bless this regime which alone, with its bayonets and prisons, still protects us from the people's wrath', caused immense indignation among the intelligentsia when it was written. Though it would be thoroughly unfair simply to 'blame' the Russian masses for the intelligentsia's plight after 1917, the latter does throw a new light on Gershenzon's words.

[100] The period in which the regime resorted to the vilest methods and infringed on civil rights in the grossest way was, not surprisingly, 1905–8. See e.g. Vassilyev, Okhrana, pp. 26, 64.

Was there a Movement for
Civil Rights in Russia in 1905?

LINDA EDMONDSON

IN those extraordinary months of intense political activity and social upheaval which have become known as the Revolution of 1905, the question of civil rights assumed an importance which, although it has been noted, has been taken rather for granted by historians.[1] The rhetoric of freedom, of personal rights, of equality before the law, and of the state founded on the rule of law permeated the writings and utterances of political activists of the left and centre. Implicit and explicit in their schemes for the regeneration of Russia were civil rights and liberties. Repeatedly in resolutions at congresses, in petitions to the government and administration, and in the many protests against 'arbitrary authority' (*proizvol*), the call for freedom of expression, freedom of association, inviolability of the person rang out loud and clear. Even by the end of 1904, before the mass protest movement of the revolution had fully erupted, references to civil rights had become so standard, so ubiquitous, that one might be tempted to dismiss them as nothing more than rhetorical devices were it not for the fact that they touched the everyday lives of people at all levels of society.

But while the political programmes and the formation of

* Research for this essay was made possible by the Economic and Social Research Council, which funded a project on civil rights in Russia before 1917 at the School of Slavonic and East European Studies, University of London, between 1982 and 1985. Additional support was provided by a Finnish government scholarship for research in the University of Helsinki Slavonic Library in 1984 and 1985. I should also like to thank Abraham Ascher and Reginald Zelnik for reading a first draft of this essay and for making very helpful comments.

[1] No one could ignore the civil rights issue, but in general it has not been singled out for attention. See e.g. S. Galai, *The Liberation Movement in Russia, 1900–1905* (Cambridge, 1973); T. Emmons, *The Formation of Political Parties and the First National Elections in Russia* (Cambridge, Mass., 1983). However, H. Rogger specifies civil rights as an issue in Russian politics, in *Russia in the Age of Modernisation and Revolution* (London, 1983), ch. 4.

political parties have been scrutinized quite closely in recent years, no one has asked what function concepts of civil rights performed in the political discourse of this period, and what significance may be attached to them. It is the purpose of this essay to discuss the civil rights issue in the context of the 1905 Revolution, and to ask whether a movement for the acquisition of civil rights can be said to have developed during this period.

One of the reasons why the civil rights issue has been rather neglected is, paradoxically, the reason why it is worth studying: by and large, the acquisition of civil rights was not a matter of dispute between political groups. It is true that the meaning of such rights and the place which they should occupy on the scale of priorities were indigestible bones of contention among (and within) the quarrelling factions. None the less, civil rights were championed, at least on paper, by all groups and parties critical of the government, with the exception of the extreme right. This point deserves emphasis: it was not of incidental significance that a detailed prescription for civil rights appeared on every political platform and in virtually every public protest issued by the left and centre during these months.[2]

But what exactly was meant by civil rights? Here we enter that realm of the elusive to which W. E. Butler refers in his opening essay. Because civil rights in modern parlance have tended to become conflated with 'human rights', we need to define more precisely what was included (and implied) in the term 'civil rights' in Russia before 1917. But even a precise definition still leaves room for disagreement and confusion, both revealing and reflecting the overall divergence of opinion among political thinkers and activists so familiar to any student of pre-revolutionary Russian politics.

For the study of the civil rights issue in 1905, this confusion should not be seen as a semantic inconvenience. If we can disentangle what people meant (and what we mean) by civil rights, we may cast a new light on some of the disputes which raged between factions and individuals over the desired ends and

---

[2] The available sources are almost excessive. All the periodical press is of use, including specialist journals (e.g. of the medical profession). Those of particular value for this essay are *Osvobozhdenie*, *Listok osvobozhdeniya*, *Pravo*, and the daily newspapers.

means of the revolution, and bring to the surface contradictions in their (and our) thinking.

It is at first sight a relatively simple task to make a list of civil rights such as one might find in a political programme or protest between 1904 and 1907. Indeed, one quickly appreciates that there developed a rhetoric of civil rights, even a predictable formula, which determined not only the phraseology appropriate to civil rights demands, but even their position within the text of a protest or declaration. A characteristic statement would invariably employ the following concepts: equality before the law of all citizens (often with the additional phrase 'regardless of nationality, religion, or sex'); freedom of speech, conscience, press, assembly, and association; inviolability of the person and the home. Frequently it would also stipulate one or all of the following: freedom of movement; freedom from arbitrary arrest and exile; trial by judicial authority before a legally constituted court. These are the classical liberal freedoms, 'the freedom of the private individual' whose essence 'is precisely the existence of a private sphere with which no state, even the most democratic, has the right to interfere'.[3]

In the many resolutions and declarations of the 1905 Revolution, a statement of civil rights demands was commonly made as the preamble to a list of political demands or at the head of such a list. A number of examples will serve to illustrate the point. The first is the resolution passed at the best known of the political banquets sponsored by the Union of Liberation in the last two months of 1904. It was held in St Petersburg on 20 November to commemorate the fortieth anniversary of the judicial reforms; 676 guests were addressed by the 'legal populists' from the journal *Russkoe bogatstvo* (including V. G. Korolenko, N. F. Annenskii, and A. V. Peshekhonov) and by the liberal I. V. Gessen. The resolution demanded: fundamental rights for all citizens (freedom of speech, assembly, association, personal inviolability, etc.); the abolition of all class, national, and religious restrictions, and the 'real equality of all before the law'; all laws and taxes to be created only with the participation and assent of 'freely elected

---

[3] A paraphrase by A. Walicki of Benjamin Constant's definition of freedom. See the thoughtful discussion by Walicki, 'Marx and Freedom', *New York Review of Books*, 30/18 (24 Nov. 1983), 50–1.

representatives from the whole people'; ministerial responsibility to a national assembly. The banquet called for the immediate summoning of a constituent assembly, a free election campaign, and a full amnesty for all those convicted of political or religious offences.[4]

Similar resolutions were passed at other banquets in the campaign, in the two capital cities and in the provinces. Many were explicitly modelled on the St Petersburg resolution in content and phrasing, or were close in spirit, like this banquet of doctors in St Petersburg: 'We are firmly convinced that no partial repairs to this regime can put Russia on the path of enlightened development; the essential conditions for this are inviolability of the person and home; freedom of conscience, speech, the press, assembly, and unions, guaranteed by a representative form of government on wide democratic principles.' The resolution called for an immediate amnesty, and a constituent assembly 'freely elected by citizens of both sexes without distinction of religion or nationality on the basis of universal, direct, equal and secret suffrage'.[5] A banquet in Kaluga resolved: '1. that all citizens of both sexes must be guaranteed personal inviolability, freedom of conscience, speech, assembly, the press, unions, as inalienable rights; 2. that all estate, national, and religious restrictions be removed and that equality of all before the law, without distinction of sex, be established.' It also called for a constituent assembly and an immediate amnesty.[6]

A banquet at the Commercial Club in Rostov-on-Don on 5 December could well be seen as a civil rights campaign in miniature. Over six hundred representatives of various professions attended the banquet, together with a group of workers' representatives from Rostov and Nakhichevani. The diners heard seven speeches, five of them by lawyers. Three were on freedom

---

[4] *Listok osvobozhdeniya*, 19 (1904), 4. T. Emmons has counted 38 such banquets and analysed their content, in particular to establish how many called for radical political change. However, he does not single out civil rights demands, referring to them usually in passing: T. Emmons, 'Russia's Banquet Campaign', *California Slavic Studies*, 10 (1977), 45–87.

[5] *Osvobozhdenie*, 63 (1905), 226–7. The specification of female suffrage in any resolution passed before the latter part of 1905 invariably indicated a position on the radical wing of the liberation movement.

[6] Ibid.

of conscience, personal inviolability, and 'the necessity of freedom of education, speech, the press, and assembly'; one was on the peasant question; and the remainder were on political reform. 'All the speeches were fired by a single burning conviction: that to live as we have done up to now is no longer possible.' Following a unanimous resolution demanding civil rights and a constituent assembly, a workers' resolution was read out. This had been drawn up earlier at workers' meetings and made the same demands, but added the freedom to strike, as well as universal, direct, equal, and secret suffrage. In conclusion, the banquet was addressed by Dr S. V. Svatikov, who called for unity between the intelligentsia and the proletariat and was enthusiastically applauded. The banquet itself proceeded without interference, and a Cossack guard outside the hall made no attempt to disperse the large crowd of workers who had gathered there. But Svatikov was later arrested for giving this speech and legal proceedings instituted.[7]

Student meetings, too, adopted strong resolutions calling for civil rights and political change. Student demonstrations were broken up by police and Cossacks—one in St Petersburg on 28 November prompted a signed protest by 120 liberal and socialist *intelligenty*, who declared that the assault on 'our sons and daughters, our brothers and sisters' was 'utterly typical of the present regime and must finally shatter the illusions of those who still have not lost hope of the possibility of the most elementary protection of the individual under the present state system'.[8]

Lest it seem that only politically radical gatherings concerned themselves with civil rights, it is worth quoting from the Eleven Theses which the privately held national *zemstvo* congress passed, early in November. This meeting found it impossible to agree on a political formula, but apparently encountered no problems in agreeing to a statement on civil rights:

To avoid the possibility of administrative abuse, it is necessary to establish and maintain the principle of inviolability of person and home. No one should be subjected to search or restriction in his movements

[7] Ibid. 228. The journal report also noted that a telegram of greeting was sent to the banquet by the Don *oblast'* Marshal of the Nobility, Denisov.

[8] *Listok osvobozhdeniya*, 22–3 (1904), 7.

except by order of a court, independent in its authority. To achieve the above ends, it is necessary to provide also for the practical implementation of the principle of administrative legality by establishing procedures for civil and criminal prosecution of officials who violate the law.

In order to make possible the complete development of the spiritual resources of the people, the full exposition of public needs and the free expression of public opinion, the following are indispensable: freedom of conscience and religion, freedom of speech and press, and freedom of assembly and association.

All citizens of the Russian Empire should have equal personal (civil and political) rights.[9]

These theses evidently reflected the views of provincial *zemstvo* assemblies throughout Russia, every one of which had, by the end of 1905, called for a fully constitutional regime based on guarantees of the 'rights of man'—freedom of speech, assembly, etc., plus habeas corpus.[10]

It hardly needs to be said that these uncompromising demands for civil rights did not diminish after the massacre of Bloody Sunday. What may be worth noting is the fact that the tone of civil rights demands did not change substantially during 1905, even though the overtly political content of protests frequently did, becoming both more outspoken and more specific as the opposition consolidated. But if the content of civil rights protests remained much the same, the pace of protest increased, as each professional and special-interest group organized itself into a union, until by early May fourteen of them joined together into a Union of Unions, committed to the summoning of a constituent assembly and the establishment of civil rights. To this end, the union was prepared to disregard prohibitions on meetings and establish freedom of speech and assembly without preliminary permission (*yavochnym poryadkom*).[11]

Thus far, my illustrations have been drawn from those political circles within which one would most expect civil rights to be

[9] Cited in S. Harcave, *The Russian Revolution of 1905* (London, 1970), 280. 14 of the resolutions passed during the banquet campaign explicitly approved the *zemstvo* congress resolutions, while 4 others were similar in wording. See Emmons, 'Russia's Banquet Campaign', pp. 55–6.

[10] R. T. Manning, 'The Zemstvo and Politics', in T. Emmons and W. S. Vucinich (eds.), *The Zemstvo in Russia* (Cambridge, 1982), 136–7.

[11] S. D. K. (S. D. Kirpichnikov), *Soyuz soyuzov* (St Petersburg, 1906).

important: from the intelligentsia and the professions. True, an outside voice speaking on behalf of a workers' group would often make itself heard, as at the Rostov banquet, and in any case, the interplay between left-of-centre liberals in the liberation movement and socialists in the labour movement which was so characteristic throughout 1905 up to the October Manifesto makes rigid categorization impossible. None the less, we have so far been dealing mainly with groups well versed in political philosophy, and with highly developed concepts of individual freedom and legality, and this might lead us to suppose, firstly, that civil rights are exclusively concerned with the relationship of the individual to society, and secondly, that as a result the 'popular masses', i.e. workers and peasants, had little interest in the civil rights issue.

To make such suppositions would be to fall into a trap. Even if we accept the assertion that civil rights can be invested only in individuals and not in groups (which is itself a matter of perennial dispute), to argue that workers and peasants could have no interest in civil rights is to perpetuate the rather condescending assumption that they had no sense of their own individuality, and that, lacking the sophisticated culture of lawyers and landowners, they had developed no conception of personal inviolability.

Recent studies of working-class and peasant life in Russia which have emphasized the power of the collective over the individual and the endurance of strong traditions of collective decision-making have made a great impact on the way we interpret Russian social history. It is one thing, however, to appreciate that peasants or workers were used to thinking in terms of the needs of the group, that they were suspicious of unfettered individual enterprise, and that they exacted conformity from their fellows (behaviour which is in any case not unique to Russian peasants and workers); but quite another to argue that individuals brought up in such traditions developed no sense of self. The fact that the most enterprising members of the commune did often break out of its bounds illustrates the limitations of collective authority in the village. Even at the most basic level of daily existence in both the countryside and the town, people resented the many small (and not so small) infringements of their personal dignity which occurred in their often unsought interactions with authority. As S. A. Smith argues in his essay on workers, the rising number of non-political complaints against 'bad treatment' in the factory indicate a lively sense of self and a growing insistence on respect for their personal rights. The evidence suggests that peasants, too, believed that they had certain basic human rights as individuals.

There is every reason to believe that pressure for civil rights during the 1905 Revolution did not come exclusively, or even predominantly, from the educated middle class and from liberal political groups. Not only were concepts of civil rights well developed in the programmes and propaganda of the revolutionary left, even before 1905; workers and peasants themselves expressed more than a fleeting concern for their rights when given the leeway to do so. It would appear that this concern already existed before the eruption of mass protest in 1905. Although Victoria Bonnell is surely correct in her perception of workers as 'increasingly preoccupied with issues concerning political and civil rights, as well as the special rights of labor to unionize and to strike' in the latter part of 1905, it seems clear that such issues were well established by the beginning of the year.[12] The experience of the Zubatov mutual aid societies and Father Gapon's Assembly of Russian Factory Workers had served to encourage workers to think in terms of collective organization and the presentation of legitimate grievances to the authorities. These grievances seem naturally to have included violations of basic rights, as is attested by the ill-fated petition to the Tsar on Bloody Sunday, which is studded with references to 'lack of rights', 'despotism', and 'lawlessness'. Still more to the point of my argument, the first six paragraphs of the petition concern civil and political rights.

The prominent placing of civil rights in the programmes and declarations of the revolutionary parties also suggests that they were not seen as the exclusive monopoly of liberal politics. The first eight points of the Social Democratic party programme, adopted in 1903, would have been acceptable to many liberal

---

[12] V. E. Bonnell, *Roots of Rebellion: Workers' Politics and Organizations in St Petersburg and Moscow, 1900–1914* (Berkeley, 1983), 171. See S. A. Smith's essay for suggestions that the labour movement was very unevenly politicized before October 1905, with civil rights not greatly in evidence in many strike demands and workers' resolutions.

members of the Union of Liberation, and were in fact very close to the opening paragraphs of the union's own programme of 1905. Likewise, the programme of the Socialist Revolutionary party stipulated 'complete freedom of conscience, speech, press, assembly, labour strikes and unions, full and universal civil equality, inviolability of person and home . . .'.[13] Granted, the issue of civil rights was complicated for socialists by their disagreement as to the possibility, or desirability, of agitating for rights and freedoms in anticipation of socialist revolution. None the less, both revolutionary parties had come to regard it as essential, at the very least for propaganda purposes, to enshrine civil and political rights in their programmes.

Unless we are to assume that socialist principles are entirely opportunist (and, conversely, that liberal principles spring entirely from the purest of motives), it is reasonable to ask whether the various factions in the Russian opposition during 1905 used a common language in respect to civil rights, or whether the rhetoric masked as much as it revealed. We should also ask to what extent workers were directly influenced by political propaganda when they drew up their strike demands or put together petitions. It is clear, for example, that those who drafted the petition which was taken to the Winter Palace on Bloody Sunday were employing the same language as both revolutionaries and liberals: 'inviolability of the person', 'equality of all before the law', 'freedom of speech, press, association, conscience', etc.[14] The language is abstract and not necessarily easy to grasp (in particular the expression 'inviolability of the person' (neprikosnovennost' lichnosti), which would hardly trip off the tongue of anyone but a lawyer or academic). For this reason it would be tempting to argue that the inclusion of civil rights demands was the inspiration of outside agitators, either socialists or Liberationists, and not a reflection of workers' perceived desires.[15]

---

[13] See Harcave, Russian Revolution, pp. 263–5, 270. The Union of Liberation programme is in Osvobozhdenie, 64 (1905). Note that the right to strike was regarded by socialists as a fundamental freedom, whereas the Union of Liberation placed it within the context of labour legislation.

[14] A text of the petition is in Osvobozhdenie, 64 (1905), 233. For an annotated translation, see W. Sablinsky, The Road to Bloody Sunday: Father Gapon and the St Petersburg Massacre of 1905 (Princeton, 1976), 344–9.

[15] It is well established that individual socialists and Liberationists worked with

The problem of determining the provenance of ideas and of assessing the extent of outside influences on a given group of people is too complex to be resolved here, but it has to be borne in mind when considering whether there was a movement for civil rights in 1905, and, if so, whether workers participated in it. But it should also be remembered that influences are rarely exclusively one-way, and that in the case of the labour movement, the demands of workers almost certainly influenced their supposed political mentors—for example, in the inclusion of the right to strike.[16]

The problem is even more acute when one attempts to disentangle the competing interests in the peasant movement. There is a wealth of material from 1905 and 1906, published and unpublished, which reveals a far greater political awareness and concern for matters besides the land question among the peasantry than has generally been recognized.[17] The extent to which one finds demands for equality, freedom of speech, assembly, and association, full amnesty, etc., as well as political demands for unconditional universal suffrage, comes as a great surprise if one has hitherto assumed that the overriding, even exclusive, concern of the peasantry was for land. Faced with all this material, it may still be more comfortable to accept statements such as the following as the sole truth: 'The [October] manifesto was solemnly proclaimed in the town cathedral on October 22. Many people had gathered there, including many

Gapon's organization and tried to influence its direction. The petition shows signs of various influences, but it would be rash to assume that because the language used to express political concepts was not the everyday language of the workers, the ideas themselves could only come from outside. See Sablinsky, *Road to Bloody Sunday*, pp. 344–9; G. D. Surh, 'Petersburg's First Mass Labor Organization: The Assembly of Russian Workers and Father Gapon', *Russian Review*, 3 (July 1981), 241–62; ibid. 4 (Oct. 1981), 412–41.

[16] S. A. Smith refers in his essay to the workers' conception of a 'constitutional factory' which mimicked the liberation movement's battle-cry of a 'constitution'. This finds strong parallels in the attempts of other social groups to democratize their working environments.

[17] See e.g. S. Dubrovskii and B. Grave (eds.), *Agrarnoe dvizhenie v 1905–1907 gg.*, i (Moscow and Leningrad, 1925); 'Agrarnoe dvizhenie v Rossii v 1905–1906 gg.', *Trudy Imperatorskago vol'nago ekonomicheskago obshchestva*, 3, 4–5 (1908); A. Kornilov, 'Fakticheskiya dannyya o nastroenii krest'yan', *Pravo*, 33 (1905), cols. 2689–99; K. Sivkov, 'Krest'yanskie prigovory 1905 goda', *Russkaya mysl'* 4 (1907), pt. 2, pp. 24–48. See also D. Dahlmann, 'The Peasants and the Civil Rights Problem in 1905', an unpublished paper given at the conference on civil rights in Russia, cited in the introduction to this book.

peasants. The reading of the manifesto disappointed them; they were expecting something "about the land". But here there were only "some kind of liberties".[18]

But if personal rights were of no concern to the peasants, what are we to make of the fact that in the months before the Tsar's manifesto, peasant petitions had not infrequently complained not only of their land hunger, but also of their lack of rights and their unequal legal status, as well as their need of basic education? Of course, in arguing that peasant protest in 1905 and 1906 was for more than land, it would be foolish to err in the opposite direction, and to exaggerate the importance of rights and liberties in peasant thinking. The land issue was of immense significance, both for urgent practical reasons and symbolically. The peasants would not be satisfied with any initiative from the government which failed to fulfil their need for land, and their interest in rights and equality was not such that they would be prepared to accept them in lieu of land. Moreover, by October 1905 many sections of society besides the peasants felt that the government was trying to fob them off with vague promises of civil rights and even participation in politics, without yielding sovereignty to the people. The promises of 'some kind of liberties' contained in the October Manifesto satisfied very few people, though still enough to split the liberal opposition.

None the less, the evidence does suggest that at least during the period of the 1905 Revolution, the slogan 'land and freedom' could be taken literally as an expression of peasant wishes. There is no reason to argue, as historians of Russia have tended to do, that demands for economic change and those for civil liberties are mutually exclusive. It may be necessary for historical analysis to isolate particular aspects of a political programme or campaign; but it is equally necessary to see the separate issues as part of an entity. In 1905 land, civil liberties, and political rights all hung together. Just as the peasant demand for land could be both an expression of perceived (and real) material need and an attempt to change the power relations between classes in the countryside, to gain autonomy, so the call for civil and political rights could be both practical and symbolic in its implications. As far as political rights are concerned, this is evident: a decisive voice in the future

---

[18] Quoted by Emmons, *Formation of Political Parties*, p. 237.

national legislature would permit the enactment of a radical agrarian law; it would formally guarantee equal citizenship to the peasant, and it would give him (and possibly her) the practical opportunity to participate in legislation affecting the peasantry as a class. That they recognized this is confirmed by the enthusiasm with which newly enfranchised peasant men went to the polls in 1906.

I would suggest that peasants saw civil rights in a similar way. Their concern about their civil status was both practical and abstract. In their *prigovory* and *nakazy* they often stipulated their equalization in law with other classes (including the complete abolition of *soslovie* distinctions); they asked to be free from the supervision of the *zemskii nachal'nik*; they wanted the right to hold meetings at which they could speak freely. By 1906, in response to the government's punitive expeditions against the villages, they petitioned for an end to martial law, an amnesty for those convicted of political offences, and in some cases for an end to 'the shameful death penalty'.[19] All of these demands related closely to the lives of peasants in a period of turmoil and physical repression.

Proof of the peasants' concern with rights rests on the evidence provided by the hundreds of *nakazy* and *prigovory* which have survived, on police reports in the archives, on newspaper and journal reports of peasant meetings during 1905 and 1906, and on articles written by members of the intelligentsia soon after the event, seeking to demonstrate the peasants' engagement in the political movements of the time. Doubts none the less persist that all this material does not tell us whether the *prigovory* really expressed the wishes and views of the mass of the peasant population, especially when one considers that some of the terminology used is clearly imported from the intelligentsia.

One could both prove and disprove the authenticity of the peasant petitions by reference to their idiosyncratic syntax and orthography and variable legibility on the one hand, and their often formulaic expression on the other. Some *prigovory* were

---

[19] Helsinki, Valtionarkisto, *Trudoviki-puolueen duuma-rhymä* (Trudovik Duma Group), box 2, folder 65. I am very grateful to Hannu Immonen for introducing me to this collection and for the assistance he gave me in using it. For texts of peasant petitions and resolutions in 1905, see also *Pravo, passim*, and daily newspapers. Many thanks also to Dittmar Dahlmann for information on published sources and ideas on their interpretation.

evidently composed by peasants themselves, some by an educated outsider; others were based on a model provided by the Peasant Union or, in 1906, by the Trudoviks, and completed by peasants or their representatives in the village. Some petitions were signed by dozens of individual peasants; others were signed by a few; in many cases, the literate signed on behalf of the illiterate.[20]

As conclusive proof at this point, and perhaps forever, is not available, one might make a very subjective observation in support of the thesis that peasants had an interest in civil rights. If we are prepared to accept such documentation as one form of evidence of the peasants' insistent demands for land, why should we suppose that specific requests for an end to martial law, the removal of the *zemskii nachal'nik*, even 'inviolability of the person' can only be foreign imports? Writing about peasant aspirations before 1861, Daniel Field makes the observation that 'the longed-for freedom, or *volnost'*, was purely negative— freedom such as Russians imagined they had enjoyed in the good old days'.[21] This concept is not so far from the notion of the 'free-born Englishman' subjugated by the 'Norman yoke' which sustained the parliamentary rebels against monarchical despotism in England in the early seventeenth century.[22] It is also reminiscent of the classical liberal conception of freedom as essentially negative: the existence of a private sphere, of personal rights which the state cannot invade or infringe. I am not suggesting that Russia's peasants in 1905 were the spiritual heirs of the English parliamentarians who opposed Charles I, nor that they were all unconscious liberals, nor even that peasant aspirations in 1905 were identical to those before 1861. What I am proposing is that peasants, at least as much as the intelligentsia, had an interest in those civil rights which would give them greater freedom of action and liberate them from external supervision.

---

[20] Welcome confirmation of the argument expressed here can be found in two recent works: T. Shanin, *Russia 1905–07: Revolution as a Moment of Truth*, ii (Basingstoke and London, 1986), ch. 3; and F.-X. Coquin, 'Un aspect méconnu de la révolution de 1905: Les "Motions paysannes"', in F.-X. Coquin and C. Gervais-Franchelle (eds.), *1905: La première révolution russe* (Paris, 1986), 181–200.

[21] D. Field, *Rebels in the Name of the Tsar* (Boston, 1976), 7.

[22] An analogy with the 'free-born Englishman' may not be as far-fetched as it appears: they share a myth of a bygone golden age, before the common people's rights were usurped. See C. Hill, *Puritanism and Revolution* (London, 1958), 58–122.

Up to this point, the rights which I have been discussing have been those which most liberals would regard as essential civil rights. But I have hardly touched upon the arguments which raged within the opposition over the very definition of rights and the means by which they should be attained. Thus far it has been possible to use the liberal definition of civil rights without encountering any major problem, and therefore to maintain the notion that civil rights can be painlessly separated from political, social, and economic rights. In reality this is far from being the case. The distinction between civil and political was not made by the parties on the far left, which took political rights (the right to vote in national and local elections, and the right to be elected) to be part of the personal rights belonging to every citizen.

The distinction was a meaningful one for liberals, however. A person's civil rights were seen to be the inalienable and unconditional personal rights which no state could infringe or negotiate. They were the indispensable pre-condition for any political settlement. In 1905 liberals meant this both in principle and practically—practically, in the sense that they understood free political activity to be impossible before the rights of assembly, association, and free speech had been firmly established. That the practical significance of civil rights was just as important to liberals as the principle seems clear. Terence Emmons notes that by the middle of 1905 the constitutionalist leadership had concluded that it would have no chance of appealing to a mass audience, and therefore of competing with the revolutionary parties, unless restrictions on free political activity were removed.[23] This consideration may partly explain why the attainment of civil rights was such an urgent issue in the political discourse of 1905, and it has led me to revise an earlier assessment of the differences between socialists and liberals on this question.

From an initial reading of the material, it seemed that for liberals the establishment of a state founded on civil liberties was pre-eminently an end in itself, whereas for socialists civil rights served primarily an instrumental purpose, in giving society the political environment necessary to pursue radical or revolutionary goals.[24] This now seems far too cut and dried. It disregards the

---

[23] Emmons, *Formation of Political Parties*, p. 37.

[24] Unpublished paper given at the School of Slavonic and East European Studies, London, Oct. 1983.

strong libertarian tradition within socialism, both internationally and within Russia itself, a tradition which dismissed liberalism less for its emphasis on rights and legality than because the liberal conception of rights was seen to be too narrow. Thus, we have to recognize that socialists too could conceive of rights as an end in themselves, and did not view the struggle for rights solely as a means to a quite different end. To see the revolutionary parties' support of civil rights as serving only an instrumental purpose also obscures the fact that socialists argued among themselves over the virtues of promoting civil and political rights in capitalist society. In other words, far from being calculating opportunists, they were not of the unanimous opinion that civil rights had any practical instrumental value at all.

It does seem clear that in certain respects there was not a great gulf between the constitutionalists' behaviour and that of the revolutionaries. Both camps had an ideological commitment to freedom and equal rights, and both used the issue of rights to gain advantage for themselves and to win the freedom to organize and propagate their ideas without prohibitions and sanctions.

But the distinction that liberals were prepared to make between civil and political rights does mark them off from the far left. In liberal thought one could separate the personal rights which are the possession of every citizen from the right to participate in politics which may or may not be extended to every citizen. While citizenship guaranteed civil rights, it conferred only the capacity, not the right, to political participation. However, radical members of the liberation movement found it hard to accept this distinction, arguing that equality was negated if some had the power to make legislation and others did not. Their unease was clearly expressed in the frequently acrimonious debates during 1905, when the Union of Liberation, the Union of Unions, and later in the year, the Constitutional Democratic party had to work out political platforms which would satisfy all their members and appeal to a mass audience.[25]

In these debates the main points relating to civil rights were usually drafted without major disagreement, and served as a

---

[25] The issue of political participation in a future national assembly occupied many pages of the press in 1905. With each new turn in Russia's political fortunes, the issue was reconsidered: e.g. after Bloody Sunday; after the publication of the electoral law for the Bulygin duma on 6 Aug.; and before and after the October Manifesto.

minimum programme uniting the disparate elements within these organizations. But the paragraphs dealing with the future political structure of Russia, and particularly the question of entitlement to political rights, provoked lengthy argument, which was sometimes left partially unresolved at the end of the debate.[26] The essence of this debate was the desirability or otherwise of mass participation in politics. I will not go into detail, since this is already a well-worn path. But the issue is significant for the discussion of civil rights, in that it exposes not only the fear aroused in many liberals by the prospect of un-fettered democracy, especially in a backward and undereducated society, but also the disagreement within liberalism over the relationship between civil and political rights.

The concept of legal equality was central to the thinking of liberals and socialists in this period. All were working within the tradition established by the French Revolution (the slogan 'the rights of man and the citizen' often appears in a resolution or protest), but the concept was seen to relate specifically to the existing social structure of Russia, which formally separated the population into estates (*sosloviya*), and excluded the peasant estate from large areas of the law code governing other citizens. In addition, the law formally discriminated between inhabitants of the empire on the basis of their nationality and religion, as well as discriminating between the sexes. Anyone advocating the establishment of civil rights in Russia assumed that freedom and legal equality were inseparable. Matching principle to concrete reality, however, proved to be more complicated.

In theory, the objections put by moderate liberals to the proposal for unconditional universal suffrage made sense. The objections took various forms according to the particular issue involved (peasant enfranchisement, women's rights, the nationalities' right to self-determination, etc.), but essentially their argument amounted to the belief that eligibility for political rights required

[26] The best-known example is the compromise formula adopted by the *zemstvo* congress in Nov. 1904. During 1905 disagreement was often signified by the absence of the 'four-tail' suffrage formula and its substitution by a phrase such as 'freely elected representatives'. At the Union of Liberation's congress in Mar. and at the Kadets' first congress in Oct. failure to agree on women's suffrage led to the addition of an amendment making the demand for women's suffrage non-binding on the minority. See L. H. Edmondson, *Feminism in Russia, 1900–1917* (London and Stanford, 1984).

in each individual both maturity and respect for the opinions of others, characteristics to be found only in a society which had already recognized the individual rights of free speech, equality before the law, and personal inviolability. Therefore, from this point of view, there was no inconsistency in proposing to establish the legal equality of all citizens without distinction, and refusing to consider equal *political* rights for all citizens without distinction. Political rights would eventually follow from civil freedom.[27]

There were obvious practical difficulties attendant on a political settlement which would give every citizen the right to free speech, but would discriminate on grounds of education, social status, nationality, sex or whatever else, in the distribution of political rights. But Liberationists on the left of the movement objected on principle, since to them the separation of personal and political rights was nonsense. In the end it proved to be politically expedient to accept the radical line, though in doing so the liberation movement split, and the most moderate liberals refused to participate further in its organizations.

The issue of social and economic rights was just as contentious. The essence of socialist objections to the liberal formulation of rights lay in the latter's apparent unwillingness to broaden the definition of fundamental human rights beyond the boundaries of 'bourgeois freedoms' to include, for example, the right to labour protection, a guaranteed wage, or the right to a 'dignified existence'. It should be noted, however, that there were strong differences of opinion among liberals themselves on these issues. Criticism of the prevailing opinion came not only from the left wing of the Liberationists, but also from the group which associated itself with Struve in late 1905 and 1906. At the second Kadet congress in January 1906, P. I. Novgorodtsev proposed (unsuccessfully) that the right to work and the right to a dignified existence should be added to the party programme.[28] Other 'right Kadets' wrote on similar themes during these months. In the first

---

[27] A. Tyrkova, herself on the right wing of the Kadets, argued that if women were ineligible to vote because of their political immaturity, then no one in Russia was eligible, as the country lacked all the prerequisites for healthy political development. To be true to their principles, every liberal politician should forgo political rights until Russia experienced civic freedom: *Zhenskii vestnik*, 5 (1906), 135.

[28] *Vtoroi vserossiiskii s"ezd delegatov konstitutsionno-demokraticheskoi partii: Biulleteni* (St Petersburg, 1906), no. 7, p. 2. For the intellectual origin of these

issue of Struve's *Polyarnaya zvezda*, S. L. Frank discussed the political and social implications of a philosophy founded on the importance of the individual personality. He argued that while guarantees of civil and political freedom and equality were essential, they were not sufficient in themselves. Society must also be responsible for the social welfare of its citizens. And S. A. Kotlyarevskii, commenting on the Kadets' social programme, argued that social freedom was as important as political liberty.[29]

Political and socio-economic rights were unmistakably part of the debate on civil rights during the 1905 Revolution. By contrast, it is quite striking to note how little was said in this debate about the right to property. Clearly, silence on this question did not indicate its irrelevance to Russian politics, since the right to private property, and especially to landed property, was being directly challenged in those very months by the agrarian movement. Besides, liberals debated the issue of property when they were discussing the land question. But it occupied an area of political discourse quite separate from that of civil rights. In the Kadet party programme, for example, property rights are mentioned only once, in the section on 'fundamental rights of the citizen': 'All Russian citizens without distinction of sex, religion, and nationality, are equal before the law. Any *soslovie* distinctions and any limitations of the personal and property rights of Poles, Jews, and all other separate groups of the population without exception must be removed.'[30]

It would be possible to infer from this paragraph that the Kadets did possess a conception of the inviolability of property, inasmuch as they deemed it an infringement of a person's fundamental rights to be deprived of his or her property on the grounds of belonging to one or other 'separate group' in society. But the paragraph was clearly addressed to forms of discrimination rather than property rights, and does not adequately compensate

concepts, see A. Walicki, 'Vladimir Solov'ev and the Legal Philosophies of Russian Liberalism', in R. Bartlett (ed.), *Russian Thought and Society 1800–1917. Essays in Honour of Eugene Lampert* (Keele, 1984), esp. 167–75.

[29] S. A. Kotlyarevskii, 'K programme konstitutsionno-demokraticheskoi partii', *Russkiya vedomosti*, 5 Dec. 1905, 1. For a discussion of the attitude of 'right Kadets' to the idea of social welfare as a component of freedom, see J. E. Zimmerman, 'Between Revolution and Reaction: The Russian Constitutional-Democratic Party, October 1905 to June 1907', Ph.D. thesis (Columbia, 1967), 74.

[30] *Konstitutsionno-demokraticheskaya partiya (Partiya narodnoi svobody): Postanovleniya II-go s"ezda i programma* (St Petersburg, 1906).

for the absence of discussion of property in the public debate about civil rights.[31]

It now remains to answer the question posed in the title of this chapter: is it possible to talk of a movement for civil rights in Russia in 1905? Before attempting an answer, I must first clarify what I mean by 'movement'. It is not my intention to propose that all groups participating in political protest, notwithstanding their bitter feuds and irreconcilable theoretical differences, were basically working towards a common goal. But it should be possible to establish whether there was a widely held commitment to the acquisition of civil rights, and whether there was any possibility of joint action between competing groups in support of these rights.

The evidence suggests widespread support for the idea from differing social groups and political factions, but a frequent ambiguity when the vague concept was put to the precise test— instances of the rhetoric of equality and freedom being modified to accommodate the particular prejudices of the speaker: peasants who petitioned for equal rights but denied them to Jews; moderate liberal lawyers who defended the autonomy of their profession but not the right of women to practise in it; printers who demanded freedom of the press but censored material from the Union of the Russian People.

Nor is there much evidence to suggest that the civil rights issue could transcend political conflict and unite, even temporarily, fundamentally opposing factions. There is no question that the obstacles in the way of establishing civil rights in the Russian Empire were formidable: both the traditions of government and administration, which discouraged the free expression of ideas or the acceptance of concepts of natural rights, and the habits of mind which such traditions engendered severely impeded the chances of a successful struggle for civil rights.

None the less, it is perhaps unrealistic to expect a completely consistent application of the principles of civil rights in any society, no matter how well developed its legal traditions and its controls over executive power. If few people in Russia were uncompromising adherents of civil rights, capable of putting into

---

[31] For a much fuller discussion of this problematic issue, see R. Wortman's essay in this volume.

practice, without amendment, the principles which they advocated, it does not follow that the whole concept was destined to
fall on barren soil. Nor, I would argue, does the fact that peasants
or workers may have had a very particularist understanding of
rights necessarily lead to the conclusion that calls for civil rights
from these sections of society were of no significance. A
conceptual system, like a political system, never springs into life
fully formed. The circumstances of Russian life after 1905 were
extremely hostile to the realization of civil rights, and hostile to
the further elaboration of the conceptual system. But this fact
should not lead us automatically to assume that the basic
aspiration to rights was lacking.[32]

Given that the civil rights issue was not sufficiently powerful to
overcome the other disagreements between social and political
groups which made collaboration so difficult, the term 'movement' may be considered a misnomer. But it may be appropriate
if we accept it as a description of an essentially uncoordinated
mass of demands presented by separate groups of the population,
each with its own axe to grind.

It is not difficult to pin-point specific civil rights issues of
concern to a particular section of the population. Freedom of
speech is a prime example. It was a focal point of the whole
protest movement in 1905, yet it impinged on the livelihoods of
journalists, publishers, and printers more directly than on any
other profession.

Writers, journalists, publishers, printers, and newspaper
proprietors saw the government's crisis as it developed after
1900, and especially when the war with Japan turned into a series
of military disasters during 1904, as an opportunity to dispose of
the cumbersome and unenforceable censorship regulations.
Increasingly during 1905 and up to the dissolution of the First
Duma they engaged with unmistakable relish in the battle with
obscurantism. While preliminary censorship was still in force,
editors would notify their readers when an item had had to be
excised, report instances of petty censorship, carry reports on
unauthorized meetings, strikes, demonstrations, etc. Since meetings and demonstrations invariably called for freedom of the
spoken and printed word, press coverage simultaneously sustained

---

[32] Many thanks to Reginald Zelnik for asking awkward questions, which I have
attempted to answer in these pages.

the opposition movement and reinforced its own advocacy of press freedom.

Writers and journalists were also prominent in political organizations during 1905. While this was clearly attributable to the fact that political activists chose journalism as a vehicle for their ideas, the impossibility of working in journalism or as a free-lance writer without coming into collision with censorship regulations and petty administrative interference in their profession made some degree of political involvement almost inevitable. Both these factors made the Union of Russian Writers, founded in the spring of 1905, an active and contentious participant in the liberation movement.[33]

The October Manifesto, with its promise of free speech, the partial dismantling of preliminary censorhips, and the establishment of new provisional regulations in November, did not silence the profession. Given greater licence during the 'days of freedom' to speak their mind, journalists became more, not less, critical of interference in their work. Moreover, press freedom was largely negated by the imposition of 'exceptional measures' of administration in about two-thirds of Russia at the end of 1905 and the beginning of 1906, and the press found itself again grappling with fines, suspensions, and even imprisonment.[34]

The interrelationship of professional interest and political involvement is almost to be expected in the case of writers and journalists. But what is striking about the upsurge of protest in Russia during the 1905 Revolution is the way in which dissatisfaction with working conditions and pay, aggravated by the everyday frustrations with bureaucratic *proizvol*, combined with the national political crisis to force people to make connections between private grievances and political oppression.

This process can be traced very clearly, for example, in the changing political stance of the Pirogov Society of Russian

[33] See *Pravo*, 17 (1905), cols. 1381–6, for the union's first congress in April.

[34] 39 provinces and regions were under partial or total martial law, 15 under exceptional protection, and 26 under reinforced protection early in 1906: *Vestnik partii narodnoi svobody*, 2 (5 Mar. 1906), cols. 103–10. For comment in the press, see Ya. Mauzer, 'Sorok dnei svobody pechati', *Pravda*, Dec. 1905, 230–42; V. Korolenko, 'O svobode pechati', *Russkoe bogatstvo*, 11–12 (1905), pt. 2, pp. 195–207. See ibid., and *Rus'*, 22 Oct. 1905, p. 6, for details of a union to protect press freedom formed in Oct. 1905. For censorship, and press tactics to avoid it, see C. Ferenczi's essay in this volume.

Doctors, which not only became very much more outspoken in its public statements at the end of 1904, but also linked the problems which doctors were encountering in their working lives to the lack of freedom in Russia overall. The connection was not contrived—doctors were indeed vulnerable to administrative tyranny. The governor of a province had the right to dismiss a doctor from *zemstvo* service, as well as the power not to confirm appointments. A doctor who found a job in a different locality could be prevented from obtaining the necessary residence permit. Doctors were bound by statute to tend patients if called upon; at the same time, a doctor sentenced to a period of exile was banned from practising for the duration of his or her sentence.[35]

The story was repeated in every occupation. Doctors complained about their 'lack of rights', teachers spoke out against the 'bureaucratic police-school regime'. Even schoolchildren went on strike. A teachers' manifesto proclaimed in February 1905: 'Without academic freedom, without security in our rights, we cannot train and educate the new generation, condemned to the same lack of rights, to obedience to the same regime.'[36] Political awareness was all the sharper for arising out of a growing dissatisfaction with the immediate working environment. One might, of course, argue that the reverse was true—that teachers, doctors, writers, or factory workers brought their own political preconceptions to the work-place, and criticized it in the same terms as they used to criticize political conditions in Russia. But, while this undoubtedly occurred, it seems clear that immediate dissatisfaction with the numerous petty restrictions in everyday life, the hierarchical structure of institutions such as schools, hospitals, or factories, the degree of arbitrary authority wielded by administrators, together with the powers of surveillance available to the police and local authorities, gave the simple concepts of personal inviolability, equality of all citizens, and freedom of speech a significance and attraction which drew

---

[35] See S. Mitskevich, 'O pravovom polozhenii russkago vracha v svyazi s obshchim pravovym polozheniem russkago obyvatelya', *Zhurnal Obshchestva russkago vracha v pamyat' N. I. Pirogova*, 6 (Dec. 1904), 600–7. See also the excellent study by N. M. Frieden, *Russian Physicians in an Era of Reform and Revolution, 1856–1905* (Princeton, 1981).

[36] Quoted by P. Alston, *Education and the State in Tsarist Russia* (Stanford, 1969), 179. See also *Pravo*, 6 (1905), col. 424; ibid. 17 (1905), cols. 1388–9.

thousands, even millions, of people into political protest during 1905. In this sense, a movement for civil rights certainly developed in the 1905 Revolution, not a coherent, planned campaign for institutional change, but a clamour for equality and freedom and an end to *proizvol*.

Civil Rights and the Provisional Government

H. J. WHITE

BETWEEN February and October 1917 civil rights (taken here to mean freedom of conscience, expression, association, movement, and assembly; equality before the law; and the right to due process of law) did not prove to be a major issue. True, it was a vital demand at the very beginning of the revolution, when all seemed in the balance. For Sukhanov, 'complete political freedom in the country, an absolute freedom of organization and agitation' was the one condition for allowing the bourgeoisie to take power.[1] Yet within a matter of days such freedom could be taken for granted as one of the 'gains of the revolution'. Lenin described the situation in his *April Theses* as 'characterized, on the one hand by a maximum of legally recognized rights (Russia is *now* the freest of all the belligerent countries in the world); on the other, by the absence of violence towards the masses'.[2] The Provisional Government worked hard to embody the new freedom in legislation, a labour attracting little attention beyond occasional criticism of the length of time it seemed to take. This criticism did betray a certain lingering fear of possible counter-revolution, or even of treachery on the part of the government itself. As the months passed, gradual curtailment of absolute freedom by the government elicited increasingly strident protest. However, far more important issues underlay the growing disaffection of the population with the Provisional Government: civil rights were little more than a touchstone in the conflict.

A brief examination of the Provisional Government's record on civil rights can be instructive, none the less. The significance which the government attached to the issue is revealing of its own political complexion, while the attempt to build a new political

---

[1] N. N. Sukhanov, *The Russian Revolution 1917*, ed. J. Carmichael (Oxford, 1955), 105.
[2] V. I. Lenin, *Polnoe sobranie sochinenii*, 5th edn. (Moscow, 1959–68), xxxi. 114.

order incorporating civil rights reminds us that the government must be seen as an actor in the revolutionary process. Attention to the circumstances under which the government had to begin this attempt also serves as a salutary reminder of the radical nature of the February Revolution. The fate of the attempt provides something of an epilogue to the study of civil rights under tsarism, a framework for considering the impact upon Russian society of the experience of developing rights.

The intention in this essay is to discuss first the context in which the Provisional Government operated: the February Revolution and the popular conceptions of rights and democracy which developed out of it. The role of civil rights in the government's own programme will then be examined, followed by an account of its attempt to realize that programme and its subsequent retreat.

If 'Bread, Peace, and Land' were the concerns that determined the course of the October Revolution, the decisive issue in February was 'Freedom'—even if bread riots in Petrograd provided the spark. It was not at all clear what positive content this 'freedom' might possess: attention was naturally concentrated on destroying the repressive and arbitrary tsarist state and its system of privilege. The demand for civil rights had been an important component of the general attack on the autocracy, and the new freedom was consequently expected to involve civil rights. These were pictured mostly in a negative sense—the guarantee of individual or group liberties against interference from the state—although the concept of equality was also contrasted to the traditions of privilege and hierarchy of the old regime. Less attention was paid to the rights of individuals or groups *vis-à-vis* each other, or to positive guarantees by the state towards individuals and groups.

The extent of civil liberty in Russia after the February Revolution was quite staggering, as Lenin had observed. Without waiting for formal legislation of any sort, groups and organizations began to appear like mushrooms. Meetings were held on every street corner, people began to swarm around the country on various personal or public missions (bringing chaos to public transport), an explosion of the printed word occurred as every new group sought to proselytize. Since no records were kept, it is impossible to quantify this sudden exercise of liberty—but any contemporary account will give the flavour. Not all of it was overtly political: Mayakovskii could publish previously censored poems, and stage a public meeting under the banner of 'Revolution-War-Futurism-Mayakovskii', while less elevated persons published obscene postcards depicting Rasputin and the former Empress.[3] The most important development of all was the emergence of the 'mass organizations' (soviets, trade unions, factory committees, etc.), and the rapid expansion of formerly banned or restricted political parties.[4]

The dramatic exercise of freedom demonstrates how swift and radical an event the February Revolution was. The coercive apparatus of the tsarist state was quite broken: within a matter of three to five days, tsarist civil authorities collapsed in every town in Russia without exception; the police were disarmed and driven off the streets; the troops of the garrisons had mutinied or been led by their officers into the revolutionary camp.[5] Once the army commanders at the Front had accepted the revolution, there was simply no going back.[6] A profound psychological break had occurred: the long-awaited revolution had come; workers, soldiers, and peasants expected the new order to help them realize their 'rights'.

With hindsight, the chances of building a new political order which could satisfy such expectations seem absurdly slim. The millenarian inflation of demands, the economic weakness of Russia, the strains of wartime would all stand against it. There was also a fundamental incompatibility between the ideas of ordinary people and those of educated 'society'. In Petrograd, the

---

[3] *Vladimir Mayakovsky: Three Views* (London, 1982), 21.

[4] The fullest account of the emergence of the 'mass organizations' is J. L. H. Keep, *The Russian Revolution: A Study in Mass Mobilization* (London, 1976).

[5] There is no adequate study in English of the course of the February Revolution in the provinces. A brief account may be found in M. Ferro, *The Russian Revolution of February 1917* (London, 1972), 79–83. Nor does there seem to be an acceptable one vol. Soviet account, apart from E. N. Burdzhalov, *Vtoraya revolyutsiya v Rossii*, ii (Moscow, 1971). There are, however, a multitude of documentary collections published in the 1920s and 1950s which deal with the events of 1917 in individual provinces. In recent years an increasing number of scholarly monographs have appeared also. To give just two examples: *1917 god na Kievshchine: Khronika sobytii* (Kiev, 1928); V. V. Vas'kin and G. A. Gerasimenko, *Fevral'skaya revolyutsiya v Nizhnem Povolzh'e* (Saratov, 1976).

[6] See T. Hasegawa, *The February Revolution: Petrograd 1917* (Seattle, 1981), chs. 24 and 25.

distrust between them was certainly expressed in the phenomenon of 'dual power'. A look at the provinces, however, gives a curiously different picture: there seems to have been a sort of basic consensus about the revolution which had an institutional reflection in the Committees of Public Organizations (*Komitety obshchestvennykh organizatsii*) which sprang up to assume local power in almost every town in the empire.[7] The real significance of these bodies is that they were acknowledged as locally sovereign by the workers' and soldiers' organizations which participated in them. In fact, the committees generally afforded a plurality, if not a majority, to what became known as the 'democratic elements' (*demokratiya*), i.e. the workers', soldiers', and peasant organizations, and the revolutionary parties.[8] This phenomenon is increasingly accepted by Soviet historians, who attribute it to a lack of political consciousness amongst the masses, identified by Lenin as a 'petty bourgeois wave' sweeping across the country.[9]

This should be recognized as an important qualification to the 'pessimistic' interpretation of Russia's social and political development, given classic formulation by L. H. Haimson, which stresses the hostility of the 'democratic elements' towards their social superiors.[10] The attitudes and expectations which underlay the consensus are worthy of investigation. No doubt there was a degree of simple political calculation: the leaders of the 'democratic elements' feared counter-revolution; their counterparts feared anarchy. Yet there was also a great deal of euphoria, with sackloads of congratulatory telegrams, and even donations of food

---

[7] Information on the committees is drawn from a wide variety of published sources (see n. 5 above). The only substantial account in a western language is W. G. Rosenberg, 'Les Libéraux russes en mars 1917', *Cahiers du monde russe et soviétique*, 9/1 (1968), or, more briefly, his *Liberals in the Russian Revolution* (Princeton, 1974), 59–63. Soviet accounts are becoming more useful, e.g. A. M. Andreev, *Mestnye Sovety i organy burzhuaznoi vlasti (1917 g.)* (Moscow, 1983), 26 ff.

[8] Moscow, Tsentral'nyi gosudarstvennyi arkhiv Oktyabr'skoi revolyutsii (hereafter TsGAOR), Ministerstvo vnutrennikh del Vremennago pravitel'stva (Otdel po delam mestnago upravleniya), f. 1788, op. 2, d. 64, contains the results of a Ministry of the Interior survey of committees in 21 provinces during the late spring, including information on composition.

[9] See e.g. V. I. Startsev, *Vnutrennyaya politika Vremennogo pravitel'stva* (Leningrad, 1980), 193 ff. Lenin's remarks occur in several places, notably in 'Zadachi proletariata v nashei revolyutsii', in *Polnoe sobranie*, xxxi.

[10] L. H. Haimson, 'The Problem of Social Stability in Urban Russia 1905–1917', *Slavic Review*, 23/4 (1964), and 24/1 (1965).

from peasant communities, to express support for the Provisional Government. There was a certain mutual deference between groups not accustomed to dealing with each other. Beyond this, two other factors perhaps held the committees together. The break with the old régime was much cleaner and more definite in the provinces, for a start: there were fewer signs that the old order was lingering in a new guise. The leaders of local 'society' had been much swifter to assume the mantle of revolution. Their optimism no doubt reflected in turn the absence of violence and the apparently favourable disposition of the lower orders, but there were also other factors. The first of Haimson's two polarizations, that between the tsarist state (*vlast'*) and society (*obshchestvo*), is too readily forgotten: there was remarkably little hesitation about whether to endorse the February Revolution, even when its outcome could hardly be certain. The old governors and police were swept away without prevarication: perhaps the old order was visibly more rotten, brutal, and incompetent at its fringes than at its centre. Moreover, counter-revolution held fewer terrors in provincial towns; once the garrison troops and their commanders had endorsed the revolution, there seemed no obvious source of it (although rumours occasionally surfaced of the spread of armed reaction from the Don Cossacks). There was thus neither the need nor the possibility of adopting some dubious intermediate position between the old order and the revolution: the Committees of Public Organizations were unashamedly revolutionary bodies, in marked contrast to the Provisional Government.

This is not to suggest that the upper classes were all whole-heartedly supporters of revolution. What almost certainly occurred was a capitulation on the part of the majority to the enthusiasm of a few, and in effect an abandonment of the strict defence of their 'class interest'. This willingness to compromise, to accept sacrifices, is reflected in their acceptance of the domination of the Committees of Public Organizations by the 'democratic elements'. It reveals some readiness on the part of the urban upper strata to abandon rural landowners, and on the part of professionals to abandon the merchants—tensions that had surely long existed in provincial society. It also reflects the reluctance of conservative members of the officer corps to become involved in 'politics' (and perhaps the absence of the most able forces of conservative provincial society at the Front). The radicalism of the committees might be seen as a function of a profound crisis in the provincial élite, seized upon by genuinely revolutionary elements.

The second factor in the success of the committees could be the presence of a radical intermediary layer, educated people of either high or humble origin who were looked to by the masses for leadership, but who were more acceptable to the upper strata than the 'dark people': intellectuals, students, co-operative organizers, worker-activists, etc. Their existence has been proposed by Allan K. Wildman, as a result of his research into the course of the revolution in the Russian army: he calls them a 'committee class', since they provided the personnel for the democratized army's committee machinery.[11] This also identifies them as Mensheviks, SRs, and other moderate socialists or 'populists' of various hues, although this is dangerous ground, for it coincides unhappily with Lenin's ascription of a fundamentally petty bourgeois nature to his socialist rivals.

Despite this promising beginning, the honeymoon of the February Revolution was short-lived: neither the attitudes nor the institutions of the provincial consensus survived. The committees were undermined in part by the Provisional Government itself, but also by the sheer chaos and economic collapse which made many of their problems insoluble. There was a sharp polarization of attitudes. The spread of political ideas from the centre was of great importance, made possible by the expansion of parties and mass organizations and of the printed word. The April crisis over war-aims sent a shock wave right through the country, although the Petrograd Soviet was already becoming identified with hopes for peace.[12] As the year passed, it was the Bolsheviks above all who seemed to present coherent ideas in tune with mass aspirations.[13]

A further process seems to have been involved in the polarization of ideas: social conflict on a local scale. This is best conceptualized by S. A. Smith, who in his study of Petrograd

[11] A. K. Wildman, *The End of the Russian Imperial Army* (Princeton, 1980), p. xix.
[12] Ibid. 321.
[13] This is of course contentious, but it is a perception widely held. See R. G. Suny, 'Towards a Social History of the October Revolution', *American Historical Review*, 88 (Feb. 1983), for a discussion of recent historiography.

workers, presents their struggle to achieve a 'constitutional'·
factory as a microcosm of class struggle in which class consciousness developed and class aspirations were defined.[14] The same
process was at work in the army: the soldiers' demands to be
treated with respect and to be given a say in the running of their
units express exactly the concept of political revolution that
ordinary people expected February to deliver. In the countryside, the link between this political revolution and social
revolution was at its most clear-cut: freedom to the peasant
meant freedom from the *barin*, the landowner.[15]

By the autumn of 1917 the upper classes were on the verge of
exclusion from the political process, and indeed under threat of
full loss of civil and political rights. They had been saved from
expulsion from central government by the indecision of the
moderate socialist leaders at the Democratic Conference, but in
many localities the 'democratic elements' responded to the
Kornilov affair by expelling members of the Kadet party from
local government, arresting anyone who fell under their suspicion,
and harassing 'bourgeois' organizations.[16]

Initial compromise had thus given way to a strongly class-
based perception of democracy, one with which absolute civil
rights could not be compatible. Indeed, the extent to which
democracy and civil rights were understood and valued at all by
ordinary people is open to question. The issue is raised in recent
studies of the working class in 1917: having reclaimed the
revolution as a democratic process, western historiography has to
account for its culmination in Bolshevik dictatorship. William G.
Rosenberg has drawn attention to the variety of explanations on
offer.[17] The earliest writers to deal with the problem, Marc Ferro

[14] S. A. Smith, *Red Petrograd: Revolution in the Factories 1917–1918* (Cambridge, 1983), 256.

[15] Ferro, *February 1917*, pp. 130–6 on the soldiers, and pp. 121–30 on the peasants, is a survey of popular demands based on petitions and resolutions.

[16] In Kiev, the soviet of workers' deputies demanded that the Special Committee for the Defence of the Revolution (set up to deal with the Kornilov threat) should arrest all counter-revolutionaries and ensure that all public offices were held only by people devoted to the revolution; further, that no Kadet representatives should be allowed on the Special Committee: TsGAOR, f. 1788, op. 2, d. 105, report by the Kiev city commissar. Other accounts of the reaction to the Kornilov affair can be found in d. 69, Ministry of the Interior circulars and memoranda.

[17] W. G. Rosenberg, review of Smith, *Red Petrograd*, in *Slavic Review*, 43/2 (1984).

and John Keep, suggest that a process of centralization and
bureaucratization occurred within the mass organizations, allowing the Bolsheviks (seen as an external force) to capture them
from above. According to this view, the masses are easily
manipulated out of democracy: it is not a strong institutional
process.[18] Rosenberg, along with Diane Koenker and David
Mandel, suggests that the workers opted for a Bolshevik
dictatorship as the only rational solution in a situation of counter-
revolution and economic collapse. The workers' idea of democracy
does not require an institutional process at all, but simply the rule
of the toilers as a class.[19] S. A. Smith argues that a process of
centralization did occur within the mass organizations, but from
below; the Bolsheviks did not constitute an outside factor, but
were themselves democratic elements forced along by the logic of
events and a weakness of theory. The practice of democracy is a
reality, but an ideology of democracy is lacking.[20]

Were the masses interested in democracy as such, or merely in
having the big issues (bread, peace, land) resolved in their
favour? The evidence from 1917 is that workers, soldiers, and
peasants did indeed hope for a political revolution which would
leave them in charge of their own lives. Their own customs were
strongly democratic—but in a traditional (peasant) way, collectivist not individual, and essentially untheorized. The political
ideas to which they were exposed were not ones likely to instil in
them essential concepts of democracy, such as civil rights as
protection for minorities and individuals from the majority, but
above all as protection against the power of the state. Marxist
theory is explicitly hostile to civil rights. The Mensheviks did not
devote much attention to them, while the Bolsheviks preached
the idea of the commune-state with contempt for 'bourgeois'
concerns for formal structures, checks and balances, or separation
of powers. The SRs did have a strongly anti-centralist tradition,
but little theory of law or democracy, and a similar contempt for
things 'bourgeois'.

[18] For the argument briefly stated, see Ferro, *February 1917*, p. 324, and his
October 1917: A Social History of the Russian Revolution (London, 1980), 272–3; and
J. L. H. Keep, *Revolution*, pp. ix ff.

[19] Rosenberg, review of Smith, and his 'Workers and Workers' Control in the
Russian Revolution', *History Workshop*, 5 (1978); D. Koenker, *Moscow Workers and
the 1917 Revolution* (Princeton, 1981); D. Mandel, *The Petrograd Workers and the
Fall of the Old Regime* (London, 1983).

[20] Smith, *Red Petrograd*, esp. pp. 258 ff.

Concepts of civil rights would thus appear to have made rather too little headway amongst the mass of Russia's population. Ironically, however, amongst the members, apparatus, and supporters of the Provisional Government it could be said they had made too much.

It is not easy to place the Provisional Government's moving ideas. The public record of the time may well have been coloured by the 'official optimism' identified by former members, while the available unpublished record of its meetings is not very informative.[21] Soviet writers assume too readily that it was no more than a restyled autocracy, devoted to the same imperialist and monopoly capitalist ends, and even using the same officials; on the other hand it has been portrayed by western historians as too radical, unduly trusting of the masses, and insufficiently concerned for the machinery of liberal democracy.[22]

Study of the domestic policy of the Provisional Government would suggest, however, that it was guided by classically liberal conceptions. Indeed, the government's programme is best understood as an attempt to build Russia into a formal western democracy: there was a positive obsession with law, civil rights, electorally based institutional structures, and private property. The Provisional Government placed itself in a middle position, rejecting both the illegality and brutality of tsarism, and the lawlessness of revolution. An extraordinary amount of time and effort went into countless commissions designed to transform Russia's legal and administrative structure. The government was dominated by lawyers and academics, in many ways representing the triumph of the professional stratum in alliance with progressive business men and landowners.[23]

[21] For 'official optimism', see e.g. V. Nabokov, 'Vremennoe pravitel'stvo', *Arkhiv russkoi revolyutsii*, 1 (1922). The minutes of government meetings, printed for internal circulation as *Zhurnaly zasedanii Vremennago pravitel'stva* (hereafter *Zhurnaly*), available e.g. in TsGAOR, Kantselyariya Vremennago pravitel'stva, f. 1779, op. 2, d. 1, contain no more than a record of decisions taken and persons present.

[22] See e.g. L. Schapiro, 'The Political Thought of the First Provisional Government', in R. Pipes (ed.), *Revolutionary Russia* (London, 1968).

[23] I have compiled data on senior Ministry of the Interior personnel from a variety of sources, which illustrate this. Only 2 tsarist department heads were retained in March, and 11 outsiders were brought in as department heads and deputy ministers. These included activists in the wartime 'Voluntary Organizations', experts on local government and economics, and lawyers. The stronghold of the (mostly Kadet) lawyers was the government's Juridical Conference, which advised on legislation.

The Provisional Government's attitude towards the people was a little ambivalent. Prince G. E. L'vov, who combined the position of Prime Minister with that of Minister of the Interior, is castigated in Milyukov's memoirs for his faith in 'revolutionary legal creativity' (*revolyutsionnoe pravotvorchestvo*).[24] It would be fairer to describe this as a cautious optimism, a hope that the masses could be guided into the correct path. Much of the government's legislative programme was evidently designed to be a blueprint for the Constituent Assembly. B. B. Veselovskii typifies the outlook: a leading expert on local government and an historian of the *zemstvo*, he was commissioned to work in the Ministry of the Interior on plans for democratic local 'self-government', which he declared would be the 'fundament of a new state order and a school for the political education of the people'.[25]

It is true that the optimism faded as the months passed, but the attempt to build a new order from above continued to the very end. The components of this new order were identified at the beginning of the year (when the liberal lawyers and experts were brought in), and changed remarkably little. The presence of socialist ministers did not materially alter the government's policies (except upon the issue of war-aims), nor indeed did the socialist ministers attempt to purge their departments of non-socialist advisers. The new order was to be based unequivocally upon civil rights, formal electoral democracy, private property, and a modicum of welfare. The main reservations that were made were connected with the war, the continuation of which was an article of faith for most liberals. (The war was a problem for liberals in all belligerent states, as the power of the state over the economic activity, property, and persons of its citizens was universally boosted.) Private property was the least explicit part of the programme, evidently being a delicate issue; the inevitability of land reform was accepted.

The Provisional Government declared its aims thus:

Realizing the full gravity of the lack of rights, which oppresses the country and hinders the free creative impulse of the people . . . the Provisional Government deems it necessary to provide the country

---

[24] P. N. Milyukov, *Istoriya vtoroi russkoi revolyutsii* (Sofia, 1921–4), ii. 67–8.
[25] Editorial in *Zemskoe delo*, 5–6 (Mar. 1917).

immediately, even prior to the convocation of the Constituent Assembly, with laws safeguarding civil liberty and equality in order to enable all citizens to apply freely their spiritual forces to creative work for the benefit of the country. The Government will also undertake the enactment of legal provisions to assure all citizens equal participation in the elections of organs of local self-government on the basis of universal suffrage.[26]

In similar vein, Kokoshkin, the Chairman of the Provisional Government's Juridical Conference (which advised it on all legislation), told the seventh congress of the Kadet party: 'Our conception of a state regime is based on three principles—the principle of the inviolability of civil liberty and civil equality, the principle of the guarantee of complete rule by popular will, and the principle of realizing the bases of social justice.'[27]

Although this programme was formally acceptable to the moderate socialist leaders, it came into conflict with popular conceptions of 'rights' on a number of issues which had not been fully anticipated or elaborated. The first of these issues to appear was the demand for civil rights in the armed forces, expressed initially in the famous Order No. 1 of the Petrograd Soviet. Here the government made more or less immediate concessions and recognized the soldiers' own version of their 'rights', excepting only their desire to elect their commanders. On 5 March the Minister of War, Guchkov, issued an order which, on 11 May, was elaborated into a formal 'Declaration of Soldiers' Rights'.[28] This order set up a formal system of committees in all military units, and allowed soldiers to be members of political organizations, to smoke in public, to ride on public transport, and to visit the theatre. Soldiers were to be addressed in the respectful second person plural (*vy*), and officers were to lose their elaborate

---

[26] Declaration of 7 March, translated in R. P. Browder and A. F. Kerensky (eds.), *The Russian Provisional Government 1917: Documents* (Stanford, 1961), i. 158. Wherever possible in these notes, references will be given to documents in translation.

[27] Ibid. iii. 1200.

[28] *Sbornik ukazov i postanovlenii Vremennago pravitel'stva* (Petrograd, 1917–18) (hereafter *Sbornik ukazov*), military/naval section, order dated 5 March—to which an 'Explanation' was added on 22 March to the effect that the entitlement to attend theatres and ride on trams did not encompass doing so without paying. For the full text of the declaration, see *Vestnik Vremennago pravitel'stva* (hereafter *VVP*), 14 May 1917.

honorific titles and were to be addressed as 'Mr' (*gospodin*), followed by their rank.[29]

The next popular demand was for recognition of the rights of national minorities—for immediate autonomy across a range of matters, extending as far as the right to have separate national military units. This was a major problem for the Provisional Government's jurists, who had strong views about the unitary nature of the empire. At first they accepted only the liquidation of the (enemy-occupied) kingdom of Poland and the restoration of the Finnish Constitution, along with repatriation of Central Asians conscripted for labour service in 1916; however, by July the government was forced to concede limited autonomy to the Ukraine, while Finland became virtually independent.[30] National military units were resisted, but they were none the less formed from below and had to be tacitly recognized.[31]

The issue of private property was initially a major problem only in the form of agricultural land: it soon became very evident that the peasantry's idea of their 'rights' included the transfer to them of all agricultural land. The government's policy was simply to stall, waiting for the Constituent Assembly. State control of private property in other sectors of the economy was accepted as a matter of necessity: the state monopoly on grain was steadily extended to other products, and rationing became widespread. Seizure of factories by workers did not become a general problem until late in the year.[32]

The final universal demand faced by the government was vaguer but none the less strident: 'social justice'. This was a demand that was sufficiently ambiguous for almost everyone to be dissatisfied. The government reorganized Russia's somewhat primitive social services under a new Ministry of Welfare, and

[29] See Wildman, *Russian Imperial Army*, pp. 291–2; and V. A. Miller, *Soldatskie komitety russkoi armii v 1917 g.* (Moscow, 1974), chs. 2 and 3. Both suggest that establishing a formal system of committees was a successful move, capturing existing soldiers' committees at least temporarily for the government.

[30] On the Provisional Government's nationalities policy, see R. Pipes, *The Formation of the Soviet Union* (Cambridge, Mass., 1964); and W. Stoyko, 'The Attitude of the Russian Provisional Government towards the Non-Russian Peoples of its Empire', Ph.D. thesis (New York, 1969).

[31] The 'Ukrainianization' of army units in the Kiev garrison is ducumented in *1917 god na Kievshchine*; see also e.g. N. Ezhov, *Voennaya Kazan' v 1917 g.* (Kazan, 1927).

[32] Smith, *Red Petrograd*, pp. 177 ff.

made a number of much-needed improvements—such as the granting of state benefits to common-law dependants of servicemen on a par with lawful wives and dependants. However, no very clear statement seems to have been made on welfare rights.[33]

The government's programme thus remained centred on formal democracy and civil rights, very much bound together in the western liberal idea of 'legal order'. It was not a programme intended purely for show: the government began to try to implement it at once.

The first problem with legal order was the legal status of the Provisional Government itself. At its first meeting, there was a discussion about whether to rule by article 87 of the tsarist Fundamental Laws, or to accept that the government should be answerable to the State Duma; the eventual decision was to regard it as being invested with sovereign power until the Constituent Assembly should meet.[34] None the less, it is significant that the government chose to operate on the basis of continuity with the old regime in the interest of preserving legal order. In the words of the legal periodical *Pravo*, the necessity was acknowledged 'so far as possible of preserving existing laws and institutions until new ones are created by the Constituent Assembly'.[35] The government operated by amending or repealing tsarist legislation, using tsarist formulas and procedures. This continuity was underscored by efforts to hold the old regime accountable to its own laws: numerous investigations were conducted into past misdeeds by central and local tsarist officials; even senatorial revisions were ordered. In keeping with this insistence upon legality, the government frequently proclaimed its refusal to prejudice the Constituent Assembly: this was a useful delaying tactic, and obscured the fact that most of its legislation was designed with the object of ratification by the Assembly.

[33] No study seems to have been made of the Provisional Government's social and welfare policy. As well as the new Ministry of Welfare, the government created a Ministry of Labour to combat unemployment and promote industrial peace. The 8-hour working day was adopted widely in Russia, but originated in a private agreement between the Petrograd manufacturers and the Soviet: see Smith, *Red Petrograd*, p. 66.

[34] Startsev has discovered a draft protocol of the government's first meeting, *Vnutrennyaya politika*, pp. 114–16. [35] A. Leont'ev, in *Pravo*, 8 (1917).

This approach to legal order had the unfortunate effect of cutting off the Provisional Government from the local revolutionary consensus which had existed in March. Legalism and obsession with detail bred delays in reform and helped to cast doubt on the government's devotion to the revolution. When the government began to appeal to continuity, this doubt grew deeper. Moreover, the rigid insistence upon legality in administration (as well as in the defence of civil and property rights) actually undermined the position of the Committees of Public Organizations, which had no official status. The relationship between the Provisional Government and the committees was marked by continual conflict, in which central government was in effect trying to assert control over the revolution, to channel it in accordance with its own programme and values.[36]

The attempt to build a new structure to contain the revolution began with the enactment of civil rights into law. The Provisional Government's record in this endeavour is impressive, despite delays and a sometimes piecemeal approach to legislation.

The commitment to equality before the law, promised in the government's eight-point programme published on 3 March, began to be honoured the next day with the abolition of all national, religious, political, and social restrictions on promotion in the armed forces, and the withdrawal of quota limits on Jews wishing to enter university.[37] A statute formally abolishing all discrimination on grounds of religion or nationality was produced by 20 March. The tsarist social estates (*sosloviya*) were not dissolved at first; this was apparently considered to be a private matter after the removal of legal distinctions on the basis of social class; in July pressure of public opinion forced the government to commit itself to their abolition.[38] There was no direct statement upon the emancipation of women, but a series of measures began to remove disabilities: it was agreed on 19 March that women should have the vote; and other decisions allowed women to become advocates, civil servants, and teachers in boys' schools, and made them eligible for jury service, although they were permitted to refuse it.[39]

---

[36] An impression of this conflict can easily be gained from reading Ministry of the Interior circulars and replies to local institutions in *VVP*.

[37] *Zhurnaly*, 4 Mar. 1917.

[38] Browder and Kerensky, *Documents*, iii. 1318.

[39] *Zhurnaly*, 19 Mar., 28 Apr., 1 June; the proposal for women to have equal

Inviolability of the person and the right to due process of law were guaranteed first of all by the dismantling of the old law-enforcement apparatus. On 4 March the Okhrana, the Gendarmerie, and special courts with class representatives were abolished; on 10 March the Police Department was closed down; on 19 March the land captains (*zemskie nachal'niki*) who had been responsible for supervising peasant administration were also abolished. Military field courts were liquidated. An amnesty was declared on 6 March which included reduced sentences for ineligible prisoners who had been freed during the revolution, if they returned voluntarily.[40] Administrative justice was overhauled, depriving railway authorities, Cossack officials, and others of punitive powers.[41] A new system of administrative courts was created, with powers that included a judicial review of administration in certain circumstances.[42] A law on the inviolability of the person, dwelling, and correspondence was still in preparation at the time of the October Revolution.[43] Cruel punishments, such as the wearing of chains, were outlawed; on 26 April the penalty of exile to Siberia was abolished.[44] The death penalty was abolished on 12 April, although it had been commuted in earlier cases; the delay may have been due to pressure from socialist elements who entertained hopes of stringing-up the former Tsar and assorted counter-revolutionaries.[45] The government also granted extensive aid to returning political prisoners and exiles.[46]

Censorship had ceased during the February Revolution, and was formally abolished on 6 March; the tsarist Chief Administration of Press Affairs had already been closed down two days earlier.[47] Military censorship was retained, but in a revised and much reduced form.[48] A statute on the press was produced on 27 April, providing for registration of all serial and individual

opportunities in the civil service was made on 8 Mar., referred to the Juridical Conference, and approved as a law on 5 Aug.

[40] *Sbornik ukazov*, 4 and 10 Mar.; *Zhurnaly*, 19 Mar.; *Sbornik ukazov*, 13 Mar.; Browder and Kerensky, *Documents*, i. 196.

[41] *Sbornik ukazov*, 14 Mar.

[42] Browder and Kerensky, *Documents*, i. 232.

[43] VVP carried intermittent reports on the progress of this and most other legislation.

[44] *Sbornik ukazov*, 17 Mar. and 26 Apr.   [45] Ibid., 12 Apr.

[46] *Zhurnaly*, 8, 14, 17, and 20 Mar.

[47] Ibid., 4 and 6 Mar.   [48] *Sbornik ukazov*, 13 Mar.

publications with a 'Book Chamber' (*Knizhnaya palata*), but not using this in any way as a restriction upon publication.[49] Reservations on the choice of school-books were ended on 17 July.[50] The only limit placed upon freedom of expression before the July Days was a decision in April to legislate against the printing of insults to religious feelings, which was regarded as the legitimate protection of freedom of conscience. When the Grand Duchess Maria Pavlovna complained to the government about slanders against her and other members of the imperial family, she was politely advised to seek redress in the courts.[51]

Enactment of freedom of association was similarly swift. On 6 March the government issued a statement on the freedom to strike and to join a trade union.[52] This was followed by a law on freedom of association on 12 April: like the press law, this provided for registration but not in any restrictive manner.[53] Workers' committees in factories were separately recognized in a law of 23 April.[54] Procedures for the supervision of public meetings and spectacles were drawn up on 27 April.[55]

Freedom of conscience was endorsed in a new law on religion which allowed a person to choose their religious affiliation on or after the age of fourteen.[56] The government encouraged a range of reforms in the Churches: divorce was reformed in the Ortho-dox Church, and the Georgian Church regained its autocephaly.[57] Disestablishment, or the dissociation of the state from religious affairs in general, did not figure in the government's thinking. The trend was away from state regulation of religious life, but ironically this might involve greater intervention in the short term: the Orthodox Church in particular had to be bullied into reform.

Freedom of movement was not, apparently, directly proclaimed: the passport system seems to have remained on the statute books, even if it can hardly have been implemented in the chaos of 1917. To some extent, the need for rationing and the control of militarily liable labour involved restrictions on movement.

---

[49] Browder and Kerensky, *Documents*, i. 228.   [50] *Zhurnaly*, 17 July.
[51] Ibid., 29 Mar.   [52] Ibid. 6 Mar.
[53] Browder and Kerensky, *Documents*, i. 226; trade unions had to be registered in order to own property or enter contractual obligations.
[54] *Sbornik ukazov*, 23 Apr.
[55] Browder and Kerensky, *Documents*, i. 228.   [56] *VVP*, 20 July.
[57] *Sbornik ukazov*, 1 May (divorce), and 27 Mar. (autocephaly).

The Provisional Government was aware that its newly granted rights had to be defensible. It was hoped that a formal, democratic, administrative structure and a reformed system of law enforcement would secure the new order. The government was committed to democracy on the full 'four-tail' suffrage, although the issue of the democratic control of central government was evaded until the autumn, and even then only an advisory 'pre-Parliament' was established. The Constituent Assembly was to be the ultimate in democracy, and was expected to set up a parliamentary republic. Meanwhile, the Provisional Government devoted enormous efforts to preparing the legislation for a new structure of local government. The only major disputes of principle occurred over the voting age (with the 'democratic elements' insisting on the age of eighteen) and over the right of garrison soldiers to vote in the town where they were stationed: the second point was conceded swiftly, but the voting age was fixed at twenty.[58]

The government's programme for building democracy began with an attempt to regularize the new agencies of power created by the February Revolution. The Committees of Public Organizations were recognized as temporary local authorities, but care was taken to homogenize them and to limit their powers—in particular to deny them the right to impose taxes. A limited amount of central-government money was made available, but its use was restricted; under no circumstances were soviets and other 'private' organizations to receive funds. The existing *zemstva* and town dumas were to be protected as the base of the permanent new order; since they had been elected on very restricted franchises, it was agreed that they could be 'democratized' by the addition of representatives of the 'democratic elements'. As soon as possible, local elections were to be held on the basis of universal suffrage and proportional representation, after which the Committees of Public Organizations would be dissolved. In addition, a long-planned, small, rural self-government unit was to be created: a *zemstvo* at *volost'* level, which would encompass people of all social classes, thus ending the isolation of the peasantry in a separate system of administration. Finally, central-government agents were expected to have an important role in

---

[58] Browder and Kerensky, *Documents*, i. 455.

local affairs: commissars were to be appointed to each province and district.[59]

It should also be noted that the government tried to extend the principle of formal democracy into other areas of administration. As already mentioned, a system of committees was created for the armed forces; an attempt was made to regulate industrial democracy through the recognition of workers' committees and the creation of arbitration procedures; a democratic presence was built into the new institutions which had been designed to prepare the land reform and to handle the procurement of food and supplies for the population.[60]

But it gradually became clear that formal democracy was not of itself going to hold the new Russia together. The attempt to control and co-opt the new institutions of the revolution was sound in principle, but counter-productive in practice because it actually undermined them. Opposing the formal democratic principle to the 'revolutionary-democratic' practice of representing groups and institutions cannot be regarded as a success. In the autumn, conditions of crisis produced new versions of the Committees of Public Organizations in a spontaneous, desperate search for 'firm authority'.[61]

The other plank of local order was to be a revitalized and democratic system of law enforcement. Here, too, the first principle was continuity: a commission was set up on 25 March to review the tsarist law codes and to bring them into line with the revolution. The 1864 judicial system was to be restored, which raised a number of problems: how to remove reactionary judges without violating the principle of judicial independence; what property or other qualifications should be applied to jurors; and whether to have elected, appointed, or co-opted judges. At the higher levels, these issues seem to have been successfully resolved; unsuitable judges and senators were quietly persuaded to retire, and in June the recalcitrant were made liable to special disciplinary procedures. The real problems proved to be at local

[59] Information on the reorganization of local government is drawn from TsGAOR, f. 1788, op. 2. A useful study of government commissars is E. P. Baranov, 'Mestnye organy gosudarstvennogo upravleniya Vremennogo pravitel'stva v 1917 g.', diss. (Moscow State University, 1975).

[60] Wildman, *Russian Imperial Army*, *passim*; Smith, *Red Petrograd*, pp. 77 ff.; Keep, *Revolution*, *passim*.

[61] cf. n. 16 above.

level, and did not offer much hope for the defensibility of civil rights.[62]

Under tsarism, local justice was mostly dispensed by land captains, peasant *volost'* courts, and urban magistrates. The 1864 system of having elected Justices of the Peace had been whittled down to only ten provinces and eight cities by February 1917. The government's first problem was to establish courts in Petrograd, which it did by creating temporary courts composed of a judge, a worker, and a soldier. This system, devised by Kerenskii, proved to be popular and was extended to other parts of Petrograd province; it was strongly disliked, however, by the government's liberal jurists, who secured its abolition in July. The next problem was rural justice: on 21 March the government created temporary Justices to take over the judicial functions of the land captains (whose administrative duties passed to district commissars); on 4 May a law revived the use of elected Justices of the Peace, who were to sit in a new court with two other members elected by the *volost' zemstvo* or town duma. Peasant *volost'* courts were not formally abolished in 1917, although peasant committees often dispersed existing courts and elected new judges. The new system of local justice was gravely handicapped by lack of finance and lack of personnel: in creating over 4,000 new vacancies for Justices of the Peace, and insisting on high qualifications for the office, the government was continuing to spread the Russian intelligentsia too thinly.[63]

On the positive side, two improvements should be acknowledged: peasant communes lost the right to expel members, and considerable efforts were made to humanize and improve the penal system. A degree of prison self-government was introduced, with elected elders, and in Moscow it was ordered that prisoners should be addressed in the respectful second person *vy*.[64]

The most important ingredient of law enforcement, the

---

[62] On the government's judicial policy, see e.g. A. S. Farfel', Bor'ba narodnykh mass protiv kontrrevolyutsionnoi yustitsii Vremennogo pravitel'stva (Minsk, 1969); E. A. Skripilev, 'Karatel'naya politika Vremennogo pravitel'stva i apparat ee provedeniya', diss. (Academy of Sciences Institute of State and Law; Moscow, 1970).

[63] The various decisions and laws can be found in Zhurnaly and/or Sbornik ukazov.

[64] On peasant communes, see Zhurnaly, 1 Aug.; on prison reform, see E. A. Skripilev, Tyuremnaya politika i tyuremnoe zakonodatel'stvo Vremennogo pravitel'stva (Moscow, 1968), 41–6.

militia, was unfortunately the least adequate to the task. The tsarist police had simply disintegrated during the February Revolution: the Provisional Government proceeded to abolish them, conscripting all former policemen into the army. They were replaced by militias composed of local volunteers and garrison troops, and also workers' militias (particularly in Petrograd). These were often democratic in structure, with elected commanders. The government was determined to regularize and professionalize the militia system, producing a law on the militia in April which set up a uniform structure and provision for central supervision. Politically, this was another occasion for interminable wrangles about who should control the militia, and whether it should have a volunteer component or a democratic structure. As a civilian police force, the militia was woefully inadequate against crime, let alone politically motivated illegalities, and it soon acquired a reputation for corruption and incompetence. The militia was basically an urban police force, since tsarist rural policing had in any case been left mostly to the peasants themselves.[65]

Reforms in the legal system also involved new provisions for ensuring legality in administration. Both the Procuracy and the new government commissars were charged with the general supervision of legality; a new law set out the civil and criminal liability of officials; and, as we have seen, administrative courts were created.[66] There was also an overhaul of military justice, with new regimental courts.[67]

In view of the problems of enforcement, defending civil rights in the new order would be no easy matter. The tsarist state had, of course, ultimately rested upon its armed forces—but by the summer of 1917 it was clear that neither front-line troops nor rear garrisons could be relied upon. The Provisional Government was thrown back upon the capacity of the Soviet's leaders to handle major problems, while minor ones went largely unanswered.

In the circumstances, the level of violation of personal rights on political grounds was relatively low. Crime, and the infringe-

---

[65] The only serious treatment of the civil militia is A. P. Zvyagintseva, 'Organizatsiya i deyatel'nost' militsii Vremennogo pravitel'stva Rossii v 1917 godu', diss. (Moscow State University, 1972).

[66] *Sbornik ukazov*, 11 Apr.; Browder and Kerensky, *Documents*, i. 232.

[67] *Sbornik ukazov*, 17 Apr.

ment of property rights on political grounds, was another matter. As to political rights, the non-socialists were often pessimistic about electoral abuse, but apart from a certain amount of rough electioneering (the tearing-down of Kadet posters and ribbons being a frequent occurrence), there does not seem to have been much infringement of rights by intimidation or fraud.[68]

If freedom of expression was generally unhindered (and a surprising amount of latitude was allowed to right-wing elements, at least until the Kornilov affair), the major day-to-day problem of civil rights was inviolability of the person and of the home. Even after the February Revolution was secure, various self-appointed bodies made it their business to arrest tsarist policemen and officials, and individuals occasionally took the opportunity to settle old scores. The 'democratic elements' continued to fear counter-revolution, and consequently continued to arrest suspects. These would usually be handed over to the militia, and after an investigation and prolonged argument they would be released. The government issued a whole series of decrees and circulars on controlling illegal arrest.[69] A further problem was the frequent raids or searches made in towns: soldiers would decide to seek out draft-dodgers or counter-revolutionaries; soviets would organize round-ups of deserters and criminals.[70] Political murders and beatings were relatively uncommon once the February Revolution was completed (even during February only a few tsarist officers and officials were lynched), though the numbers began to rise in the autumn; violence against the person was most frequent in rural unrest.[71]

Crime, on the other hand, became endemic with the collapse of policing and order; the emptying of the prisons during the February Revolution no doubt played a part as well. The result was heightened insecurity and lawlessness, which often turned against the perpetrators. Vigilante groups were formed in some places, but most of the retribution upon suspected or apprehended

---

[68] See e.g. W. G. Rosenberg, 'The Municipal Duma Elections of 1917', *Soviet Studies*, 21 (Oct. 1969). There are frequent reports on local elections in the journals *Gorodskoe delo* and *Zemskoe delo*, and summary reports in *VVP*.

[69] See e.g. *Zhurnaly*, 5 and 22 Mar.

[70] *Odesskiya novosti*, 18 July, reported repeated raids for deserters in the town, claiming that every citizen had probably been stopped 3 or 4 times.

[71] On rural unrest, see e.g. G. J. Gill, *Peasants and Government in the Russian Revolution* (London, 1979).

criminals was by angry mobs. This lynch law (*samosud*) is impossible to quantify, but it formed the theme of frequent militia reports and articles in the local press.[72]

Most of the violations of legality in 1917 concerned property, landed or industrial, as a result of obvious social conflict. As well as 'seizure', property owners found themselves arbitrarily subjected to illegal 'taxes', or simply informed by their tenants that rents had been lowered. The government was forced to concede a moratorium on land transactions and the transfer of 'untilled' land to local peasant-dominated Land Committees.[73] Usually the Provisional Government defended private property behind the scenes, ordering local commissars or militia commanders to deal with complaints, and seeking to avoid confrontation—especially over what might constitute 'untilled' land.[74] In some cases, infringement of property rights had civil rights implications; for example, when people were evicted from their homes, or newspaper presses were expropriated. Such incidents were relatively rare, although some notorious cases attracted great attention. The Bolsheviks camped out in the Petrograd dacha of the ballerina Kshesinskaya; a group of anarchists selected Durnovo's dacha further up the river, but were forcibly removed after staging an armed seizure of the *Russkaya volya* presses.[75]

By the summer of 1917 the Provisional Government's efforts to build a new political order were in full swing, although the capacity of this order to contain and to resolve social and political conflict was debatable. It is impossible to quantify the instances in which 'legality' was violated, but the general atmosphere was one of insecurity and uncertainty. In Petrograd, the government began to achieve a successful working relationship with the leaders of the 'democratic elements', and in a spirit of growing frustration began to try to use its new allies and its new apparatus

---

[72] A typical incident reported in *Odesskiya novosti*, 10 June, concerned a man who beat up his mistress: hearing her cries, passing soldiers broke in; the man then seized an axe and wounded a soldier, whereupon a crowd gathered and beat him insensible.

[73] Gill, *Peasants and Government*, ch. 3.

[74] Many such cases appear in TsGAOR, f. 1788, op. 2, d. 103 ff., correspondence between the Ministry of the Interior and local commissars.

[75] A touching account of Kshesinskaya's efforts to evict her squatters is provided in Sukhanov, *Revolution*, pp. 209–11; for the Durnovo dacha affair, see A. Rabinowitch, *Prelude to Revolution* (Bloomington, Ind., 1968), 61 ff.

to impose law and order. Civil liberties would, if necessary, be curtailed to ensure the survival of the state.

The liberals, who continued to dominate the machinery of government at the centre, were becoming less and less ambivalent. Talk of 'revolutionary legal creativity' was eclipsed by a strong sense of the tutelary role of the state over the masses. Rosenberg has termed this the politics of 'state consciousness' (*gosudarstvennost'*).[76] It reflected a basic fear that the revolution would end in anarchy, defeat in the war, and the collapse of hopes for a democratic future. The government slowly adopted a more aggressive position as it faced the rapid escalation of peasant and national-minority demands, and the spread of what it perceived as totally destructive and anarchic tendencies amongst workers and soldiers. The phenomenon of 'republics'—areas where government authority was simply repudiated—was particularly alarming. The first of these to appear was Kronstadt, but in the early summer there were miniature seizures of power in Nizhnii Novgorod and in Tsaritsyn.[77] The final straw came with the July Days in Petrograd, even though there were remarkably few echoes of it elsewhere in the country.[78]

In June the Provisional Government had begun to make noises about defending the revolution by force if necessary, having in mind particularly the plans by Bolsheviks and anarchists for a demonstration which was eventually prevented by the Soviet.[79] The immediate response to the July Days was to prosecute offenders, and an investigation was ordered by the Petrograd procurator (later entrusted to a Special Investigative Commission). The most worrying feature for the government was the involvement of troops; the workers were not yet well armed, since the Red Guard was mostly organized rather later. It was against the army that most of the repressive action was directed, although the Bolsheviks were also identified as the organizers, and were subjected to harassment and arrest.

On 8 July the War Ministry was authorized to ban *Pravda* and other 'subversive' newspapers from the Front; three days later

[76] Rosenberg, *Liberals*, ch. 5.
[77] On Tsaritsyn, see D. J. Raleigh, 'Revolutionary Politics in Provincial Russia: The Tsaritsyn "Republic" in 1917', *Slavic Review*, 40/2 (1981).
[78] Rabinowitch, *Prelude*, is the best account.   [79] Ibid. 72–3.

the death penalty was restored at the Front, and on 31 July it was extended to the navy. There was provision for appeal against the death penalty to the relevant army commander, although this was subsequently modified to an automatic review of death sentences by the Army Commander and the Army Commissar, with any disagreement being resolved by the Commissar to the Commander-in-Chief. On 12 July the press law was amended to allow the Ministers of War and the Interior to suppress and prosecute newspapers which incited dereliction of military duty, violence, or civil war. Military censorship was tightened on 14 July. On 19 July incitement to disobedience of lawful orders on the railways was made a criminal offence. On 28 July the Ministers of War and the Interior were empowered to ban meetings or congresses which endangered military or state security, and to order the arrest of individuals by administrative procedure; street meetings in Petrograd were also banned.[80] These measures were accompanied by arrests and reassignments among the troops involved in disturbances.

It is not easy to discover how extensively these measures were implemented. It was widely believed that the death penalty was never used, but there are references to cases in White *émigré* sources.[81] The arrest of Bolshevik leaders is well documented, but the scale of other arrests is uncertain. Soviet sources refer loosely to widespread arrests, particularly amongst soldiers; there were said to be 750 soldiers from the Western Front in one Moscow prison in September. The power to ban meetings was used in Petrograd during August; during the Kornilov affair the government tried to stave off illegal requisitions of property by imposing fines and administrative arrest. Kerenskii ordered the closure of *Pravda* and *Okopnaya pravda*, and of at least one provincial Bolshevik paper, the Tsaritsyn *Bor'ba*.[82]

Even allowing for fairly numerous arrests of soldiers, it cannot be contended that this repression was either particularly extreme or particularly effective. The negative impact it made on mass opinion, however, was huge. The death penalty was the worst

---

[80] These measures are recorded in *Zhurnaly* and VVP.

[81] See e.g. V. Manakin, 'The Shock-Battalions of 1917: Reminiscences', *Russian Review*, 14 (July 1955), 221–2.

[82] See e.g. Farfel', *Bor'ba*; Skripilev, 'Karatel'naya politika'; Rabinowitch, *Prelude*, ch. 7; Raleigh, 'Revolutionary Politics', p. 203.

blunder; a certain degree of action against Bolsheviks and anarchists was widely acceptable, and was backed by the moderate socialists. But in the eyes of the people the Provisional Government seemed to be reverting to repression of positively tsarist dimensions; rumours began to spread of a new Okhrana, of plans to encourage a military coup or to surrender Petrograd to the Germans.

During the autumn the Provisional Government's retreat became more marked as their state structure collapsed around them. There was increasing resort to direct military repression of the 'republics'; for the first time, significant numbers of troops were made available specifically for internal policing, and arrangements were made for local-government commissars to call upon them. This tougher line is also reflected in a series of relatively minor changes with adverse civil rights implications: it was made a criminal offence to insult representatives of the Allied powers, foreign travel was further restricted, and the right of residence in Moscow and Petrograd was curbed in the interest of food supply.[83]

At this point, the disintegration of the army had gone too far to permit effective repression. It is evident that many local military commanders chose to co-operate with the revolutionary organs given a new lease of life by the Kornilov affair, rather than strictly to obey the Provisional Government. In such circumstances, the government itself collapsed, concluding that a formal western democracy was not going to work in Russia. One part of it was more or less secretly hoping for an external miracle, such as military dictatorship; the other was moving towards the acceptance of popular demands on the big political issues, although it never quite got there.

The development of civil rights in Russia up to 1917, while undoubtedly contributing to the collapse of tsarist autocracy, did not culminate in a new order built around them. Neither the ideology, nor the institutions, nor the social base for such an order could be found. One might reflect, though, upon the 'near miss': in social terms, the spread of the 'committee class'; in institutional terms, the flowering of mass democratic organs, and

[83] See e.g. *Zhurnaly*, 12 July and 5 Aug.

the ideology of freedom and dignity—all of which belonged not
to the liberals of the Provisional Government, but to the
'democratic elements'. It is, of course, an absurd anachronism to
chide the Russian masses and revolutionary intelligentsia for not
having thought out the relationship between freedom and
socialism, but their fate might be instructive.

INDEX

Index compiled by Peva Keane